MW00852455

SELLING
THE PROFESSION

Focusing on Building Relationships

SELLING

THE PROFESSION

Focusing on Building Relationships

8th Edition

DR. DAVID J. LILL & JENNIFER LILL-BROWN

Contact the authors if you would like information on how to access all aspects of the curriculum developed exclusively to assist you in the preparation of lecture material, tests, case studies, and other classroom or lecture activities.

www.sellingtheprofession.com

This book may be purchased for educational, business, or sales promotional use. For information or to place an order, please contact:

DM Bass Publications
6635 Broken Bow Drive
Cane Ridge, TN 37013
615.941.2747 (business)
615.476.5035 (direct)
615.941.2458 (fax)

ISBN-13: 978-0-9652201-8-7

EIGHTH EDITION

Library of Congress Cataloging-in-Publication data on file
Lill, David J. and Jennifer Lill Brown
Selling: The Profession / Focusing on Building Relationships /
Dr. David J. Lill and Jennifer Lill Brown

Cover Design/Interior Layout: Marisa Jackson

Printed in the United States of America

To Martha

We love you so much.
You are the best wife, mom, and grandma ever.
We are so blessed to have you!

TABLE OF CONTENTS

INTRODUCTION

Welcome to an exciting new time in your life!

Whether you are a fledgling salesperson, a seasoned veteran, or a college student who is interested in pursuing the absolute best job on the planet, we salute you for recognizing the power of knowledge.

It is said that we all sell every day, but let's be honest: some people are better at it than others. That is because selling is an art, a craft, and a trade and like any trade, you only get better with training and practice.

This book is the perfect mix of learning and application to take your reading experience from static to dynamic. The ideas, concepts, and style are the result of a combined 45 years of engaging in selling, teaching professional selling at the university level, coaching and consulting, writing dozens of business and success books, giving keynotes, and conducting sales training and seminars.

As entrepreneurs, professionals and seasoned salespeople who love the sales environment and endeavor for selling to be viewed as the respectable and valuable career it is, we wanted a textbook that would:

1. Give you *transferable, tangible skills*, no matter your industry or experience level.
2. Convince motivated students that selling is a *phenomenal, lifelong career* to consider—not just a job you do until something better comes along.
3. Show you how sales can be a *source of tremendous financial and personal fulfillment.*

Selling: The Profession focuses on building relationships—because sincere connections are what spell success for salespeople operating in a highly competitive environment and dealing with buyers who demand fast and accurate answers to complex problems. We break the sales process down into its most basic components to simplify the complex buyer-seller interaction that takes place in any selling situation, with the result being an eight-step Relationship Selling Cycle. These eight steps are detailed in chapters 8 to 15.

A critical foundation is being able to better control your time and activities. This is really all about personal organization and self-management. You cannot manage time, but you can manage yourself and your personal activities. Administrative ability on the part of the salesperson is fundamental to success. The inability or lack of desire to become organized is responsible for the vast majority of failures.

Communication and social style expertise are also necessary foundational elements. An understanding of these concepts allows you to more readily appreciate the complex, dynamic behavioral relationships that take place in selling. Success in relationship selling depends on accurately getting your message across to prospects. Understanding social styles is an especially useful tool for gaining insight into how prospects are thinking. It is a method for finding the best way to approach a prospect and to set up a working relationship with that person.

You will be introduced to the usefulness of social media and its countless applications in the world of selling. As global competition brings new challenges, technology brings new tools that help sales professionals sell more effectively and efficiently.

You will see the real world of selling through sales studies, personal experience, and insight from successful sales professionals who put the theory contained in the book into everyday practice. As one top salesperson said:

"Practice without theory is blind and theory without practice is sterile."

Relationships can be more important than the actual product being sold. Customers don't always know the components of a product, how your company functions, or how they will be treated after money changes hands, but they can make an assessment about a salesperson and about the relationship that has occurred over the course of the selling cycle. Ultimately, customers' decisions are based on the fact that they trust and believe in what a salesperson says.

Therefore, the quality of relationships with your customers is the competitive advantage that enables you to stand out in a sea of similar products and services.

Your ability to develop and maintain long-term relationships is the key to your success as a person, a student, and a business professional. For customers, a buying decision means a decision to enter into a relationship with a salesperson and their company. It is very much like a business marriage.

Selling: The Profession shows you how to bring about that union.

About the Authors

DR. DAVID J. LILL has forty years of professional sales, sales training, and teaching experience. He earned his Ph.D. degree in Marketing from the University of Alabama, and he taught selling and marketing classes at Baylor University, Belmont University, New Mexico State University, and Nichols State University. Dr. Lill is also a business and sales consultant who conducted seminars and training courses for two decades on sales and marketing related topics. His relationship selling model is used by companies throughout the country in a wide variety of industries including insurance, telecommunications, real estate, publishing, banking, hospitality, chemical, and automotive.

Dr. Lill is the founder and president of DM Bass Publications through which he wrote, publishes, and promotes his acclaimed textbook, *Selling: The Profession.* He owned and operated an advertising firm in Louisiana where he developed and implemented advertising and marketing campaigns for a number of companies including financial institutions, car dealerships, retail department stores, and a dental practice.

Dr. Lill is the co-author of *Cause Selling: The Sanford Way (2nd edition), The Handbook for Relationship Selling,* and *The Official Handbook for Health Club Sales.* In addition, Dr. Lill has published 65 articles in various academic, trade, and professional publications. These include: *Selling Power, Journal of Advertising, Journal of the Academy of Marketing Science, Sales & Marketing Management, Business Topics, Nashville Business Journal,* and the *Journal of Pharmaceutical Marketing & Management.*

Dr. Lill sold successfully for a telecommunications company, specializing in marketing information technology. He also worked for the Milwaukee Journal in their Advertising Laboratory Division. While there, he brought in prestigious clients such as

General Mills, General Foods, and Nabisco and conducted marketing studies using Milwaukee as a test market for new product launches.

David lives in Nashville, Tennessee with his wife, Martha. They are blessed to have two exceptional children, David, Jr. and Jennifer, and five grandchildren. David is an engineer with TVA in Chattanooga, Tennessee where he lives with his wife Amber, and their daughter, Madelyn, and son, David Matthew. Jennifer is a published author, ghostwriter, and entrepreneur.

JENNIFER LILL BROWN comes from a background of sales, entrepreneurship, and authorship. She is a renowned and prolific ghostwriter who has helped more than 40 prominent professionals and public figures put their passions into words (**www.jenlillbrown.com**). Some of her more notable clients include NFL Hall of Fame quarterback Joe Theismann, Dr. Josh Axe, Jordan Rubin, James Malinchak, Dr. David Jockers, John Crowley, Michael Drake, Scott Keffer, and Dr. Asa Andrew. She has a unique talent for researching and writing from the perspective of virtually anyone from any background.

Jennifer has also co-authored four books of her own. She and her father's most recent endeavor is *Cause Selling: The Sanford Way*, which is based on the vision of billionaire philanthropist T. Denny Sanford. She was also the co-founder, along with former business partner Tom Black, of the Tom Black Center for Selling Inc. While working with Tom, she edited and produced his sales book, *The Boxcar Millionaire*.

While obtaining her degree in finance from the University of Alabama, Jennifer sold for one of the most respected sales organizations in the country, The Southwestern Company. She sold educational products door-to-door by relocating and fully running the business from concept to sales, delivery, and customer service. She was the awarded "Top First Year Dealer Award" and facilitated the recruitment and training of new recruits, as well as formulating and developing a system of lead finding and a unique delivery method.

Jennifer lives in Nashville, Tennessee with her husband Will, and their three homeschooled handsome sons, Porter, Wyatt, and Jesse. Her parents, Martha (Grandma) and David (Papa), live next door and are proud, devoted grandparents.

Acknowledgments

Since one of our primary goals was to produce a text with real-world concepts and applications, we could not have been successful without the assistance of all those in sales who took time to share their thoughts, as well as a team of supportive friends and family. The insightful comments made by the sales professionals highlighted throughout the book add an important dimension to student learning. The success they have achieved in all areas of their lives through hard work and dedication, while upholding high standards of business ethics, should serve as a model for young, aspiring business professionals.

DAVID'S ACKNOWLEDGMENTS

A Special thanks to six individuals who have been true blessings to me: Deryl Bass, Jimmie Carter, Don Evans, Charlie Kromer, Dan McGinley and Bob Tight—friends and sales professionals, who each in their own way have had a profound effect on the way I think and the actions I take.

The 32 cases in the 7th and 8th editions are the work of Dr. William Barnett. I cannot thank him enough for the exceptional case studies he provided.

My thanks and appreciation to the following professors, business associates, and colleagues. Their insightful suggestions and encouragement added significantly to the content of this textbook: Gary Benson, Southeast Community College (NE); Dr. Kenneth Blanchard, founder of *Blanchard Training & Development*; Frank Bingham, Bryant University; Bob Bricker, Pikes Peak Community College (CO); David Braun, L.A. Pierce College (CA); Patricia DeCorte, Delta College (MI); Sandra Fields, University of Delaware; Bert Fisher, COO, Our Community Credit Union (WA); Robert Garber, Florida Atlanta University; Wil Goodheer, president of International University (Vienna, Austria); Shawn Green, Aurora University (IL); Desiree Cooper Larsen, Weber State University (UT); James Lollar, Radford University (VA);

Dr. Morris L. Mayer, University of Alabama; Dan McGinley, former Director, Sanford Institute of Philanthropy (National University, CA); Dan Moore, President, The Southwestern Company; Judith Nickel, WCTC (WI); Steven Osinski, San Diego State University; Dr. Norman Vincent Peale, author of *The Power of Positive Thinking*; Robin Peterson, New Mexico State University; John Robbins, Winthrop University; Michael Powell, North Georgia College & State University; Allen Schemmel, WSM-AM/FM Radio (Nashville); Bob Tangsrud, Mayville State University (ND); Chet Trybus, Ferris State University (MI); William Youngs, SUNY College at Cobleskill (NY); Brian Williams, Southeast Tech Institute (SD).

My Family:

To my wife, Martha, you are the love of my life, my best friend, and my favorite person in the whole world! There is no way to express the depth of my gratitude and admiration for sticking with me through it all and for setting the example of what a Godly woman looks like for our kids and grandkids.

To Dave, what a phenomenal son, father and husband you are. You and Amber love your children (Madelyn and David Matthew) so much and your mom and I couldn't be prouder!

To Jennifer, what a remarkable daughter and fantastic mother to our grandsons, Porter, Wyatt, and Jesse! My co-author and editor-in-chief for *Selling: The Profession*! I am so very proud of you and Will. You are quite the team!

There is no way this book could have been completed without their love and support!

JENNIFER'S ACKNOWLEDGMENTS

To my father, Dr. Lill, Dad, thanks for giving me the opportunity to work on the various book projects with you to watch the master at work! And my deepest gratitude for your love and belief in me.

To my mother, Martha, Mom, you are my best friend and sounding board for all things big and small. I love you more than words can express.

To my husband, Will, I love you! Thanks for being my buddy and for giving me your unconditional support and being my biggest fan.

To my sons, Porter, Wyatt, and Jesse, you guys made my life so full of joy. Every day is an adventure with my boys.

To Allison, thanks for *all* the things and for being my friend.

To my clients, including John Crowley, Dr. Josh Axe, Jordan Rubin, Joe Theismann, Michael Drake, James Malinchak, Tom Black, Kevin Clayson, Dani Williamson, Scott Keffer, and JM Ryerson: helping you write your books has shaped my life and my impact on this world. Thank you!

PART I

SELLING SUCCESS FUNDAMENTALS

Salespeople are influencers! You have chosen an exciting and vital profession to study. Part I provides you with a foundation for success in professional selling.

Welcome to the world of Relationship Selling! In Part I, we explore the foundational pieces needed for building a long-lasting and rewarding career. In order to provide the most value to others, you need to gain a full understanding of what a career in selling involves, to know how to efficiently manage your daily activities, to understand how to best communicate with others within and outside your organization, and to recognize what drives people to buy.

You'll learn more about yourself and your customers, as well as how to effectively communicate with prospects in a way that fosters real, lasting relationships. We will study the selling landscape and how its changes can affect your career and your interactions with customers and prospective customers. We'll also discuss time management and how to set goals that better help you succeed, one day and one customer at a time. Finally, we'll discuss the four social styles and their role in helping you to create more genuine connections.

YOUR CAREER IN PROFESSIONAL SELLING

OVERVIEW

In a world in which we seem to be more and more disconnected, the job of a salesperson is more important than ever. People still thrive on connections! A selling style that focuses on relationships is interactive, encourages prospect participation, employs empathy, and helps everyone win. Positioning yourself as a consultant rather than an order taker creates a partnership with customers—peers working to solve problems together.

OBJECTIVES

- Appreciate the importance of selling in the modern business climate.
- Understand the purpose of personal selling.
- Examine professional selling as a viable career opportunity.
- Recognize the different types of sales jobs and the requirements for success in each.
- Identify the personal characteristics required for success in a selling career.

You Are Already Selling

Countless daily interactions between people involve the act of selling in some way. We universally recognize many of these interactions as selling. For example, a retail salesperson sells you clothes, furniture, or a smartphone, an auto dealer sells you a car, and an insurance agent sells you a policy.

A company is not in business until somebody makes a sale.

However, other everyday transactions that are not typically considered "selling" involve the same skills, goals, and behaviors that professional salespeople use. Examples include servers who convince you to get dessert, politicians who persuade constituents to vote for them, and celebrities who push their ideas through social media. Don't forget about family members who influence decisions such as who gets to use the family car, where to go on vacation, and what to fix for dinner.

In other words, you are already selling. You are selling yourself, your ideas, and your desire for cooperation and companionship to almost everyone you engage in anything more than the most casual conversation.

Partnerships, relationships, strategic alliances, and networking are more than mere phrases to sales organizations. They are tools that help create winning strategies. Competitiveness among the world's major corporations will only continue to grow, and using outdated sales strategies is dangerous and ineffective.

You need the latest and best sales practices if your goal is to gain new customers and keep existing ones. That could mean checking in with customers and prospects through LinkedIn or Facebook, doing regular email drip campaigns, and launching a social media sales campaign.

A true sales professional does not succeed on the merits of personality traits or skills alone, but on the ability to handle change, to harness technology, and to respond to customers' evolving needs. The sales profession must rise to the challenge because, as hotel magnate Conrad Hilton once said, "Success seems to be connected with action. Successful people keep moving."[1]

0%
"Our study concludes that this is the percentage of
our customers who will buy from us without
any effort whatsoever on our part."

Keep growing and moving forward to become a solutions provider.

It is crucial to understand the business world today and know what challenges customers face so that you can become a genuine *solutions provider*. Sales professionals demonstrate their value to customers by providing valuable information and helping solve problems.

The Value of Salespeople

We see new products and services popping up every day. With the hectic pace of life, neither individual consumer nor businesses can expect to keep up with all the innovations that become available. Instead, they must rely on salespeople!

A salesperson's job is to identify prospect needs, determine ways those needs could be met, and then share that information with the prospect. Salespeople can also serve customers even when their offering is not the right fit. Through open, honest relationships with customers, salespeople can discover where their product or service needs improvement and relay that information directly back to their company. In this way, they will be able to serve future customers better.

Salespeople who consistently bring a sincere approach to their work build trust and loyalty with customers and become an invaluable resource to their company.[2] Therefore, they are facilitators of the information who keep their company and customers competitive.

Compensation Potential

Because of their vital role in business, salespeople are among the best-paid employees of a company. More salespeople earn above

$100,000 annually than professionals in any other occupation.[3] According to an annual survey of telephone sales representatives, the average salary in that field is approximately $65,000.[4] According to different studies on sales and marketing salaries, product managers in sales positions have an average base salary of more than $98,000.[5]

These are just averages—some salespeople make less, while some make significantly more. Salespeople are the catalysts of the economy. They are responsible for keeping goods, services, and ideas flowing.

In short, selling is the most critical job in any organization.

Importance of Sales Training

In today's competitive environment, many companies provide ongoing sales training, and many of these companies spend considerable amounts of money on their training programs. Corporate skills training is increasing at more rapid rates than ever before. The reason? Research suggests that more than 70 percent of organizations cite "capability gaps" in skillsets as one of their top five challenges. Also, many companies say it takes three to five years for a sales professional to become fully productive.[6] That makes the right training even more critical to shorten the amount of time it takes to become a valued contributor to your organization.

Sales training is no longer an option, but an imperative. According to Simon Bartley, CEO of UK Skills, neglecting to train *today* will lead to a decline in economic growth *tomorrow*. Companies must see the importance of building up each salesperson, for the good of the entire organization. "On the ground is where skills allow an individual to achieve their goals of having a better quality of life and a real sense of personal achievement," says Bartley. Companies cannot cut corners and expect to have the same results as their better-trained competitors.

Training is not just an excellent way to stay competitive.[7] Truly future-focused corporations view training as an *investment* rather than an expense. The reason is that proper training almost always leads to increased profits and improved customer satisfaction.[8]

A study by the Society for HR Management reported that hiring unsuccessful salespeople costs companies approximately $20,000 for intermediate positions, $100,000 for senior management, and $300,000 for sales representatives. These figures include both the hard and soft costs of recruitment, training, and lost opportunity costs.[9] That makes a well-trained salesperson an indispensable commodity!

After spending considerable amounts of money and time on training, companies have made a significant investment in each salesperson. By providing intensive hands-on training programs, companies build confidence in their sales force, enabling them to create superior product presentations. The proper training is also evident to customers—they know they are dealing with a product expert who genuinely knows how to solve their problems.[10]

The Positive Nature of Selling

Any seasoned sales manager will tell you: it's hard to find and keep talented salespeople. One of the contributing factors to this may be the historically negative perceptions and attitudes toward selling as a career that is prevalent among college students. Employers say many young workers are uninterested in sales—a field they perceive as risky and hyper-competitive.[11]

Why do negative perceptions about the profession exist? It may be because many people have not had the opportunity to observe career salespeople at work. Their primary contact with salespeople is with retail salespeople (many of whom have little to no sales training) and telemarketers that call during dinner.

Unfortunately, these are the models we see when we think of sales, and consequently, many people view selling as a job to accept if nothing better is available.

Sales is not an easy job, but the rewards are well worth the challenges. However, in order to get the most out of the position, there are four specific characteristics that every successful salesperson must possess:

Personal Integrity

Long-term success in sales requires the highest possible ethical standards in dealing with prospects, customers, and your company. A salesperson who lies or deceives customers will tarnish their reputation as well as that of the company. An outstanding salesperson has high values and always operates in the most ethical manner.

Positive Self-Worth

Sales is a demanding career, which is why you must have a positive self-image and a persevering spirit. A person who is unable to accept the reality that not every prospect becomes a client will be devastated by failures and feel an overwhelming sense of personal rejection. The persistent myth that salespeople are arrogant, overbearing, and excessively aggressive contradicts reality. Successful salespeople are, instead, highly interested in people and their needs and eager to be of real service to others.

Relationship Focus

As a salesperson, you are not required to pretend, to conceal your personality, or to become a doormat for customers. Success in professional selling does not call for assuming an inferior position socially, psychologically, or financially. Companies may spend millions on customer relationship management (CRM) systems to monitor customer retention. But all the expensive systems in the world could never be as effective at fostering loyalty as a relationship-focused salesperson.[12]

Thirst for Learning

Success in sales requires you to be able to understand a customer's needs quickly. Then you must be able to interpret those needs and suggest viable solutions. The development of these skills requires not only intelligence but also ongoing training, the willingness to be flexible and adapt to change, and the ability to grow beyond preconceived beliefs in an ever-changing business climate.[13]

More accurate information and education are helping to improve attitudes toward sales as a career. Recent surveys reveal that more students believe that sales careers require creativity, offer career opportunities, foster personal integrity, and provide attractive financial incentives.[14]

The Basics of Personal Selling

How do you define the type of personal selling that forms the basis of this book? Here is a comprehensive definition:

PERSONAL SELLING is the process of ***seeking*** out people who have a need, ***assisting*** them in recognizing and defining the need, ***demonstrating*** how a certain product or service satisfies the need, and ***persuading*** them to use that service or product.

This definition is broad enough to include any selling in which you may engage. It describes the commercial aspect of selling a product or service, as well as the process used to solicit funds for nonprofits or enlist leaders for youth organizations. It also includes the activities of athletic coaches, political parties, clergy, and personnel officers in all kinds of organizations.

A sales career is both exciting and demanding, and it provides regular opportunities to develop and enhance skills and sales strategies. The potential for personal and professional growth never ends. Because prospects have diverse needs, interests, and decision-making abilities, selling is different in almost every situation—and this creates unique possibilities and increased income potential.

Salespeople are Made, not Born

When someone quits a sales job after a few weeks or months, chances are, they did not make an effort to learn the skills required for success. Such people are quick to throw in the towel, claiming they just weren't born to be salespeople. They are "90-Day Wonders" because, after 90 days, they wonder why they ever got into the sales business.

On the other hand, professional salespeople read books, take courses, ask questions, study the techniques of successful salespeople, work hard for their customers, and continually strive to outperform themselves.

Don't be a 90-Day Wonder. Instead, do your job so well that it makes people wonder how they can get hired as well!

Selling requires a working knowledge of psychology, sociology, communication, and persuasion. It is not a natural process to close a sale. It is a skill to be learned, just like anything else. Even experienced salespeople can fail if they get to the point where they think they know it all. Success in selling is a constant learning process. You must always be a student of your profession. Successful salespeople are made, not born. They find success through concentrated attention, repeated practice, sincere desire, and goal-directed action.[15]

Exhibit 1.1 illustrates the ongoing debate—*can you teach someone how to sell, or is it an innate skill?* We are all like computers in that we are only as good as we have philosophically, emotionally, and intellectually programmed ourselves to be. Becoming a master salesperson takes time and effort. Even the best salespeople continually adapt and refine their skills throughout their careers.

EXHIBIT 1.1 **Can Selling Be Taught?**

Absolutely! In Daniel Pink's book, *To Sell is Human*, he says that human beings cannot avoid influencing and being influenced by other people. People are going to be moved to make a decision—the trick is to make sure that the ideas and products with genuine merit do the moving.[16]

Selling is an art for many successful salespeople, but it is also a skill that must be honed and practiced. If you want to become good at influencing others, then you need to learn how. It's not magic, and it's certainly not innate. It may sometimes feel instinctive, but that's because people are often able to pick up on effective strategies implicitly through experience and observation. Not realizing you are learning makes your abilities feel natural, even when they aren't.

Learn from seasoned salespeople and get the most out of your training. Then, armed with the knowledge of what works in the field, practice it. Everything gets more comfortable, more automatic, and more natural with practice. You have what it takes; now you need to learn to use it.[17]

Sales Career Benefits

The once-popular Wide World of Sports television program promised the viewer "the thrill of victory, the agony of defeat." This thrill of victory makes sales an exciting and satisfying career, but the excitement comes not just from earning the monetary rewards or beating out the competition. Those are minor parts of the satisfaction of successful selling. What makes a career in professional selling so rewarding is a combination of three things:

1. Independence and Variety

A sales career frees you from a mundane daily routine. Salespeople work in a variety of places and deal with prospects who have widely different personalities. What works for one customer may alienate another. Consequently, you must always be aware of unique preferences and adjust quickly. The great news is selling is never dull!

Salespeople can exercise a more considerable measure of control over their time and activities than many other professionals. Sales is not a nine-to-five job. The hours are often flexible. However, because there is no strict structure in day-to-day sales activities, they must also be self-starters and stay motivated.

2. Advancement Opportunities

Effective salespeople do not have to conform to one static career path. Almost any option for career advancement is open to those who are motivated to be successful. Exhibit 1.2 illustrates a potential career path for a highly motivated salesperson. As you move up the corporate hierarchy, the various options require a different blending of personal skills and characteristics. As a result, there is no guarantee that a successful salesperson will also make a successful manager. Many talented salespeople refuse promotion to higher managerial positions. They love what they do and can often earn more money selling than they could in a management position.

Entrepreneurship. Sales is an ideal career for those who plan to one day own and run a business. No business can survive without a viable marketing organization. An owner or chief executive with a background in sales

EXHIBIT 1.2 Potential Career Path for Professionals in Selling

"Bob, have sales do that thing where profits go up."

is in an excellent position to launch and manage a successful enterprise. An entrepreneur can find people who understand manufacturing and finance, but the sales and marketing staff must share the founder's dream if the concept is to become a reality.

Promotion to Sales Management. A sales manager may have either limited or comprehensive duties. New sales managers may supervise just two or three salespeople, but as they prove themselves, they may earn more responsibility. As a sales manager, you may be required to monitor the team's activity, provide on-the-field training, and recruit additional salespeople. You may have to perform these duties while continuing your own sales activities. Other sales management positions involve managing a local, regional, or nationwide sales division. Such jobs might include budgeting, training, recruiting, and other executive duties.

Top Management Positions. Sales experience makes an executive a valuable member of the management team. Although chief executive officers (CEOs) have traditionally come from the financial and legal ranks, companies are increasingly tapping into the sales and marketing departments to find their leaders. Organizations are looking for CEOs who are not only effective leaders and skilled strategists, but who also have excellent interpersonal skills and initiative.[18] Many skills used in selling resemble those needed in top management. Both jobs require great people skills. It is essential in both positions to maintain control under stress, to recognize opportunities and threats, and to locate, and analyze vast amounts of information.[19]

3. Job Security

Companies will always need salespeople. Selling is also more recession-proof than other professions; sales jobs were among the first to recover from the 2008 economic crisis in America.[20] Companies are always in search of ambitious salespeople and typically provide excellent rewards for top sales performers. They know that quality salespeople who become dissatisfied can leave and possibly take their established customers with them.

Because companies usually pay salespeople according to performance, they can directly affect their income by deciding how much time and effort to invest in the job. Thus, a salesperson's job security comes from personal decisions about how hard and how efficiently to work. Work, in many ways, is like money: *if you are willing to expend enough of it, you can have almost anything you want.*[21]

Sales Career Challenges

Like any other profession, a sales career has reasons why it may not be right for everyone. The work qualities some may see as advantages are distinct disadvantages to others. Some people view a fixed salary as more secure than a commission-based income that is dependent upon performance. Some people prefer careers that don't seem to be as tied to the global economic climate. Others dislike the irregular hours and travel often required, and plenty of people prefer work that doesn't require as much initiative or creative energy.

Probably the most difficult situation faced by every salesperson is handling rejection. Not every presentation and close produces a sale. Not every prospect needs the service or product, and an ethical salesperson never presses for an order from a prospect whose needs will not be met by that product. No salesperson can ever be 100 percent successful in closing sales, even when a prospect truly needs the product or service. The best salespeople learn that rejection is not personal.

Prospects who do not buy are refusing the product or service, not the salesperson.

The decision seldom has anything to do with the salesperson's worth. Even the occasional prospect who reacts negatively to a salesperson does so as a result of the prospect's personal opinion—an opinion that may be affected by prejudice or completely unfounded. Rejection is not proof that the salesperson is undeserving or inadequate. Salespeople who cannot separate their worth from what they sell may become paralyzed by the fear of being rejected.

Sales Job Classifications

Sales jobs are so diverse that they fit a wide variety of personal needs and interests. A great deal of variance exists from industry to industry. The responsibilities of a salesperson who calls on large manufacturing companies are vastly different from those of the real estate salesperson who sells single-family homes. Sales careers also vary within industries. For example, a residential real estate agent is in a different world from that of a real estate developer who puts together multimillion-dollar offers for office complexes or shopping centers. As diverse as sales jobs may be, they all share some basic similarities:

- The need to understand the prospect's problem.
- The need for relevant technical and product knowledge.
- The need for the discipline to successfully execute a sales plan.
- The ability to translate features into benefits.

There are many ways to classify different types of sales jobs: Business-to-business (B2B), business-to-consumer (B2C), direct selling, indirect selling, or personal selling, to name a few. No matter how you label the different types of selling, they can be broken down into the same basic categories.

The sales classification format developed by Derek Newton is the standard organization model for careers in professional selling because of his empirical research with over 1,000 sales executives from manufacturing, wholesaling, retail, and service firms. Newton's model is presented here as the basis for the four types of selling found across this variety of industries.[22]

1. Trade Selling

The trade seller's primary responsibility is to increase business from present and potential

customers through merchandising and promotional assistance. They usually deal with buyers who are resellers (wholesalers and retailers). Long-term relationships are essential for success. In addition to delivering orders and replenishing inventory, a trade salesperson's tasks may involve: persuading clients to provide additional shelf space, setting up product displays, and conducting in-store demonstrations for shoppers. Companies typically expect trade sellers to indirectly increase sales by assisting clients in moving a large volume of inventory.

2. Missionary Selling

The missionary salesperson's task is mostly one of educating those who ultimately decide what product the consumer will use. One standard example is a pharmaceutical sales rep who calls on physicians to introduce a drug company's products and persuade doctors to prescribe a new medication to patients. In addition to pharmaceutical companies, food and beverage manufacturers, transportation firms, and public utility companies employ missionary salespeople.

3. Technical Selling

An ever-growing class of salespeople is the technical specialist group: the engineers, scientists, and others with the technical expertise to clearly explain the advantages of the company's product. These salespeople sell directly to the firms that use their products.

They are especially vital in complex industries such as chemicals and machinery.

They act like management consultants in that they identify, analyze, and solve their customers' problems. In the past, technical specialists were more concerned with explaining the product than with securing the order. Today, however, more companies are teaching these salespeople some essential selling skills to help them make better presentations and close more sales.

4. New Business Selling

This type of salesperson seeks out and persuades new customers to buy for the very first time. They are incredibly vital to organizations that are focused on growth. New business selling includes selling brand-new products to existing customers or existing products to new customers. The characteristics discussed later in this chapter—perseverance, empathy, ability to ask questions, initiative, and resourcefulness—are vital to sales success for this category.

Order Takers vs. Order Getters. The *order taker* responds to requests, while the *order getter* is a creative problem solver. An order-taking salesperson merely reacts to customers' expressed desires. Inside sales positions (such as in retail sales) are generally order-taking by nature. Outside order takers are service salespeople who mainly assist retail clients in delivering orders or replenishing inventory.

An order taker may engage in *suggestive selling* by asking you to purchase an additional item. The next time you stop at a Chick-fil-A drive-thru and the person asks, "Would you like a cookie or lemonade with that?" You are observing suggestive selling in action. By being helpful and pleasant, retail workers may create a few sales, but more often, they only assist customers in completing the purchase of goods they have already chosen.

Order getting, or creative selling, requires ingenuity and the ability to generate demand for a product or service among potential buyers. The product may be tangible such as automobiles or real estate, or the product may be intangible such as investment services or advertising. Creative personal selling generally offers the most significant potential because it demands the highest level of individual skill, dedication, and effort.

If you are interested in a profession filled with order getting instead of order taking, social networking may help you find the right fit—which you will read about in this chapter's *Social Media Connection.*

Attributes of Successful Salespeople

There is no single list of traits that accurately describes every successful salesperson. They are as diverse as members of any other profession. They include both extroverts and introverts, and all the degrees in between. However, specific characteristics seem to be present in most successful salespeople, despite the numerous ways individuals express those characteristics and adapt them to their styles and purposes.[24]

Enthusiasm

Ralph Waldo Emerson said, "Nothing great was ever achieved without enthusiasm." One of the essential characteristics in salespeople is *enthusiasm*—but there is a difference between people who are enthusiastic about their product and those who are only excited about their commission. Enthusiasm in salespeople is based on a genuine belief in the product and a conviction that it will serve the needs of the prospect.[25] Such energy is communicated both verbally and nonverbally to prospects. Enthusiasm may be expressed as a calm, quiet confidence, or as an exciting action. Genuine enthusiasm is highly attractive and reassuring to prospects.

Empathy

Empathy, the ability to understand another person's concerns, opinions, and needs, whether sharing them or not, provides salespeople

The Social Media Connection

USING SOCIAL MEDIA TO LAND YOUR DREAM SALES CAREER

Is it possible to tweet your way to a new career? It may not be quite that easy, but career experts recommend leveraging social media sites such as Facebook, Twitter, and LinkedIn as a part of your job search.

Carisa Miklusak, principal of Ingenium Consulting Group and co-founder of SoMedios, suggests that job seekers use social media every step of the way. If you are new to the job market, social media is a useful way to research the culture of companies that interest you. While a corporate website can provide helpful information, a company's social media presence can offer additional insight into their culture and how they interact with employees and customers.

"On Facebook, for example, a job seeker may be able to read about the organization on the

Information tab, see pictures of a recent team outing to get a feel for the culture, and follow recent conversations between customers and the company—all critical factors in making a decision," Miklusak said. "Candidates should use these tools to pre-interview companies and determine if they are a true fit."

Once you get an interview, use social media sources to learn about the decision-makers you will be meeting. "By conducting a LinkedIn or Google search, a candidate will likely be able to gather a great deal of information about the background of their interviewer," Miklusak said. "This is becoming a widespread practice and prepares the candidates to customize their talk track and interview presentation to what they've learned about their interviewer. It also empowers candidates to come prepared with better questions."

At the offer stage, use social media to reach out to current or past employees. This is becoming common practice and can allow for real-time discussions of standard salary ranges, work assignments, and conditions.

The reach and influence of social networking are only getting higher and stronger. So, go ahead and see what social media can do for you during your career search.[23]

with the sales advantage of being able to follow and understand the prospect during a sales call. Empathy is the ability to pick up on the subtle clues and cues provided by others in order to accurately assess what they are thinking or feeling.

Empathy is useful when handling objections and unexpected presentation changes made by the prospect. Empathetic salespeople can sense changes in prospects and adjust their presentations accordingly. By careful listening, effective salespeople absorb prospects' reactions, generate an upbeat environment, and sell themselves to prospects. The combination of sincerity and compassion enables them to tailor the presentation to mesh precisely with the prospect's stated needs throughout the sales cycle.

Goal Direction

The best salespeople stay focused on their goals through the course of their daily activities. They understand how personal goals and organizational goals are interrelated, and they work to make both types of goals happen.[26] Goal-directed salespeople respond positively to incentives such as money, prestige, and recognition. When these incentives fit into their overall plan for achieving the goals that represent self-actualization for them, salespeople go all-out to win them.

Ability to Ask Questions

Good salespeople ask questions; poor ones keep talking. You need to remain in control of the sales interview, and the person who is asking questions is the one in control. When you ask the right questions, you will gain new prospects, discover valuable qualifying information, uncover hidden buying motives, and anticipate most objections. Questioning is your best tool for keeping the interview on track and moving toward a successful close, while also giving the prospect the feeling of remaining in control of the situation.

Resourcefulness

Top salespeople are the ones who are most resourceful. They can quickly think of new ways to make a point, new applications and creative uses for products, and different reasons for a prospect to make a buying decision. They can think on their feet under pressure. For these people, resourcefulness is an automatic response, like a reflex. Resourcefulness comes from an agile and analytical mind and allows you to stay on the right side of the fine line between being just right and very wrong.

The right word or phrase clears away the fog and reveals the solutions. The wrong word or phrase is like putting a drop of ink into a glass full of water: It obscures everything!

Administrative Ability

Effective self-management, especially the management of time, is essential to success in selling. Your most productive time is spent face-to-face with prospects. But you are also required to attend meetings, travel, wait, prepare for interviews, read, study, attend to paperwork, and conduct after-sale follow-up and service.

Salespeople must engage in many non-selling and administrative tasks. They, therefore, spend only a portion of their precious time in direct contact with prospects and clients. Efficient time management can make the difference between success and failure. Time and territory management is one of the most critical issues for salespeople today. According to a survey of more than 840 salespeople among companies with large sales forces, high-performing salespeople find ways to increase time with customers and maximize the effectiveness of their time spent on administrative duties. In a comparison of high-performing companies and low-performing companies, salespeople for the high-performers spent 40 percent more time with their best potential customers and 30 percent less time on administrative duties.[27]

Initiative

The best salespeople have a powerful, unrelenting, internal drive to excel. This intrinsic motivation can be shaped and molded, but

it cannot be taught. This type of motivation is what keeps great salespeople with their heads above water when others are sinking during tough economic times.[28] Successful salespeople are self-motivated. They are self-starters who exercise initiative. They do not wait to be told to prospect, to be assigned calls to make, or to be urged to end the presentation with a close. They see the work that needs to be done and take personal responsibility for doing it.

Perseverance

Setbacks often outnumber triumphs, and when this happens, salespeople must have reserves of strength and resilience to fall back on. Depending upon the type of sales activity and the product or service, the number of sales closed compared to the number of presentations made usually ranges from 5 percent to 50 percent or more. Salespeople need perseverance in several areas:

- The ability to keep going to another prospect no matter how many have said no.
- The ability to make repeated presentations to the same prospect.
- The ability to continue asking for an appointment until the prospect agrees to meet.

Pleasant Personality

The way to make a friend is to be one. People will always prefer a salesperson with a friendly, outgoing disposition. A key to forming a pleasant personality is to like people and genuinely enjoy knowing as many different kinds of people as possible.

Department store entrepreneur J.C. Penney said, "All great business is built on friendship." How do you build friendships in today's competitive sales climate? Find out what the buyer needs, then make every effort to deliver it. Ask yourself: "What would I do if I wanted to be friends with this person?" The answer will tell you how to build a long-term relationship.

SUMMARY

Selling is an essential part of human interaction that involves discovering needs and providing solutions.

Salespeople are well-paid professionals who make a significant impact on their organization's success.

Partnerships, relationships, and alliances are more than words—they are tools you can use to form winning strategies.

Professional selling offers opportunities that involve many different skill levels and diverse roles.

Selling is a demanding career that offers substantial rewards and outstanding opportunities for personal achievement.

Social media is an incredible tool for landing a sales position, from the initial search process to the offer stage.

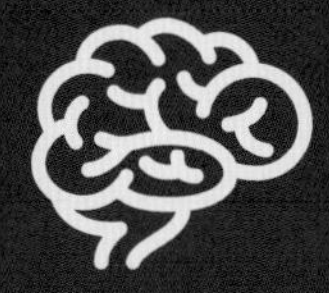

All personality types can be successful in sales, but specific characteristics enhance the likelihood of success.

If you are pleasant and genuinely desire to solve problems for your customers, you are well on your way to success.

Review Questions

1. In the sense that all persuasion is a form of "selling," name the types of situations in which you most frequently "sell." In which of these are you most often successful? If persuasion is an essential part of selling, is selling a form of leadership? Explain your answer.
2. What career limits exist within sales? Illustrate.
3. Are salespeople born or made? Justify your answer.
4. Why is a feeling of rejection a problem for salespeople? Is this feeling an inevitable part of a sales career?
5. Describe the four broad classes of sales jobs and give examples of each.
6. In addition to securing orders for products, in what ways do companies depend upon salespeople?
7. What responsibilities belong to the salesperson after the order is signed? How does the discharge of these responsibilities affect the entire sales process?
8. Salespeople are interdependent with other individuals in their company. Why is this true concerning the following factors: product changes, pricing, shipping, and competition?
9. Name some qualities that seem to be shared by the most successful salespeople. How do these traits contribute to success? Can they be developed, or are they innate? Does this mean that there is only one type of personality style that is successful in sales?

IN-CLASS EXERCISES

These exercises help build teams, improve communication, and emphasize the real-world side of selling. They are meant to be challenging, to help you learn how to deal with problems that have more than one correct answer, and to help you utilize a variety of skills beyond those used in a typical review question.

EXERCISE 1.1 What Do Salespeople Think?

Pair up with another student whom you do not already know. Contact a salesperson who does *not* work in retail sales (that is, avoid department stores, electronics stores, auto dealerships, etc.) and arrange an interview. During the meeting, ask the salesperson what sort of knowledge, skills, and personal characteristics contribute most to that person's success. How is success measured or determined? Ask what the most significant challenges or obstacles to success in that person's current position are. How does the person try to deal with these challenges or obstacles? Feel free to follow up with additional questions.

In class, be prepared to role-play the results of your interview; at the very least, be ready to discuss what you learned that pertains to lessons from this chapter.

EXERCISE 1.2 Who Are You?

You will work individually on this exercise. Copy the brief survey on the next page onto a sheet of paper, and then make five copies of that survey (or save it as a screen shot on your phone). Rate yourself on each of the personal characteristics, and put the results aside.

Enlist the help of five friends outside of this class. Give or send each friend a copy of the survey to answer about you. Remind them to be honest in their appraisal since you will use their responses to decide whether you are suited for a particular profession (do not mention sales or selling).

After all five people have completed and returned the survey, compare the results to your self-rating. Are there any discrepancies between your friends' ratings and your own? If so, how do you account for or explain them? Do the results confirm or weaken your confidence in pursuing a career in sales? Which personal characteristics do you think you need to work on to become more successful? Be prepared to discuss such questions in class or online.

Please rate the person who gave you this survey according to the following personal characteristics by circling the appropriate response. Since your friend will use the results to help determine whether he/ she is suited for a particular profession, you must be candid. When you finish, return the completed survey to your friend.

1. Enthusiastic

Always *Usually* *Seldom* *Never*

2. Empathetic, Able to Understand Others

Always *Usually* *Seldom* *Never*

3. Goal-Directed

Always *Usually* *Seldom* *Never*

4. Able to Ask Good Questions

Always *Usually* *Seldom* *Never*

5. Resourceful, Creative

Always *Usually* *Seldom* *Never*

6. Well Organized, Efficient

Always *Usually* *Seldom* *Never*

7. Self-Motivated, Responsible

Always *Usually* *Seldom* *Never*

8. Persevering, Determined, Tenacious

Always *Usually* *Seldom* *Never*

9. Pleasant, Personable, Outgoing

Always *Usually* *Seldom* *Never*

Case Studies

These case studies present you with selling scenarios that require you to apply the skills discussed in the chapter and give you training through practical learning situations. They are meant to be both engaging and challenging, and like the exercises, don't have one right answer.

CASE 1.1—Whom Would You Recommend?

Imagine you are a corporate recruiter who has been retained by a large electrical equipment-manufacturing corporation to find a new salesperson for the corporation's regional sales force. Your job as a recruiter is to select and pass along the résumé of the single applicant whom you judge most likely to succeed. You conduct your search under conflicting pressures: on the one hand, you have time to interview only three candidates; on the other hand, the one you recommend must be retained by the corporation for at least three months, or your firm will be required to return its fee.

1. **Greg** strikes you immediately as a go-getter. Upon entering your office, he strides confidently across the room, with his arm outstretched to shake your hand. Greg makes eye contact and announces how pleased he is to meet you. Before you can invite him to sit, he perches on the edge of the chair in front of your desk and launches into a list of reasons why he is qualified for this job. As Greg talks, you become aware that he is pleasant, well dressed, outgoing, and very enthusiastic about working for your client. He researched the company and marshaled all of the factors in his background that make him a good match for the position. Although you haven't said much, you didn't need to, since Greg has done an excellent job of anticipating your questions and concerns. After about 20 minutes, he asks if you need anything else and stands, thanking you for such a pleasant interview.

2. **Martha** presents a somewhat reserved demeanor. Although pleasant and friendly, she is nervous despite her impressive résumé. As you ask about her prior experience, Martha reveals that her last employer terminated her for the inability to meet her sales quota. Martha claims that she never received significant product training or positive support from management when she couldn't produce. Nevertheless, because of

her previous success as a B2B (business-to-business) representative for a hardwood importing company, she feels that she would thrive in a similar B2B environment. Martha proudly explains how she cultivated customers for as long as two years and how she always followed up with clients to ensure she continued to meet their needs. Before she leaves, she briefly summarizes her B2B selling success and hopes that her lack of technical knowledge won't prevent her from being considered for this position.

3. **Cynthia** is an older applicant who wants to change careers. There is a direct, no-nonsense air about her as she explains why. For 17 years, she worked as a mechanical engineer for a major tool and die manufacturer, rising to the level of design supervisor. When her position was outsourced to a plant overseas, she found herself at a crossroads. Frankly, she was tired of working in a design lab with the same dozen people all day, and similar jobs in her field were becoming rare. Although she admits that she has no sales training whatever, she is hoping that her technical background will gain the attention of the company's sales manager. At the end of her interview, she points out that working for the same company for 17 years testifies to her perseverance, dedication, and ability to work with others. You assure her that her application will receive every consideration.

With your own firm's fee on the line, which applicant will you recommend, and why? Which applicant most closely approximates your personality and style, and why?

CASE 1.2—The Dejected Colleague

Mike was on a rampage. Having knocked over the water cooler in the copy room, he proceeded to kick in the front of one of the copiers. Hearing the commotion, Frank, his friend and colleague, burst through the closed door, finding Mike slumped over and in tears.

"Hey, buddy, what's the matter? What's wrong?" Frank asked, putting his arm around Mike's shoulder.

"I just can't take it anymore," Mike managed to choke out between sobs. "I'm a failure. I'm going to quit. I've failed my family and myself."

"Has anything in particular happened?" Frank knew that Mike had been in a sales slump, but he didn't know the details of the struggle.

"I've lost two big accounts. I can't take the rejection anymore," Mike sobbed. "And the long hours and travel are killing my family life."

"I understand," said Frank softly as Mike's sobbing subsided. "Here, let me help you clean up this mess. Then, let's go get a cup of coffee somewhere so we can talk about all this."

What should Frank say to Mike in the coffee shop? Mike is having some problems with aspects of the sales profession in general. Are these problems the sort of thing that salespersons can reasonably expect to encounter? What should Frank help Mike call to mind that would get Mike back on the right track? How can Frank be empathetic without allowing Mike's dejection to continue to be overwhelming?

RELATIONSHIP SELLING

OVERVIEW

For most salespeople, a lot goes into getting a yes. A successful sale represents moving through multiple steps promptly and doing so in a manner that benefits everyone involved. This chapter introduces the eight-step Relationship Selling Cycle that makes up the last half of the book. If you fully understand what each step entails, you will experience success in selling much more quickly than those who stumble through the process without a road map.

OBJECTIVES

- Understand the role of relationship selling and how it differs from past stereotypes of selling.
- Learn what fosters relationships and what damages them.
- Compare and contrast relationship selling and traditional selling.
- Learn the steps in the Relationship Selling Cycle and the purpose of each step.
- Examine the usefulness of continuous quality improvement in a sales organization.
- Understand the importance of relationships in our multicultural world.

The Heart of Selling

The profound effects of the Internet and technology on professional selling are impossible to deny. According to reports, online sales continue to increase at a yearly rate of 14.8 percent, while brick-and-mortar sales are growing at just 1.9 percent.[1]

With all the changes in business, it's easy to see why some speculate that online sales and technological advances may soon make traditional salespeople obsolete. But it's not salespeople that have become obsolete; it's old sales techniques.[2]

As a salesperson, are you at risk of being replaced by a website? Unless you are genuinely helping your customers achieve results that they would not be able to accomplish without you, what you do *is* at risk. That doesn't mean that the sales profession is going away. It will only continue to grow once more salespeople realize that their job descriptions have changed.

Sales professionals can no longer be order takers. Instead, they must see their role as being the ones to help customers find and develop new opportunities. Today's sales force must assume a far more significant role in the success of their customers and clients—and relationship selling is the way to achieve that.[3]

View yourself not as the conveyor of information, but as the developer of opportunities.

The role of the salesperson has never been more critical. Sophisticated buyers require skilled advice and expertise, and it is here that face-to-face selling has been and will continue to be the most effective channel to the customer. Even web-based companies such as Charles Schwab and Dell Computer have on-the-ground sales forces to reach market segments that require complex customized products and services. This new selling is all about value creation: *How the selling process itself can be used to create value for the customer.*

Relationship selling isn't a novel idea; the concept has been around for a long time. In recent years, there has been a notable shift toward relationship-centered selling, and it's easy to see why. With the decrease in consumer confidence and the increase in online sales, more companies are searching for ways to build value in the eyes of customers.[4] The willingness and ability to meet each client's needs in a way that builds trust and loyalty is the cornerstone of building partnerships.

Build or Break a Relationship

Partnership is a positive word that makes customers feel that you are looking out for their best interests. The relationship between customer and salesperson is not a legal partnership but an informal one that symbolizes trust and cooperation. The best salespeople take the time to get to know the customer's business situation, needs, decision-making process, and the competitive environment. For customers, a buying decision usually means a decision to enter into a long-term relationship with salespeople and their companies. It is much like a "business marriage." They have a variety of options and choices open to them, including not buying anything at all. When customers decide to buy from a salesperson, they become dependent on that sales rep. And since they have likely had unpleasant buying experiences in the past, they are often uneasy and uncertain about getting into this kind of dependency relationship.[5]

Exhibit 2.1 illustrates the key elements that can build or break this trust-bond relationship between buyer and seller. Relationship selling allows you to grasp a company's needs by putting yourself in the customer's shoes. *You are first a diagnostician.*

EXHIBIT 2.1 How to Build or Break a Relationship

RELATIONSHIP BUILDERS

1. Treat donors like lifelong partners.
2. Become a solutions provider.
3. Deliver more than you promise.
4. Schedule regular service calls.
5. Develop open and honest communication.
6. Use the "we can" approach.
7. Take responsibility for mistakes made.
8. Be an ally for the customer's business.

RELATIONSHIP BREAKERS

1. Focus only on making the sale.
2. Wait for a problem to develop.
3. Over-promise and under-deliver.
4. Wait for customers to call you.
5. Lie or make exaggerated claims.
6. Use the "us vs. them" approach.
7. Blame somebody else. Knock a competitor.
8. Focus on personal gain.

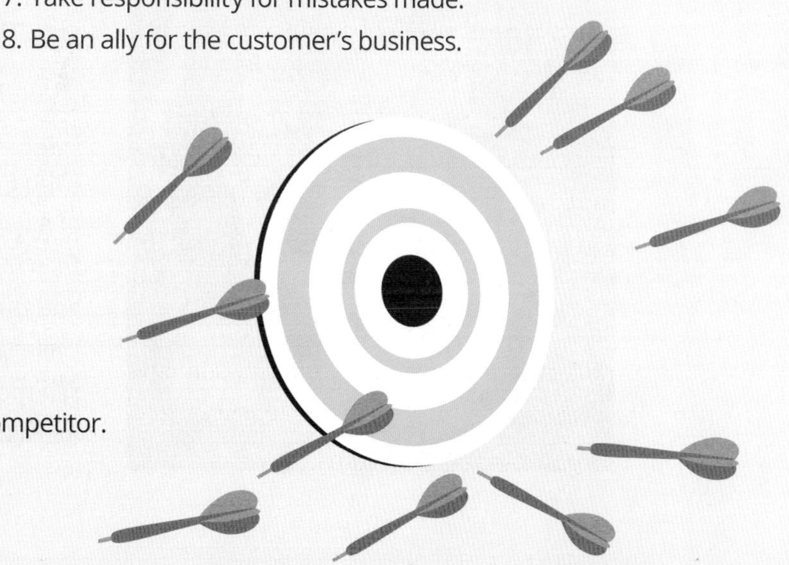

Relationship salespeople create an information transfer, support for client goals, and enthusiasm for their success. The top salespeople have escaped the "selling" mentality and encourage the customer to share their needs. In the face of increased competition in the software space, Huddle—a provider of secure, cloud-based collaboration software—knows that the customers' needs come first. They know that roughly 80 percent of a company's future revenue comes from just 20 percent of its existing customers. Therefore, it's essential to think about what the customer wants and needs and creating the offering accordingly.[6]

That is the precise mentality that will guarantee a company's survival. It isn't always about who has the better product or best price, but who can best provide solutions to the customers consistently, and on their terms.

To be a consultant rather than just a salesperson, you have to be a creative resource and a value provider to clients. The relationship salesperson works hard helping others succeed—not merely helping them spend their money. Unless you are willing to commit to excellence, you will never experience the satisfaction that comes when everyone wins. Here are some key characteristics of relationship selling:

- Discover and understand the customers' problems and needs.
- Partner with your customers and become a valuable resource for information.
- Demonstrate to customers how they can achieve their goals with your product or service.
- Have a genuine conviction that your company, your product, and your services are the best for your customers.
- Believe in yourself because a positive attitude makes it all work.

Relationship Selling vs. Traditional Selling

If you learn the Relationship Selling Cycle steps and what it takes to perform each action well, you will experience higher rates of success and enjoy your job much more than those who stumble through the process without a plan. The portion of the sales cycle that occurs face-to-face between the salesperson and the prospect includes these four steps:

1. The Approach
2. Identifying Needs
3. Making the Presentation
4. Handling Objections and Gaining Commitment

Exhibit 2.2 contrasts the amount of time the relationship salesperson and the traditional salesperson spend in each step. You can see from the figure that the old pyramid model of selling has been turned upside down. The 40 percent of the equation for the traditional model that used to be closing is now building trust in the relationship model. Meanwhile, reassuring the customer and closing has shrunk to just 10 percent in the new model.

The relationship salesperson spends the majority of time in the first two steps—building trust and asking questions—whereas the traditional salesperson spends most of his time presenting features and trying to close. The goal is to learn how to communicate with your business partners and establish an alliance that is extensive in scope and relevant to the customer's vision.[7]

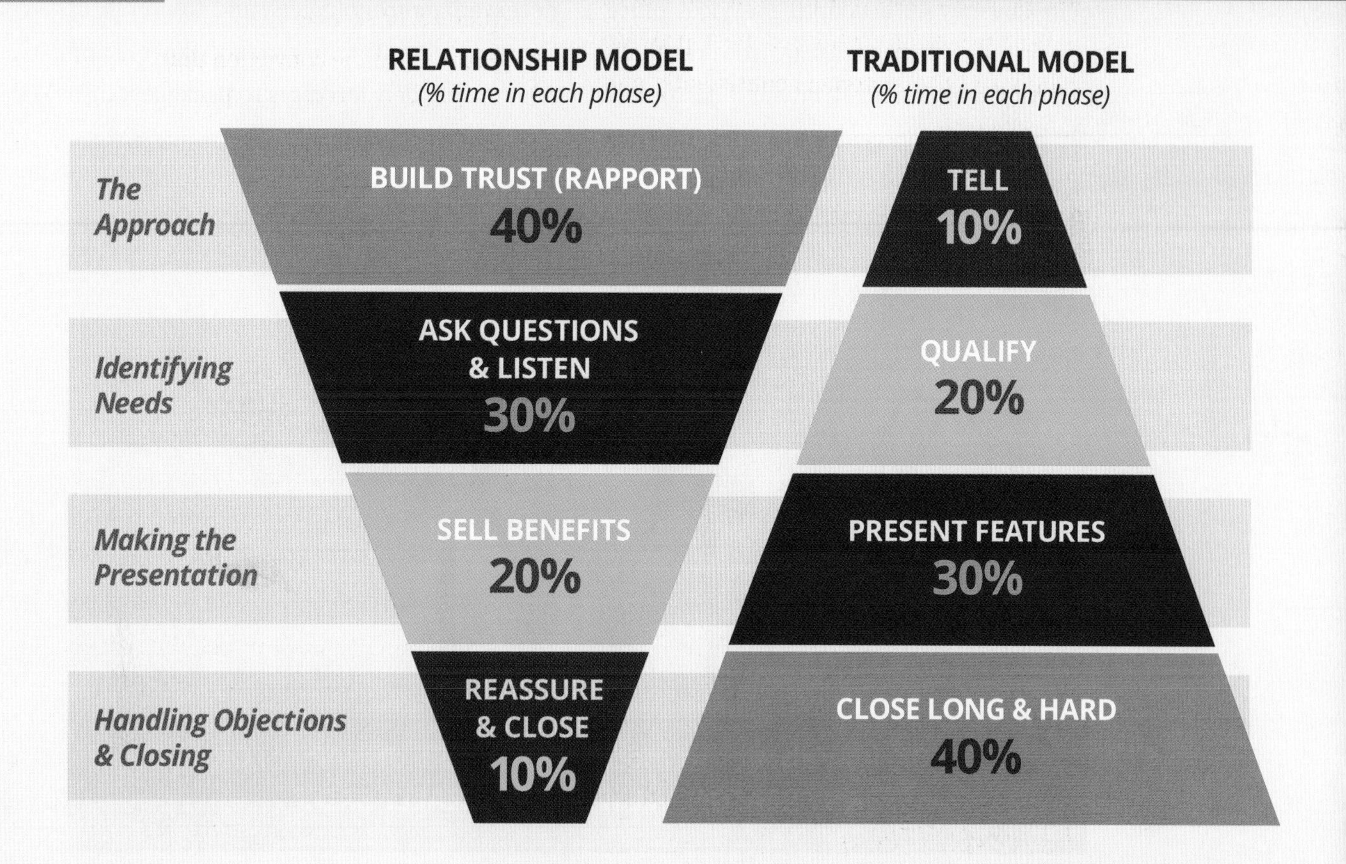

Customers Buy Solutions

Customers can now conduct many of their transactions online and have little need for a salesperson that doesn't add value to the overall process. Therefore, relationship salespeople must possess a much more sophisticated and complex set of skills that caters to modern, busy customers.

Low-end selling—which is essentially transaction processing and order taking—continues to fade away in favor of more efficient, cost-effective online selling options. But this doesn't mean that the Internet will replace the professional salesperson; selling is merely becoming more strategic. It's moving up the food chain, and the need for relationship selling is increasing. Your company may sell accounting services, office equipment, or website design. However, that's not what customers are buying—customers are trying to increase sales and improve efficiency. By demonstrating how you can help customers achieve the goals of their organization, you distinguish yourself from competitors. Selling is still about relationships, and people buy from people they like.[8]

Order takers will vanish, but creative relationship-focused salespeople will flourish.

The Relationship Selling Cycle

You can gain a better understanding of the entire sales process and the problems it generates by breaking the sale into its principal tasks. This text will present these steps in a logical sequence, but they are not necessarily chronological, and the order of the steps will vary. The ebbs and flows of any relationship defy attempts to package it into nice, neat compartments.

"OK, how about this motto: 'IF YOU ARE UNHAPPY FOR ANY REASON, WE WILL FEEL REALLY BAD'."

Regardless of account size or potential, you are sure to perform certain predictable tasks each time. These tasks, such as identifying prospects and determining needs, may be called the "steps" in the selling cycle. When organized into a prescribed sequence, they comprise an overall structure rather than a lock-step approach to selling. The eight basics of successful selling described in Exhibit 2.3 are the focus of chapters 8 through 15, and they represent your guide to a successful sales career.

Phase One

Identifying a Qualified Prospect. *Prospecting* is the process of searching for someone with a need for the product or service, the ability to pay for it, and the authority to make a buying decision. One of the best ways to find qualified prospects is to review current accounts to see who needs service, who might need more than they currently have, and who may not know about new products or services you offer. At the same time, survey your territory to

EXHIBIT 2.3 The Eight-Step Relationship Selling Cycle

identify new leads and find out information on the businesses in your area that might be interested in your product. The reason for this step is simple: Sales professionals must study the people they want to approach.[9]

Planning Pre-Approach Activities. After you identify qualified prospects, establish a definite purpose for each sales call. To accomplish this, you must evaluate your potential customers' needs and also determine who the decision-makers are in the companies you have studied. These activities equip you to interact with the customer and then develop an action plan and call schedule to set appointments.

The Social Media Connection

HOW SOCIAL MEDIA CAN MAKE COLD CALLING A LITTLE EASIER

If you've ever been to a chiropractor, you know that they like to take x-rays and observe your posture before they ever make their first adjustment. Such pre-checks make the entire experience more helpful and relevant. Similarly, if you jump in and try to 'fix' a prospect's problems without the proper pre-approach, you will not get through to as many people as you should.

The good news is that by using social media "touches" before your next sales call, you will have a higher likelihood of making a genuine connection—and hopefully securing that first appointment. The best part is you will seem more professional and less intrusive. Here are some great ways to use social media to get on your prospects' radar to turn a cold call into a warm call:

- If they have a blog, comment on a relevant post.
- Follow that prospect on Twitter.
- Send a LinkedIn request before your first call so that your name is familiar.
- Retweet or mention your prospect in a tweet.
- Join the same LinkedIn group and contribute to a conversation within that group.
- Like a comment made by the prospect.
- Endorse them for a skill on LinkedIn.

Phase Two

Approaching the Prospect. What happens during the opening minutes of the face-to-face encounter affects the success of the whole presentation. Some people do not thaw out immediately, which means you may need to find icebreakers that help them feel more at ease with you. Spend time finding the prospect's comfort level.[10] Most first-time meetings between a salesperson and a prospective customer produce an *egocentric predicament.* The dilemma arises from the salesperson's fear of being rejected and the prospect's fear of being sold something he doesn't need. By redesigning your approach to selling, you can calm the prospect's fear of buying and reduce your fear of selling.

Treat prospects as individuals and not as carbon copies of everyone else.

Discovering Needs. During this step of the sales encounter, you and your client learn together whether the client needs or wants something that you can provide. Because the success of the whole process rests on this fundamental discovery, spend whatever time is necessary on this stage. Ask questions to get to know the prospect's needs and problems. One of your primary goals in every sales situation should be to *create an atmosphere within which an act of trust can occur.* Tell yourself that you want to build a relationship, not just close a sale. You want customers who have confidence in your integrity and ability and confidence in your company and its product or service. You don't talk prospects into a sale; you listen them into a sale.

Making the Presentation. Your evaluation of the prospect's situation should lead you naturally into the presentation of product benefits that fit the needs previously expressed. Every product or service has both features and benefits. A *feature* is any fact about the product or service, tangible or intangible. For example, a feature of a particular automobile may be front-wheel drive. However, prospects want to know about *benefits* rather than features. The front-wheel-drive feature is meaningless unless it satisfies a need, solves a problem, or provides an advantage. Instead of saying, "This car features front-wheel drive," you could instead say, "The front-wheel drive provides ease of handling and safety, which we discussed was a primary concern of yours." In other words, tie each feature back to a previously stated need.

A prospect does not buy without being sure that what you are saying is true. That is why you do not create sales; instead, people buy based on their expectations. No one likes to be sold. They want to see the value of what you offer and then make their decisions based on their assessment of whether your product satisfies their needs. The salesperson who holds confident, positive expectations closes far more sales than the one who expects rejection.

> **"In professional selling, as in medicine, prescription before diagnosis is malpractice."**
> *Tony Alessandra*

Handling Objections and Gaining Commitment. Now is the time to verbally clarify and confirm what both you and the client will do to make the solution work. This part of the overall process helps to avoid misunderstandings by bringing any objections that exist out into the open so that you can address them. Each clarification and confirmation adds weight to the case in favor of a favorable buying decision. As shown in Exhibit 2.4, when the scale of decision tips far enough toward the positive side, the prospect says yes. When that happens, everyone wins—the client, you, and your company. Relationship selling is a matter of presenting positive benefits that respond to a need, use, and value. Selling in this manner reduces your need to deal with resistance, answer objections, or haggle over price. Since the client has been an active participant throughout, the commitment and close should be the natural conclusion to a successful sales interview.

Phase Three

Service After the Sale. The final step of relationship selling is service after the sale. "Whether you call it customer retention,

EXHIBIT 2.4 **The Scale of Decision**

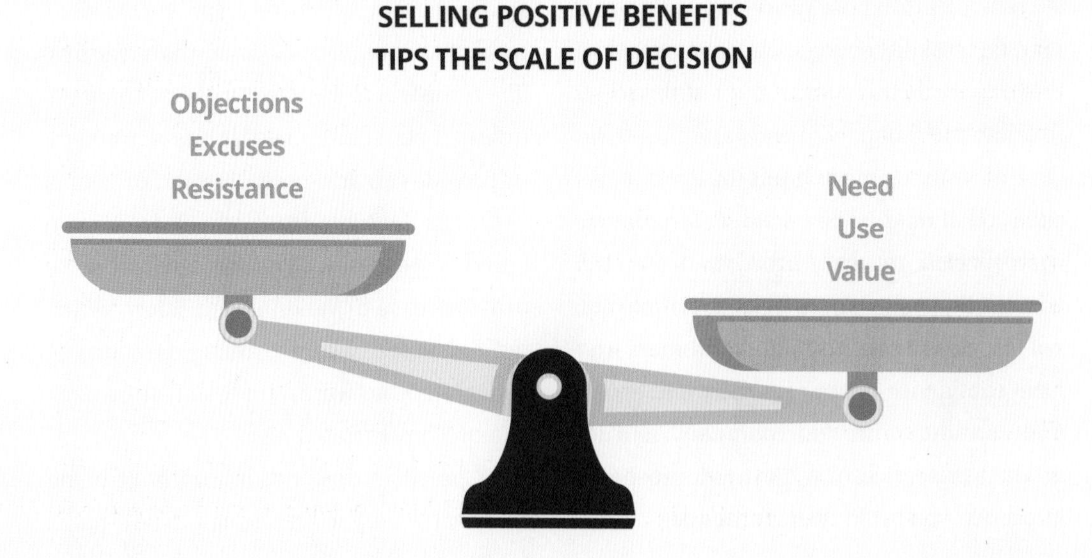

account management, or just staying in touch, developing a strategy so that you don't lose the customers you have is vital to the success of any business," says Rhonda Abrams, CEO of The Planning Shop, a book publisher for entrepreneurs.[11] Service, service, and more service is what counts and gives you a competitive edge. Plenty of satisfied customers do not come back unless you create a trust-bond relationship.

Ultimately, you should look at customer satisfaction as an economic asset, just like any other asset of the company. Consider service after the sale to be another essential step within the sales cycle.[12] Creating customer satisfaction is an income-producing endeavor. Clients must sense that you genuinely care about them. Service after the sale is your way of expressing appreciation for their business. Service makes the difference—and is as essential as the quality of the product.

Continuous Quality Improvement

Total Quality Management (TQM) has been a popular topic for years. The idea has been around for so long that leaders often fail to see just how relevant and compelling it still is today. The scope of a typical TQM program covers three main areas: 1) The quality system, 2) The process of continuous improvement, and 3) The development of the staff involved.[13] TQM is an essential building block for relationship selling, and the principles have practical implications for salespeople.

How does TQM fit into relationship selling? Most organizations have a robust strategic plan in place to achieve excellence and make sales. Where they struggle is in the execution. Organizations achieve their goals only when they successfully hardwire excellence across all operational areas. One way to accomplish this is through TQM implementation.[14] With TQM, the center of all discussions is the customer; everyone inside and outside the company is a customer. Continuous quality improvement is a philosophy, an overall style of management that focuses on customer satisfaction.

FedEx CEO Fred Smith states that "We aim for 100 percent customer satisfaction and all FedEx employees must have an 'above and beyond' attitude when doing their jobs. The attitude of doing whatever it takes to serve the customers is reflected from top to bottom in the organization's structure. This kind of spirit is integral to the FedEx work culture."[15] But even before they can service customers, Smith states, "Employee satisfaction is a prerequisite to customer satisfaction."[16] Therefore, TQM not only focuses on fostering healthy relationships with customers but also on building connections within organizations.

The list below highlights the main points of TQM that deal directly with fostering relationships and building lasting associations. While there are variations in the language and scope of TQM programs, it is possible to target these five principles that are especially relevant in the practice of relationship selling:

1. **Listen and learn from your customers and your employees.**
2. **Continuously improve the partnership.**
3. **Build teamwork by establishing trust and mutual respect.**
4. **Do it right the first time to ensure customer satisfaction.**
5. **Improve communication in your own company to broaden the utilization of your company's resources. Everybody is involved in the relationship.**

The 85/15 Rule

TQM is practiced today thanks to the pioneering work of W. Edwards Deming. One of Deming's most important lessons is his "85-15" rule.[18] When things go wrong in the field, there is an 85 percent chance the system is at fault. Only about 15 percent of the time is it the individual salesperson's fault. TQM means the organization's culture is defined by and supports the constant attainment of customer satisfaction, through an integrated system of tools, techniques, and training.

Service Quality

The concept of *service quality* has two dimensions: 1. The process of delivering the service, and 2. The actual outcome. What must an organization do to provide exceptional service quality that creates a favorable outcome, and how does the salesperson fit into the process? First, in order for everyone in your company to become customer-oriented, they must think in terms of the whole process rather than just their individual tasks. The goal is to develop a customer, and that's a process in which the salesperson is only one player. The process includes every department in your organization, from finance to HR to customer service. Therefore, solving a customer's problem is not the salesperson's job alone; the whole organization gets behind the effort. Building customer relationships is everybody's responsibility.[17]

It is essential to focus on how you relate to plant and office employees because this can make a difference in the way they treat your customers. It pays to be liked and appreciated by staff people, especially those in sales support, credit, billing, and shipping. Take a moment from time to time to compliment and thank the support people in your company for the great job they are doing.

Prospects and customers notice and think about everyone they come in contact with during the sales encounter. The relationship between perceived effort and customer service is a powerful one. When you and the customer interact, the quality of the interaction itself is an integral part of the relationship. If the customer feels that the salesperson is empathetic during their interaction, it translates more naturally to customer happiness.[19]

> **"I can live for two months on a good compliment."**
> *Mark Twain*

Most business success stories involve taking an old idea or product and doing a better job with it than the next company. Amazon didn't invent online selling; they just did it better, giving customers the ability to have convenience, speed, and a customer-centric approach to returns. Then there is Southwest Airlines! They aren't the oldest airline around, but they are indeed the ones with a reputation for having no hidden fees

or hassles. They figured out how to offer passengers consistent service without extra charges in a way that has kept them profitable while other airlines struggle to survive.

The overall point is, you can get a lot out of a current product or service if you change the processes around it, or change how you deliver it. The objective is to change those processes enough that you are providing more value to your customers or, at the very least, holding on to those customers by offering a fair price.

The $332,000 Customer

A Passion for Excellence author Tom Peters says, "A customer is not a transaction; a customer is a relationship."[20] The missing link in service often is an intense awareness of the customer's point of view. The process of handling the problem is as necessary to customers as the solution to the problem itself. In other words, companies must organize their delivery system to answer every customer's implied question: "What are you going to do for me today?"

Peters uses the example of former Dallas Cadillac dealer Carl Sewell, who wrote a book called *Customers for Life*. Sewell claims that the value of a single lifetime customer at his dealership is $332,000. However, he goes on to suggest that happy lifetime customers generate four or five other satisfied lifetime customers. So, one Cadillac customer is roughly a 1.5 million dollar customer.

Two investments Sewell made illustrate his understanding of the value he places on customer satisfaction. Number one, he bought a street sweeper to keep the front of his dealership clean. First impressions count for everything, and people judge his dealership by its cleanliness. Secondly, he convinced an upscale local restaurant to open a branch in his service bay. When it's a simple repair, a lot of his customers come in and enjoy a hot meal while they wait.

Some salespeople will read about TQM and say, "This is nothing new; it's common sense stuff." They are right, but it has taken many years for men such as W. Edwards Deming, Joseph Juran, and Genichi Taguchi to refine and perfect this philosophy.[21]

Selling in a Multicultural World

With all of the talk about the globalization of markets, it can be easy to forget to look within our own companies for evidence of growing cultural diversification. The truth is that while other professions have seen jumps in their numbers of workers from diverse ethnic backgrounds, the sales profession has been slow to follow.[22] But according to the latest U.S. Census data, the number of minority business owners now totals over 22 percent. It's safe to assume that an increase in the diversity of the sales force will naturally follow.[23]

Today's Diverse Workforce

These changes are exciting! Think of the benefits your company has to gain from the knowledge and experience of salespeople from diverse cultures. The varied backgrounds of your sales staff may even serve as bridges to developing more meaningful relationships with customers from around the world.[24] And, while no individual should ever be stereotyped, it may be helpful to understand the broad characteristics of different cultures to better connect with others.[25]

Relationships remain at the heart of developing trust and partnerships in a multicultural sales setting.

An Emphasis on Diversity. Understanding the multicultural perspectives of your sales force and your customers does not come without effort. For this shift in understanding to take place, companies will need to focus on ways to make improved relationships with multicultural partners a priority. As with other aspects of communication coming from your company, this shift needs to happen in a way that reminds customers and employees alike that you value them as individuals. No

"Every one of your employees is human.
You have a rather narrow definition of 'diversity', don't you?"

one likes to feel used. One such company that has made a strong commitment to ethnic diversity is technology titan Apple Inc. They believe that:[26]

> *"Great ideas push the world forward. And they can come from anywhere. At Apple, we rely on our employees' diverse backgrounds and perspectives to spark innovation. So we're hiring more inclusively, choosing partners who make diversity a priority, and creating opportunities for the next generation."*

Equipped for Understanding

Once companies have made multicultural relationships a priority, they must take active steps to make it happen. Employee education is essential! Depending on the level of interaction with people from varied backgrounds, the training may involve only a small component of new employee orientation. For others, it may mean the need for ongoing training. Nissan Motor Corporation has been offering language training to its employees for years because the company recognizes the value of cross-cultural training and skillsets.[27]

A fundamental principle behind TQM is that customer satisfaction begins inside your company with employee satisfaction. Only when you understand, respect, and support salespeople from all backgrounds can you know and relate well to your customers.

The evidence of improved relationships is in the sales figures. A study published in *Personnel Psychology* shows that minority salespeople working in pro-diversity firms increase their annual sales by $21,000 to $27,000 per individual. Patrick F. McKay, from the School of Management and Labor Relations at Rutgers University, says, "A pro-diversity climate is important to mitigate discrimination among African-American and Hispanic employees because they are most likely to experience discrimination." If salespeople know their company supports them, they feel more confident, and this, in turn, is reflected in their enhanced job performance and increased sales.[28]

SUMMARY

Selling has evolved from the art of persuasion to the psychology of relationship selling.

The relationship cycle of selling includes: the approach, need discovery, the presentation, objections, the close, and follow-up.

The three phases of the sales cycle represent the effort required before you meet, during face-to-face time, and after the sale.

The purpose of relationship selling is to discover prospect needs and become a solutions provider!

Selling at its best is customer-oriented and requires extensive knowledge of the prospect.

Build relationships and foster extreme customer loyalty through continuous quality improvement.

Promote the mindset that everyone inside and outside the company is a customer through a TQM approach.

Understand the diverse perspectives of today's marketplace to improve relationships with co-workers and customers.

Review Questions

1. Compare and contrast the stereotype of traditional selling and professional relationship selling.
2. What questions must a salesperson answer 'yes' to before it is possible to make a recommendation to buy?
3. What is the difference between the features of the product and its benefits? Which is most useful in the selling situation? Why? Should the other, then, be mentioned at all? How?
4. Name at least three reasons why a prospect may resist making a buying decision. For each reason, tell how the salesperson could have prevented this particular type of resistance.
5. If a salesperson encounters sales resistance, how can he or she close the sale in spite of the opposition? Is this always synonymous with "hard sell"?
6. What is the purpose of service after the sale? What does it include? Whose responsibility is such a service?
7. Who needs to be acquainted with the organization's underlying philosophy of business? If all members of the organization do not understand that philosophy, what types of problems might result? Why?
8. To what extent must a sales rep agree with the company's commitment to continuous quality improvement?
9. Why is multicultural diversity within companies important for businesses today? What impact does increased diversity have on the customer?

IN-CLASS EXERCISES

These exercises help build teams, improve communication, and emphasize the real-world side of selling. They are meant to be challenging, help you learn how to deal with problems that have more than one correct answer, and help you utilize a variety of skills beyond those used in a typical review question.

EXERCISE 2.1 Can You Spot "Relationship Selling?"

Divide into four-person teams for this exercise. Working individually, conduct an online search to find two sales training videos that reflect traditional selling techniques and two sales training videos that demonstrate relationship selling techniques. Exchange your results with your other team members (this can be done online as well). Discuss everyone's findings and, as a team, decide which single example of each approach is best or most obvious, and why.

Be careful that your team's final selection includes two videos that focus on the same part of the sales cycle (e.g., closing vs. closing, approach vs. approach, presentation vs. presentation). Otherwise, when you present your videos to the rest of the class, they would have no logically compelling reason to decide between them; they would be comparing apples with oranges, as it were.

In class (utilizing available technology), present your team's two selections and invite discussion of each by the class. Encourage the class to consider each example in light of the two approaches to selling described in Chapter 2. Without presuming that one approach is superior to the other, ask the class which approach they find most effective, and why. No matter which video the class seems to prefer, see if you can convince them otherwise!

EXERCISE 2.2 Enjoyable Selling

For this exercise, pair up with another student whom you do not already know. Agree between you that for this exercise, one of you will adopt the role of a traditional seller, and the other the role of a relationship-focused seller. Outside of class, develop a complete sales script from approach through closing for selling your counterpart a new home entertainment system. Your script should be developed according to traditional sales methods or relationship sales methods, as outlined in Chapter 2.

In class, take turns making your respective sales pitches to one another. Regardless of whether a sale was closed successfully in either case, jot down a brief response to each of the following questions. Think about the reasons for your replies, and be prepared to discuss them in class or online.

- What difficulties arose as you employed your script to sell the home entertainment system to your counterpart?
- Can you attribute any of these difficulties to the method of selling—traditional or relationship—that you used?
- As a customer, what did you find annoying, if anything, about your partner's approach to selling?
- As a seller, what did you find most annoying about your approach to selling?
- Given your total experience in this exercise, which approach to selling do you prefer, and why?

Case Studies

The following case studies present you with selling scenarios that require you to apply the critical skills discussed in the chapter and give you training through practical learning situations. They are meant to be both engaging and challenging, and like the exercises, don't have one right answer.

CASE 2.1—The Nervous VP for Sales

As vice president for marketing and sales for Netwerx, Inc., a firm specializing in videoconferencing equipment and software systems, Tom Nelson was nervous. He had just left a meeting with the company's chief financial officer, Brad Poindexter, that had not gone well. Tom had passed along the news from one of his sales managers that a major account was on the verge of going sour. The sales manager had reported that Secure Title, a title search and insurance company with offices in 50 major metropolitan areas, had not responded to communications regarding the renewal of their annual contract. The account was worth $450,000 per year to Netwerx; and in the current business climate, they could not afford to lose it. Worse, word on the street was that Secure Title was aggressively shopping for a lower price since its own business had fallen off due to the commercial real estate collapse. Brad, the CFO, had pushed Tom hard: "What in blazes is the matter with your people? Tell 'em to get on the horn and find out what's going on. If we lose this account, heads will roll, starting with yours, Tom!"

Tom had been worried for quite a while before this crisis. From a friend in R&D, he knew that Netwerx was about to roll out an improved, more efficient software package that would run on their existing videoconferencing hardware, but no meetings with marketing and sales had been held. Moreover, other vendors with inferior products were touting their lower price with some success. Netwerx had already seen a 17% decline in annual revenues. With no Christmas bonus last year, some of his salespeople were getting restless.

Ever since the annual meeting of the National Marketing and Sales Association last fall, Tom had been mulling over the desirability of shifting strategies for Netwerx. At the meeting, he had been exposed to a series of presentations on "relationship selling" and TQM. Netwerx had never entertained such an approach. Up to this point, the company had focused on touting the superior features of their system, giving their clients tickets to sporting events and golf outings, and aggressively closing sales. But Tom feared that such a traditional approach might not be effective in a sluggish economy. A meeting of Netwerx's executive committee was scheduled for next week. The CFO had made it clear that he expected a positive report from Tom.

What should Tom say to the executive committee? Which factors should Tom consider as he decides what to do?

CASE 2.2—Four-Leaf-Clover's Transition

The "boiler room" at Four-Leaf-Clover, a 66-year-old financial planning firm, was aptly named. Hour by hour, day in and day out, the phones never stopped. Using automatic dialers connected to a high-end CRM (customer relationship management) system, the sales force continually called random prospects to elicit new business. Typically, after a few perfunctory questions, attention would turn quickly to a presentation of the features and advantages of new financial instruments structured for wealthy individuals who were not averse to risk. The psychological temperature of the stress-filled room was high. Most staff members quit after less than a year; those who stayed more than two years were called "veterans." What worked in the past, however, was no longer as effective, especially in a volatile economy plagued by recent financial scandals.

Jasper Harrington, vice president for sales at Four-Leaf, has just convinced his superiors that something different, called "relationship selling," should be tried. Harrington wants to

begin with a select group of six high-producing salespersons to see if they can outperform their colleagues regarding total revenue acquired over six months. If the project is successful, the new program will be rolled out company-wide. The only catch? Harrington must train his trial group himself.

How should Harrington structure his training? What points should be emphasized for the sales group? Where do you think Harrington will encounter the strongest resistance from this group? What can Harrington say that might convince the trial group to make the switch to becoming consultants, rather than just salespersons, for their clients?

As the project goes forward, how should Harrington measure the performance of the trial group in terms more meaningful than total revenue produced? What are other performance criteria essential for assessing the success of relationship selling?

ETHICS IN SELLING

OVERVIEW

This chapter examines the need for a strong ethical and moral character in sales. Few professions expose you to more potential rejection daily than selling does—but the rewards for your persistence are great! They are so great that some salespeople do whatever it takes to stay ahead and edge out the competition. When in doubt, choose honesty. Acting in a way that is ethical and respectful builds a loyal client base and makes you happier, too.

OBJECTIVES

- Learn sound principles upon which to base ethical behavior.
- Identify the sources of influence on ethical behavior.
- Understand your role in maintaining the ethical position of the organization and also behaving ethically toward customers.
- Discover what company loyalty requires if your employers are involved in questionable ethical behavior.
- Know the implications of federal and local laws regarding ethical standards.

Ethics in Modern Society

Erin Hood is at war with herself. The pharmaceutical company she works for is pressuring her to meet a sales quota 20 percent higher than last year's target. She is a single parent with two children, and she sees an opportunity to meet her quota if she can beat out a competitor for a sizable order from a drugstore chain. Erin is considering planting some carefully worded negative comments about her competitor in the ear of the store chain's purchasing agent. If she doesn't meet her quota, that could mean no Christmas this year for her kids. What should she do?

Erin is facing an ethical dilemma. Because salespeople are relatively free and independent operators, they encounter a higher number of ethical problems than many other professionals. For this reason, you must be clear on your moral and ethical standards before getting caught up in something that escalates beyond your control.

Ethics is an old subject, but it is certainly not obsolete. Greek philosophers suggested that "A merchant does better to take a loss than to make a dishonest profit." Ethics is a long-debated subject for salespeople. In the early 1900s, con men tried to sell parts of the Brooklyn Bridge to immigrants. It's the origin of the phrase, "If you believe that, I've got a bridge to sell you!"[1] The image of salespeople, dating back to even before the bridge scammers, is usually filled with words like deceitful, pushy, fast talker, liar, and more.

Given the myriad of scandals in business—from subprime mortgages to insider trading—most people assume that corruption is prevalent worldwide.[2] America certainly seems to be continually reeling from the shocking, unethical activities of business and government leaders.

It is not companies, institutions, and political organizations that are unethical; individual people are unethical. Ethics is a

personal matter, and the ethics of a business, government, or organization is merely a reflection of the combined value systems of its members.

Business ethics is an aspect of *societal ethics.* Traditional values seem to have given way to a widespread sense of anything goes, and "sell at any cost" was the mantra the early salesperson learned.[3] Making matters worse is the now-pervasive idea that one should be able to, "Do *what* you want *when* you want to." As a result, many Americans want immediate personal gratification and will act in whatever manner seems to promise it.

Some say that business ethics is an *oxymoron,* a contradiction in terms. They suggest that business and ethics are incompatible because ethics is values-ridden and grounded in philosophy and religion, while companies need to be ruthless and dishonest to finish first.[4] This thinking is ludicrous! The notion that honest businesses and salespeople finish last is poisonous and untrue. You *can* be an ethical salesperson who works for an upright organization. And, if you are among the ethical ones in business, you will enjoy a longer, more satisfying career.

The Origin of Ethics

A *legal standard* is a rule that is enforced by laws and statutes, but an *ethical standard* is an outgrowth of the customs and attitudes of a society. Most of us have a shared idea of what we mean by ethics but defining it in a way that everyone would accept is difficult. Essentially, ethics is a systematic effort to judge human behavior as right or wrong in terms of two primary criteria: *truth* and *justice.*

The root of the word ethics derives from the Greek word *ethos,* which means the character and ideology of the community. A society cannot exist unless people agree fundamentally on what is right and wrong, just and unjust. Without shared norms of behavior, we would have anarchy in our political system and chaos in our lives. The three most critical value-forming institutions in America are home, religion, and education. Many people believe that the changing roles of these three institutions have produced a society with lower ethical standards than those of its earlier history.

The Bases for Ethical Systems

Philosophers and ethicists point to two systems to describe ethical thinking. The first of these is *deontological* ethics. This system relies on the use of expressly stated rules, such as the Ten Commandments or the Golden Rule. Some believe these rules come from a higher power, some believe the rules are intuitive, and others maintain that we discover the rules through fundamental reasoning.

The second system for making ethical decisions is the *teleological* approach. This system defines right and wrong only in terms of outcome. For example, research shows that executives tend to respond to ethical issues in a pragmatic way that is independent of their organization's guidelines or personal moral codes.[5] They simply seek to solve problems in a way that benefits the most people.[6] This utilitarian behavior is illustrated by the idea proposed by Jeremy Benthem in the 19th century that society's goal is to produce "the greatest good for the greatest number."[7]

According to the teleological approach, the individual should assess what good or harm would come to those involved and act in a

"Welcome to the Business Ethics course.
Today we're going to start with the basics."

way that would have the most positive results for most people. Several studies have found that if an employee violates the company's stated rules, their manager will react more harshly if the outcome is negative—but the punishment will be less severe if management sees the result as beneficial.[8]

With these two bases consciously and unconsciously affecting us, we can expect to experience some indecisiveness when faced with ethical decisions.

Guidelines for Ethical Behavior

Today, no matter the specific method of ethical decision-making, most Americans embrace three basic guidelines: universal nature, truth-telling, and responsibility for one's actions. Without them, the free enterprise system would be threatened, and any kind of business exchange would be difficult. Our society would disintegrate into a dog-eat-dog environment.

Universal Nature. The universal nature guideline is a derivation of the Golden Rule. We want others to play by the same basic rules by which we would play in a similar situation. This guideline sets up a basic level of trust between people and makes life predictable.

Truth Telling. Prospects and customers need to believe that what others say is true. The idea of honesty may originate in a set of rules we learned, but truth-telling makes sense on purely logical grounds as well. Trust facilitates cooperation, buyer commitment, and the development and maintenance of long-term, client-salesperson relationships.[9]

It's not always simple to be truthful with prospects. At times, it is easier to tell a white lie if it means setting up the all-important face-to-face interview or getting a commitment over the phone. For that reason, some salespeople's cold calling techniques have become entrenched in lies. Would you trust someone who lies in their initial conversation with you? No—and neither would your prospects.

Responsibility for Your Actions. President Harry S. Truman kept a sign on his desk, stating, "The buck stops here." He reminded himself that he had no one to blame when things went wrong. Individuals may choose to live by this attitude and accept personal responsibility for their actions, or they may attempt to follow the impulse of the moment and blame someone else for the consequences. If we demonstrated a higher level of credibility based on our willingness to accept responsibility for personal

actions, the entire system would work more efficiently and with less mistrust.

Influences on a Salesperson's Ethics

Although individual salespeople may know what is right and wrong according to their underlying value system, they encounter many new influences and pressures on the job. A stated set of ethical guidelines provides direction for decision-making and a much-needed standard for judgment for salespeople.[10] Knowing what to expect and understanding how to balance, personalize, and integrate such guidelines makes ethical decisions easier for everyone.

Unethical behavior occurs in sales because people forget the real purpose of professional selling: to satisfy the needs of others.

Company Code of Ethics

Most respectable companies have codes of ethics. Some of these companies adhere strictly to their system as part of corporate culture, and they provide ethics training for new employees. They may also have an ethics committee to rule on ethical dilemmas. A recent study examined the relationships among ethics code awareness, perceived corporate values, and organizational commitment, and two key findings emerged. First, those who were aware that their organization had an ethics code viewed their company as having more values than those who were not aware of an ethics code in their company. Second, respondents showed higher levels of commitment when they were aware of the presence of a formal ethical code within their company.[11]

The United Professional Sales Association (UPSA) is an organization of sales professionals whose overall mission is "to advance the profession of sales." They designed an Ethics Selling Framework upon which its members must abide. This structure reflects best practices and points out what is not permissible in today's business climate. Portions of their ethical code of conduct include:[12]

- I will maintain high standards of integrity and professional conduct.
- I will accept responsibility for my actions.
- I will continually seek to enhance my professional capabilities.
- I will sell with fairness and honesty.
- I will encourage others in the profession to act ethically and professionally.

Exhibit 3.1 discusses a day of national observance that the UPSA put into effect to emphasize the tremendous importance of ethics in selling.[13]

Driven by government actions, fear of punishment, and the desire to improve public image, companies are paying more attention than ever to their employees' behavior. Ethics is a monetary issue as well! For example, a study conducted by researchers at the University of Central Missouri found that ethical behavior in business-to-business selling had positive economic impacts. When salespeople act with strong moral judgment, they help build customer-oriented relationships that result in long-term success.[14]

EXHIBIT 3.1 A New Holiday?

The UPSA has declared May 24th to be International Stop Selling Day. It's a day to highlight the critical shortcomings in the sales profession that have arisen due to the lack of customer focus, ethical codes, and universal rights for buyers.

"We encourage all salespeople to pause and reflect on their professional responsibilities on International Stop Selling Day. We encourage our members and non-members who consider themselves sales professionals to participate in this important event. There is a difference between being a salesperson and being a sales professional. We also believe that many salespeople do not receive adequate sales training that focuses on the critical competencies required to be productive. We're doing something about that by providing real-time access to top-notch sales trainers and thought leaders in a global forum," says Brian Lambert, UPSA Founder and Chairman.

Do you think your sales organization would support International Stop Selling Day? Tell your manager about it and see if your company wants to celebrate a new holiday!

Some companies make their code of conduct a part of daily operations; some never consider their code; some have no ethical system at all. Issuing a code of conduct statement communicates to salespeople (and their customers) that their companies have high moral standards. Organizations can gain several benefits when they adhere to a core set of ethical values embodied in a code of conduct:

- **Greater motivation among co-workers.** Although many employers have yet to recognize the significance of staff morale, 94 percent of surveyed employees declared company ethics to be a critical aspect of their work lives.[15]
- **Demonstrated respect for the law.** When top management makes a formal commitment to support an ethical company culture, the subject becomes considerably more significant. Consequently, a company's personnel pay greater attention to staying compliant with the laws and regulations affecting their organization.
- **Improved business relationships.** Due to pressures exerted by investors and consumers, we have seen an increase in campaigns to boycott the products of individual companies that have displayed unethical standards. From this perspective, a clearly defined ethical culture is a valuable way to become the kind of business other people want to partner with and support, not boycott.

As a salesperson, you need to know where the company stands and whether its stand is consistent with your own. The time to determine this is before you work for them.

Corporate Social Responsibility

Ethics codes fit into the broad, popular framework known as Corporate Social Responsibility or CSR. CSR focuses on the managerial processes needed to monitor, meet, and exceed ethical norms within a company. It also focuses on the development of products and policies that reflect good corporate citizenship. That could mean sponsoring a fundraising event like a charity run. It could also mean choosing products or developing procedures that reflect the company's environmental goodwill, which is often called "going green."

A growing number of companies are making CSR a significant component of their product pitches. Because products must have key benefits to the consumer, companies are hoping to tap into the consumer's concern for the environment. In other words, especially in green marketing, doing well by doing good is the new mantra of the socially responsible bottom line.[16]

Starbucks knows the powerful impact of being environmentally responsible. They strive to combine consumer-driven demands with ecologically and socially responsible production methods. Starbucks CEO Howard Shultz wrote about the heart of this method in his book *Onward: How Starbucks Fought for Its Life without Losing Its Soul:*[17]

> *"Valuing personal connections at a time when so many people sit alone in front of screens; aspiring to build human relationships in an age when so many issues polarize so many; acting ethically, even if it costs more, when corners are routinely cut—these are honorable pursuits, at the core of what we set out to be."*

Executives as Role Models

The likelihood that unacceptable selling practices will occur in an organization has much to do with how its executives behave. If a sales manager gives the impression that his or her team must do anything possible to make a sale, salespeople assume that unethical behavior is acceptable.

More than anything, an organization's culture influences sales reps' behavior with clients. That is why sales managers must emphasize ethical selling behavior in both their words and actions.

The company's top executives must keep in check the pressure the managers put on their salespeople. If the CEO comes around once a year with a pep talk on moral behavior but proceeds the rest of the year to use underhanded methods of doing business, salespeople get a mixed message. Ethical conflict may also arise when salespeople's moral values differ from those perceived to be held by their immediate supervisors or top management. Here are some ideas to consider that may foster ethical behavior within an organization:[18]

- When a company communicates its code of ethics effectively, this will likely result in more ethical behavior.

"Boss, I admire you because you never ask me to do anything you wouldn't do yourself."

- Ethical behavior is associated with the presence and enforcement of written codes of ethics.
- Corporate goals and stated policies strongly influence managers' decisions on whether to act ethically or unethically.
- More ethical behavior will exist when the corporate climate creates ethical values and behaviors that are cultivated, supported, and rewarded.

"As a manager, the important thing is not what happens when you are there, but what happens when you are not there."
Dr. Kenneth Blanchard

Colleagues and Competitors

In the course of your sales career, you may witness colleagues or competitors who are acting unethically. Imagine that you are riding in a cab, and a colleague asks the driver to provide a receipt for expense account purposes and to indicate a figure higher than the actual fare. Do you join in the activity, rebuke the colleague, report the colleague—known as *blowing the whistle*—or ignore it?

A customer reports that a competitor has said you have an alcohol problem and are therefore undependable. Do you deny the charge, or do you retaliate by making detrimental remarks about your competitor? These are tough questions, so decide now where you stand on such issues to avoid doing so on the spot, based on peer pressure or other social forces.

The Bottom Line

A company's future will be in jeopardy if it does not establish common values or hold its salespeople and other employees accountable for their actions. An unethical company could increase short-term profits through unethical behavior, but at what cost? All it takes is one lawsuit or a little attention from the media to

discredit the company's reputation. The top priorities must be the long-term success and good name of the company.

Groupthink and Gamesmanship

Groupthink refers to the pressure exerted on salespeople to be part of the group and not to buck the system—to be team players, no matter what. Being a team player is beneficial if the team has noble goals and plays by ethical rules. However, if the group's thinking contradicts your code of ethics, you must weigh your options carefully. Psychologist Irving L. Janis warns against groupthink because it can often lead to flawed judgment.[19]

Instances of groupthink exist in every profession, and the pharmaceutical industry is certainly one example. Two salespeople and three pharmacists recently pleaded guilty to their roles in a scheme involving the illegal sales of drug samples to pharmacies in New Jersey and New York. The operation generated more than $1 million in illegal profits. The salespeople, former Procter & Gamble reps, stole samples from doctors' offices and sold them to the pharmacists. They also paid doctors and office personnel to obtain supplies.[20] A few people conspired to cheat others and convinced themselves that what they were doing was okay, or at least that the rewards were worth the risk.

Gamesmanship is becoming caught up in winning only for the sheer joy of victory and a dislike of losing. Our culture nurtures this type of competitive spirit—from winning the high school football game to beating a friend at golf. The typical gamesmanship-driven salesperson looks for shortcuts and is willing to use any technique to increase sales. To them, winning means doing whatever is necessary to make the sale.

One case study demonstrated that employees in a workplace where the gamesmanship mentality runs rampant often use their feelings to survive. The study showed that many people were forced to use irrational emotions as strategic tools of defense against their aggressive and hostile workplaces.[21] Do your best to avoid the temptation to cross over the line into unethical or illegal behavior.

Developing a Personal Code of Ethics

Many competing forces that influence a salesperson's decisions have an ethical dimension. Situations often arise in which a clear right or wrong is not readily apparent, and discretion in behavior is up to the individual. Because the influences on salespeople often contradict one another, each salesperson must develop

a personal code of ethics that supersedes all other claims.

Responsibility to Self

In the final analysis, the small voice of conscience is the arbitrator of conflicting ethical claims. It provides the ability to say that you have made the best decision under the circumstances and take full responsibility for it. Listen to that voice and don't brush it aside as insignificant. That voice often knows you better than you know yourself!

Responsibility to the Company

Salespeople sometimes rationalize that cheating here or there in their dealings with the company doesn't hurt. After all, the company makes lots of money, and what they do would never be noticed. Several areas especially lend themselves to temptations to be less than ethical:

Accuracy in Expense Accounts. Padding expense accounts is relatively easy. A salesperson can add extra mileage, submit charges for a meal at a friend's house, or take their family out and report it as a business dinner. Abuse of expense accounts is prevalent in both government and business circles. Falsification of expense accounts is not only unethical, but it can also lead to dismissal if detected. As a practical matter, it unnecessarily increases the costs of the company and may put it at a competitive disadvantage.

Honesty in Using Time and Resources. The temptation to shop between sales calls, linger over a third cup of coffee, and sleep late in a hotel room are examples of ways a salesperson may misuse time. Such actions ultimately hurt both the salesperson and the company. Not to mention that many consider dishonesty in expense accounts to be theft. According to the FBI, internal theft is among the fastest growing business crimes and is responsible for the failure of one-third of businesses.[22]

Responsibility to Competitors

Being honest and refraining from taking unfair advantage are the basic guidelines when dealing with competitors. Making untrue, derogatory comments about competitors or their products is bad business. At the very least, the legal implications of this behavior make the risks too high.

In the same sense, pumping a competitor's salesperson for information at a trade show in an attempt to steal their customers is not ethical. Some salespeople go so far as to use sabotage, espionage, and dishonest tricks to gain an unfair advantage over a competitor. These tactics include planting spies to hear a competitor's sales presentation and persuading a customer to put out a fake bid request to see what other salespeople submit. The underlying theme in this area is to gain customers fairly by providing quality products and superior service.

Responsibility to Customers

Behaving honestly and providing quality information and services are the primary ingredients for establishing mutually satisfying relationships with customers. Fortunately, the stereotype of the smooth talking, deceptive door-to-door salesperson is slowly disappearing. Still, many opportunities for unethical tactics exist.

Overselling or Misrepresenting Products. Some salespeople persuade customers to buy more than they need to meet a quota or to win incentive prizes such as a gift card or paid vacation. Overselling for personal gain will eventually catch up with the salesperson when customers realize that they have far more than they need. Lying about product capabilities, delivery date, or warranty specifics are all unethical ways to win a sale. They also put you at risk for legal action or permanent loss of loyal customers.

Gift Giving. Although giving a customer a small thank-you gift is customary, the intent with which you offer a gift reveals its true nature. If you give something as a bribe, that is unethical and probably illegal. Sometimes a salesperson may even give an "under-the-table" gift to secure a sale.[23] The value

of the offering, in comparison to the sale, is also something to consider. In America, the general rule of thumb is that no gift should exceed $25 to $50. One study suggested that in the pharmaceutical industry, even small gifts such as pens and notepads can unknowingly influence the decision-making processes.[24] It may be wise for salespeople to explore the ethics behind giving gifts of any size.

Entertaining Clients. Policies regarding entertainment are similar to those that cover gift giving. In some industries, entertaining a client with a meal, an excursion, or tickets to the theater or a football game is customary. If the intent is to say thanks or to help develop a more personal relationship, providing entertainment may be acceptable and even expected. It is essential to find out the rules of behavior in your particular industry and company.

Operating in a Global Environment

Many international salespeople operate with-in cultures that have different ethical standards from those in America. Which criteria should salespeople follow: their own or that of the country in which they are working? In some cultures, "grease" or "speed" money makes the wheels of a government agency or a company move faster. In Japan, they view gift-giving as a time-honored tradition rather than a bribe.

A company usually has guidelines for an employee to follow in a foreign country, but bribery is universally condemned and is, in fact, illegal, whether it is practiced at home or abroad.

Exhibit 3.2 on the next page provides an excerpt from computer tech giant Hewlett Packard's global gift and entertainment policy.

While customs and practices vary among cultures, giving simple gifts can be a useful way to create goodwill and establish trust in business relationships. We have a responsibility to make sure that gift and entertainment practices are reasonable and consistent with thoughtful, well-intentioned guidelines.[25]

Ethics and Job Tenure

It's imperative to affiliate yourself with a company you can stand behind and support. Disagreements or issues of unethical behavior on the part of the company may, however, emerge after you are hired. Deciding how to handle conflicts involving ethics can be stressful because your decision may mean either your termination or resignation.

When is it time to look for a new job? Weigh the options carefully and determine who the decision helps and who it hurts. Are there any alternative, creative options that minimize risk and allow you to accommodate both your career and conscience?

EXHIBIT 3.2 Hewlett Packard Gift and Entertainment Policy

Subject to the specific rules outlined further in this policy, the following business amenities are generally permitted:

- Pens, calendars, mugs, t-shirts, and memo pads.
- A local sporting event or entertainment valued at less than $50.
- Gift cards or coupons for HP products and services valued at less than $50.
- Gift cards for products and services that do not compete with HP's products or services valued at less than $25.
- Any travel, meals, and entertainment must be reasonable and directly related to the promotion, demonstration, or explanation of HP's products or services.

The following business amenities are never permitted:

- Cash, loans, stock, stock options, and cash gift-cards.
- Any gift or entertainment provided in direct exchange for reciprocal action.
- Any item or entertainment that is illegal or sexually explicit, involves gambling, or would otherwise violate our values or our Standards of Business Conduct.
- HP employees may never accept cash (or cash equivalent) in return for advocating or selling products from a partner, except commissions and customer loyalty programs, as allowed under HP's Conflicts of Interest Policy.
- You may not accept any combination of gifts/travel/meals/entertainment totaling more than $500 per person from the same non-HP source more than once per quarter.

Whistle Blowing

According to business keynote speaker Nancy Hauserman, "In the pursuit of the goals of productivity and consumption, we have failed to preserve individual and community values. The individual has been reduced to a cog in the corporate wheel, a capital investment, a corporate property."[26] This attitude can make salespeople feel unimportant and fear that their ideas and suggestions are not valid. This type of reaction is particularly relevant if an employee's superiors ignore his or her attempts to pass on valuable information.

Consider the Following Situation:

Sandra Baker landed a job as a software company sales rep. She is required to go on frequent business trips with her manager across the country. On the second trip, her manager books a dinner with a potential client at a posh restaurant. She does a quick tally of the meal, appetizers, drinks, and desserts—it adds up to over $300. She's just familiarized herself with the company code of conduct policy, which states client meals should be under $100. She decides this must be an exception, but also chooses to watch her manager more carefully. On her next trip, the manager engages in the same kind of behavior. This time, Sandra questions him. He responds by saying he'll report there were more people at the meal. He also implies that, as a new hire, she should be careful not to jeopardize her reputation or job. What should Sandra do?

In Sandra's situation, there are several options to consider:

- Make discreet inquiries into how common this type of expense is in the company and then decide how to proceed.
- Talk to her manager about the gift-giving and see if they can implement a more ethical way to entertain clients.
- Blow the whistle on the manager by reporting him to his superior.
- Ignore the whole situation and continue selling.
- Look for another job.

As careful as a salesperson may be when selecting a company, an ethical dilemma may arise. In the best-case scenario for Sandra, the company leaders would expose the violation and punish those who are responsible. But what if pointing fingers at someone causes the whistle-blower to be fired, resulting in tremendous career and financial difficulties?

On the surface, the wiser course appears to be to keep quiet and let the problem resolve itself. Sometimes, the best policy is to keep quiet until you can accumulate substantial evidence or identify the co-conspirators. However, silence as a long-term strategy is a bad idea. The violation is likely to be exposed at some point, and being part of a cover-up is not a desirable position.

In some cases, inaction can even be grounds for legal action.

Ethical Considerations for Management

The company may treat its salespeople as partners aligned by a common mission or regard them as collateral damage in the field. Salespeople are precious resources and deserve fair treatment. They also deserve to be informed by their managers of decisions that affect them and protected from situations in which they might be forced to make unethical decisions. Here are some ideas for preventing unethical behavior among sales managers.[27]

1. **Avoid setting up management-incentive systems in a way that makes fudging the data tempting for executives and managers.**
2. **Encourage managers to be accessible to salespeople so that they can see early warnings of troublesome developments.**
3. **Set up appropriate controls, not only on financial accounts but also in customer complaints, salesperson dissatisfaction, and expense accounts.**
4. **Set sales goals that are motivating but not impossible to achieve.**

If salespeople know management values their ideas and judgment, they feel ownership in the organization and want to do a better job. According to *Forbes Magazine*, Google is the number one employer worldwide in the area of employee satisfaction.

"Google stepped up their game in support of work-life balance and families," said Glassdoor co-founder and CEO Robert Hohman. "Increased maternity and paternity leave, reworked on-site daycare—they've made an effort to allow people to have strong families as well as give their best to Google. That came through loud and clear and seemed to be what pushed them over the edge this year."[28]

Companies like Google and In-N-Out Burger (who came in at #8 on the list that year) know that workers need to feel valuable, and they treat their employees not as forces to control, but as individuals to empower. Treating them in this manner unshackles their skills, talents, and potential.

Managing the Sales Territory

Some of the most excruciating decisions salespeople and their managers face are those concerning territories. A salesperson may have spent years cultivating customers in a region, only to have it divided by management or even taken away. The most important thing is to treat salespeople with respect by involving them in territory decisions.

Fortunately, today's data-rich environment provides access to all kinds of information for helping sales managers address the problem of assigning fair and balanced territories. A first step is creating a database that captures a sufficient account workload for the entire sales team. Then, by analyzing that data, it's possible to identify territories with gaps in customer coverage and those that are not already saturated.

Through using a structured territory design process, sales managers can make informed account assignment decisions that close coverage gaps.[29] In the end, more customers will get the attention they deserve, and more salespeople will increase their earning potential. It will also be easier to identify and reward top performers.

Workplace Harassment

Another part of building and participating in an ethical business is the development and adherence to workplace harassment and discrimination guidelines. The United States Government's Equal Employment Opportunity Commission (EEOC) defines *workplace discrimination* as, "Engaging in acts that prevent people from being hired, from keeping a job, or from receiving an

equitable wage based on their age, gender, disability, national origin, pregnancy, race/color, or religion."

Workplace harassment is defined as any act—including offensive remarks, unfavorable treatment, and creating a hostile work environment—that may eventually lead to the employee resigning or being fired. The EEOC further defines sexual harassment, which violates Title VII of the Civil Rights Act of 1964, even more extensively:

> *"Sexual harassment can include unwelcome sexual advances, requests for sexual favors, and other verbal or physical harassment of a sexual nature. Harassment does not have to be of a sexual nature, however, and can include offensive remarks about a person's gender. Both the victim and the harasser can be either a woman or a man, and the victim and harasser can be the same gender.*
>
> *The law doesn't prohibit teasing, offhand comments, or minor isolated incidents. However, harassment is illegal when it is so frequent or severe that it creates a hostile work environment or results in an adverse employment decision (such as a firing or demotion).*
>
> *The harasser can be the victim's supervisor, a supervisor in another area, a co-worker, or someone who is not an employee of the employer, such as a client or customer."*

Sexual Harassment in Action

In our modern litigious business environment, an organization's failure to recognize the consequences of workplace sexual harassment can be devastating. For employees in organizations that lack sound policies, the negative impact of sexual harassment—including liability, embarrassment, and lost productivity—can be extensive. Here are three real-world examples of what harassment looks like in the workplace:

- *Anna Garcia, a bank teller, reported that a female supervisor was allegedly talking nonstop about male and female genitalia and graphically describing sexual encounters. "It didn't feel like a bank," says Garcia. "It felt almost like a nightclub."*
- *A woman reported that her boss announced, "Come to dinner with me." It wasn't a request. When she asked, "In what context?" he replied, "You know what context."*
- *A married male sales manager reported that a female sales rep*

> *came into his office one day and started to rub his shoulders. On another occasion, she said she wanted a hug and proceeded to place her arms around him. In a few other instances, she came up behind him and roughly jabbed her fingers into his side to tickle him.*

"With the advent of social media, there is a much more casual relationship between co-workers and supervisors, and that absolutely creates more opportunity for people to cross the line between professional and unprofessional conduct," says David Lowe, a San Francisco employment lawyer.[30]

Ethics is Good Business

Ethical behavior may sometimes appear to be an unattractive alternative. After all, for every inside trader, fraudulent salesperson, or immoral politician who gets caught, perhaps even more get away with unethical behaviors. However, the recent slew of ethical scandals in corporate America has brought with it a renewed concern for ethics. Much of the newfound conscience in corporations has filtered down to salespeople.

Gary Edwards, former president of the Ethics Resource Center, says that ethics is receiving more attention, partially because of awareness of the tremendous costs of unethical activity in legal fees, increased government regulation, and damage to company image.[31]

In short, companies are paying attention to ethics because it happens to be a good business strategy. In this chapter's Social Media Connection, you'll learn more about how to use your social profiles to enhance your reputation as an honest and ethical professional.

The Social Media Connection

USING SOCIAL MEDIA TO PROMOTE ETHICAL PRACTICES

It takes a lifetime to build a good reputation and only one second to destroy it. This idea has never been more accurate than it is today, in an age when everything we say and do may be shared instantly through social networking. If you want to maintain and build on your ethical reputation (both yours and your company's), then post carefully on social media, even on your personal, non-work-related profiles. You never know who's watching.

NAVEX Global and PwC recently sponsored a groundbreaking study from the Ethics Resource Center around social networking in the workplace. The study concluded that having a policy and conducting training on social media can help change employee behaviors online. For this reason, more organizations should teach their employees what is acceptable and, more importantly, what is not acceptable to post online. Here are a few ways to use social media to promote yourself and your organization:

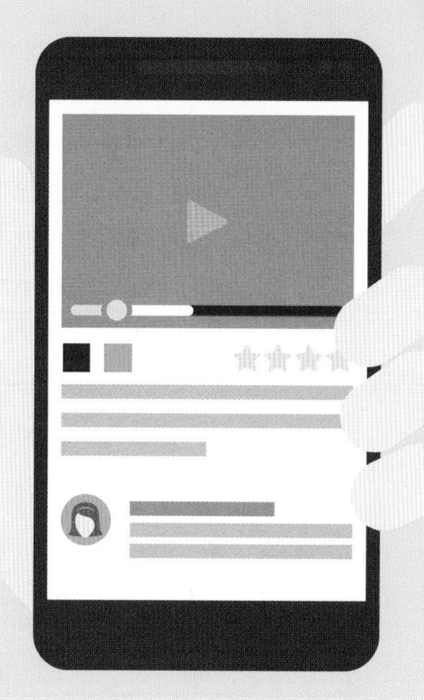

- Use social media tools such as Facebook and YouTube to publicly share your organization's good deeds and commitment to ethics.
- Start a company blog dedicated to ethics and compliance.
- Host a moderated conversation group on LinkedIn and allow compliance professionals to post content, ethical questions, and stories—and then employees can respond.
- Ask employees to submit nominations for fellow co-workers whose actions demonstrate high levels of integrity. Share the submissions on YouTube after they have been approved.

Checkpoints in Ethical Decision Making

Professional salespeople who are honest and authentic in relationships with employers, customers, and competitors become trusted and valued partners. The key to making repeat sales is to build these kinds of relationships and maintain them. A well-defined personal code of ethics as a basis for behavior is an invaluable asset. When faced with an ethical conflict, it is helpful to use a standard set of questions to ask yourself. Use the checklist here to guide your thinking:

A Five-Question Ethics Checklist

1. ***Is it legal? Look at the law and other standards.***
2. ***Is it fair to all concerned?***
3. ***Would I want someone else to act this way toward me?***
4. ***How would I explain my actions to someone else?***
5. ***How will it make me feel about myself?***

These questions are designed to activate your sense of fairness and rationality, and they require careful evaluation regarding existing standards and your sense of personal responsibility. Realize that your feelings are important to the process, because negative emotions adversely affect performance. Ultimately, if a truthful response to any of these questions troubles your conscience, then you should probably avoid the action in question.

You can also apply this ethics checklist to the activities of a company. Don't ever think you are trapped selling products and services for a company that condones unethical practices. If you don't like their policies, go find a workplace whose values and ethics align with your own.

"Explain it to me one more time. What's the difference between ethical behavior and being an annoying goody-two-shoes nerd?"

Legal Issues Facing the Salesperson

Companies face a serious problem today thanks to the complexity of antitrust laws and inadequate legal guidance. We would have no need for these laws if all businesses played by the same ethical rules. However, too many firms and individuals find the temptation to violate regulations to be irresistible. Their violations fall into two broad categories:

1. Monopolistic actions, such as price-fixing and competitor takeovers.
2. Deceptive actions, such as false claims about products or services and disparaging remarks about competitors.

Several laws have been passed to preserve fair competition, such as the Sherman Antitrust Act, the Federal Trade Commission Act, and the Clayton Act. These government regulations are designed to protect both sides of business transactions. First, they protect the consumer by preventing monopolies that could lead to price gouging. They also protect businesses by establishing rules that protect small companies from bullying and other unethical practices.

When in Doubt, Spell it Out

If the product you sell has a component that could be dangerous, you must fully and clearly warn customers of any potential hazard connected with product use. A warning like, "The use of this equipment at improper voltage levels will result in damage to the product and could lead to operator harm" may not be sufficient. A more comprehensive statement might be, "The maximum voltage allowed during use of this product is 115 volts. If used at a higher voltage, parts may come forcefully dislodged and lead to injury or death."

If a serious accident were to occur, the courts might rule that the vague wording in the first statement is analogous to a sign in a snake-infested yard that reads, "Please keep off the grass." That is a grossly inadequate warning if you know that the grass conceals poisonous rattlesnakes.

Given all the laws affecting business, sales representatives can say or do many things to get themselves and their companies into trouble. Since jail sentences for those who break antitrust laws have doubled in the last few decades, and the fines are much higher, it's safe to say that crime doesn't pay. Exhibit 3.3 presents six tactics for salespeople to consider following as protection for themselves and their companies.[32]

The Uniform Commercial Code

In addition to federal antitrust laws, many other laws deal directly or indirectly with professional selling. One set of regulations that is enforced in all 50 states is the Uniform Commercial Code (UCC). The UCC is a collection of guidelines that spell out the conditions under which a sale can be made. The rules cover most business transactions and govern the following aspects:[33]

1. An offer to sell may be legally binding if made in writing, conveyed electronically, or stated orally. A distinction is made between a legitimate offer to sell and an invitation to negotiate.
2. The financing of the product or service must be explained clearly and thoroughly.

EXHIBIT 3.3 **Protect Yourself Against Violating Anti-Trust Laws**

1. **Know the difference** between exaggeration (sometimes called "sales puffery") and statements of fact made during the sales presentation.
2. **Read all promotional literature** on the products you sell carefully. Challenge what you consider to be untrue or exaggerated claims.
3. **Know the technical specifications,** capabilities, design peculiarities, and unique characteristics of the products you sell.
4. **Study the company's terms of sale.** Overstating your authority to establish prices can lead to legal troubles.
5. **Stay current on all federal and state laws** that affect warranties and guarantees.
6. **Educate customers** on all aspects of the product before completing the sale.

Salespeople must know the legal ramifications of any credit arrangements made with customers. Truth in lending also requires full disclosure of finance charges before closing the sale.
3. The salesperson must know the legal responsibilities if either party fails to live up to respective contractual obligations.

The UCC also governs warranties and guarantees offered by sellers and defines both express warranties and implied warranties. *Express warranties* are statements and promises found in the advertising, sales literature, labeling, and oral statements made by salespeople. *Implied warranties* are a result of state law and the assumption that the product complies with those laws. Implied warranties are in effect unless a disclaimer is made. The salesperson should state what is promised as well as what is not guaranteed to avoid any legal issues. The warranty statement should also set time or use limits and specify who is providing the warranty.

Despite any short-term gains that could result from unethical behavior, doing the right thing is the only sensible choice. Unethical behavior is selfish. When you abide by honest practices, you can rest easy, knowing that you have other's best interests at heart.

There is no pillow as soft as a clear conscience.

Which Race Are You Running?

One of most the important books published in the area of business ethics is *The Power of Ethical Management.* Written by Dr. Kenneth Blanchard and Dr. Norman Vincent Peale, this book is of particular significance for salespeople who are on the firing line between customers and employers.

Dr. Kenneth Blanchard is the co-author of *The One Minute Manager* and *The One Minute Manager Library.* He is also the founder of Blanchard Training and Development Inc., a management consulting firm in California. The late Dr. Norman Vincent Peale authored 34 books during his distinguished career. His book, *The Power of Positive Thinking,* is one of the most widely circulated books ever published.

The underlying message of *The Power of Ethical Management* is simple: You don't have to cheat to win! You may get farther in the short run by cheating. But in the long term, where it counts, you never gain by unethical conduct. The authors remind us that "nice guys may appear to finish last, but usually they're running in a different race."

When salespeople focus on their purpose —solving problems and helping customers be more successful—they understand the need for ethical behavior. Cheating, lying, and short-changing customers may produce a profit today, but that is a sure way to bring failure in the future.

SUMMARY

It is essential to develop a personal code of ethics but also be aware of the ethical guidelines of your company.

Ethics is a smart business decision because salespeople who are honest in relationships become trusted and respected business professionals.

Salespeople who witness ethical violations at work must decide whether to blow the whistle, stay quiet, or find another job.

Sexual harassment is a serious issue in the workplace. Report any harassment immediately and avoid inappropriate relationships with co-workers.

When faced with an ethical conflict, use a standard checklist of questions to guide your thinking.

Numerous laws have been passed to preserve fair competition, including the Sherman Antitrust Act, the Federal Trade Commission Act, and the Clayton Act.

The Uniform Commercial Code describes the conditions under which a company can make a sale. It outlines requirements for financing, truth in lending, and a salesperson's responsibilities.

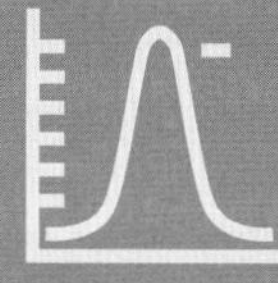

When you behave unethically, you may benefit in the short run. In the long run, however, it is a losing strategy.

Review Questions

1. We have heard much about questionable corporate activities, insider trading scandals, health risk cover-ups, and so on. Does this mean that the bottom line takes precedence over moral responsibility? Why or why not?
2. What kinds of management tactics make salespeople more likely to exhibit unethical behavior?
3. In the real world where salespeople compete for sales, is a code of ethics practical? And do salespeople need channels of communication and support structures along with an ethics code?
4. A priest once attended the luncheon meeting of the Sales Executives Club of New York. He talked at length about the importance of honesty in business dealings. Asked why he did this, he replied, "What sales executives have to do puts them, among all businesspeople, at the greatest risk of losing their souls." Do you agree with his statement?
5. A half-century ago, the medical department at Johns Manville Corporation began to receive information implicating asbestos inhalation as a cause of chronic lung disease. For 50 years, Manville managers concealed this information from employees. The company was eventually brought down by questions of corporate ethics. How can you explain this behavior? Did Manville executives behave immorally for decades?
6. When specific safety precautions are needed in connection with using a product, what are the responsibilities of the salesperson in giving this information to customers?
7. Do you believe you would ever be at risk of succumbing to groupthink or gamesmanship? Have you ever been persuaded by peer pressure to do something you later regretted? What can you do to lessen the possibility of compromising your ethics?

IN-CLASS EXERCISES

These exercises help build teams, improve communication, and emphasize the real-world side of selling. They are meant to challenge you, help you learn how to deal with problems that have more than one correct answer, and help you utilize skills beyond those required for answering typical review questions.

EXERCISE 3.1 What is the Effect of Company Codes of Ethics?

Pair off with another student with whom you have worked previously in this class. After briefly conducting online research to locate major companies in your area that have codes of ethics (you might have to contact their human resources office to obtain a copy), identify one company to scrutinize further. Interview a sales manager at that company and ask the following questions:

1. Does your company have a code of ethics for employees in sales? Do you have a copy?
2. Is the content of the code included in sales training for new employees? Are they tested on their understanding of it? Are they required to indicate their acceptance of the code?
3. Do you use or refer to the code when deciding whether a particular sales practice should be adopted or followed? If so, does the code influence your decision? If you don't use or refer to the code, why not?
4. In your opinion, does the code of ethics help or impede the company's ability to succeed?

After the interview, interview a salesperson for the same company, but without the sales manager's knowledge. Ask the same four questions and later jot down a record of the responses. In class, for each question, role-play the response of the sales manager and the salesperson. See if the class can account for any differences between them.

EXERCISE 3.2 Crossing the Line?

You will work independently on this exercise. As a class, in groups, or individually, view the film *Disclosure* (1994), starring Michael Douglas and Demi Moore. Take notes and be prepared to discuss the following questions:

1. Was Tom Sanders (Michael Douglas's character) a victim of sexual harassment according to law, or was Meredith Johnson (Demi Moore's character) merely aggressive in pursuing a consensual relationship?
2. At what point might Meredith have crossed an ethical or legal line?
3. What actions might Tom have taken to prevent any inappropriate behavior, and when?
4. Given Tom and Meredith's previous relationship and their current positions, was there anything that Tom could have done to preserve his dignity and still retain his job?
5. To what extent was the company liable for protecting Tom against Meredith's predatory behavior?
6. By reversing stereotypical gender roles, has this film created a distorted picture of sexual harassment that amounts to an injustice against female employees?
7. If you were in Tom's shoes, what would you do?

EXERCISE 3.3 Ask an Attorney

Invite an attorney that works with sales contracts, and a sales representative he or she is acquainted with, to class. Ask the attorney and sales rep to present several real-life scenarios of borderline sales activities from their personal experiences. Let the students decide (in writing and orally) if those involved acted ethically and legally and explain why.

Case Studies

The following case studies present you with selling scenarios that require you to apply the critical skills discussed in the chapter and give you training through practical learning situations. They are meant to be both engaging and challenging, and like the exercises, don't have one right answer.

CASE 3.1—Selling Off-Label

In the pharmaceutical industry, off-label marketing involves selling prescription drugs for purposes and conditions that are not identified on the FDA-approved label and accompanying specifications. In other words, a drug that has been approved and tested for efficacy and safety for specific uses may be often marketed and prescribed for purposes that have not been deemed safe. Accordingly, selling drugs off-label violates relevant ethical codes for the industry and is considered a criminal offense.

Over the past several decades, pharmaceutical companies have been found in violation of such laws and codes. In recent years, several major companies—Johnson & Johnson, AstraZeneca, Eli Lilly & Co., and Pfizer—have paid enormous fines and been subjected to other penalties for such violations.[34] Since 2004, Lilly, Bristol-Meyers Squibb, and four other companies have paid $7 billion in fines and penalties. Most spectacularly, Pfizer alone paid $2.9 billion in penalties and settlements in 2009 for this practice.[35] Despite the sanctions,

billions more were retained as revenue from off-label sales. With such sums at stake, the pressures on company representatives are immense.

Gwen Olsen was a sales representative selling Haldol (Haloperidol) for McNeil Laboratories. Haloperidol is an antipsychotic drug that is also used to treat verbal and motor tics as in Tourette's disorder, as well as explosive behavior in children. When Gwen found that her sales quota for this drug was going to fall short, thereby disqualifying her for a big bonus, she asked her manager what to do. He recommended marketing the drug to nursing homes and physicians who cared for their patients. The suggestion worked, and Gwen increased her sales by 25 percent.

Nevertheless, she noticed that the drug was being used for off-label reasons, mainly to control the behavior of elderly patients who were difficult to manage. The extreme decline of one patient whom Gwen had befriended caused Gwen to undergo a crisis of conscience for her role in the unapproved use of the drug. For the full account, watch Gwen's description of the situation that she faced by following the link: http://www.youtube.com/watch?v=v5jYU20dH4A&feature=player_embedded.

After watching the video, come to class prepared to discuss the following questions:

1. Was what Gwen did unethical or illegal? Citing principles discussed in Chapter 3, explain your answer.
2. Should Gwen be upset at her behavior? Doesn't most of the responsibility fall on her manager and the company?
3. Knowing how difficult it is to find high-paying sales positions, do you think Gwen did the right thing by leaving pharmaceutical sales? Would you? Explain.
4. Leaving questions of legality aside for a moment, should selling drugs off-label really be considered unethical? If society's collective ethics are simply the sum-total of individual decisions, and if selling off-label continues to be widespread in the industry, how can anyone say that a strategy that is routinely adopted by so many is unethical?

CASE 3.2—Boxed In

As the smoke curled up from the small fire in his boss's ashtray, Nick Roberts realized that he faced a predicament. Having just graduated from college, he had recently moved to Dallas, Texas, with his wife and infant son. He had majored in economics and history as an undergraduate and, through connections provided by his wealthy father-in-law, had landed a lucrative position as a corporate salesperson with Southwestern Container Corporation. The company manufactured and sold corrugated containers to businesses throughout the southwest. He and his wife were thrilled about his new job and their prospects for the future. But now, Nick wasn't so sure.

You see, the fire in the ashtray served a legitimate purpose and was no accident. Nick's boss had just concluded a phone call in his office with his counterparts at two other companies. As the 20-minute conversation among the three competitors proceeded, Nick and the other sales staff were allowed to listen via speakerphone. The sole topic discussed was the price structure for various grades and sizes of corrugated containers for the region.

The three companies thrived on competing for business accounts based on service, but they had come to realize over time that competing on price or price plus quality reduced their profits. If they could agree on the price, they could sell boxes more cheaply to larger customers and more expensively to smaller customers. Overall, they could keep costs elevated without having to worry about being undercut by a competitor. Life was more comfortable, more straightforward, and more lucrative that way. After the conference call, Nick's boss touched a match to his notes and dropped the burning paper into his ashtray.

As the meeting broke up, Nick was sweating. What should he do? If Nick sold containers according to the agreed price structure, was he acting unethically? Could he even go to jail? After all his father-in-law had done to get him this job, how could he walk away? How would his young family survive? Should he blow the whistle on the entire company? Nick's mind was swirling. What would you advise him to do, and why?

WINNING TIME MANAGEMENT SKILLS

OVERVIEW

You cannot manage time, but you can manage yourself and your actions. This chapter shows you how to get better control of your time and your activities. Success is ultimately about personal organization and self-management. If selling were all you did, managing your time would be easy. But most salespeople also have paperwork, travel time, meetings, and more. So, it's up to you to make the most of your time to work on the highest priority items—the actions and conversations that will foster relationships and increase sales.

OBJECTIVES

- Develop a positive time management attitude.
- Identify interruptions in a typical workday and what you can do about them.
- See the need to organize your activities as a means of controlling your time.
- Develop a procedure for getting organized.
- Understand the importance of a fully integrated organizing system.
- Discover a prioritizing system that allows you to be more productive.
- Learn how to manage travel time in your sales territory.

Your Most Prized Possession

The term *time management* is a contradiction. Because every minute has 60 seconds and every hour has 60 minutes, time itself cannot be managed—it can only be used. What *can* be managed, however, are you and your activities. Time management is an area of personal development that involves four primary actions discussed in this chapter:

1. Cultivate a time-positive attitude.
2. Get organized and take control.
3. Establish an organizing system.
4. Prioritize your schedule.

Time is a precious commodity. Although it seems like an unlimited resource, that notion is deceptive since time can't be stored for future use or reclaimed if wasted. When you realize life itself consists of time, the value of time becomes apparent.

Time is made up of a series of events. The key to managing it is controlling these events to your advantage.[1] You can learn the art of time control. You can also manage your thoughts and actions. Even though we are each capable of controlling our time, it is an area of great struggle for many. Here are some symptoms of time mismanagement. See if any of these sounds familiar:[2]

- Letting paperwork and emails pile up in your inbox
- Procrastinating and delaying decisions
- Getting a little farther behind every day
- Working late and on the weekends

Most of us can relate to these symptoms. Here is a visualization exercise that may help you better understand the worth of time:

"The key to time management is strict and disciplined adherence to a rigid schedule, while remaining flexible enough to let anything happen at any time."

Visualization Exercise

Your bank has just informed you that you have been chosen to receive a special prize. Every day, for the rest of your life, they will deposit $86,400 into your account. The only stipulation is that you must spend it all every day. Anything left at the end of each business day goes back to the bank.

Those first few weeks are exhilarating. By the end of the first month, you've received over $2 million. After a while, however, you begin to have trouble spending that much every day. Think about how you would feel the first time $20,000 slipped away from you and went back to the bank because you failed to spend it all. You would quickly realize that using this much money every day calls for serious planning.

This visualization exercise is grounded in some truth. Time is money! Every day, you get 86,400 seconds deposited in your account. You can't save any remaining time for another day. How many of your 86,400 seconds goes to waste depends entirely on your skill in planning and managing your time. The critical considerations become how you will *spend* your time, and how will you *invest* your time. For example, investing time in your family and causes that are close to your heart could never be wasted time. Those are investments in your future and your legacy, not as a salesperson, but as a partner, parent, friend, sibling, and any other role that means something to you.

> **"Dost thou love life? Then do not squander time, for that's the stuff life is made of."**
> *Ben Franklin*

Cultivate a Time-Positive Attitude

We all wake up with the choice to use time wisely or to waste it. *Desire* is the variable that dictates which path we will choose. In other words, like most success factors in selling, effective time management depends on the conscious choice to adopt the right attitude. The first line of defense to protect your time is to identify precisely how it can be wasted, and then learn effective means for managing it.[3]

Nearly everything that we think, say, or do is governed by patterns of behavior that we develop over the years. We develop most of them early in life and rarely change them. The only way to lose a habit is to stop practicing it.[4] If you want to achieve high-quality results in professional sales, establish healthy habits and patterns. The people who most efficiently control their time have the best idea of what they want to accomplish.[5]

Time management is a matter of *personal choice* and *responsibility*. Mental preparation is necessary to win the race against time. Developing a time-positive attitude helps overcome life's obstacles. Just as Olympic champions practice diligently to perfect athletic techniques, you can practice time management techniques to maximize the benefits of professional and personal pursuits.[6]

The 'Gain a Day' Test

Pick three days out of the next five-day workweek to arrive at work by 5:00 am. Do all of the "busy work" that you normally do during working hours that require no human interaction (email, reports, more emails, social networking), and then from 8:00 a.m. to the end of your workday, spend all of that "extra" time reaching out to prospective and current customers.

It is estimated that the typical salesperson spends an average of only two hours a day engaged directly in selling. Your job involves a lot more than just selling. But should it—or perhaps more importantly, to what extent? Merely increasing the time spent with customers isn't the solution. It's what you do with the time that matters. That is why one of the greatest weapons salespeople have at their disposal is *focus*. You won't get to every last thing on your to-do list each day. What you must do is *focus* your time so that it matches opportunities.

Here is a test to compare the actual results of your typical workweek to expectations.

Time Analysis

At the beginning of the week, write down the key deliverables you expect to accomplish during the next five days. As the week progresses, keep track of what you do. Organize each day according to specific areas and track the time spent on each. Here are some recommended categories to track:

- Calling on existing customers
- Calling on prospective customers
- Customer email
- Internal email
- Non-specific email
- Personal social media use
- Job-related social media use
- Coffee, food, lunchtime
- Talking with colleagues
- Work meetings
- Travel/drive time
- Paperwork/reports

Don't change your routine. Just track it, hour by hour. At the end of the week, compare what you did to what you wanted to accomplish. List the five habits or attitudes that were the biggest obstacles to the achievement of the results you wanted. Write out a plan for changing these habits or attitudes. Conduct another time analysis study in a few months and compare the two. Determine whether you are making progress in replacing these habits or attitudes with new ones.

Conducting a detailed personal time-analysis study at least twice a year is a good habit to establish. Just as doctor check-ups keep you aware of maintaining your health, time management check-ups keep you informed of how well you use your time.

Get Organized and Take Control

Many salespeople have the skills to be successful, but they are often held back by their bad habits. If you are disorganized or inefficient, the first step towards getting organized is to determine what type of *time abuser* you are. There are three types:[7]

1. **Procrastinators.** Do you often leave assignments until the last minute then throw yourself into a panic, working around-the-clock in a vain attempt to meet a deadline?
2. **People Pleasers.** Do you regularly take on more and more responsibility out of a fear of confronting authority and eventually commit too much time to unproductive projects?
3. **Perfectionists.** Do you take more time than allotted to satisfy extremely unrealistic but deeply internalized standards of excellence?

Once you identify what type of time abuser you are, you must lay the groundwork for effectively handling the onslaught of information you daily encounter. The following techniques can help you manage the information in the most efficient way possible.

Remove the Clutter

You can think more clearly and more creatively if you remove electronic and physical clutter from your life and your living space. Remove unnecessary paperwork from your work area—your desk, bag, and car. Even if the piles on your desk are neat, they promote a subconscious psychological tendency to review and think through the items. According to a national Harris

Interactive survey, more than 84 percent of salespeople consider themselves to be *pilers*. They regularly stack files around their office instead of archiving them.[8]

In a few seconds, you can think through all of the tasks represented by a sizable stack of paper or a group of flagged emails. For all practical purposes, however, your mind does not differentiate between doing a task physically and doing it mentally. Be kind to your brain and remove the clutter, which includes trash, food containers, drink cups, dishes, and more. Turn your office into a clean, minimalist nest of productivity. Once you decide to dispense with clutter, tackle the job at once. Follow this plan to eliminate the disorder from your surroundings and your life:

1. **Collect.** Gather up all the clutter that affects you and take it to one work area. In addition to your office, empty your car, pockets, and any other place where you store things. Dump all the clutter into one container. If it's your email that needs to be de-cluttered, set aside an afternoon where that is all you do. Silence your phone and get ready to sort and delete.

2. **Sort.** Divide the clutter or email into two categories: time-critical material (items with a specific due date) and someday material (things with no specific due date). Removing someday items allow you to think more clearly and creatively.

3. **Prioritize.** Deal first with the time-critical items that are due within 30 days. Examine each of the items you have identified as time-critical. If an item involves a meeting or a specific hour of the day, put it on your calendar immediately. Each day review your schedule to see which action items you need to do to be ready for upcoming meetings or deadlines. *That* is your priority—not connecting on social media or chatting with co-workers.

4. **Categorize.** Come up with categories for the someday material and emails. Set up tabs on your desktop or within your email server with specific folders for each type of someday item. For paperwork, create folders with labels and file them away. If your office still uses paper, perhaps you can recommend to leadership that the office go green so that all paperwork is digital. Just remember that if a someday item does need to be addressed eventually, set a reminder on your phone and place it on the higher priority list.

Handle Interruptions

To handle interruptions properly, you must first determine whether an occurrence is an interruption or part of your job. Only when you understand this difference are you able to control your attitude toward the people and the circumstances that threaten to get in your way. Once you determine that an interruption is necessary, decide whether it is more important than what you are currently doing. That will help you keep your priorities straight and reduce procrastination.[9]

Interruptions typically fall into three categories, each of which you can handle with the right attitude. Exhibit 4.1 lists the three

EXHIBIT 4.1 **Types of Interruptions**

PAPER
Emails
Notes/Reports
Projects
Other Messages

PEOPLE
Superiors
Co-Workers
Customers
Friends & Family

ENVIRONMENT
Phone Calls
Social Media
Visual Distractions
Comfort Factors

types of intrusions and examples of the most common ways that people experience them.

People Interruptions. People interruptions are the most frustrating because they are the most difficult to overcome. The person who does the interrupting also makes a difference in the way you respond. If your superior disturbs you, you should probably address his or her requests. If you are working on an item with a tight deadline or are headed out to a meeting, however, you can ask respectfully whether your superior might wait. It's okay to say no to your superiors.[10] Because your work is essential to their success, most leaders consider such a request to be a mark of self-confidence.

When a client interrupts you, adopt the attitude that this contact is not an interruption. Don't alter your entire day based on a client's whim, but do give full attention to that conversation and do what is necessary to take care of the situation (as long as you don't sabotage the rest of your day).

Your customers, superiors, and co-workers are not the only ones who can disrupt your day. Family members and friends can wreak havoc on productivity. When choosing whether to answer calls, texts, or emails from people outside work, consider how much that interruption may set you back. When possible, give yourself a window of time (perhaps during lunch) to connect with friends and family members.

"The average American worker has 50 interruptions a day, of which 70 percent have nothing to do with work."
W. Edwards Deming

Paper Interruptions. No matter how virtual things become, paperwork will still be a part of your life as a salesperson. Just as you do with any other kind of interruptions, prioritize paper interruptions. If you need to fill out physical paperwork or cloud-based paperwork, do so as the first or last activity of your day so that it doesn't interfere with your workflow. If someone needs you to review a report or project, ask right away when edits need to be done. If it's not urgent, make a note to yourself to handle the edits after you've completed the task at hand.

Social networking for personal reasons is a notorious time zapper, which we discuss in this chapter's Social Media Connection. Consider limiting your use during the day. Next, take the time to audit incoming emails, and don't be afraid to be selective. Set aside specific periods to deal with it. Turn the sound off on your computer and turn push notifications off on your phone so that you are not alerted every time a message arrives.[11] Then the remainder of the day is free for more productive activity. When you have a particularly important task to complete, go to a place where you can work without any interruptions.

Environmental Interruptions. Distractions in your workspace can wreak havoc on productivity if not properly addressed and controlled. Instead of feeling overwhelmed by environmental distractions such as frequent phone calls, you can schedule time blocks on your calendar each day to set appointments and do other sales-related tasks.

Factors such as temperature, clothing, and lighting play an essential role in your productivity. If your clothes are uncomfortable, if your office is too hot or cold, or if the fluorescent lighting gives you a headache, all of these issues must be addressed. If you work remotely at a coffee shop or shared workspace, research and try out different locations to find the quietest, most comfortable spot.

Establish an Organizing System

The challenge for salespeople is to discover organizational methods that work for them and their unique needs, tastes, and preferences. What's important is that you take the guesswork out of the sales process and your daily task list and replace that with a defined business process that sets you up to win.

The Social Media Connection

HOW TO USE YOUR TIME WISELY ON SOCIAL MEDIA

A study found that the average social network user spends 3.6 hours on social media every day. Considering you may only be awake for 16 hours each day, this means nearly 25 percent of our waking time is spent on Facebook, Twitter, and the rest. It's not reasonable for most people to cut social media entirely out of their workday, especially considering what an important role it plays in finding leads and staying connected. What that means, then, is you must give yourself strict time limits on how much time to devote to social media during working hours. So, what if you only had 30 minutes? Here are some ideas for making the most out of a half-hour on social media:[12]

5 MINUTES TO CHECK YOUR MENTIONS

For your first five minutes, dive into an app called Mention to see all the times your name or your company's name has appeared on social media, in blog posts, and across the Internet. Mention is an app that provides real-time media monitoring for you and your product or company. Mention will track everything, and you can respond and reply right from your Mention dashboard.

5 MINUTES TO CHECK YOUR NOTIFICATIONS

For the next five minutes, hop into the notifications section inside Facebook, Twitter, Google+, LinkedIn, and your other social media channels. For everything that slipped through the cracks with Mention (direct messages or being added to Twitter lists, for instance), here's your chance to follow up.

15 MINUTES TO RESPOND TO QUESTIONS AND SEEK OUT INFLUENCERS

Next, the 15 minutes to respond and react can include a bit of carryover from the first two items. If you happen to have a sea of notifications or mentions, definitely spend the time addressing each one. Then, hop onto your account and start engaging:

- Respond to the comments on your posts
- Respond to any direct mentions and @-mentions
- Answer any questions that involve your product
- Answer questions about your niche and industry (tip: use a saved hashtag search to track these)
- Engage with your VIPs, be it customers or influencers (tip: create a Twitter list for these)

5 MINUTES TO ROAM

The last five minutes can be spent being free. If you've worked efficiently during the previous 25 minutes, it's nice to experience social media in real-time, responding, and engaging with whatever catches your eye at the moment. Just keep your eye on the clock!

Success is a percentage game, particularly in sales. Just because you have a clean desk and an organized system won't guarantee you will make more sales—but it certainly won't hurt. If you find a system that works for you, keep doing it. In other words, repeat successful behaviors.[13] That is a secret of success at any level of competition.

Selling is not a game that requires perfection. You only need to figure out ways to stay ahead of the competition. Identify the behaviors that will consistently improve your performance, and you will be well on your way to creating a powerful sales discipline. To stay ahead of the competition, you must first remove the unnecessary disorder from your environment. Once you remove the clutter and control interruptions, you will use two simple tools to organize your day and activities:

1. Master Calendar

Your master calendar should list specific time commitments such as appointments with clients and meetings. You may also choose to use your calendar to plan your day. For example, you can set a time block of 7:00 a.m. to 8:00 a.m. to check emails and 5:00 p.m. to 6:00 p.m. to do paperwork. Sync your master calendar with your smartphone and other devices so that when you update the calendar in one location, it auto-updates everywhere. Use the notes feature in your calendar or a note-taking app that integrates with your schedule to enter any additional information about an appointment. If you want to get it done, put it on your calendar.

I'd like to schedule a time-management seminar on my calendar—as soon as I can find time to buy a calendar.

2. Daily To-Do List

The second organizational tool you will need is a daily to-do list. Be sure to prioritize each item on your list. There are numerous "getting things done" software and app options that you may find useful. For example, ZenDone is fully integrated with both Evernote (a popular note-taking and task management app) and Google Calendar (a popular calendar app) and features an easy way to prioritize tasks. You either do them, delegate them, or defer them.[14]

Your to-do list becomes even more valuable when you use it not only to identify tasks but to establish priorities for them. Putting top priorities first is the only way to be sure that your activities are making a direct impact on your goals. Sales success depends on establishing and steadfastly pursuing a series of goals. When you develop specific and measurable growth goals, you gain the determination and drive it takes to succeed.[15]

Charles A. Coonradt, the author of *Game of Work*, says, "In the absence of clearly defined goals, we are forced to concentrate on activity and ultimately become enslaved by it." Using a to-do list helps you develop the automatic habit of attaching a *when* to every thought, idea, commitment, or promise.[16] When it comes to using a do-list and prioritizing your day, remember that the app or system itself is not nearly as important as the practice!

As much as you may want to, no one can alter time. The trick to managing your time is to manage not your time, but your activities. Keep a daily to-do list of what needs to be accomplished and use the list to make sure you are moving the sale forward.

The Integrated System

Make your life as easy and streamlined as possible by using technologies that work together. Take your time and find the note-taking app, master calendar, and to-do list that all work seamlessly together. It's worth the time and a little research to find a system that works for you and makes your day more efficient. It's nice to be able to put low-priority tasks out of your mind and know they are there on your list for later.

Together, all of your organizing tools form an integrated system that makes the organization of your daily activities an automatic process. At the close of each day's work, you should spend a few minutes transferring any leftover items from today's list to the next day. Then check your notes and your master calendar to find all the things you have scheduled for tomorrow. Confirm any specific times associated with those items, such as the time for an appointment or meeting. Now you are ready to begin work tomorrow without even thinking about what to do first.[17]

Prioritize Your Schedule

The *Pareto Principle* (also known as the 80/20 Rule) states that 80 percent of effects come from 20 percent of causes. Italian economist Vilfredo Pareto came up with this notion in 1896 to show the connection between population and wealth. He wanted a simple way to explain why 80 percent of the land in Italy was owned by just 20 percent of its people.

Since that time, the principle has shown itself to be true in other areas. It's certainly true in life, in that 80 percent of results come from just 20 percent of our time and activities. Businesses generally recognize that

80 percent of sales come from 20 percent of clients, 80 percent of complaints come from 20 percent of customers, and 80 percent of productivity comes from 20 percent of employees. Here are some examples of the Pareto Principle in action:

IN MEASURING VALUE, YOU RECEIVE:

80% of:	From 20% of:
Sales	**Customers**
Productivity	**Activity**
Profit	**Products**
Referrals	**Clients**
Commission/Income	**Orders**

IN MEASURING FRUSTRATION, YOU EXPERIENCE:

80% of:	From 20% of:
Absenteeism	**Employees**
Errors	**Workers**
Complaints	**Customers**

Likewise, 80 percent of your success comes through the achievement of the top 20 percent of your goals. That speaks to the power of conscious, purposeful activity, prioritization, and a time-conscious attitude. By focusing on the top priority items in your day, you can transform your entire life and career.

In managing your time effectively, you must recognize which items you complete, not how many items you complete, determine your success. To identify which activities have the highest potential for producing success, practice establishing different categories of priorities. Here is one possible categorization system:

A-priority items are the **"do it"** tasks that are the most urgent. They include things with impending deadlines and actions required for an upcoming presentation. Failure to do

these tasks would damage the reputation of your company, or your credibility, if you failed to accomplish them.

B-priority items are the **"delegate it"** tasks. They include items that can be done at any time within the next week or month without causing any repercussions.

C-priority items are the **"defer it"** tasks. They would be nice to do at some time when you have nothing else pressing to do, but you would suffer no real loss if you never got around to them.

You want to give first attention to your A-priority tasks and carefully number them in the order of importance. Your goal is to complete as many A-level priorities as you can each day and supplement them with any B-level items if you have time.[18]

Time Goals

Once you have established the habit of using a to-do list, begin to record next to each item your estimate of the amount of time you will need to complete it. Estimating the required time lets you judge whether you can achieve everything. If you can't, you have the possibility of getting someone else to help before you fail to complete an essential task. Time studies show that even people who prioritize still waste an average of 15 minutes between tasks through simple procrastination, or in trying to decide what to do next.

A second benefit of estimating completion times is to help in avoiding procrastination. A deadline—even an informal estimate of the time required—pushes you to complete the work in the allotted time. Northcote Parkinson, a British naval historian and author of *Parkinson's Law*, is noted for his observation that work expands to fill the time allowed for its completion.

PARKINSON'S LAW states that work expands to the time allowed for its completion.

Something about a stated time allotment seems to establish a mental state that causes you to use that precise amount of time. If the time is short, you work efficiently and push for completion. If the time allowance is too generous, you procrastinate and encounter a dozen small interruptions that ensure you don't finish too early. By estimating times for completion, you eliminate the tendency to procrastinate.

If you expect sales success, you should also anticipate hard work and long hours. However, there is a difference between working hard and working right. If you always have more work than working hours, you may be due for a refresher course in time management. These eight techniques can't give you more time, but they can help you make the most of what you've got. Follow them to help you get—and keep—time on your side.

1. Place a Time Limit on Meetings. If you tend to dread meetings, maybe it's because they drag on too much and accomplish too little. Knowing your meeting lasts only an hour should help keep things moving. Before each gathering, encourage leaders to decide on a limited number of topics to discuss and a limited period for addressing them. Exhibit 4.2 provides six powerful tips for getting the most out of sales meetings.[19]

2. Set Deadlines and Beat Them. When you've got a lot to do and not a lot of time

EXHIBIT 4.2 **How to Run a Dynamic Sales Meeting**

Sales teams have a lot of meetings—and many salespeople have come to view meetings as interruptions. It doesn't have to be that way. Below are six keys to make your next meeting a place where decisions get made, and you leave feeling energized and motivated:

1. **Give people a reason to be there.** Start the meeting off with a short trivia game for which the winner gets a gift card. That will give people a reason to get there on time!
2. **Add value.** Add value by providing the team with quick sales tips, and help the team better execute on a key sales skill that will help them close business.
3. **Set rules for individual updates.** To ensure individual updates don't monopolize the entire meeting: set time limits for sharing, briefly summarize key learning points, and quickly recognize when to take individual issues offline.
4. **Motivate and reward.** Make motivation a part of every team meeting. It isn't about significant gifts; gratitude often has the greatest impact.
5. **Do a capability activity.** Every sales meeting must stretch and challenge team members' skills. Capability activities typically focus on a part of the sales cycle such as prospecting or closing. It's all about ongoing skills development.
6. **Follow a set agenda.** Follow a format for each meeting so that you'll have a consistent and easy-to-follow agenda keeping everyone focused. This will reduce meeting preparation time dramatically.

to do it in, deadlines can help you to stay on schedule. Prioritize your tasks, and then draw up a plan for completing them. Don't make the mistake of waiting to start on a job just because the deadline seems far away. Chances are, something will come up to fill the extra time you think you have.

3. Take Advantage of Your Peak Time. To be most efficient at the jobs you like least, tackle them at the time of day when you feel most productive. Pay attention to your moods and work output throughout the day to find out when you're most productive, and save your worst jobs for when you're at your best.

4. Don't Overload on Overtime. If your work-week consistently exceeds a reasonable number of hours, ask yourself why. Identify the tasks that take up the most time and look for ways to complete them more efficiently. Also, compare the number of hours you're working to what you're getting done. A too-small return on your time investment indicates a problem.

5. Do Some Delegating. Don't feel guilty about delegating responsibility. If you take on a job that someone else could handle more effectively, you're not making the best use of your company's resources.

6. It's Okay to Say No. When it comes to time management, many of us are our own worst enemy. You'll never have enough time to finish your work if you're always biting off more than you can chew. When colleagues ask you to take on extra projects that are not your responsibility, you have every right to say no. If you agree to take on too many jobs for others, you will limit your income potential and create needless frustration and resentment in your life.

7. Put It in Writing. To remember critical details from a meeting, important dates, or anything else, write them down or, better yet,

put them into your integrated organizing system. Freeing your mind of clutter helps you think more clearly, and concentration is key to productivity.

8. Cultivate Helpful Relationships. Create and keep lasting relationships that result in people gladly working to assist you, and this can be one of your most potent time-management strategies.

Managing Travel Time

One of the essential considerations for field salespeople is protecting their time for making those vital sales presentations. Travel through a territory is, in a sense, non-productive, although necessary time. The key to maximizing travel time is to weigh the amount of time on the road against your other daily activities. In other words, ensure that you are spending enough time doing the things that matter. The way to begin to do that is to keep track of your time. Keep a log that creates a snapshot of how you spend your time. It's vital to include on this log the amount of time you spend traveling, and then try to keep that time to a minimum.

As you learned earlier, the Pareto Principle says that 80 percent of your business will come from 20 percent of your customers. Thus, you must determine how much time and energy each account receives. It may be helpful to divide accounts into categories (such as A, B, C, and D accounts) and spend a fixed amount of time with each level of account.[20] Here is a graphical representation of this prioritizing system:

	Description	Time Spent
A	High-volume, repeat customers	40%
B	Moderate sales volume, reliable customers	30%
C	Lower volume accounts, one-time customers	20%
D	Accounts that cost too much time and energy compared to the payoff	10%

Outside salespeople travel all day long, so it will help if they set themselves in motion on the most efficient route between customers and prospects. Sales professionals pay close attention to the routing and scheduling of their calls.[21] They take into consideration the proper mix of accounts on each trip. Prioritizing is useful for determining a profitable blend of account visitation and servicing. A common mistake is to call on D-level accounts simply because they are located near A-level accounts and require little travel. These customers do not need to be called on with the same regularity as the A-level accounts. Instead use your time to prospect for new high volume, repeat customers.[22]

Ultimately, it's all about balance. If you are going to be a productive time manager, you need to balance the driving forces with the limiting forces in your life. Live within the zone between these two pressures so that you can be your most effective all the time. You need self-discipline from the time you wake up in the morning until you go to bed at night.

Spending your time more wisely starts with paying attention to how you spend it. Once you decide to take control of your time, you'll have the power to stop squandering it. Time is like talent. You can't create more of it—you have to make the most of what you've got.

**Ordinary people think merely of spending time.
Great people think of using it.**

SUMMARY

The ability to manage time effectively involves having the right attitude, getting organized, removing interruptions, and prioritizing.

Time is money. If you seek sales success, developing a time-positive attitude is one of the smartest things you can do.

If you want to excel, first remove the clutter from your office, home, car, and devices.

Many people, paper, and environmental factors interrupt productivity, so handle them with planning and control.

An ideal system for managing your day is a fully integrated one that includes a master calendar and daily to-do list.

Utilize technology to find apps that fully sync with one another—and avoid personal social media use during working hours.

Use a priority classification system to determine which tasks are: A (do it), B (delegate it), or C (defer it) priorities.

Delegate tasks that someone else could easily do so you can get back to higher priorities.

Review Questions

1. Write a 100-word statement giving your opinion about the importance of effective time management and its possible impact on your future in professional selling.
2. What four activities must you do to effectively manage your time?
3. How does a cluttered desk or email inbox affect time use?
4. How does the appearance of your car or briefcase affect professional credibility?
5. What three primary sources of interruptions cause time problems? Give some strategies for handling each type.
6. Describe an effective method for scheduling tasks and handling incomplete tasks.
7. What can you do to limit the time you spend on social media and telephone calls?
8. Describe the necessary elements of an effective organizing system.
9. How can you maximize travel time in your sales territory?

IN-CLASS EXERCISES

These exercises help build teams, improve communication, and emphasize the real-world side of selling. They are meant to be challenging, help you learn how to deal with problems that have more than one correct answer, and help you utilize a variety of skills beyond those used in a typical review question.

EXERCISE 4.1 Doing A, B, C

You will work individually on this exercise in class. Whether you're a full-time or part-time student, whether you're working or have family responsibilities (or both), you are busy. Chapter 4 offers several suggestions for managing your activities more efficiently. During the next 20 minutes, you will construct and think about one of them: the to-do list.

On paper or in Microsoft Excel, create a grid with three columns:

A—Do it
B—Delegate it
C—Defer it.

Add three rows, one row for each of the next three days.

- "Do it" means that an activity must be completed by a specific time within the three days.
- "Delegate it" means that an activity must be completed anytime during the next week, or it's something you can easily pass off to someone else.
- "Defer it" means that an activity can be completed at a later time if you have some extra time.

Next, enter activities in each cell of the grid and note an estimate of how long it will take to complete each activity. (You can allow time for daily activities such as eating and sleeping, but don't enter them into the grid.) During the next three days, keep an accurate record of which activities in each column were completed. Examine which activities were not completed and the reasons why. What challenges regarding the management of your activities did your analysis of this brief to-do list reveal?

Case Studies

The following case studies present you with selling scenarios that require you to apply the critical skills discussed in the chapter and give you training through practical learning situations. They are meant to be both engaging and challenging, and like the exercises, don't have one right answer.

CASE 4.1—The Pesky Client

While she was busy working at 3:30 p.m. to complete two spreadsheets that she had to forward to her sales manager by the end of the day, Janice's phone rang. With a groan, she reached for it, "Yes, Alice? What is it?"

"I'm sorry, Janice," replied Alice, "but it's Mr. Caruthers again. He called earlier around noon, but you were out."

"Do you know what he wants?" asked Janice.

"Something about those bearings that he talked about with you last week. I tried to refer him to Ed, but he said that he would only deal with you."

"Okay, Alice. I'll take care of it." Janice was perturbed. She had to submit her bi-weekly sales report and expense report by 5:30 p.m. Otherwise, she wouldn't get paid, and the numbers wouldn't make it into the company's monthly totals. Caruthers was one of her largest accounts, but he could be a blowhard and take up too much time.

Janice looked at her reflection in the small mirror that she kept next to the phone, put on a big smile, and pushed the lighted button. "Hello, Mr. Caruthers. It's nice to hear from you again. I'm sorry that I was out when you phoned earlier. What can I do for you?"

"Hi, Miss Stokes. I'm calling about those bearings that you promised me last week. I told you that if I don't get them by next Tuesday, I'll have to shut down the line. Here it is, Friday, and I haven't heard anything from you." Caruthers was upset and worried.

"I'm sorry, Mr. Caruthers. I do know how important delivery of the bearings is to your operation. Let me check with our people, and I'll get right back to you," Janice replied in her most reassuring tone.

"All right. But I can't wait much longer." With that, the line went dead.

What should I do? Janice thought. If I discover that there's a problem with meeting Caruthers's deadline, there's nothing I can do about it today. But if I call him back with that news, he'll never get off the phone. I might as well trash my reports.

On the other hand, if there is no problem, I'm confident that Caruthers will be so relieved that he'll talk forever. He knows he's a good customer, and he expects me to give him a lot of attention. Either way, I'll miss my deadline.

What would you advise Janice to do? Should she take care of her reports before dealing with her best customer's problem? Or should she handle the Caruthers matter and explain the circumstances to her manager, hoping he'll understand? What would you do, and why?

CASE 4.2—"I'm Late, I'm Late, for a Very Important Date"

The White Rabbit's song in *Alice in Wonderland* had become the mantra for Roberta's current existence. No matter how hard she tried, she just couldn't get her act together. It seems she was always late getting to the office, late for appointments with clients, and late meeting her boyfriend for dinner. And this morning was no exception: at 9:20 a.m., she was just pulling into the parking lot. Greg, her manager, was sure to be on her case.

And he was. "Nice of you to work us into your busy schedule, Roberta," Greg growled.

"I know. I know. No matter how early I leave, I always get stuck in traffic." Even as she said it, Roberta realized how lame that sounded.

"Well, I can't let it slide. My boss has been reviewing timesheets, and you know what that means." Greg softened his demeanor a bit. "Come on in, and let's chat about it."

After they both settled in with their lattes, Greg asked, "So tell me, why do you think you have such a problem being on time?"

"I don't sleep well, Greg. I go to bed at a reasonable hour, but then I wake up around 1:00 or 2:00 in the morning, worrying about what I didn't get done and what needs to be done for the next day. I sometimes watch the clock tick over to 4:30 before falling back to sleep."

"Not good. Not good at all. You must be exhausted," Greg replied with some sympathy.

"And I know that telling an insomniac to get more sleep doesn't help."

"I know," said Roberta. "I've tried prescription and over-the-counter sleep aids, but nothing gets me through the night. I really don't know what to do. When the alarm goes off, I can barely drag myself out of bed, let alone to work."

"Maybe your problem is stress. And it sounds to me like your stress might be occurring from lack of organization," remarked Greg. "What do you think? Shall we try to work on that a little?"

"Okay. I've tried everything else," Roberta admitted plaintively.

In light of the discussion of activity management in Chapter 4, what do you think Greg suggested to Roberta to relieve her stress? What suggestions would you make to someone in similar circumstances? How do you manage stress so that you can get sufficient rest to function at a high level? If a lack of organization is a problem, what can you change to manage your affairs better?

PURCHASE BEHAVIOR AND COMMUNICATION

OVERVIEW

As a salesperson, you must understand why people buy and communicate with them in a way that builds meaningful relationships. The more you know buyers and their decision-making process, the more readily you can help them. Because success in selling depends on accurately getting your message across to prospects, this chapter describes how to break through communication barriers. Excellent communication is the cornerstone of a healthy relationship, and when it comes to professional selling, it's not optional.

OBJECTIVES

- Become familiar with the purchase decision process.
- Learn the differences between individual and organizational buyers.
- Understand which environmental influences affect the purchase decision process.
- Discover what goes into successfully sending and receiving messages.
- Learn ways to overcome communication barriers.
- See the importance of using your voice as a tool.
- Explore the effects of body language and proxemics.

Small Words Make a Big Impact

> *"Four score and seven years ago, our fathers brought forth on this continent, a new nation, conceived in Liberty, and dedicated to the proposition that all men are created equal.*
>
> *Now we are engaged in a great civil war, testing whether that nation, or any nation so conceived and so dedicated, can long endure. We are met on a great battlefield of that war. We have come to dedicate a portion of that field, as a final resting place for those who here gave their lives that that nation might live. It is altogether fitting and proper that we should do this.*
>
> *But, in a larger sense, we cannot dedicate—we cannot consecrate—we cannot hallow—this ground. The brave men, living and dead, who struggled here, have consecrated it, far above our poor power to add or detract. The world will little note, nor long remember what we say here, but it can never forget what they did here. It is for us the living, rather, to be dedicated here to the unfinished work which they who fought here have thus far so nobly advanced. It is rather for us to be here dedicated to the great task remaining before us—that from these honored dead we take increased devotion to that cause for which they gave the last full measure of devotion—that we here highly resolve that these dead shall not have died in vain—that this nation, under God, shall have a new birth of freedom—and that government of the people, by the people, for the people, shall not perish from the earth."*

You just read the Gettysburg Address, given by President Abraham Lincoln on

November 19, 1863. The speech lasted about two minutes, with a total of 268 words, 198 of those words being only one syllable. Despite the lack of complicated verbiage, Lincoln's speech is the classic model of great oratory.

When asked to explain Britain's wartime policy to Parliament, Prime Minister Winston Churchill said, "It is to wage war, by sea, land, and air, with all our might, and with all the strength that God can give us." As Neil Armstrong first set foot on the moon, he said, "That's one small step for man, one giant leap for mankind." These world-changers demonstrate that you don't have to use big words to make a big impact.

Not only are small words more understandable than big words, but they also add elegance to your speaking and writing. Realize and appreciate the persuasive power of a well-written sales proposal. Just think about how much more you could sell if you could talk and write equally well. If you must choose between a big word and a small word, pick a small word every time. Take a lesson from the highway safety department. Place a sign at the boundaries of your speech that reads, **"Caution—small words at work."**

Why People Buy

A retail salesperson working at an Apple store in Las Cruces, New Mexico convinces a middle-aged couple to purchase a MacBook Air by emphasizing his parents' enjoyment of and success with the product.

A prominent philanthropist is widely known to love and support children's causes. A fundraiser for the San Diego Zoo presents a new program that will give inner-city public schools access to live video feeds from all of the best animal exhibits. The kids will even have virtual access to the staff and veterinarians for questions. The fundraiser convinces the philanthropist to donate $1 million to fund the program.

Yum! Brands, the company that owns Kentucky Fried Chicken, Taco Bell, and Pizza Hut, has decided to upgrade their registers in a test market of 13 states. If the new, high-tech registers are a success, they will implement the systems nationwide, and possibly in their international markets. The capital investment requires consideration by top executives, tax specialists, production personnel, and marketing personnel. Three competing salespeople will have direct, frequent contact with all of these Yum! Brands personnel and will call in technical experts to assist. The process will take many months to complete.

These three situations involve consumer behavior and illustrate some diverse aspects of the purchase decision process. *Consumer behavior* is the set of actions that make up an individual's consideration, purchase, and use

of products and services.[1] The term consumer behavior includes both the purchase and the consumption of products or services. Your role as a salesperson is vital in the process of matching your offering to the prospective buyer's needs.

Countless factors determine whether a prospect will decide to spend personal or company funds on a purchase. For physical products, one major determinant of a brand's competitiveness is how consumers perceive a product's packaging. For organizations that sell a service without packaging, a company's overall branding and marketing plays a significant role.

Brand usage and familiarity are potent forces, which is why future-focused companies test proposed brand changes in the market before changing a well-established brand. Notable alterations to the appearance of household names such as Cheerios, Tide, or Kraft would not happen without consumer research to assess new design options.

The difficulty lies in accurately measuring the marketplace impact of a design or branding change for your product or service. Surprisingly few companies take a disciplined approach to evaluating the performance of their current packaging and product presentation. As a result, companies tend to make significant changes to a brand's appearance based on intuition or in response to something the competition did. In other cases, unnecessary redesigns may waste resources and risk confusing or alienating users.[2]

However, the process does not end with the sale of a product or service presented in a well-designed package. Companies and salespeople must be equally concerned with customer satisfaction after the sale. This chapter introduces a model of the consumer decision-making process, examines environmental factors that influence this process, and examines the communication process to determine how to send and receive messages effectively.

The Purchase Decision Process

Consumers make many decisions every day, and each decision depends on how they process information.[3] The model in Exhibit 5.1 provides a useful tool for examining the buying process. It presents a view of the buyer as someone observed not in a single act, but a complex problem-solving process. This model cannot provide all the answers for salespeople, but it is useful as a guide for understanding prospects and deciding how you can best assist in the decision-making process.[4]

Anthony faces another difficult decision...

EXHIBIT 5.1 Model of the Purchase Decision Process

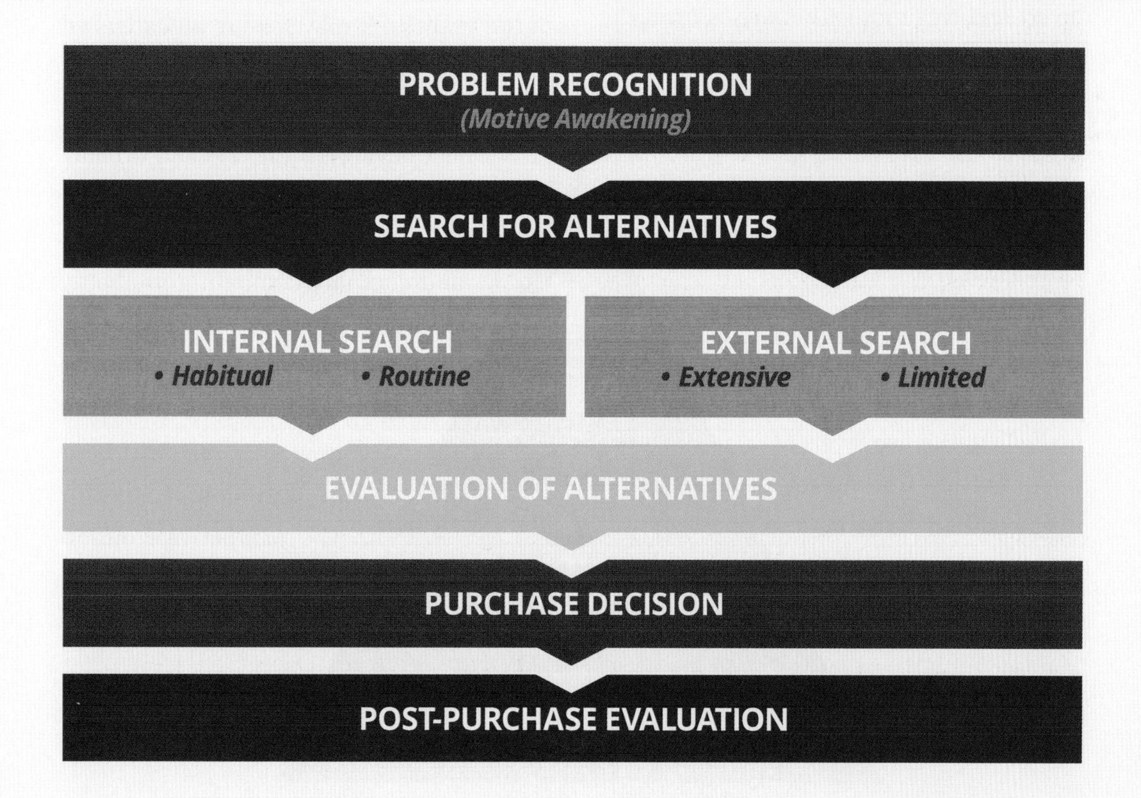

To understand why an individual makes a specific purchase decision, you must look at events leading up to and then following the purchase act itself. A buyer passes through five stages:

1. Problem recognition
2. Search for alternatives
3. Evaluation of alternatives
4. Purchase decision
5. Post-purchase evaluation

STAGE 1

Problem Recognition. The purchase process begins with conscious recognition that a problem or need exists and must be satisfied. A need may be something regarded as necessary or something that the individual wants or desires and therefore perceives as a need. No one takes action until motivated to do so, and this motivation arises from the awareness of a need.

Therefore, salespeople must recognize needs that are already active or find a way to create or stimulate recognition of a need that the prospect may not even know exists.

All sorts of requirements affect buying decisions. In Abraham Maslow's *Hierarchy of Needs*, he defined the five levels of needs as physiological, safety, social, esteem, and self-actualization. The pyramid seen here shows the most fundamental needs at the bottom, with the need for self-actualization at the top. Some buyers will not be aware of the nature of their needs until a salesperson brings them out into the open.

SELF-ACTUALIZATION
ESTEEM
LOVE/BELONGING
SAFETY
(money, security, shelter)
PHYSIOLOGICAL
(food, sleep, water)

Search for Alternatives. After recognizing an unsatisfied need, the buyer begins to search for information on available alternatives. The search may involve both internal and external sources. The internal search makes use of the buyer's previous experiences, learning, and attitudes, and often occurs without conscious effort.

Even in organizational buying, purchasing is often routine. Buyers can accomplish a great deal of it through online catalogs or a quick phone call to a supplier. However, the external search increases the complexity of the process. It may require an extensive information search or a more limited search for alternatives.

Online buying is the norm today in many industries since it provides near-countless options and makes it easy to research and compare competing products. More companies are looking for ways to implement social media into their marketing campaigns to grow their customer base and stay competitive in the competitive online marketplace.[5]

Evaluation of Alternatives. The search process typically results in numerous alternative products or services. Individual consumers have specific criteria they use for making a decision—or personal mental rules for matching alternatives with motives. These criteria are learned by experience with the product or by information obtained from word of mouth, online resources, or literature provided by the company.

If you can determine the buyer's decision-making criteria, you can tailor the presentation to focus on specific product or service benefits that differentiate your product from those of the competition.

Once you have matched the prospect's buying motives with what you have to offer, the primary determining attributes come into play: price, reputation, service capacity, and design. Identifying the dominant buying motives that determine a buyer's behavior in the decision-making process is vital to closing the sale.

Purchase Decision. After evaluating all the alternatives discovered during the search process, the buyer is ready to make a purchase decision—actually, a whole set of decisions. Buyers want to minimize their risk and simplify the decision-making process as much as possible. The professional salesperson knows this and assists the buyer in any way possible. Find out how the product or service fits into the buyer's system by asking questions like: Who else will use the product/service? How will it be used? Where will it be used? How often? What products complement this one?

Your role in assisting prospects in reaching a favorable buying decision is what makes selling such a rewarding and fulfilling career.

Post-Purchase Evaluation. The purchase decision process continues after the customer

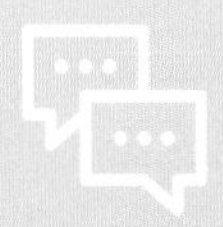

The Social Media Connection

LEVERAGE PROFESSIONAL NETWORKS TO INFLUENCE THE PURCHASE DECISION

Complex business decisions are inherently filled with risks. To increase trust and confidence in high-stakes purchase decisions, successful business-to-business (B2B) sellers leverage their professional networks through social media. Global research finds that "online social networks play a vital role in the purchase process of 84 percent of the most senior B2B buyers." In the final stage of the purchasing process, when stakes are highest, online professional networks like LinkedIn are the number one information preference of buyers.[6]

This statistic is especially crucial to salespeople since some believe that virtual communication has destroyed many of the face-to-face opportunities in sales. And, on the surface, it may seem like salespeople are becoming increasingly irrelevant. The most recent "IT Buyer Experience" study reported that nearly 50 percent of the purchasing process for technology solutions is complete before a salesperson ever becomes involved.

Fewer face-to-face encounters may not be the only change. Asking for referrals and getting recommendations are also shifting online. If you want to increase trust and influence the purchase decision, get ahead of the game by making genuine connections on all of the professional social networks. If you make a good connection online, you can eventually earn the right to meet face to face.

decides to buy. The buyer evaluates the purchase in terms of pre-purchase expectations and determines whether it has been satisfactory. Sometimes, the buyer experiences post-purchase anxiety or *cognitive dissonance*, also known as *buyer's remorse*. The magnitude of the anxiety depends on how important or costly the decision was and how many alternatives exist. You can help lessen this feeling by providing exceptional customer service and follow-up after the sale.

Influences on the Decision Process

You may not be able to see buying motives directly, but you can infer them from observed behavior. Exhibit 5.2 illustrates some of the many psychological and sociocultural factors that influence a buyer's purchase decision process. You must understand the significance and impact of these factors at the various stages of the decision-making process:

1. **Psychological factors,** such as the mood of the moment, attitudes, and perception of oneself, combine with sociocultural factors to influence purchase decisions.
2. **Sociocultural factors,** such as culture, physical environment, and social class, influence the nature and scope of the information search.

You can utilize these factors by becoming skilled in the art of communication—the sending and receiving of messages in a manner that results in understanding, productive discussion, and fulfillment of a want or a need.

Psychological Influences

Numerous psychological factors affect a prospect's buying decisions. You must be aware of these factors and understand the role they play in the process. Once you learn how these factors influence the sales process, you can use them to your advantage to read a prospect's disposition more accurately.

Perception. Individual behavior is an organized and meaningful response to the world as that particular person sees it. We perceive situations according to our own needs, values, expectations, experience, and training.

How many squares do you see in this image? Check the answer in the chapter endnotes.[7] If you didn't see that many squares, then you may have used *selective perception.* What prospects perceive as important to them may not be what you think is most important. Clients and prospective customers have significantly higher service expectations today than ever before. You may need to broaden your horizons to see what they see.

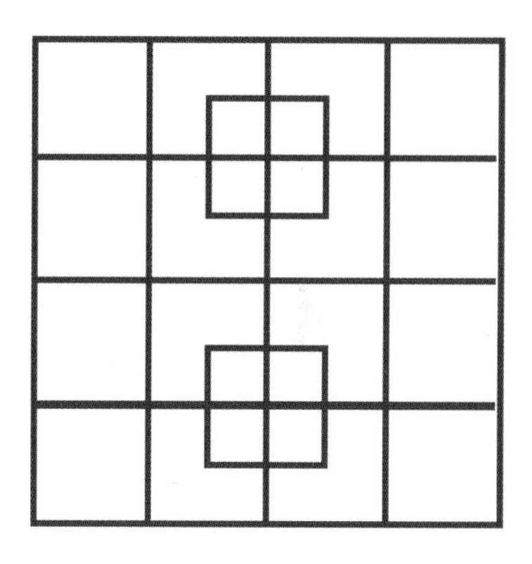

Current Mood. A person's psychological state or the mood of the moment can also

EXHIBIT 5.2 Influences on The Buyer's Decision Process

PSYCHOLOGICAL INFLUENCES
Perception
Mood
Attitudes
Self-Image

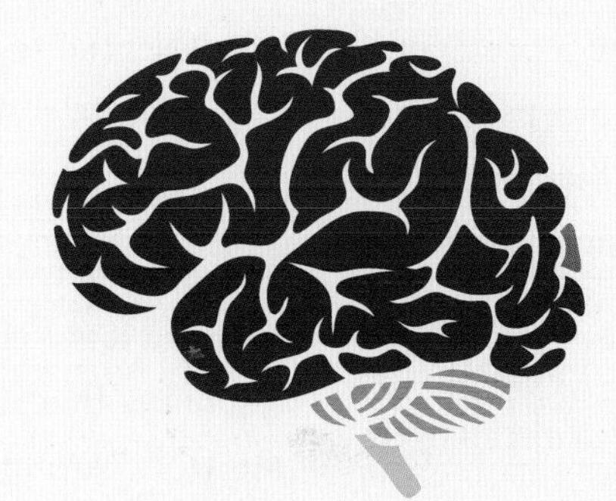

SOCIOCULTURAL INFLUENCES
Culture
Customs
Physical Environment
Social Class

influence decisions. On some days, you can easily shrug off a minor mishap, but if nothing has gone right all day, the same situation may make your blood boil.

Attitude. Attitudes are habits of thought and habitual patterns of response to stimuli and experiences. Because we use them so often, they become automatic to save time that would otherwise be required to think about a situation and make a decision. For example, some prospects believe that what worked in the past is what will always work in the future. In other words, they view change as a bad thing, which can be a problem if you are trying to convince a prospect to try a new product. Any position that makes the purchase decision more difficult creates a barrier to overcome.

Negative attitudes are problematic because we typically convey them instinctively. People develop habitual negative reactions based on experiences, and, at some point, those feelings become so ingrained that the individual is unaware they even exist. In contrast, prospects who adopt attitudes of enthusiasm, innovativeness, and willingness to explore new ideas are easy to work with and open to hearing what a relationship-focused salesperson has to say.

Self-Image. Self-image is an individual's unique self-appraisal at a given moment in time. It affects what you perceive as reality and, as a result, how communication takes place. Therefore, in choosing how to communicate, you must consider not only what is true, but also what a person believes is true.[8]

Self-image has a tremendous influence on a prospect's tendency to be a conspicuous consumer. *Conspicuous consumption* is when consumers spend money on unnecessary or unproductive leisure expenditures and big-ticket items that are considered more showy than practical. Experts say that one motive for practicing conspicuous consumption is to compensate for a negative self-image. Regardless of the reason, be aware of this powerful buying motive.[9]

Sociocultural Influences

In addition to psychological influences, it is essential to understand the impact of socio-cultural influences on communication.

Culture. Culture is a way of looking at life that is handed down from one generation to the next. It is a combination of behavior and responses that we learn through observing the world around us. You can witness the effects of culture in what people do, see, and use, and in how they reach judgments about people, events, and experiences. Individual values then develop as a result of reactions to the environment.

The cultural environment exerts a powerful influence on how we send and receive messages. A large percentage of Americans attach a positive meaning to concepts such as success, competition, efficiency, freedom, and material wealth. However, the positive response to these words is not universal.

Even more pronounced are cultural differences that affect communication among people from different parts of the world, a fact that has broad implications for salespeople who interact with different cultures.[10] Exhibit 5.3 illustrates that selling to and dealing with prospects from overseas demands cultural sensitivity.

A Global Perspective. Foreign cultures adhere to business customs, protocols, and body language used in communication that differs significantly from American traditions. If your company has global operations and you plan to sell overseas, you must learn the customs and preferences of your customers. Insensitivity to other customs and ways of communicating may derail your best efforts. As a salesperson representing your company to the world, you are responsible for learning what cultural differences you will encounter and how to best use those differences to benefit everyone involved.[12]

Language preferences and also body language vary significantly among cultures. Winking, giving pats on the back, and more can be easily misconstrued by those who are not used to such gestures. In other words, body talk does not have a universal language.

EXHIBIT 5.3 Business Card Blunder

Jane Seigel's firm had been courting a large Tokyo-based meeting planning company for the past six months. At a National Speakers Association convention, Seigel had the good fortune (or so it seemed) of meeting with the firm's representative to discuss the services Jane offered. "She handed her business card to me in the traditional Japanese way," Seigel recalls—extending the card while holding onto both corners. "I took the card, and, during our conversation, scribbled a note on the back of it."

Much to her dismay, Seigel looked up to find the woman appalled at what Seigel had just done. "I quickly put it away and then apologized profusely, but the damage had been done." The end result was Jane lost a sale worth $100,000 to her company![11]

According to Diane Ackerman's book, *A Natural History of the Senses*, "Members of a tribe in New Guinea say good-bye by putting a hand in each other's armpit, withdrawing it, and stroking it over themselves, thus becoming coated with the friend's scent." Thank goodness that when we say goodbye to a client, we can simply shake hands!

Or can we? In France, the traditional American handshake is considered too rough; they prefer a quick handshake with slight pressure. In Latin America, however, the greeting is often more exuberant, and a warm embrace is common, regardless of gender. They may even follow it with a slap on the back. In Ecuador, greeting a person without shaking hands is a sign of particular respect. In India, it is considered rude to touch women, so do not offer to shake a woman's hand. Exhibit 5.4 provides a few more interesting business differences among cultures.

EXHIBIT 5.4 **Cultural Business Differences**

1. Avoid slang or sports metaphors such as, "That proposal is way out in leftfield!" or "Are we in the ballpark on price?" They may mean nothing to other cultures.
2. Always use your last name when answering the phone in Germany, as in, "Schultz speaking." And when you call a customer, say your last name first, as in, "This is Waters, Jamie Waters."
3. In France, Italy, Switzerland, and Japan, the business card is an extension of the person who gives it, so treat cards with respect.
4. In Latin America and China, you can only proceed with business after you establish the relationship.
5. In Japan, you can never be too polite, too humble, or too apologetic. Apologizing is a sign of respect, not weakness.
6. Always appear to be less informed and less skilled in the negotiation process than you are. In many Asian cultures, there is no such thing as a quick deal.
7. The British and Russians are masters at using the pressure of silence. Don't speak until your prospect has responded to your last comment.

Organizational vs. Consumer Buying

Business-to-business (B2B) buyers include all organizations that buy products or services to use for themselves, to resell to other organizations, or to sell to the ultimate consumer. While a B2B buyer and an ultimate consumer share many similarities, an organizational buyer follows a more complicated purchase decision process. The following are the four areas where fundamental differences exist between consumer and B2B purchasing:

Decision Maker. The ultimate consumer is typically the sole decision-maker in a purchase. In an organizational setting, a team called a buying center often makes the decisions. The *buying center* is an ad hoc, cross-departmental, decision-making unit consisting of all individuals who play a role in formulating a purchasing decision.

Buying Criteria. Individual consumers have a more limited set of factors to weigh in making a buying decision. Conversely, business markets often require products that are complicated, expensive, and needed in larger quantities.

Scope of Relationship. Organizational buyers desire to stay with suppliers longer to help reduce the need for recurrent negotiation. This interdependence drives the need to build lasting, mutually beneficial relationships. As a result, many business buyers and sellers form long-term strategic business alliances.

Buying Motives. Every purchasing decision made, no matter how complex, is based on a dominant motive. Buying motives may be rational or emotional. Your presentation and relevant selling points may be, in fact, completely irrelevant if they don't match the customer's reasons for buying.[13] Individual consumers often buy based on emotion and later attempt to rationalize their decisions. For organizational buyers, however, rational motives are usually dominant, though they may take emotional motivations into account as well. The following table provides some underlying motives that lead to consumer and organizational purchases.

Consumer Buying Motives	Organizational Buying Motives
• Alleviate fear	• Economy
• Secure social approval	• Flexibility
• Satisfy bodily needs	• Uniformity of output
• Experience happiness or pleasure	• Salability
• Gain an advantage	• Protection
• Imitate	• Utility
• Dominate others	• Guarantees
• Enjoy recreation	• Delivery
• Improve health	• Quality

Multiple Buying Influences

The responsibility for organizational buying decisions may lie with more than a single individual. Organizations often set dollar limits beyond which purchase decisions must involve additional executives, red tape, and excessive paperwork. Buying committees or teams comprised of members from various departments may also become involved in decision making.

Members of a *buying center* share common goals and knowledge relevant to the purchase decision. One way to connect with a buying center is to determine the key person or persons who most strongly influence final decisions. Researchers have identified five roles played by members of a buying center:[14]

1. **Users.** These individuals will use the product or service purchased. For example, it could be a telemarketing sales team who will be the end-users of a proposed new telephone system.

2. **Buyers.** Buyers often have formal authority to make a purchase. They may also be called purchasing agents.

3. **Influencers.** Influencers provide information, directly or indirectly, to members of the buying center. For example, the supervisor for the telemarketing division may suggest certain essential features in a telephone system that will make calling more efficient.

4. **Deciders.** This role is played by those who have the power and authority to choose from among the various suppliers. They make the final decision.
5. **Gatekeepers.** Gatekeepers influence and control the flow of information that buying center members need to make a decision. Gatekeepers are invaluable to the group's decision-making process.

As much as possible, do your best to determine the members of a buying center before you meet with them. Doing so will allow you to prepare and cater to each of their needs, preferences, and motives.

The Communication Agenda

Relationship selling thrives on excellent communication. *Communication* is the verbal and nonverbal passing of information between you, the sender, and your prospect or customer, the receiver. For effective communication to take place, each person must understand the intended message. Thus, a mutual understanding is the ultimate goal of communication.

Exhibit 5.5 shows the channel through which communication must flow in a selling situation. At each intersection, the potential for both roadblocks and opportunities exists. Although the model considers communication from the salesperson's perspective, in any successful relationship, both parties participate meaningfully in an active two-way process.[15]

Encoding the Message

Encoding is the process through which a salesperson converts an idea or concept into symbols a buyer can clearly understand.

EXHIBIT 5.5 The Communication Model for Verbal and Nonverbal Messages

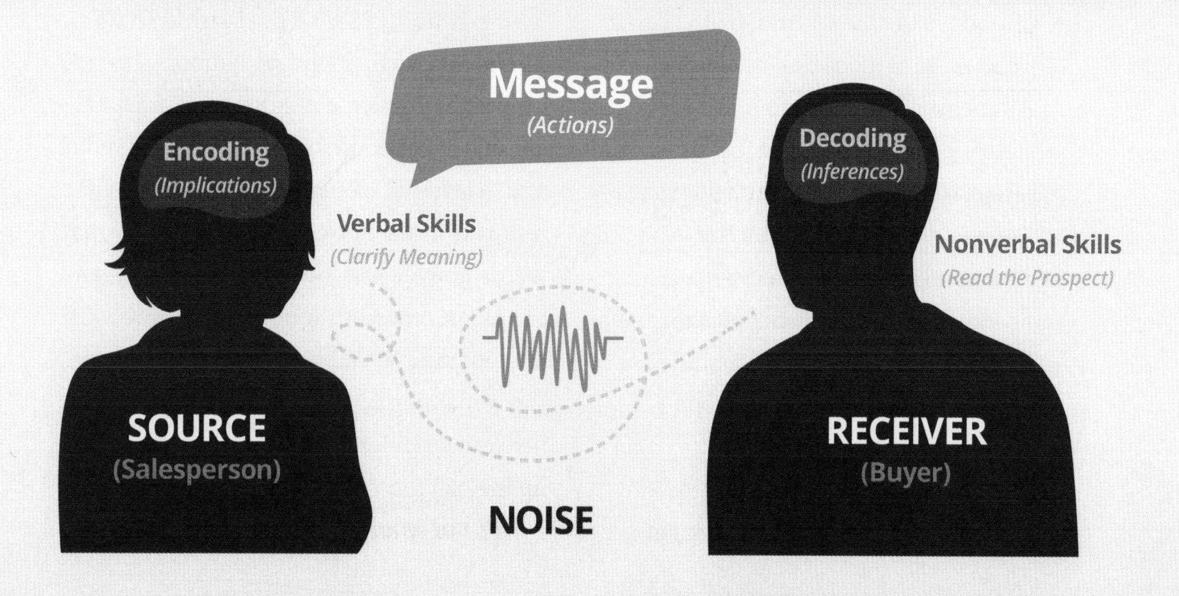

You know what you are trying to say; the real challenge is getting your point across. To express your meaning correctly requires the proper mix of symbols. There are three primary purposes for *encoding* your message:

1. To influence the attitudes and behavior of the prospect.
2. To move the buyer through a sequence of mental shifts until the buyer feels ready to make a buying decision.
3. To reach a shared understanding and agreement about the five fundamental buying decisions:
   a. *Need:* the problem you are there to solve
   b. *Product:* the way you hope to solve it
   c. *Source:* the technical questions that include origin
   d. *Price:* the big question on every prospect's mind
   e. *Time:* the timing of delivery and ease of setup

The most common symbols used in delivering a message are words, pictures, numbers, sounds, touch, smell, movement, and taste. You must encode the message, organize it, and put it into a format that the prospect will understand and accept. Communication takes place if the symbols you choose make it possible for the prospect to understand.

The ultimate challenge is to transfer your thoughts, ideas, and intentions without distortion or omission. Communication is often far from perfect because it is affected by the assumptions and needs of both parties, as well as by outside factors such as time constraints, interruptions, environmental factors.

You can achieve successful message encoding only through a thorough knowledge of the prospect's needs.

The Message: More Than Words

The *message* is a blend of symbols that are used to influence a change in a prospect's attitude or behavior, and it involves both verbal and nonverbal elements. Albert Mehrabian reports in his book, *Silent Messages*, that words convey just 7 percent of feelings and emotions! A person's tone of voice conveys 38 percent, and visual communication carries the remaining 55 percent.[16] In other words, nonverbal elements in the presentation make up the majority of the total impact.

It's not what you say but how you say it.

If verbal and nonverbal messages conflict, the listener relies more heavily on the nonverbal message. Exhibit 5.6 illustrates the contribution of various factors to messages and the amount of control we maintain over each one. The factors most easily controlled are ironically those that have the least effect, and those with the most significant impact are the most difficult to control because they happen unconsciously.

EXHIBIT 5.6 The Ability to Manage Communication Dimensions

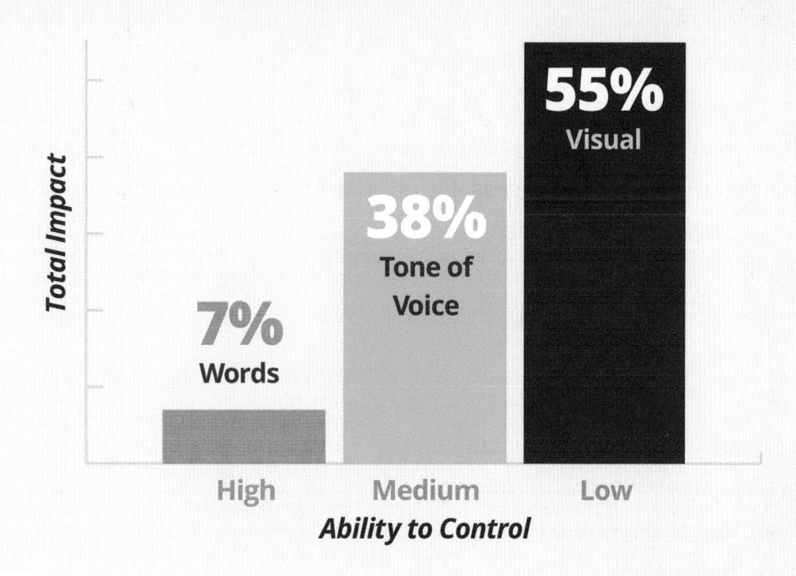

The process of delivering the message begins with visual impressions because they happen first. Consider this scenario of a salesperson walking into a prospect's office for the first time:

> *Ron, a technical salesperson, shuffles hesitantly into Allison's office wearing a listless, slightly worried expression. Ron was up all night with his sick toddler, but Allison doesn't know that. All she knows is that Ron's appearance doesn't convey confidence or trust, and so she is immediately wary. Ron unknowingly provided an instantly unappealing visual message. Ron then extends a clammy palm with a dead-fish handshake. He forces a smile but delivers his boring presentation with little or no inflection in his voice.*

In this scenario, the cluster of negative nonverbal cues masks the real message. Allison will never understand what Ron means to say, even if she does need what he is selling. Research suggests that if the first 30 seconds of communication results in a negative impression, you must spend the next four minutes overcoming that impression before any real communication can begin.[17]

Unfortunately, the prospect may decide not to buy before you succeed in undoing the damage that a negative first impression can cause.

Decoding the Message

Decoding is the mental process by which prospects figure out the meaning of a message. It is how prospects attempt to translate the symbols used in your presentation into something that relates to their needs. If the message was obviously both understood as intended and accepted, there is no problem. At this stage, either real communication or misunderstanding will occur.

Your prospects listen to your message and then make inferences or conclusions. If prospective customers fail to understand the message, the result is called *noise*, which represents a breakdown in communication. Noise happens when there are barriers to effective communication like the ones discussed in the following section.

Common Communication Barriers

Seldom will a buyer interpret the precise meaning you intended, and when the result of decoding is different from what you encoded, noise will be present. *Noise* is anything that interferes with or distorts understanding of the intended message, and it can take many forms and affect any part of the communication process. There are a few probable causes for why your sales message may not be understood or accepted. Here are some reasons for such miscommunication:

Words. All language is a code. Even if you and your prospect use the same words, you are likely putting out different meanings. Electronic forms of communication are particularly easy to misinterpret.[18] *Noise* will be created when words are inappropriate or

written confusingly. For example, profanity, veiled insults, overly technical language, obscure language, lack of punctuation, and more may confuse and offend the reader.

Distractions. Any element or interruption that may focus the prospect's attention on something other than the message is a distraction. Consumer behavior experts inversely correlate the effectiveness of marketing and sales efforts to the level of distraction they cause.[19] Some typical distractions are inappropriate clothing, uncomfortable room temperature, loud noises, confusing verbiage in marketing materials, or a nagging problem occupying the prospect's mind. Telephone calls, people interruptions, and emergencies are all interruptions that reduce or distort a message's impact.

Timing. If a prospect has some reason for not wanting to listen, no amount of communication skill on your part is enough. The prospective customer may be feeling sick, preoccupied with an unpleasant task, or facing a pressing deadline. Some people need time to warm up before getting down to business; others want to get right to your proposal and skip the small talk. If you detect the timing is not right, it may be best to reschedule.

Technical Erudition. Information overload often complicates a message. Prospects need time to process information from different sources. Salespeople often have the unconscious need to appear knowledgeable. This need may result in a salesperson

And *that* is why we lift on three.
COMMUNICATION

talking too much, poorly organizing the presentation, or wrongly assuming that the prospect has adequate knowledge. As a result, the prospective customer fails to see a need for the product or service. Never assume that a prospect knows industry slang and avoid using technical terms or jargon without clarification.[20]

Listening Habits. If the prospect is a poor listener, you must deal with the monumental challenge of designing and delivering a message effectively for someone who won't hear much of what you say. The other end of the spectrum is the salesperson does not listen well and never picks up on prospect cues that could be keys to wording a message effectively.

The buyer will make conclusions based on the messages received and react accordingly. Recognizing this *feedback* is crucial to a salesperson's success. During face-to-face

communication, verbal and nonverbal feedback is immediate and telling. Become skilled in receiving feedback so that you can adapt your sales presentation to fit each buyer's requirements. Use their feedback as a loop to bring you closer to understanding what each participant is saying. The goals are to filter out the noise and engage in clear communication.[21]

Your Voice as a Sales Tool

Voice is a big part of first impressions and factors in significantly to your success. When you call for an appointment, your speech is all you have. A pleasing and confident way of speaking is a tremendous asset.[22] Several essential components of verbal communication deserve your attention:

Articulation. In the classic movie *My Fair Lady*, Professor Higgins came up with a highly unusual way to help Eliza Doolittle improve her speech. He put marbles in her mouth and made her talk! She was forced to form her words with extreme care if she wanted him to understand her. As a result, her articulation improved. When you speak, do people hear distinct words and syllables, or *"doyourwordsallruntogether?"* A salesperson with poor articulation leaves prospects confused and bewildered.

Volume. The standard speaking volume varies during a conversation. The same is true of a sales presentation. Stressing a benefit may call for increased volume. Whispering may produce a dramatic effect that causes the prospect to lean forward (a body position that signals agreement or approval) to avoid missing what you have to say next. Variation in volume enhances the message—as long as it's not overdone.

Silence. Silence is a powerful selling tool. Use it to give the prospect time to absorb the full impact of what you have said. Slight pauses between significant points in the presentation suggest that you are thoughtful, intelligent, and analytical. Breaks also allow the prospect to comment, ask a question, or think about how to apply the idea you have presented to an existing need or problem. Avoid becoming so enamored with the sound of your voice that you talk all the time.

Rhythm. The rhythmic pattern of your speech comes from your style and also current emotions. Some voices seem to flow in long, continuous sentences, whereas others come in short, choppy pieces. Just as the rhythm in music changes to indicate that something new is happening, the same thing happens in speech patterns. Be alert to any changes in your or the prospect's speech patterns. Changes can be even more revealing than original patterns. If the prospect suddenly shifts to a more drawn-out rhythm, for example, the message may be, "Let me think more about that" or "I don't believe what you're saying."

Rate. The tempo of your delivery should be comfortable for you and your listener. Speaking too rapidly may cause you to lose prospects who talk slowly. They may feel that your fast pace is pushing them for a decision without allowing time for consideration. On the other hand, speaking too slowly may make the prospect want to find your fast-forward button. A moderate pace will enable you to enunciate clearly, establish natural rhythmic patterns, and speed up or slow down for proper emphasis of some point.

Selling Without Words

Although people have the option not to speak, they are, nevertheless, always communicating. Nonverbal signals are a rich source of information. Your nonverbal behavior can help you connect in a more meaningful way than words can accomplish. It also tells prospects and customers exactly how you feel about yourself and what you are selling before you ever open your mouth.[23]

People have wildly different levels of competence in nonverbal communication skills, and some professions require more skill than others. The success of a professional gambler depends on the ability to exercise strict control over nonverbal messages to

disguise a bluff. A mime depends exclusively on nonverbal skills to deliver a message. However, to achieve excellence in the sales profession, you must be well skilled in both verbal and nonverbal communication. Two particularly important components of nonverbal communication are body language and proxemics.

Body Language

Body language is the process of communicating nonverbally through conscious or unconscious gestures and movements. The essential elements of body language include shifts in posture, facial expressions, eye movements, and body movements. It consists of every action and gesture, from a subtle eyebrow-raising to the forward-leaning of an interested listener. Through body language, prospects express their emotions, desires, and attitudes. That makes body language a valuable tool for discovering how prospects genuinely feel.

You are far more likely to succeed when you become aware of what a prospect's body language is saying to you.

The Language of Gestures. Important signals to watch for involve body angles, hand, arm, and leg positions, and facial expressions—especially noting changes in the eyes and lips.[24] Observe all of the separate factors as a cluster of gestures that combine to state a message. Prospects sitting with arms crossed may be communicating doubt or rejection, or they may merely be sitting comfortably. In this case, you must also observe whether they have crossed their legs, are leaning back, and are glancing sideways

"Your body language says you've lost interest."

with an eyebrow raised. All of these signals combined suggest doubt or rejection, but one of them in isolation is inconclusive.

Body Signals. A hunched figure, rigid posture, restless stance, or nervous pacing may contradict what a person says verbally. Prospects allow you to sit closer if they feel comfortable and lean toward you if they like what you are saying and are intent on listening.

John Molloy, the author of the bestselling book, *Dress for Success*, compared the non-verbal body language of successful and unsuccessful salespeople. One mannerism difference he noted was the relative calmness of professional salespeople in comparison to those who were less successful. Their body movements were smooth and unhurried; there were no jerky motions, most notably when sliding a contract or a pen across the table. Each movement was smooth and gradual. The less successful salespeople exhibited jumpy, nervous movements that prospects either consciously or unconsciously noticed.

Look for changes in body posture and gestures. For example, a prospective customer who is ready to buy shows signs of relaxation, such as: nodding in agreement, mirroring your movements, moving to the front of the chair, extending their palm outward toward you, and uncrossing legs. Your posture and gestures also communicate your feelings to the prospect. If you sit in an open, relaxed position, you are likely to be more persuasive and well-received than if you sit in a tight, closed posture.

Hand Movements. Rubbing the back of the neck may indicate frustration, but it can also suggest that the prospect has a sore or stiff neck from painting the bathroom ceiling over the weekend. Next time you are speaking with a client, notice his or her hand movements and use those as indicators of what he or she is feeling. People can say so much with simple, unthinking hand motions. Evaluate the following hand gestures in the context of other nonverbal clues.

1. **Hand and head gestures.** Tugging at the ear suggests the desire to interrupt. Pinching the bridge of the nose and closing the eyes says that the prospect is thinking seriously about a matter.

2. **Posture.** Leaning back in the chair with both hands behind the head communicates a sense of superiority.

3. **Involuntary gestures.** Involuntary hand gestures that contradict facial expressions

are likely to reveal true feelings. Tightly clasped hands or fists indicate tenseness.

4. **Steepling of the hands.** Fingertips together, forming what looks like a church steeple, often indicate smugness, self-confidence, or feelings of superiority.

Facial Expressions. Eyebrows, eyelids, eyes, lips, jaw, mouth, and facial muscles all work together to communicate feelings and emotions. Research attributes as much as 70 percent of nonverbal message sending to the muscles of the face.[25]

The face is a highly reliable indicator of attitude. A person may avoid eye contact when trying to cover up true feelings. Increased eye contact signals honesty and interest. Be sure to maintain eye contact at critical moments of the presentation. For example, if you are describing the technical characteristics of a product, direct the prospect's eyes to the product itself or the presentation screen. In contrast, when stressing the benefits of using the product, maintain direct eye contact.

Lack of eye contact sends a negative message that neutralizes the impact of the intended benefit. Proper eye contact makes a positive statement that words alone cannot. In a survey conducted by Incomm Research, 80 percent of trade show attendees said they were more likely to view a company or product positively if its representatives smiled.[26]

Tightness around the cheeks or along the jawline are indications of suspicion and anger. Muscle movement at the back of the jawline just below the ears indicates an angry gritting of the teeth. A sudden flush of facial redness may warn that the situation has taken a wrong turn; embarrassment or hostility may be radiating under an otherwise calm exterior.

An isolated gesture or posture is seldom a reliable indicator of attitude or feelings. You have to take a look at the buyer in the context of the whole situation. A person may fold his or her arms to be more comfortable. Generally, if there is an objection, however, the entire body will become more rigid. When a cluster of gestures is consistent with a prospect's verbal messages, it is generally safe to accept their validity.

Proxemics

Proxemics is the distance individuals prefer to maintain between themselves and others. Most people consider body distance awareness to be a matter of courtesy. Violations of distance comfort risk closing down the communication process. Highly successful salespeople tend to move closer to clients when they are about to close a sale. The general rule of thumb is this: carefully test for the existence of comfort barriers, and then place yourself just outside those barriers.

Exhibit 5.7 shows the four primary zones or ranges that apply in a typical sales situation. Generally speaking, the intimate zone is about two feet (hence the expression, "Keeping someone at arm's length"). Enter this range only if invited. Moving inside the intimate zone, except for a handshake, is not a good idea.

Beyond that, we all have a personal zone, which is an envelope around us, extending from two to four feet. Move into the buyer's personal zone only after you have been invited, which typically occurs after you

EXHIBIT 5.7 How to Respectfully Use Space

INTIMATE RANGE
Up to 2 feet
Too close for business situations.
PERSONAL RANGE
2 to 4 feet
Use only if prospect is comfortable.
SOCIAL RANGE
4 to 12 feet
Allows prospects plenty of room for gestures.
PUBLIC RANGE
12+ feet
Good for group presentations or giving a speech.

establish rapport. The outer shell is the social zone, which extends up to 12 feet.[27]

Numerous factors help determine the amount of space various individuals need. Cultural differences, age, gender, and personality are factors. You must also take into consideration the type of relationship that exists between the salesperson and the client. Peers tolerate a closer range of contact than people with a wide gap in age or status. Conversations between two women occur at a more intimate range that those between two men or between a man and a woman. People with outgoing, open personalities are willing to be closer than those who are shy or withdrawn. Salespeople can move closer to existing clients than to new prospects.

If you have never considered how many factors affect a buying decision until now, you are beginning to see the complexities of the process. And frankly, we have just scratched the surface in this chapter. Human beings are multifaceted and unique. However, in many ways, we are also predictable. Take the time to become a master of body language. You can even use your phone to record yourself doing a sales presentation to see what your body language says to prospects. Anyone can sell—but it takes time, patience, and intention to do it well!

SUMMARY

The purchase decision process involves five stages: recognition, search, evaluation, purchase, and post-purchase evaluation.

Organizational buyers must abide by specific procedures and often make decisions through a buying center.

Successful salespeople learn how to discover buying motives and present benefits that relate to those motives.

Always be sensitive to psychological and sociocultural influences on a sale.

Communication is the vehicle for delivering your message in a manner that the buyer comprehends, accepts, and believes.

When there is a barrier to effective communication, the result is called *noise*.

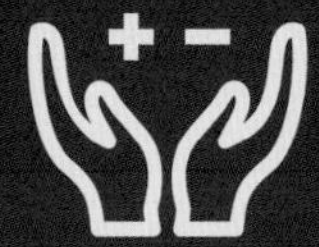

We send the majority of our messages in daily communication through nonverbal means. We are always communicating!

Understand body language and how salespeople use their space to communicate effectively with prospects.

Review Questions

1. Formulate a brief definition of consumer behavior.
2. Why must salespeople understand consumer behavior?
3. What are the five stages of the buying decision process? What is a salesperson's function in each of these stages?
4. What is cognitive dissonance? How can a salesperson prevent it?
5. What differences exist between individual and organizational buyers?
6. What is a buying center?
7. What are the three primary purposes a salesperson may have in encoding a message to be presented to a prospect?
8. How can you be sure someone has received, understood, and accepted your message?
9. What is the role of perception in the buying-decision process?
10. What are some of the psychological influences on the purchase decision process?

IN-CLASS EXERCISES

These exercises help build teams, improve communication, and emphasize the real-world side of selling. They are meant to be challenging, help you learn how to deal with problems that have more than one correct answer, and help you utilize a variety of skills beyond those used in a typical review question.

EXERCISE 5.1 Learning from Advertising

Divide into four-person teams. Outside of class, conduct an online search for two TV ads: one that exhibits consideration for the psychological, behavioral, and socio-cultural influences on customers' purchase decisions, and one that seems insensitive to those factors. As a team, explain why each video did or did not sufficiently consider the many influences. Be prepared to show and discuss your videos in class, pointing out features of each video that your team found to be effective or ineffective, and why.

EXERCISE 5.2 Brief Selling Situations

Appoint three students to participate in an active role-play in class. Divide the class into teams and give each group a brief selling situation. Give each group fifteen minutes to prepare a presentation and invite the three students in the role play to present their case to the class. Allow each team to critique the performance in terms of their ideas and the following:

- The model of the purchase decision process
- The ultimate consumer or organizational buying motives
- Any psychological or sociocultural influences present
- The communication process in general
- Barriers to effective communication

EXERCISE 5.3 Choose Your Words

Does word choice affect understanding? What common saying has been re-worded in each of the statements below?

- A single in-and-out movement of a small cylindrical object with an oblong opening in one end through which an elongated fiber is passed produces the fortuitous circumstance of precluding the necessity of performing nine such procedures at some future date.
- A wildly gyrating fragment of consolidated solid mineral matter is never encapsulated in a cutaneous layer of bryophytic living organisms that do not possess locomotive qualities in themselves.
- You may succeed in conducting a large, solid hoofed herbivorous mammal of the family Equidae to the brink of a reservoir of liquid oxide of hydrogen, but there is no surety that you will succeed in coercing said mammal to imbibe a potation.
- Members of the populace who sojourn in habitations of an amorphous inorganic transparent material made largely of silicates are well advised to eschew propelling concretions of earthy or mineral matter.

Case Studies

The following case studies present you with selling scenarios that require you to apply the critical skills discussed in the chapter and give you training through "real world" practical learning situations. They are meant to be both engaging and challenging, and like the exercises, don't have one right answer.

CASE 5.1—The Return

Ben's manager was not happy. "Do you realize what you just cost this company?" he growled at Ben. "We just took back a $1,600 home entertainment system from some guy named John Stafford. He was hot. Said that Ben Walker had just pressured his wife into buying this piece of crap and that he'd never do business here again. What happened, Ben?"

"I don't know," Ben replied. "Mrs. Stafford seemed very content with the purchase. Said her husband had wanted something like this and that she wanted to surprise him. She signed the contract and paid with her credit card. No problem as far as I could tell."

"Well, there was a problem, all right!" Ben's manager hissed. "Mr. Stafford didn't like the features on this system, especially the audio. It wasn't like anything he'd been looking for. So now we have to eat the restocking costs, and you're out the commission. This had better not happen again. I want you to go think about it and tell me what went wrong and how

you're going to avoid this kind of mess in the future." With that, the manager stormed back into his office.

Ben was perplexed. For the eleven months that he'd worked at Ocean Front Appliances, he had come to enjoy selling the three major product lines they carried. Sure, there was pressure, but the commission structure was high enough to make it worth enduring. In the case of Mrs. Stafford, he thought he'd done his job, at least well enough to get the sale. Over lunch, he confided in Marcia, another successful salesperson, that he didn't understand what had happened.

"I remember her," Marcia replied. "I was just on the other side of the display while you were working with her, and I thought at the time that this one could go sour."

"What do you mean?" Ben asked.

"Well, Mrs. Stafford was clearly nervous. She kept saying, 'I just don't know.' And then, you'd explain some other feature, and she would respond, "Do you think my husband will like this?"

"I remember. I kept having to reassure her," Ben said. "So, I thought I'd just move on and show her how terrific this system really is."

"I know, Ben, but when she kept backing up, you should have recognized the clue that she really wasn't ready. You closed her, but I think she appeased you to get out of the store."

That stung. Ben was going to have to think about this some more.

Given the above scene, what do you think, in light of what you've read in Chapter 5, that Ben should consider? Specifically, where did Ben go wrong concerning the customer's decision process, the customer's motivation for buying, and communication?

CASE 5.2—X-Ray Vision

Carla was furious. As a representative of MediTech, she had just spent the better part of three months cultivating the purchasing agent for a regional medical firm in her territory to buy the latest upgrade of MediTech's fMRI (functional MRI) machine, only to be told when she tried to close the sale that he would have to "consult others."

Todd, the purchasing agent, had never mentioned consulting anyone before now. For him to brush her off like that, Carla fumed, was insulting. When she stormed into her sales manager's office with her tale of rejection, however, he remained unperturbed.

"What do you mean, 'I should have known better?'" Carla exclaimed. "How could I have known that Todd would resort to such a transparently cheap dodge?"

"Look. I know you just came over to us recently from pharmaceutical sales," replied her manager, "but that experience should have taught you something."

"What?"

"Well, for starters, think about what you're selling. It's expensive, and the time before it becomes obsolete isn't all that long."

"But Todd knew all that some time ago. I never hid anything from him. He didn't bat an eye when I told him what their five-year projected cost would be," said Carla.

"Maybe not. But he's not the one who is most impacted by increased cost. Think about who will use the new fMRI. Physicians, that's who. And you know even better than I how much physicians like to be in control," the sales manager pointed out.

He continued, "Unless they're convinced that there's a huge medical benefit that will justify the higher fees they must charge, they'll revolt. Those issues are outside Todd's responsibility."

Even though Carla's manager was accurate in pointing out the details that he mentioned, what was Carla missing in her general approach to Todd? What should she have done differently? Why should the points that her manager raised with her have caused her to change her approach? What can she do not to remedy the situation and get the sale?

DISCOVERING YOUR SOCIAL STYLE

OVERVIEW

Effective salespeople learn as much as they can about what motivates the driving force of their business, which, of course, is customers. An especially useful tool for gaining insight into how customers think is the Social Styles Model. This chapter examines the four dominant social styles through which we send and receive information. Reading social styles is an excellent way to discover how best to approach a prospect and set up a working relationship, and ultimately, close more sales while forming lasting relationships.

OBJECTIVES

- Recognize the four different behavioral styles.
- Identify your dominant and secondary social style.
- Appreciate the roles that responsiveness and assertiveness play in each style.
- Learn how to deal with those who operate from each of the various styles.
- Understand versatility and how it affects your ability to relate to different social styles.
- Become familiar with gender issues in selling.
- Understand how to use neurolinguistic programming to read a prospect's physical cues.

A Conflict of Styles

Several weeks into her job as a fund-raiser for a nonprofit that provides care for special needs children, Allison Meek was feeling disenchanted. The problem was not with the work itself. The issues started once she was face-to-face with donors.

Allison went into every meeting ready to wow them with her organized, thorough, and detailed presentation, complete with charts and graphs to back up all points. In the middle of her presentation, prospects often interrupt her with questions that seem irrelevant to the points she is trying to make, which complicates her carefully laid out plans.

She tried not to appear irritated, but most prospects didn't seem interested in what Allison had to say. "People just aren't giving like they used to," Allison would sigh as she'd head back to the office empty-handed from yet another prospect presentation.

Some might call such incidents a few cases of bad luck. Others would say that perhaps those prospects were never going to donate in the first place. Maybe Allison is not doing a good enough job of explaining her cause, or perhaps she is over-explaining it.

On the other hand, maybe we should call Allison's problem what it is—the inability to connect to different social styles. Allison, as you will learn in this chapter, has an *analytical* social style. Unknowingly, she had communicated disrespect to some of her prospects who had entirely different methods of communicating.

This lack of understanding and knowledge concerning behavioral styles can cause lost sales (or donations, in Allison's case) and damaged or ruined relationships. Does Allison need to change who she is to fix this problem? No. She does, however, need to learn the art of *social style flexing*. In

other words, she must be versatile enough to adjust her pace and priorities to facilitate communication with another person of a different style. You can only accomplish such a *flex* through a good understanding of the four styles discussed in this chapter.

The Social Styles Model

Because of the importance of communication, successful salespeople continuously search for new ways to make their messages more effective. They are eager to learn how to anticipate and avoid conflict situations. Accurately gauging your clients' personalities will undoubtedly help you communicate more effectively and connect with prospects and customers, and thereby enrich your career.[1]

A *sales transaction*—whether it involves products, services, or ideas—is, at its core, a successful communication exchange. In this exchange, two parties develop a mutually desirable solution to a problem about which both are concerned. The best possible result is when a selling transaction develops over time into a long-term relationship full of mutual trust and credibility. If that is the goal, the relevant question then becomes:

"How can I sell so that I demonstrate respect for my customer, build credibility for myself, my product, and my company, and set up a mutually beneficial situation?"

The answer to this question lies in understanding and appealing to a person's unique social or behavioral style. Psychologist Carl

Jung first introduced the concept of social styles in 1933, based on Sigmund Freud's theories of the adult ego state.[2] Jung's work resulted in a personality theory in which he described all human behavior as a combination of four primary functions:

1. **Sensing:** wants facts and relies on the five senses
2. **Intuitive:** trusts hunches and looks for the big picture
3. **Feeling:** focuses on human needs and values harmony
4. **Thinking:** decides things based on logic and principle

Since Jung's landmark theory, several other experts have expanded upon his work and presented their derivations. David Merrill and Roger Reid began the development of their "Social Styles Model" in the early 1960s. Dr. Paul Mok, working independently of

Merrill and Reid, developed what he referred to as the "Communicating Styles Technology Model." The Wilson Learning Corporation and Dr. Tony Alessandra and Associates Inc. later expanded and added their research to these original models. The material in this chapter is a compilation of these approaches.[3]

In your personal life, you have plenty of time to learn how to best connect with friends and family members. In a business or social situation, you have far less time to evaluate and adjust your social skills. Because you are not yet familiar with prospects' styles, their responses and mannerisms may be deceptive. As a result, you may miss what they are saying.[4] The Social Styles Model provides a useful tool for making such an evaluation in the shortest possible time.

The better you understand personality types, the more successful you will be in communicating with the various people you meet.

People use four basic styles to deal with the world around them. Each is based upon one of four primary functions of human personality:

DRIVER: *The driver style is based on the* ***sensing*** *function of taking in all available sensory information and reacting to it in a results-driven way.*

EXPRESSIVE: *The expressive style is based on the* ***intuitive*** *function of imagination and abstract thought that can appear spontaneous and even impulsive.*

AMIABLE: *The amiable style is based on the **feeling** function of personal and heart-led, emotional reactions to experience with an emphasis on building connections.*

ANALYTICAL: *The analytical style is based on the **thinking** function of organizing and analyzing information logically and doing so cautiously.*

Each person has a *primary style* of communicating that is blended or complemented by a *secondary style*. These primary and secondary styles shape other people's perceptions and filter your opinions of other people. Everyone uses each of the four functions, but the frequency of use differs significantly.[5]

It is also important to note that people tend to switch from one pattern to another as their mood, nature, or moment changes.[6]

Another dimension of this model comes into play when you are under stress. When you are under pressure, you may shift to a different style of behavior. These shifts often happen unconsciously, or you may be aware of the change yet feel unable to prevent it.

Like adults, young children process experience according to their styles, which is why you can observe social styles in young children and even in babies. Behavioral patterns, Carl Jung claimed, are largely genetically determined and can, therefore, be witnessed in infants.

Behavioral Styles in Selling

Four fundamental concepts support the behavioral styles communication model presented in this chapter. These four ideas are guidelines that can help you succeed in communicating and connecting with prospects and clients. They are:

1. **We interact via our unique social style.** A *social style* is a person's overall approach to receiving and sending messages. Each of the four styles consists of verbal, nonverbal, and behavioral elements. Everyone uses a blend of the driver, expressive, amiable, and analytical styles.

2. **We all have a primary and secondary style.** Every person communicates the majority of the time through a *primary style*. Likewise, everyone also has a *secondary style* or *backup style* that may replace or modify the original style.

3. **Observable clues indicate our primary style.** You can identify someone else's style by observing *common behavioral clues* that are unique to each style. These clues include the use of time, manner of speech, standard reaction to others, and approach to job performance.

4. **Some styles complement each other, and others clash.** People respond favorably to similar or complementary styles. When a salesperson's style differs significantly from that of the prospect, the resulting conflicts can be disastrous.[7]

People tend to use one or two styles, and that choice affects everything they do and say. It also affects what prospects hear and believe during a presentation. Understanding the strengths and liabilities of your primary style and learning to be versatile can help you more effectively communicate with those around you.[8]

Exhibit 6.1 illustrates that your most damaging weaknesses (-) are merely exaggerations of your strengths (+). Your behavior responds to circumstances like the volume dial of a radio. When you use a social style in moderation, the volume is just right, and the sound is pleasant. In that instance, your style is a *strength*. However,

EXHIBIT 6.1 Social Styles Strengths and Weaknesses

CONTROLS

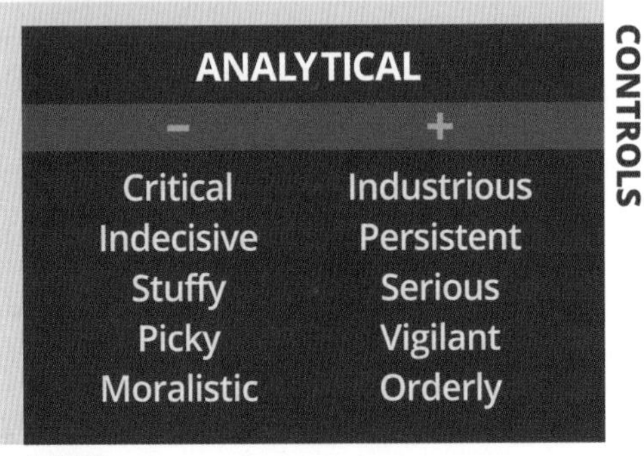

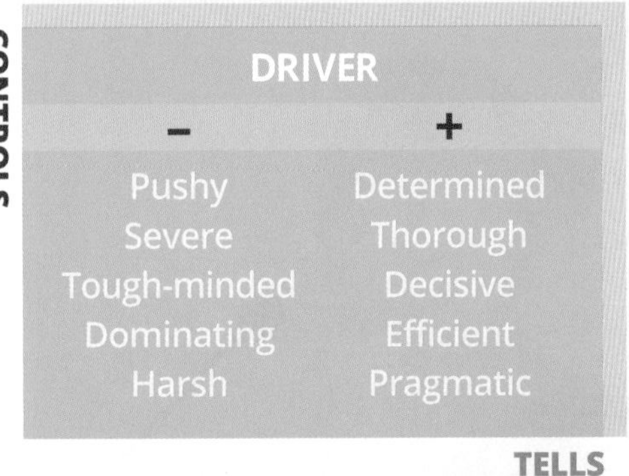

ASKS TELLS

AMIABLE –	AMIABLE +
Conformist	Supportive
Reserved	Respectful
Pliable	Willing
Dependent	Dependable
Unsure	Agreeable

EXPRESSIVE –	EXPRESSIVE +
Manipulative	Personable
Excitable	Stimulating
Undisciplined	Enthusiastic
Reacting	Dramatic
Egotistical	Gregarious

EMOTES

when you abuse or refuse to flex your style to accommodate others, (when the volume is too high), it becomes a *weakness* that leads to ineffective communication.

Professional selling is all about managing relationships. Most people don't even think about working on relationships in their daily lives. On the other hand, relationship salespeople take time to think about and understand the people around them. The relationship selling approach will strengthen and enhance your selling style by turning you into a relationship-oriented facilitator of information and value. The relationship style of selling is the modern approach to helping clients and prospects win.

A customer is not a transaction. A customer is a relationship!

When you interview for your next job, you will likely be asked to take a personality test. The popularity of personality inventories in career selection has grown substantially in recent years. A recent meta-study investigated the relationship between personality traits and job performance and found convincing evidence that personality inventories are highly effective in finding the right fit for a position.[9] Although personality style is not an accurate predictor of overall work performance, it can predict success in specific occupations or relate to specific criteria.

The social styles model does not describe a person's complete personality because it omits reference to the individual's beliefs, ethics, abilities, and intelligence. However, experts say that our habits and attitudes control as much as 90 percent of our actions.[10] That makes social style cues a useful way to learn key personality traits quickly. Social style analysis is also worthwhile because it reveals the two primary attributes of behavior, which are *assertiveness* and *responsiveness.*

Two Attributes of Behavior

When you meet someone, your mind subconsciously notes two behavioral characteristics: assertiveness and responsiveness. *Assertiveness* represents the effort a person makes to influence or control the thoughts and actions of others. *Responsiveness* is the willingness with which a person outwardly shares feelings or emotions and develops relationships.[11]

Levels of assertiveness and responsiveness vary from person to person. The table below lists the characteristics most commonly associated with both ends of the spectrum:

LOW IN RESPONSIVENESS
- Formal and proper
- Fact-oriented
- Guarded, cool, and aloof
- Disciplined about time
- Seldom makes gestures
- Controls body language

HIGH IN RESPONSIVENESS
- Relaxed and warm
- Open and approachable
- Dramatic and animated
- Flexible about time
- Oriented toward relationships and feelings

LOW IN ASSERTIVENESS
- Introverted
- Supportive, a team player
- Easygoing
- Avoids taking risks
- Good listener
- Reserved in their opinions

HIGH IN ASSERTIVENESS
- Risk-taker
- Swift in decision-making
- Willing to confront others
- Very competitive
- Take-charge attitude
- Expresses opinions

Attribute Mapping

Combining the assertiveness and responsiveness characteristics makes it possible to develop a map of what each social style will likely do or say next. Exhibit 6.2 shows the relationships among the four social styles.

The *horizontal axis* (labeled A through D) in the exhibit is the range from the *most to least assertive*. Assertive people take a stand and make their position clear to others. Because they are ambitious, competitive, and quick to take action and express strong opinions, they are located on the *Telling* end of the social style axis. Nonassertive people tend to be cooperative, silent, and slow to act. Thus, they are located on the *Asking* end of the axis. The least assertive individuals are in quartile D, and the most assertive in quartile A, with quartiles B and C representing moderate levels of assertiveness.

The *vertical axis* (labeled 1 through 4) in the exhibit is the range from *least to most responsive*. Nonresponsive individuals, those in quartile 1, are on the *Controlled* end of the spectrum. They are mostly indifferent to the feelings of others, reserved, and have no-nonsense attitudes. The responsive individuals found in quartile 4 are on the *Emotional* end of the responsiveness spectrum. Highly responsive individuals are subjective people who are incredibly relationship oriented. Individuals who land in quartiles 2 and 3 of the exhibit tend to display more moderate levels of responsiveness.

Identifying assertiveness and responsiveness levels is not a foolproof way to determine a person's real personality. With study and practice, however, you can become as much as 70 to 80 percent effective in using your observations to predict habitual behavioral patterns. Then you can be well prepared to use that knowledge to improve your communication efforts.

EXHIBIT 6.2 **Assertiveness and Responsiveness Quartiles**

NONRESPONSIVE (Controlled)
Wants facts and figures, precise about time, task-oriented, objective and reserved

ASSERTIVE
(Telling)
Fast, active, risk taker, verbal, directive, competitive

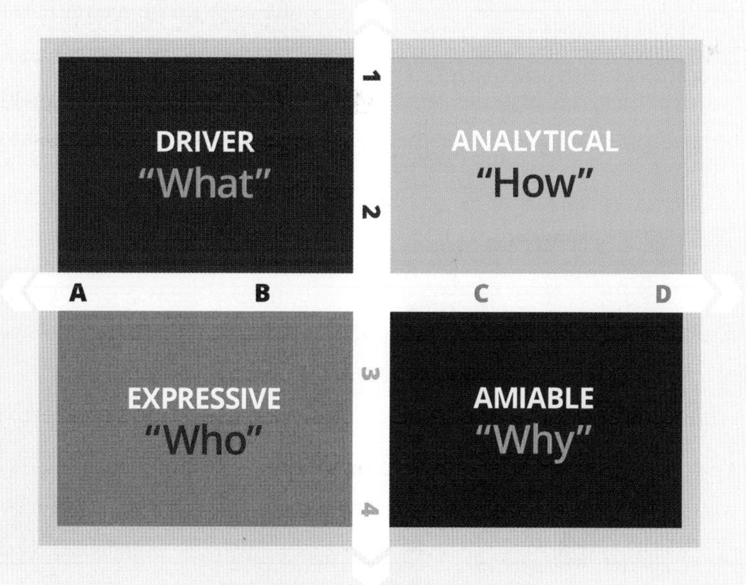

NONASSERTIVE
(Asking)
Inquisitive, slow-acting, risk averse, nonverbal, cooperative

RESPONSIVE (Emotional)
Expressive about feelings, wants feelings and emotions, imprecise about time, people oriented, subjective

Pace and Priority Choices

Assertiveness and responsiveness play a profound role in how people choose their pace and priorities. *Pace* is the speed at which a person prefers to move. Those who are low in assertiveness (analyticals and amiables) prefer a slow pace. Those high in assertiveness (drivers and expressives) prefer a fast pace in conversation, deliberation, and problem solving.[12]

Priorities indicate what a person considers to be most important. The way we prioritize is often related to how responsive we are. If you are low in responsiveness, you put *tasks* at the top of the priority list. If you are high in responsiveness, you put *relationships* at the top.

You will typically find that you can handle conflicts involving only priorities or only pace with relative ease. However, significant communication discord may occur when your style conflicts with a prospect's style in both pace *and* priority. If you interact with every customer via the same style, your closing percentage will be low, because you will only connect with complementary styles. If you learn how to relate to all four styles, however, you can significantly increase your closing ratio.[13]

In a conflict situation, most people tend to move to the extreme dimensions of their primary style. For example, an expressive may attack verbally. A driver might become overbearing, pushy, and dictatorial. An amiable could submit to avoid conflict but feel resentment and distrust. An analytical may withdraw into flight rather than fight.

Salespeople who do not adjust their behavior to meet the needs of clients will become easily frustrated with what seems like disinterest from prospects. If you are unwilling to adjust your pace and priorities to fit your prospects, it is not a lack of interest that you experience—it's a failure to connect. For example, an analytical prospect could interpret an expressive salesperson's questions

as a personal challenge or attack. If the analytical prospect responds to the questions merely to avoid further discomfort, the expressive salesperson may be encouraged by the responses and ask even more questions. That unsuspecting salesperson now runs the risk of pushing the analytical into a more significant conflict that almost guarantees a "no" at the end.[14]

How to Identify Pace and Priority

How do you go about determining someone's pace and priorities? Ask yourself these questions and observe the answers:

1. **How fast do they make decisions and get things done?**
2. **How competitive are they? Are they competitive in a conversation and fight for airtime in a meeting?**
3. **How much feeling do they display in their verbal and nonverbal communication? Are there broad smiles and gestures or few discernible emotions at all?**

Your goal is to identify pace and priorities accurately and respond appropriately. How can you more directly and efficiently find out your prospect's information preferences? You may find it helpful to use one of these statements:[15]

> *"Ordinarily, I get right into my presentation to be respectful of your time, but we could also get to know each other first. What would you prefer?"*

> *"I usually like to spend a few minutes learning more about your company's needs, but I'm prepared to get right into my presentation if that works better. What do you think?"*

> *"Thanks for sharing the concerns you have about your current product. I know we can satisfactorily address each of those issues! So, would you prefer I start with the end in mind and then work backward, or would you like to hear the step-by-step details first?"*

The expressive and amiable styles would more than likely indicate a desire to chat and get to know one another and take the slower route. The driver and analytical styles would want you to begin your presentation and get to the facts more quickly. Ask these questions and choose pace and priority according to what best suits your prospects' preferences rather than your own.

> **"Personality is to a man what perfume is to a flower."**
> *Charles M. Schwab*

Behavioral Styles Profiles

The four social styles are linked to distinctive and unique habits of behavior. The name given to each style reflects general characteristics rather than a comprehensive description. Keep in mind that no one style is better than another. Each has its strengths and weaknesses, and successful and unsuccessful people and a diverse range of backgrounds exist in each style group.[16] Before detailing each style, here is a summary of the four social styles:

1. **Drivers control and tell.** They are highly assertive and unresponsive. They command others by telling them what to do and regulate themselves by remaining objective. They are task-oriented and combine personal power and emotional control in relationships with others. They are *control specialists.*
2. **Expressives tell and emote.** They are highly assertive, but they are also high in emotional responsiveness. They attempt to tell people what to do but place more emphasis on their relationships with people than they do on the task itself. They are *social specialists.*
3. **Amiables ask and emote.** They are not assertive but highly responsive. They rely on an emotions-based approach to get things done. They are *support specialists*, combining personal reserve and emotional expression.
4. **Analyticals ask and control.** They are neither assertive nor responsive. They tend to be highly task-oriented but soften that approach by asking rather than directing. They are *technical specialists* who combine personal reserve with emotional control.

You can determine a person's primary social style with reasonable accuracy by observing both verbal and nonverbal clues.[17] Identifying one's social style does not provide a crystal ball that precisely predicts an individual's future actions and decisions. However, it does provide a basis for forming expectations about behavior and provides you with clues for how to best respond.

All About Drivers (Sensing)

Drivers exhibit minimum concern for other people's feelings. Here is an excellent example of how drivers think: a vice president of marketing for a large theme park was overheard saying, "My executive assistant drives me nuts! I'll ask her how her weekend went, and she tells me—in detail! All I want to hear is fine or not fine."

Those are the words of a real driver. If you say something harsh, they don't even seem to notice. They consider yes-people to be weak. Drivers' feelings are not easily hurt because they do not take things personally. Respectfully stand up to drivers. Make an impression by showing them substantial evidence of what your product or service can do.

Drivers tend to be intense, competitive, fast-paced, and goal-oriented. They pride themselves on the ability to get things done. They are willing to accept risks and want to know the estimated outcome of each option. Convince them that your proposed action works and that it will provide all the benefits promised. They are more impressed by what they see and hear than by what you say.

Drivers are action-driven, resourceful, organized, and pragmatic. They also tend to impose high standards on themselves and others. As a result, they may seem impatient or tireless. They push to perfect their skills but also invest time and effort in coaching other people.

At their worst, they give inadequate consideration to the long-range consequences of their actions. They draw criticism for seeking to impose on others their expectations for drive and speed. Under stress, drivers can seem anti-intellectual and defensive to opinions differing from their own, especially to those who move at a slower pace. Drivers are likely to feel that any failure is evidence that others were not loyal enough or willing to work hard enough to make the project a success.

Presentation Strategies for Drivers

1. Spend less time attempting to relate on a personal level.
2. Move fast and isolate the bottom-line benefits that can be verified.
3. Do not make a lengthy presentation. Be brief and stress the bottom line.
4. Any visuals you choose to show must be relevant to vital points.
5. Ask questions to involve them, get them to talk, and allow them to lead.
6. If you challenge drivers, challenge the concepts rather than the person.
7. Answer objections immediately, and never try to bluff.
8. Present several solutions that give them the ability to choose.
9. A compelling close is one that highlights an immediate, tangible benefit.

All About Expressives (Intuitive)

Expressives temper their assertiveness with concern for the feelings of others. They are motivated by recognition, approval, and success. They desire success but are recognition motivated. You must compliment them and show them how to win. Let them talk, and they often sell themselves. Tell them who else uses your product. Testimonials from well-known people or people they respect are significant to them.

Expressives pride themselves on originality, foresight, and the ability to see the big picture. Reinforce their self-image as visionaries and idea people, and they will be receptive to your ideas. Expressives often see new possibilities and present fresh ideas and approaches to problems.

Expressives thrive on spontaneity. The expressive's love of risk-taking makes it easier for them to take a chance on your product. Refer to the product as a "sure bet" or guarantee that you will "make this risk pay off big." To reach them, you must emphasize the importance of taking risks in the pursuit of progress. Show expressives your product's payoff potential by sharing what it can do and what that means to them. When you have a qualified expressive whose needs match your product's benefits,

Presentation Strategies for Expressives

1. Show them how they and their company can win.
2. Open with innovative ideas for them to grow through your offering.
3. Ask open-ended questions that allow them to talk, then relate benefits to their priorities.
4. Seek feedback to convey respect for their insight—but don't patronize them.
5. Use showmanship. Go with impressive big-picture features over details.
6. Never argue or back them into a corner.
7. Ask if they want you to respond to a concern (it may have been just a passing comment).
8. Use testimonials, especially from well-known people.
9. Allow them to carry out their game plan, not yours.

you should not have to do much persuading because expressives are intuition-driven.[18]

At their worst, expressives seem to base decisions on opinions, hunches, or intuition rather than on facts. They want to delegate the details to someone else so that they are free to dream. They may be impatient when others demand documentation before accepting the vision or ideas they offer. Under stress, expressives run the risk of seeming detached. They appear indifferent to problems and seem to be living in their own private world. They may spend time defending their ideas instead of trying to make them work.

All About Amiables (Feeling)

Amiables are submissive, people-oriented, and willing to go along with the crowd. They need time to get to know you personally, so allow plenty of warm up time. They are undisciplined in the use of time. Agreeable in nature, they are also easily hurt. They want to be liked.

Amiables tend to be alert and observant individuals who are concerned with whether they like you, trust you, and can picture a positive long-term relationship with you. They are highly people-oriented in their management style and resent doing business with anyone who makes them uncomfortable or is unresponsive to their feelings. Their business decisions are markedly influenced by how their various options might impact the people in the organization. Before they accept your proposal or idea, you must convince them that you believe in it, too. They must also know what risks are involved—especially those to personal relationships.

At their best, amiables are conscientious listeners, skilled communicators, and empathetic supporters. Their insight enables them to navigate organizational politics well. At

Presentation Strategies for Amiables

1. Plan to approach with as much personal information as possible.
2. Avoid a rigid or canned approach and presentation.
3. Make an informal presentation with visuals and testimonials integrated.
4. Show that you understand and accept their feelings.
5. Spend some time relating. Move to a first-name basis quickly.
6. Be open and candid. Develop a personal relationship and never skip rapport building.
7. Offer them money-back guarantees and personal assurances.
8. Avoid asking directly for their business. Instead, suggest a natural next step.
9. Be prepared to use third-party references and case histories that link them to others.

their worst, they seem more concerned with interacting than with understanding the matter at hand. They appear to be too spontaneous and not focused on weighing the pros and cons. They seem to regard their own emotions as facts and act based on their feelings. They may be criticized for being defensive, over-reactive, and too subjective.

Belonging to a group is essential to amiables. To sell effectively to them, you have to show them that you are a team player. Position yourself as their newest team member by first building rapport, then working side-by-side to accomplish the goals they've set. To minimize an amiable's insecurities, talk about the problems your product can solve. Then show how those solutions will help improve performance, which will enhance leadership's image of them. It is the amiable's job to nurture the team, so don't forget to outline what your product will do for the people in the company.

All About Analyticals (Thinking)

Analyticals are thinkers. They need time to assess and assimilate what they hear and see. They want to know just how things work and often say they want time to think things over. Product information is crucial. Know everything possible about your product, and don't expect to hear them say much.

Analyticals tend to be highly logical, organized, and unsentimental. They tend to be fact oriented and value accuracy. Their contribution to the management team is their ability to solve difficult problems and make sound, rational business decisions based on evidence and intelligent inferences rather than on imagination or gut feelings. They take a logical approach to responsibilities.

The more supporting data you can provide for your ideas, the more likely you are to sell to them. They have little interest in your opinions and more in your ability to assemble and organize supportive data for use in weighing options and arriving at a systematic, well-thought-out solution to problems.

At their best, analyticals appear to be a consistent force for progress. They are top-flight planners and doers. They can cut through untested ideas and emotional enthusiasm to find the core truth. They are capable leaders for research and planning tasks. They are valuable in executing logical, meticulous projects. At their worst, they are overly cautious and conservative.

Analyticals emphasize deliberation over action. They may become so involved in evaluating all the details of a situation that others may regard them as indecisive stumbling blocks to innovative activity. Under stress, analyticals can become rigid and insecure. They may fear taking risks. They seem more concerned with being right than with seizing opportunities.

Presentation Strategies for Analyticals

1. Know their business thoroughly.
2. Use a logic-based, low-key style of relating, with plenty of facts.
3. Be sure prospects understand the structure of your presentation.
4. Emphasize tested, proven, and well-documented aspects of your product's benefits.
5. Make use of visual aids in the presentation and leave literature with them for later.
6. Present your information in a controlled, professional, organized fashion.
7. Point out the pros and cons of your offering. They will be thinking about them anyway.
8. Present a detailed summary of significant points, and use the summary as your close.
9. Avoid the phrase, "In my opinion..." They don't care about opinions, just the facts.

Versatility as a Communication Tool

When people of different styles meet and behave strictly according to the characteristics of their styles, conflict often results. An amiable salesperson and a driver prospect can quickly arrive at a crossroads and end up going nowhere. A driver prospect wants to hear facts and to accomplish the task at hand, while an amiable salesperson intends to cultivate a personal relationship.

In an ideal situation, both parties are willing to move toward a middle ground, but that rarely happens in real life. In such cases, the salesperson must be capable of making most of the adjustments by engaging in style-flexing.

Versatility (also called behavioral flexibility) is a person's willingness to flex their style by controlling personal behavior patterns and adapting to other people as a means of enhancing communication.[19] The salesperson's style does not change, but instead, he or she applies techniques that work in a particular situation.[20] For example, when meeting with an analytical prospect, an expressive salesperson can use versatility by talking less, listening more, and focusing on facts.

Never equate versatility with insincerity or imitation of a prospect's style. Versatile salespeople seek a reasonable compromise, but they do not become so highly changeable that they continuously neglect their own pace and priority preferences.[21]

Strive for *psychological reciprocity* with prospects by making the initial attempt to relate to their style.[22] When you make the first move to adapt your style, that motivates prospects to reciprocate. Real communication and understanding will then occur much more quickly than when each person stays firmly rooted in his or her style.[23] The following aspects of a face-to-face interview often require the need for you to remain versatile, responsive, and willing to adapt and change to fit each situation:[24]

- **Comfort.** Does the prospect seem nervous? What can you do to help them feel more comfortable? Are you moving too slowly for their style? Too quickly?
- **Tension.** Is there an air of stress or general discomfort? It may be that you have not spent long enough building rapport. Back out of the presentation if necessary and ask more open-ended questions to get the prospect talking.
- **Assertiveness in asking questions.** Does the prospect provide you with valuable information by asking questions that may reveal a way to sell them? If not, how can you help prompt them to ask more questions?
- **Presentation responsiveness.** Is the prospect with you or noticeably preoccupied? If a prospect is not responsive to your presentation, you may have misread his or her social style and need to re-assess.
- **Level of openness.** Is the prospect sharing pertinent information that will help you better discover how to serve his needs? If not, ask more open-ended questions and give them plenty of time to answer. Or ask if they'd rather you move right into the presentation.

We are all in the people business. As a salesperson, you observe and verify behavior and have a constant need to become an expert at interpreting what you see. In any relationship, everyone has his or her particular point of view. When you understand behavioral styles, you can adapt your style to meet the needs of others.

Most experts believe that styles are fixed early in life—it's what you do with your style that makes a difference. Style flexing is a great way to complement the other person's style and create a mutually beneficial environment.

Gender Style Differences

While it is essential to recognize and adjust to different social styles, it is also necessary to acknowledge the contribution that gender makes to our communication in the business world. The issue of *proxemics*, which is the distance individuals prefer to keep between themselves and others, also becomes more critical when meeting with someone of the opposite gender.[25] That is why we must be sensitive to gender issues and adjust to them just as we do for social style differences. If not handled correctly, these seemingly insignificant differences can

"Look, let's just be gender-neutral about this and build a snow*person*."

break down communication lines and damage relationships.

Although there have been numerous studies conducted over the years concerning which genders are best suited for specific roles, the results remain inconclusive.[26] Research does show that women are more responsive to *contingent rewards* (rewards for meeting identified goals). Contingent reward behavior may be a predictor of effectiveness, which could suggest that those who are responsive to reward systems may possess a leadership advantage.[27] Research by Siguaw & Honeycutt also found that women were engaged more frequently in relationship-centric selling than were their male counterparts.[28]

A research study by Russ & McNeilly concluded that managers who treat male and female sales reps the same miss the potential benefits that gender styles provide.[29] The key is to be sensitive to gender differences and open to learning from all personality types and people.

Despite significant advances in gender relations, inequalities still exist in business that sometimes makes it difficult for men and women to relate to each other. In a study conducted through a survey of women professionals, the researchers examined two possible ideologies that could explain gender inequalities:[30]

1. **The first potential theory states that gender inequalities are a result of differences in training, experience, and personal motivation, and suggests that women who fall behind only do so because of individual limitations.**

2. **The second proposed ideology states that inequalities are a result of various underlying factors such as discrimination, stereotyping, and exclusion from social groups and networks.**

In reality, both theories likely play a role in gender differences and perceptions. We must, therefore, work to overcome deep-seated stereotypes of gender roles and let people's work speak for itself.

Acting on generalities, regardless of gender, can kill a sale more quickly than anything else.[31]

Do your best not to take every nonverbal cue at face value. While there are some fundamental differences in how men and women interact, there are no absolute truths. Be careful about making assumptions based solely on gender. While the best strategy is to cater to your prospect's social style first and foremost, exhibit 6.3 provides some suggestions for dealing with subtle gender differences.

EXHIBIT 6.3 Gender Flexing in Sales

- **Speak confidently and clearly.** Men tend to interrupt, especially if the speaker seems tentative or unsure. So, speak with confidence.
- **Stop interrupting.** Interrupting is an excellent way to lose a sale. Learn to listen.
- **Practice your humor.** Women may use humor less frequently than men in a business setting. Being funny at the right moment is essential.
- **Watch your language.** Consider steering clear of overtly masculine or feminine vocabulary. Words like "lovely," "charming," or "adorable" might not resonate with a male audience. At the same time, don't use crude or foul language.
- **Feel the sale.** If you sense someone is more interested in the emotional rewards of buying, mix facts with emotion to find the perfect combination.
- **Watch how you address people.** Never use the words "honey," "dear," or "sweetie." Even though these words are relatively common in some areas, such language might be offensive to those who are not used to hearing them.

No one can make a sweeping statement regarding all women or men. It's vital to communicate in a way that is meaningful to that individual—and gender is just one piece of the puzzle to help you determine what your customers value most.[32]

Culture Style Differences

To succeed in the global market, sales managers and teams need to understand how cultural differences affect behavior and business. According to cross-cultural expert and author Sinan Caykoylu, sales managers and sales teams cannot adopt a "one size fits all" approach to training. They need to be able to diversify their strategy in a way that allows them to understand how different cultures and genders react to certain behaviors.[33]

In many Middle Eastern and Asian countries, for example, it is critical to follow the customs of the area to avoid offending those with whom you are dealing. It is essential to learn the customs and personal cultural background of your prospect before your presentation or even your first introduction. Without this knowledge, your words, actions, and body language may inadvertently offend your prospect, costing you the sale and possibly, your good reputation.

Reading the Prospect's Environment

You can find important clues to a client's style in the environment as well as in verbal and nonverbal actions. Observe how the office is decorated and arranged and what seating arrangements are available.

Suppose that upon entering a prospect's office, you notice family pictures, nature posters, a circular desk, and a separate seating area with four comfortable chairs. What is your first impression of that client's behavioral style? Did you say *amiable*? If so, you are right. You can then verify or adjust your initial impression by observing the prospect's actions and speech. If the prospect rises to greet you and sits in a comfortable chair, you can confirm your amiable impression.[34]

Let's try another example. You enter the prospect's office and notice a diploma, an achievement plaque, and a poster on the wall that says, "Why not?" The desk contains jumbled stacks of paper and a chaotic appearance. There are overstuffed chairs by the open side of the desk, a bookcase with stacks of books, and a plant on the file cabinet. The disorganization, the wall decorations emphasizing achievement, and the comfortable and accessible seating suggest that this office houses an *expressive*.

Neurolinguistic Programming

An entirely different approach to communicating effectively and understanding more about prospects is offered by *neurolinguistic programming* (NLP). NLP is the brain-child of linguist John Grinder and psychotherapist Richard Bandler. It looks at how people create the results they want. In your career, this understanding can be the difference between success and a lost sale.[36] The primary focus of NLP is to pinpoint a prospect's feelings through eye-movement cues. These cues also indicate whether a person is a visual, auditory, or kinesthetic learner.[37]

When it first began to attract attention, NLP was considered a pop-psychology craze that used sneaky ways to "read" people to control and influence them. In reality, what NLP does is offer another way to observe people and understand their needs. It is entirely different from the study of behavioral styles, but in no way contradicts it.

The Social Media Connection

CAN SOCIAL MEDIA REVEAL SOCIAL STYLE?

Social media has changed the way businesses operate. It can also change the way you prepare for your next meeting with a prospect. You may be able to use your prospects' social media pages to determine their social styles before you meet them. Here are some interesting findings from a recent study conducted by *CPP*, the official publisher of the Myers-Briggs Type Indicator:[35]

In general, individuals with a preference for *feeling* (amiables) reported spending more time engaging in personal activities on Facebook in their time than did individuals with a preference for *thinking* (analyticals). When it comes to LinkedIn usage, those with a preference for *intuition* (expressives) and *thinking* (analyticals)

reported using LinkedIn more often than individuals with a preference for *sensing* (drivers) and *feeling* (amiables).

The study also showed that 29 percent of amiables and expressives interacted at least once a week on social media, and 17 percent of them shared information about their professional life at least once a week. In contrast, only 16 percent of drivers and analyticals interacted at least once a week on social media—and only 8 percent of them shared information about their professional life at least once a week.

As for Twitter, more individuals with a preference for *intuition* (expressives) reported being active users of Twitter than individuals with a preference for *sensing* (drivers).

What does this all mean? Well, it could indicate that, although not the case in every situation, a person's proclivity toward posting, liking, tweeting, commenting, and recommending may tell you what personality type he or she favors. *What does your social media presence say about you and your personality?*

Identifying Learning Modes

Neurolinguistic programming is the science of how the brain learns, and it is based on recognizing and then appealing to a person's dominant mode(s) of learning or perception. We all use these modes to map reality and build a model of what the world is like that can guide us through our environment. Each person has a primary learning mode: *visual*, *auditory*, or *kinesthetic*. We use each style at various times but generally favor one method.[38]

1. **Auditory.** Some people prefer to perceive the world through *hearing*. They learn more quickly by listening than by reading or seeing. Their brains may even translate experiences presented through other senses into an auditory mode. These are the people who test ideas on how they sound. They often use responses like, "I hear what you're saying," "It sounds good to me," and "I'm hearing a lot of complaints about that situation." If you want to reach this style of learner, use webcasts, podcasts, and discussion groups.
2. **Visual.** Other people prefer to perceive the world through sight. They learn and form opinions based on what they see. They are the ones who originated the saying, "Seeing is believing." They create mental pictures of their experiences as a means of interpretation. They frequently use phrases like, "I see what you mean," "I'm in a fog about the whole concept," and "Do you get the picture?" This visual style responds best through videos, graphs, pictures, diagrams, and illustrations. Other ways to reach this

style are through the use of videos and in-person demonstrations.

3. **Kinesthetic.** A small number of people perceive the world through the sense of touch. They feel life. Everything has a texture that either attracts or repels them. Some of these kinesthetic learners use their gustatory (taste) and olfactory (smell) modes in conjunction with touch. Those operating in the kinesthetic mode say things like, "This deal just feels right," "That was a smooth presentation," "That transaction left a bad taste in my mouth," and "I smell something rotten about this deal." Tactile or kinesthetic learners respond best when they can directly interact with information. For this reason, you may want to use interactive surveys, demonstrations, websites, and even games.

NLP creators Bandler and Grinder first used this information to teach therapists how to build rapport and successfully convey messages to patients quickly. They soon realized that this powerful communication tool would work for people other than therapists. They began to train people on how to teach these techniques.

Unfortunately, some people use NLP as a powerful manipulative tool for their benefit to the detriment of others. When used ethically, however, it is a helpful method for cutting down the time needed to build trust and rapport—a necessary process in relationship selling.[39] NLP is one more tool you can use to help you interpret people's behaviors and motivations to help them solve a problem.

Some salespeople seem to have an innate ability to identify a prospect's behavior and personality traits and adapt to them. It's like they have an internal radar that sends out test signals, interprets the feedback, and instantly chooses the best tactics for establishing rapport. If you do not naturally have this ability, learning how to connect with people can be one of the most challenging parts of becoming successful in selling. Fortunately, NLP is a great technique you can use to develop this ability.

Using Eye Cues to Read Prospects

Our eyes are rarely still. The direction they move during a conversation reveals the system of perception that is active at the moment.

Exhibit 6.4 illustrates the various eye cues that help to identify a person's primary mode of learning. Fortunately, these instinctive eye movements are universal and can, therefore, almost always be reliable indicators of a person's learning style.[40] It's important to note that some left-handed people reverse their right and left eye cues. Every valuable tool comes with some limitations, but once you have established a person's dominant hand, you can use this chart with confidence.

Between the extremes of each dimension are many degrees of responsiveness and assertiveness, and therefore, pace and priorities.

To avoid distrust and breakdowns in communication, you must meet the needs of your prospects, especially their behavioral style needs. Treat them as they want to be treated and move according to the pace and priority they desire. The most successful salespeople help customers verbalize problems and create a solution that customers would not have developed on their own.

There's an old saying—if you want to get better at something, learn more about it. Learn about social styles and NLP and study people and their wide variety of reactions. Eventually, your understanding of social styles will become a powerful sales tool.

EXHIBIT 6.4 **Eye Direction as Thought and Learning Clues**

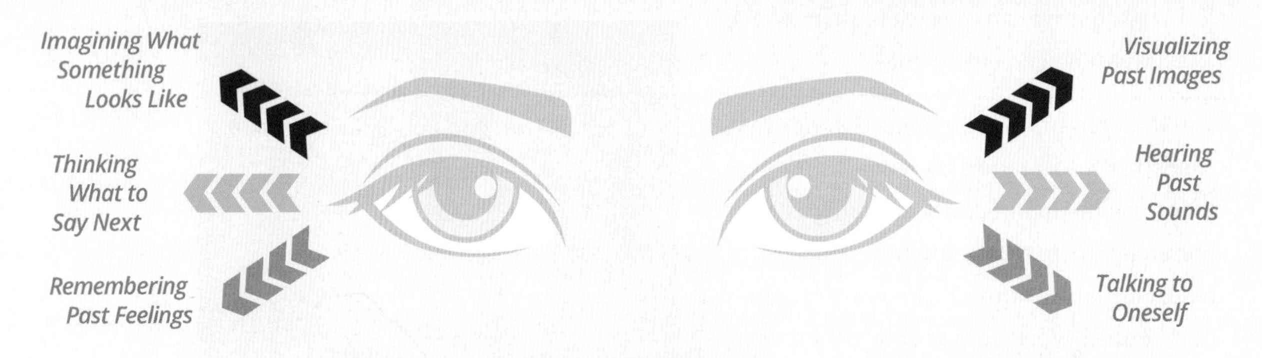

VISUAL PERCEPTION

Looking Up and Left—Visualizing (remembering) from the past; picturing the past mentally

Looking Up and Right—Visually creating an image to see what it would look like

KINESTHETIC PERCEPTION

Looking Down and Right—Remembering past feelings

AUDITORY PERCEPTION

Looking Sideways to the Left—Hearing sounds or voices from the past (remembering)

Looking Sideways to the Right—Constructing a future conversation; thinking of the right words to use

Looking Down to the Left—Holding an internal dialogue with oneself; how something sounds

SUMMARY

The Social Styles Model is a useful tool for gaining insight into the thinking of buyers.

Recognizing behavioral cues makes it possible to classify people into one of four styles: driver, expressive, amiable, or analytical.

The Social Styles Model utilizes a person's assertiveness and responsiveness levels to assess social style.

Versatility is your ability to adjust your pace and priorities to facilitate interaction with a person of another style.

Take the lead in finding common ground with prospects by using psychological reciprocity.

Never attempt to adopt a style that is an artificial imitation of a prospect's style.

Gender differences may require you to flex your behavioral style muscles to enhance communication.

Neurolinguistic programming (NLP) uses eye cues to discover the perceptual learning field a person prefers.

Review Questions

1. How do assertiveness and responsiveness factor into a person's behavioral style?
2. Which style is characterized by each of these pairs of dimensions?
    a. Low assertiveness and high responsiveness
    b. Low assertiveness and low responsiveness
    c. High assertiveness and high responsiveness
    d. High assertiveness and low responsiveness
3. What is a backup style, and what is its importance to the salesperson?
4. Explain this statement: The strengths of a particular behavioral style are the source of that style's typical weaknesses.
5. Point out some strengths of each of the four behavioral styles and show how they can be used as assets in selling. Identify some of the weaknesses of each and tell how they can damage sales effectiveness.
6. Are there any "absolute truths" in the ways that women and men will always behave in a business situation?
7. What social style is associated with excellent planning skills and a tendency to be risk-averse?
8. What social style is known to delegate tasks, and is recognition motivated?

IN-CLASS EXERCISES

The following exercises help build teams, improve communication, and emphasize the real-world side of fundraising. They are meant to be challenging, to help you learn how to deal with problems that have no single right answer, and to use a variety of skills beyond those employed in a typical review question. Read and complete each activity. Then in the next class, discuss and compare answers.

EXERCISE 6.1 Reading Your Sales Staff

Many of you will eventually become sales managers or leaders in your organization. How well you succeed will largely depend on how well you can "read" other people, to determine their basic personality orientation and to respond appropriately. You might as well begin to practice that skill now when there is relatively little risk.

Using the chart in Exhibit 6.2, write down where your dominant social style falls on the chart. Briefly describe why you characterize yourself in the way that you do.

Next, pair up with another class member whom you do not know. It is essential for this exercise that you not know the other person in any significant way. As your instructor directs, in class or before, the two of you should chat for ten minutes about any topic(s) whatever. After the chat, jot down your partner's probable social style. Briefly add the most important reasons for your decision.

Do gender differences play a role in your analysis? Your partner should do the same for you.

Finally, based on what you've learned from Chapter 6, describe what you believe to be the most significant challenge your conversation partner may face in relating to others. Why? What suggestions would you offer to help your partner in becoming more versatile in relating to others? Be insightful and constructive in your comments.

EXERCISE 6.2 Learning Styles vs. Presentation Styles

For this exercise, divide the class into teams of four people each. Each group should break out for a 20-minute discussion of the learning styles of each team member. Do some team members respond better to auditory means of communication rather than visual? Are there primarily visual learners represented on the team? What about the kinesthetic aspects of communication and learning? During the discussion, team members should share anecdotes about the most memorable presentations they have witnessed, and why.

Following the initial discussion, the team should then spend ten minutes critiquing modes of communication in this course. Do the class presentations in this course favor auditory learners, visual learners, kinesthetic learners? Based on the principles of neurolinguistic programming (NLP), briefly list constructive suggestions for improving communication and learning in this course. Finally, for the remainder of the class, the teams should come together to discuss their findings, especially their suggestions for improving communication in the course.

Case Studies

The following case studies present you with fundraising scenarios that require you to apply the critical skills discussed in the chapter and give you training through practical learning situations. They are meant to be both engaging and challenging, and like the exercises, don't have one right answer.

CASE 6.1—The Client Who Wouldn't Say Anything

Jimmie Caldwell was frustrated. He had just returned to his office after meeting with Marjorie Styles, owner of a local jewelry store. After visiting his company's website, Marjorie had phoned to request an appointment at her office to discuss creating a new website for her store. Jimmie was a web designer and one of the founding partners, along with Alice Stallings, of the firm that had now grown to bill over $750,000 per year. Clearly, they knew what they were doing.

As Jimmie barged into Alice's office, slamming the door behind him, Alice looked up. "I take it that the meeting didn't go well," she said calmly.

"Boy, that's an understatement!" Jimmie declared. "Marjorie Styles is really exasperating. I don't know whether we can work with her."

"Why? What happened?"

"Well, when I walked into her office, I noticed that she had pictures of her family—you know, husband, kids, the family dog—on her desk. So I remarked, as I usually do, on how nice her family looked and asked about where they like to go on vacation. Marjorie said, 'Oh, anywhere,' and sat down. I tried a little more informal chit-chat, but she sort of stared over my shoulder. The entire meeting went downhill from there."

"What do you mean?" Alice asked.

"What I mean is that the woman wouldn't say anything! At least not anything helpful. For instance, when I asked her why she wanted to change her website, she said, 'Because the one I have now stinks.' I followed up and asked if she could be more specific, and she said, 'No, this website just doesn't work for me anymore.' 'What, exactly, don't you like about it?' I asked. 'Everything,' came the response. What am I supposed to do with that?"

"Well," Alice prodded, "what did you do with that?"

"I couldn't think of anything else. So I launched into a description of what we could do. You know, that we could change the color palette, insert some video on the home page, make the navigation more intuitive, improve email management, yadda, yadda, yadda. I then handed her a copy of our fee schedule."

"And her response to all that was what?"

"Virtually no response. All she said was that she would have to think it over and that she would get back to me. I asked if she minded if I followed up in a few days, and she said, 'No, that would be ok.' And that was it."

Based on what you have read in Chapter 6, where did Jimmie go wrong? Specifically, what cues did Jimmie pick up on with Marjorie, and why do you think he misread them? Based on the admittedly sketchy information in Jimmie's report to Alice, how would you characterize Marjorie's basic social style? What is Jimmie's style? Why might their differences in style have resulted in miscommunication?

What should Alice do in response to this situation? Should she try to help Jimmie understand why Marjorie might have responded to him as she did? Should she have Jimmie contact Marjorie to meet with her again in a few days to try a different approach? If so, what should that approach be, and why? Or should Alice contact Marjorie herself, taking Jimmie out of the loop, and try to repair the situation? How might Alice's approach differ from Jimmie's? What could Alice do to obtain Marjorie's business?

CASE 6.2—Another Boring Meeting

Human beings have probably been complaining about boring meetings ever since sitting around the fire in front of their cave. Today's sales meetings are no exception. Derek Johnson's last sales meeting turned out to be a model for inducing sleep among his sales force. The meeting lasted for 90 minutes. And, despite the assistance of a steaming vat of coffee, several people were dozing by the end. On the way down the hall back to his office, Derek overheard comments such as, "Boy, that sure was a waste of time!" and "I hate meetings when we're told to be enthusiastic while the meeting itself is dead." Rather than endure more disrespect, Derek was tempted to cancel sales meetings altogether and just let everybody sink or swim on their own.

Nevertheless, as a low ranking sales manager, Derek knew that his vice president would never tolerate his running a sales team without meetings. Besides, the software company for which Derek worked, Cloud9 Strategies, was trying to take a share of the market from its biggest rivals in the CRM space with its new program, EverReach. He knew this year's numbers would make or break them and even determine whether he had a job this time next year. To make sure that his team understood EverReach's features and would promote it vigorously, Derek concluded that he needed to have yet another sales meeting.

This time, however, he determined that things would be different. In the first place, he invited the company's best salesperson to help explain EverReach's features. The rep promised to bring a 30-minute video that would thoroughly present EverReach in the most favorable light. Derek had previewed the video online and knew that the music and visuals were excellent. No one would be sleeping through that! He also had new promotional literature to hand out to everyone. This meeting would indeed be different!

From what you have learned from Chapter 6, would you say that Derek is on the right track? What theoretical principles underlie Derek's new approach to the EverReach sales meeting? If you were attending the meeting, what more should Derek do to keep you from falling asleep? What could Derek do to make the session even more effective in generating enthusiasm and improving learning?

FIVE TOOLS EVERY SALESPERSON NEEDS

OVERVIEW

Before you call on a new prospect, there are several essential steps to take. These steps are a part of the all-important processes that must occur before you ever make your first sales call. Chapter 7 prepares you for success by presenting the five tools every salesperson needs for success. These include knowledge, technology, networking tools, positioning strategies, and a plan for staying motivated. When you start your day fully prepared, your chances of success significantly increase, so arm yourself with the tools that will help you win.

OBJECTIVES

- Study what type of product knowledge you need for success in selling.
- Appreciate how tech tools impact salespeople and how to use them to your advantage.
- Examine social networks and know which ones to focus on as a salesperson.
- Understand the concept of product positioning.
- Identify three types of motivation and how they operate in affecting behavior.
- Learn how to accept personal responsibility for staying motivated and exercising initiative.
- See the importance of setting and achieving goals.

Preparing for Success

If you wish to have a lucrative, long-term sales career, you are going to need more than a little company sales training. The best salespeople don't rely on others to make them the best—they gather the tools they need and make a personal commitment to excellence.

Because the company's bottom line and your livelihood depend upon your efforts, your level of preparedness is a notable mutual concern. The Relationship Selling Cycle detailed in chapters 8 to 15 is the most direct way of building a sustainable track record of success. However, five tools don't directly relate to a step in the sales cycle but will benefit the cycle and your career significantly. They are:

1. The right knowledge
2. The right technology
3. The right networking
4. The right positioning
5. The right motivation

Some aspects of these areas may be your company's responsibility, but some are primarily your responsibility. No matter who bears the obligation, both you and your company are active participants. Too much is at stake for either party to take a passive approach to preparation.

Success in sales involves more than getting a person to say yes. If it were that simple, every salesperson would be successful. Do you have what it takes?

1. The Right Knowledge

New salespeople may have a general knowledge of their company's industry and may even have some understanding of the product they sell. However, companies often hire salespeople with little or no experience or knowledge of the company and its products.

Obtaining product knowledge is one of the first prerequisites to success. A study conducted among buyers about their perceptions and attitudes toward salespeople

indicated that what they like least of all is an *unprepared* salesperson.[1]

Ultimately, two things must happen for you to achieve the level of preparedness that buyers want and deserve. First, your company must provide you with enough information to make you feel confident in representing the product. Second, and more importantly, you must internalize that knowledge so you can provide real value to your customers.

What do you need to know about the product? One answer is everything! Nevertheless, you cannot wait until you've learned everything to start selling. In most cases, it is impossible to learn every last detail, especially if your product is complex or is subject to policy changes.

After you start selling, don't stop learning! Just because you are now "in the field" with customers, you must still commit to learning more about the product or service you sell and how it solves problems for customers. Gaining product knowledge is an ongoing process.

Product or Service Knowledge

Product knowledge begins with the product itself: its features, its benefits, and its acceptance in the marketplace. Product knowledge includes knowing all available options, how it can adapt to a customer's needs, and how it performs under varying conditions. Detailed product knowledge prepares you to answer any question a customer might have and offer whatever advising is necessary to help the customer reach a decision.

When you thoroughly learn about the product, you can answer detailed technical questions from expert buyers. You can also explain it in simple terms to someone who is considering such a purchase for the first time. Only in the rarest cases would you tell a prospect every detail about a product. However, knowing all the information gives you a storehouse from which you can select the best features to highlight that fit a customer's unique situation. It's not only what you know but how you use it! Exhibit 7.1 shows how two salespeople can use the same product knowledge with vastly different results.

Performance Knowledge

Performance is another vital area of product knowledge. How long will your product last? If it's a physical product, what kind of wear and stress does it tolerate? How easy is it to upgrade? How much training is necessary for an employee to operate or use? Can it be repaired? Who performs the needed maintenance? Are spare parts readily available? These are all questions relating to performance issues. Even if your customers don't ask about them, rest assured they are thinking about them.

In technical industries, salespeople should have access to company engineers and advisors who furnish engineering and technical information when needed.

EXHIBIT 7.1 **A Tale of Two Salespeople**

A cloud-based software sales rep named Tim called on the owner of a small business who needed an automated solution for a shipping process that still relied on processing physical paperwork. Tim had been well trained in product knowledge and was eager to demonstrate his expertise. He overwhelmed the prospect with tech jargon—management interfaces, middleware, API-driven communication, and more. Tim left without an order.

Later, another technical salesperson called named Ashley. She told the business owner how quickly her software could be implemented and how easy it is to learn, even for the least tech-savvy among them. She also explained that the owner would receive daily reports that are designed to reveal both sales trends and upsell opportunities—in other words, numbers that grow his bottom line and make life easier for his sales force!

It's not hard to guess who got the order. Ashley listened to the prospect and catered to his specific needs. She knew all the tech jargon that Tim used, but she also recognized that customers want to be heard, not intimidated.

"I know nothing about the product, but I'm happy to give you my expert opinion."

Therefore, product knowledge also involves knowing who to call on and when to ask for help. Never use industry jargon or complicated words to explain what you sell. Pretend you are selling it to someone who has never used it before. If you confuse your prospects, they will not be quick to say yes to something they don't understand.

Manufacturing Knowledge

Product knowledge also includes knowledge of the manufacturing methods and processes that affect the performance or durability of the product. These vital ingredients of quality affect buying decisions. Understanding the manufacturing process may enable you to explain why a price that seems high to the prospect is reasonable, or why delivery takes longer than the buyer had expected.

Distribution Knowledge

The company's distribution methods are another critical area of product knowledge. What are the delivery channels used? Are exclusive dealerships granted in certain areas? Is selective distribution used? Do discount houses and chains sell the product in competition with other retail outlets? Another vital element of distribution concerns pricing policies. Such policies include dealers' costs, quantity discounts, applicable credit terms, and whether the company will consider negotiating exclusive deals.[2]

Company Knowledge

Product knowledge also involves gaining as much information as possible about the company you represent. You need to know the history of the company. That includes:

who founded it and when, how the present product line evolved, the company's past and current position in the market, and its performance track record. You also need to study the company's target demographic, so you can more easily detect what information may interest your prospects. Knowing the history and performance of your company will help you sell more effectively.[3] It is essential to be aware that your prospects may be almost as knowledgeable about your company and its products and performance as you are. Do your best to be an endless source of knowledge about the company you represent.

The Social Media Connection

IS YOUR COMPANY PUTTING THE RIGHT KNOWLEDGE OUT THERE?

Social media marketing, or SMM, is a form of online marketing that implements various social media networks to achieve marketing communication and branding goals. Forward-thinking companies are those who figure out how to leverage their social media presence and their SMM to increase sales.

It makes sense to market online, given the fact that so many prospects conduct online research before they buy to compare companies and learn more about the organizations that interest them. You and your company can leverage this fact by ensuring that your company's posts have the following attributes:[4]

- **The content is planned.** Consider keyword research and brainstorm content ideas that will interest your target audience.
- **The content is valuable.** Content reigns supreme when it comes to social media marketing. Make sure you are offering useful information that your ideal customers will find interesting.
- **Posts have a consistent image.** Using social media for marketing enables your business to project its brand image and core identity across different online platforms.

- **Your company regularly blogs.** Blogging is a great social media marketing tool that lets you share a wide array of information and content with readers and keep them coming back for more.
- **Your posts contain links.** Social media marketing relies primarily on your business sharing its own unique, original content, but it's also great to link to outside articles. Linking to other sources improves trust and reliability, and you may even get some links in return.
- **Can be measured via analytics.** You can't determine the success of your social media marketing strategies without tracking data. Google Analytics is a great social media marketing tool that will help you measure your social media marketing techniques.

Service Knowledge

Once you make a sale, your responsibilities have just begun. Outstanding after-sale service will cement the relationship and ensure repeat orders—and repeat commissions! If you sell a product, you must know the company's service policy regarding renewals, repairs, updates, and replacements. Are there service charges? Who performs the service? Late fees? Licensing considerations? What kind of service is available to adapt or adjust the service or product to the customer's changing needs? Your customers will inevitably ask some or all of these questions, so it is imperative that you know the answers.

Competition Knowledge

Another overlooked area of product knowledge is information about the competition. Learn about your major competitors' product lines; know their credit terms, their prices, their delivery schedules, and their reputations for service. Most buyers—either personal consumers or company purchasing agents—are not weighing the advantages of buying a product against those of not buying. Instead, they are trying to decide *which* product or service to buy, yours or the competition's offering. The following story is an example of how one salesperson used his knowledge of the competition to make the sale:[5]

> *Ken Andrews was involved in a highly competitive bidding situation for his company that makes next-gen AI for automobiles. Ken knew his competitor had a lower-quality product—but offered it at a substantially lower price. Ken's product has superior attributes. It is also far more straightforward to use and comes with free lifetime upgrades, therefore giving him the edge*

in capabilities, quality, and service. He knew that the other company would lead with its notably lower price. So, Ken presented to a major car manufacturer by projecting an increase in car sales over the next five years after implementing their tech—the best AI on the market. Who needs AI that doesn't work? Cheap isn't always better. Ken won at a higher price through a better product offering.

One of the advantages of studying your competition is that it reminds you of your product's best features and what makes it unique. Learning about the other companies operating in your space will refresh your presentations, especially if you have been selling the same thing for a long time. Once you know what makes your product better than the competition, you can stress those areas where your product excels and gain a lasting advantage over your competition. Exhibit 7.2 provides an overview of the four areas of competitive advantage.

EXHIBIT 7.2 Differential Competitive Advantage

PRODUCT SUPERIORITY

- Versatility
- Efficiency
- Storage
- Handling Time
- Safety
- Adaptability
- Appearance
- Design
- Mobility
- Packaging
- Life Expectancy

SERVICE SUPERIORITY

- Delivery
- Inventory
- Credit
- Training
- Merchandising
- Installation
- Maintenance

SOURCE SUPERIORITY

- Time Established
- Competitive Standing
- Community Image
- Location
- Size
- Financial Soundness
- Policies and Practices

PEOPLE SUPERIORITY

- Personal Knowledge and Skill
- Support Personnel Skill
- Integrity and Character
- Standing in Community
- Call Schedule Flexibility
- Interpersonal Skills
- Mutual Friends
- Cooperation

2. The Right Technology

Technology is imperative in any career, but it is perhaps even more so in sales. Thanks to the many jobs of a salesperson—from administrative work and scheduling to direct customer contact and follow-up—sales achievement requires you to use every available advantage to make your job a little easier or at least a little more efficient.

It is, however, essential to remember that the heart of sales will always be the face-to-face time with customers. Therefore, it is wise never to allow technology to become a crutch. It doesn't do your job for you; it's more like a sales partner. It is also about being more than tech-savvy. It's about finding the right tech tools to do the job well.

Social media, CRM software, lead generation software, and email management systems are just a few of the tools that salespeople use every day to communicate with the world. However, merely using something doesn't guarantee it will benefit you. Remember the adage of "garbage in, garbage out." Technology doesn't solve problems by itself. If you automate a mess, all you have now is an *automated* mess.[6] Unfortunately, some companies don't take the time to determine what tools will best fit their processes before introducing technology. When that happens, they create unnecessary problems for their sales force.

In order to keep up with the increasing demands of the changing marketplace, salespeople are expected to become more productive at everything they do. They must see more prospects, provide more value, and do a better job with each customer. Technology relieves salespeople of many administrative duties that would typically rob them of precious time. It also allows them to analyze and transmit information to customers and management quickly and efficiently.

If you want to become more productive, take the necessary time to learn how to use each piece of technology thoroughly. Do the tutorials, read the online help and tip pages. Do the work, and technology will begin to work for you. Once you find the right tech for you, your schedule, and your industry, you will experience improvements in four key areas:

1. Improved Training

The best way to improve at anything is through practice. In the past, the best you could hope for from your company might be periodic training events and seminars.

Afterward, they would hastily send you back to your job with no practical application. That's like a quarterback throwing passes for a few days and then deciding that's all the training he needs for the season.

The problem of inadequate training continues today. In a recent study, researchers found that one out of seven companies never train their salespeople, while more than half train their employees just twice a year.[7] Another study found that more than 33 percent of second-year salespeople receive four days of sales training annually, while 39 percent of seasoned professionals receive just two days per year.[8]

Because selling is a career that requires a lifelong commitment to learning, this is unacceptable. The answer to this dilemma has been around for a long time but is still being underutilized. It comes in the form of web-based sales training or eLearning. Web-based technology makes training more accessible and more affordable by maximizing flexibility and effectiveness for both the sales force and sales managers. The benefits of web-based training include:[9]

- Constant and convenient access to training programs.
- Increased interactivity among large or remote sales teams.
- Instant access to new product information and product updates.
- Direct performance measurements with immediate feedback.
- Reduced travel costs for airfare, hotel stays, and convention expenses.
- Focused attention on particular areas of need.

The companies that find ways to respond quickly to customer needs and make information readily available to their business partners will gain the all-important competitive edge. The implementation of an effective sales force automation program provides benefits that relate directly to improving the bottom-line.[10]

2. Improved Communication

Laptops, tablets, and smartphones allow you to bring your business and all of your favorite tools with you everywhere you go. Our devices are indispensable for maintaining constant access to important contact information, sales scripts, emails, and more. They also enable more productivity during flights or commutes.

It's also becoming easier to connect virtually via videoconferencing using popular programs such as Skype and Zoom. Try getting face to face with your sales leaders and customers without leaving your desk. It is a cost-effective way to communicate, connect, and even present a proposal or discuss a deal.

Working remotely or *telecommuting* is a work arrangement in which employees do not commute to a central place of work. It is a practice that is widespread today, thanks to the advances in communication technology. If you work for a company with a cloud-based CRM system rather than an in-house system, you can do most of your communicating from the comfort of your home office or a Starbucks. Many companies still encourage their salespeople to conduct business from the office, but for more disciplined salespeople, this is an excellent option.

3. Increased Productivity

Customer relationship management (CRM) is a broad term that covers concepts used by companies to manage their relationships with customers, including the capture, storage, and analysis of customer information. CRM is more than just contact management software; it is a tool that can move companies to a higher level with customers. Salespeople use well-integrated CRM systems daily as the central point of customer contact.[11] The leader in the industry is Salesforce.com, which offers a cloud-based solution to organizing your business and reaching out to prospects and clients.

With the number of quality CRM programs available, the key is to find one with which you feel comfortable working and can easily understand. Websites such as www.compareCRM.com have reviews and comparisons of the latest contact managers on the market to assist in making the best decision for your needs. CRM-related apps are also available for managing contacts on the go and for coordinating sales information among members of a team.

4. Improved Leads

In the old days, salespeople worked from long lists of names with no other information other than a phone number. That was how cold calling worked. Today, lead generation has moved to the web, since most searches for products and services begin online. That's where lead generation software comes into play.

Lead generation software is a type of software that enables you to target your ideal customers. It's a technology that allows you to call on fewer unqualified leads and be able to focus on qualified or at least partially qualified prospects. In the world of professional selling, efficient prospecting is a game changer! By automating the process of generating, segmenting and following up with leads, lead generation software accelerates the entire sales process.[12]

3. The Right Networking

Salespeople have the incredible opportunity to relate to customers and prospects daily through social media. According to recent data, the average user logs 2.5 hours per day on social platforms. That is up almost an hour from just five years earlier. Facebook leads the pack at 1.4 billion users daily and is only growing in popularity. Despite reports that young people don't use Facebook anymore, almost 60 percent of Facebook users are between 18 and 34 years old.[13]

Savvy salespeople and innovative companies use social media to their advantage. As with other technology tools, the question isn't, "Should I use social media?" but "How should I use it?"

Every individual has preferences and styles that determine their personality and what makes them unique. Some people prefer

a low-key, one-on-one conversation, while others are most comfortable in a loud group discussion. The same goes for social media preferences: People have their preferences and favorite features about each social networking site. Therefore, companies must stay open-minded and flexible to meet the needs of their customers. Salespeople, too, must pay attention to communication preferences and work to communicate in the way that is most comfortable for the customer.[14]

The following is a discussion of the most commonly used social media sites that are beneficial for salespeople and tips for using them to your advantage in professional selling:

Facebook

When Facebook was created in 2004, its original purpose was to provide a way for students on college campuses to network with one another. Today, however, there are over 1.4 billion active daily users who log in to Facebook across the world.[15] Companies and salespeople utilize Facebook fan pages to build profiles of their products and services and to keep their brand prominent in the daily newsfeed of Facebook users. When it comes to Facebook, it pays to write regular, fresh posts, and include engaging topics, not just pictures or personal thoughts. Here are a few tips for salespeople to get the most out of Facebook:[16]

Useful Facebook Tips for Salespeople

1. **Like your clients' Facebook pages.** Doing so is a great way to stay aware of what those businesses are talking about in public, which can help you understand what they are trying to accomplish.
2. **Organize your Facebook friends into custom lists.** Create a list for current customers and clients that you are already connected to on Facebook. Create a second list of potential customers and clients. Creating lists allows you to isolate posts from the people on your lists and quickly chime in on conversations they are having by commenting or sharing.
3. **Search for prospects using a Facebook graph.** Did you know you can easily find out which friends work at a specific company, or if they have friends who work for that company? Go to your Facebook page and search for, "My friends who have friends that work at Company X" and see what you find.
4. **Post something related to your work.** As long as you keep 80 percent of your posts personal in nature on your page, you can do some posting about what's happening at work. Of course, keep things positive and remember you're doing this with a business purpose in mind.

LinkedIn

LinkedIn is the business side of social media. On LinkedIn, you won't find photos from your college roommate's vacation or status updates about what's for dinner. As the world's largest online professional network, LinkedIn has over 575 million users, with more than 260 million monthly active users, including executives from all Fortune 500 companies.

If you are ready to get serious about LinkedIn, take a long hard look at your contacts. Contacts are the currency of LinkedIn. If your contacts are predominantly family, friends, and old school pals, you've got some work to do.

Perhaps one of the most important things to remember about LinkedIn is that *connections breed connections.* Your "first-level" contacts open up a route to a wide range of second and third-level connections. That is how you scale your network. Strike while the iron's hot—whenever you meet anyone (online or off) always follow up quickly with a connection request while you are still fresh in his or her mind.[17]

Twitter

For many people, LinkedIn comes to mind when talking about social media for professionals. However, according to some studies, Twitter has edged out LinkedIn—even if by a small margin—to become the most used social tool for salespeople. Twitter has always been associated with community building and sending brief messages, but there's more to it than that. Twitter is a more natural and spontaneous way to strike up a conversation

with people, which is why 100 million people use it every day.[18]

LinkedIn, while it lets you connect with other professionals, isn't so great when it comes to *engaging* with them. Twitter also allows you to get into a conversation with anyone you want. Since Twitter offers users the option to receive direct messages from non-followers, the opportunities for salespeople to communicate about their brands or businesses is broadened significantly.

Aside from the sites listed above, dozens of other social networking sites cater to almost any need. YouTube has long been recognized as one of the most useful sites for business and personal use. Depending on the field, a salesperson may want to join more niched sites as well. For example, publishing professionals may wish to relate to potential readers on Goodreads.com, while those in the music industry have found sites such as Noisetrade.com to be useful for connecting to listeners. Whatever the product or service is that you sell, it is imperative to find out the latest ways to network with other salespeople and customers.

4. The Right Positioning

The level of competition today is astounding. It's a fast-paced race, and the competition is coming from all over the world. That makes *positioning*—the marketing strategy of differentiating a product or company in the mind of prospects—more critical than ever.

Once a business identifies what makes it unique in the eyes of the consumer, that element should become the focus of its entire marketing and sales strategy. What makes your company and your product line different? Here are a few key actions for finding the answer to the question on your prospects' minds, which is, "How is your company better than the others?"

1. **Realize** what qualities of your products and services are most important to your customers. Use that information to custom-design a unique niche for yourself.

2. **Reinforce** your differentiating factors (those things that set you apart) via an integrated marketing communication message that reinforces those attributes in the customer's mind.

3. **Remember** the way you service or sell to your customers can make a significant difference. For example, if you provide a personalized approach to customer service when everyone else is just sending automated emails, you will stand out for all the right reasons.

4. **Respect** the power of competition and keep an eye on how your competitors are positioning themselves. Be ready to respond to their claims to maintain a differential competitive advantage.

Positioning refers to developing a specific marketing mix to influence potential customers' overall perception of a brand, product line, or organization. The term was popularized by authors Jack Trout and Al Ries, in their book, *Positioning: The Battle for Your Mind*. Positioning is the place a product occupies in potential customers' minds relative to competing offerings. Once a position is selected, product, price, place, and promotion strategies and tactics are designed to reinforce that position. These marketing mix components represent a bundle of individual dimensions that are designed to work together to create a competitive advantage.

Positioning on a company-wide scale does not typically fall under the responsibility of salespeople. Fortunately, the best companies use *integrated marketing campaigns* in which all elements of their operation work together to form a consistent positioning strategy.

5. The Right Motivation

Salespeople often find that they have the right knowledge and skills but have trouble using them consistently, or they find little satisfaction in their accomplishments. The missing ingredient is motivation.

There are numerous definitions of motivation. Perhaps the simplest is this: motivation is a reason for taking action. We can expand this definition to say that motivation is the *impetus* to begin a task, the *incentive* to expend effort in accomplishing the task, and the *willingness* to sustain the effort until the task is completed.

One of the most common question sales managers ask is, "How can I better motivate my salesforce?" The answer is, "You can't." The question implies that there are secret strategies or gimmicks that, once discovered, will double or triple motivation and productivity. However, genuine and lasting motivation is not something management *does*, but rather a *process* that management fosters.[19]

The primary responsibility for developing and sustaining motivation rests with the salesperson. The company's role is to provide a supportive climate for motivated employees. Bob Nelson, author of *1001 Ways to Reward Employees*, says, "What motivates people the most takes just a little time and thoughtfulness." Recognize them as individuals, and you're giving them what they most crave. Read "The Lighthouse Story"

The Lighthouse Story

Jonathan Berger, sales manager for the Carrier Corporation, once had a salesperson close a critical account that put a significant bonus in the sales rep's pocket. Berger decided to make the sale a truly memorable triumph. He knew the sales rep's wife had a passion for lighthouses, so he sent her a small crystal lighthouse with a note thanking her for the time and support she invested in her husband. The sales rep's wife wrote Berger back and said, "Never has anyone in any company acknowledged my existence or the contributions I make to my husband's career." There is no doubt she will think of Jonathan and his thoughtful gesture every time she looks at the lighthouse.

about how one sales manager found a creative way to inspire and motivate a deserving employee.[20]

Practical Motivation for Salespeople

Most motivational theories agree that drive arises as a response to either an external or internal stimulus. Recognizing those stimuli can help you discover ways to control them or your reactions to them in a way that produces a positive, sustained motivational drive.

Motivation may arise from the *fear* of punishment or withholding of acceptance if one's behavior does not conform to expectations. It may come from an *incentive* or the promise of reward for desired behavior. The most effective type of motivation comes from *attitude*, which dictates behavior using personal values and standards as guiding principles.[21]

Fear Motivation. Fear is a natural emotion designed to help protect us from danger, and using it as motivation has some value. Fear motivation protects a person from self-destruction or harm and protects society from the effects of undesirable or illegal behavior. Fear motivation can also serve as a quick way to get the desired reaction.

In spite of these advantages, fear motivation has serious disadvantages that more than offset its benefits:

- **Fear motivation is external.** It is useful only as long as the enforcing power is present. When the parent, police officer, teacher, or sales manager is out of sight, fear motivation no longer has the same power.
- **Fear motivation is temporary.** Threats or punishment may control behavior for a time, but people tune out warnings if they discover that penalties are not regularly carried out.
- **Fear motivation is negative.** With fear motivation, you either do the task or face the consequences. That

transforms the task into an imposed duty rather than a chosen activity. A warning not to do something creates a void that may be filled by another equally undesirable behavior.

Incentive Motivation. The use of incentives for motivation is usually considered more progressive than the use of fear. Sales organizations commonly attempt to produce motivated activity by offering incentives. Such incentives may be increased commissions, contest rewards, plaques, bonuses, better sales territories, and perks such as a reserved parking place, private office, personal assistant, or company car.

Incentives must mean something to each individual, or they do little to encourage action.[22] Like fear motivation, incentive motivation has advantages. Incentive motivation inspires effort. When a promised reward is highly desirable, salespeople will exert extreme effort to win it. It is positive in that it promises something beneficial. Salespeople are not frozen into inaction by fear of being punished or deprived.

Like fear motivation, however, incentive motivation carries built-in disadvantages.

- **Incentive motivation is external.** It is the dangling carrot, not internal drive or desire that spurs initiative. When the carrot is gone, what happens then? There is no intrinsic drive to continue.
- **Incentive motivation is temporary.** A salesperson may exert tremendous effort to win a sales contest or some desired reward but not continue that level of activity once the contest is over. Additionally, if a promised reward is undesirable, it does not motivate action.
- **Incentive motivation can backfire.** Incentives, once earned, often come to be regarded as rights instead of special privileges for outstanding performance. For example, salespeople who qualify for a company car feel incensed if leadership increases the requirements for earning the vehicle, and they fail to meet the new quota.

> **"People often say that motivation doesn't last. Well, neither does bathing—that's why we recommend it daily."**
> *Zig Ziglar*

Attitude Motivation. Attitude motivation operates on the concept that the only lasting universally compelling motivation is the personal ambition that comes from a person's internal structure. This type of motivation is based on a healthy self-image and a belief in the possibility of success. Attitude motivation is self-motivation. All great salespeople inherently possess this powerful, internal drive.

You can shape and mold a self-motivated person, but you can't teach internal motivation.[23] *Self-motivation* is the result of the choices to respond positively to outside influences. Fear and self-doubt are the habitual attitudes of some people, but others choose to react to life boldly. For example, some salespeople who hear they're too inexperienced for a position immediately lose confidence and find a job where someone tells them what to do.

However, others respond to statements of doubt by choosing to believe that their condition is temporary. As a result, they are willing and eager to try different activities, stretch their imaginations, and attempt new goals. They do not wait for someone else to motivate them; they are always reaching out for new experiences. These salespeople are self-motivated.

What you are, then, is not a result of what happens to you. You are the result of your choices, and your reaction to events (both good and bad) is always a choice. The advantages of attitude motivation are the opposites of the disadvantages of fear and incentive motivation:

- **Attitude motivation is internal.** Because attitudes come from within, you do not need to wait for an outside stimulus to make appropriate choices and take action.
- **Attitude motivation is permanent.** A specific attitude, once thoroughly established, continues to operate on an automatic basis until you do something to alter it. Self-motivation is the only kind of motivation that can be sustained over a long period.

If your perspective in life is that things are hard, they will always be hard. If you choose to believe that your failures are merely steppingstones to the next success, you will find life to be much more rewarding. Choose to believe in yourself and your abilities. Life is all a matter of perspective, anyway.

Attitude Motivation Through Goal Setting

The single most important tool for developing self-motivation is a program of personal goals. A personal goals program creates desire—one of the most potent emotions operating in human experience. If you want to be able to choose where you will go with your sales effort, and how you will get there, you need clear goals and strategies. Only then will you have the power to direct your efforts.[24]

A Matter of Perspective

Two salespeople fell on hard times and ended up penniless in a small town in Montana. They learned that the local trading-post paid $20 apiece for wolf pelts and decided to seize the opportunity. That night, they set out with a couple of clubs and a tent and made camp in the distant hills. They were no sooner asleep than one of the men was startled by an eerie sound. He crawled outside the tent to find himself surrounded by hundreds of snarling, hungry wolves. The man scrambled back into the tent and shook his friend. "Wake up!" he cried. "We're rich!"

Paul J. Meyer, who was the founder and former chairman of the board of SMI International, developed his "Million Dollar Personal Success Plan" in 1947 at just 19 years old. Since then, it has had a profound effect on business motivation theories and is the classic model of practical goal setting. It has five distinct parts that work together to provide a roadmap for achieving success in selling:

1. Crystallize your thinking.

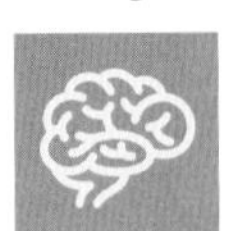

Determine what specific goals you want to achieve, and then dedicate yourself to their attainment with unswerving singleness of purpose. If your goals are hazy and undefined, you cannot plan concrete action steps for their achievement. You must write down and date your goals. Monitoring your status keeps you focused.[25] Without specific action plans, you will waste far too much of your time and effort.

2. Develop a plan for achieving your goals and a deadline for their attainment.

Plan your progress carefully, as detailed as hour-by-hour. A written plan of action keeps you on track and headed toward achievement. A written plan also reveals conflicts between various goals so that you can plan and make a reasonable schedule for the time and resources needed to reach all goals. Deadlines give you a target.[26] Target dates help draw out more potential and use it to bring desired goals into being. Deadlines also eliminate distractions and help you to think creatively.

3. Develop a sincere desire for the things you want in life.

A burning desire is the most excellent motivator of every human action. The desire for success implants a "success consciousness," which creates a dynamic and ever-increasing "habit of success." A burning desire to achieve the goals you want often makes the difference between a wish and a goal. A *wish* is something you would like to have, but you are not willing to invest enough time or effort to achieve it. A *goal* is something you want so intensely that you will exert whatever effort is needed to reach it.

4. Develop supreme confidence in yourself and your abilities.

Confidence enables you to undertake challenging goals and believe you can succeed. Begin every activity without acknowledging the possibility of defeat. Concentrate on your strengths, instead of your weaknesses, on your powers instead of your problems. Self-confidence lets you see challenges as opportunities and obstacles as stepping-stones to success. Self-confidence builds your credibility and makes it easy to ask for the sale—not once, but again and again. The secret to developing this kind of confidence is a growing list of goals accomplished.

5. Develop a dogged determination to follow through, regardless of obstacles, criticism, or circumstances.

Determination to stick to a plan of action is an outgrowth of desire and confidence. When you have

If you put your mind to it, you can eat more garbage, sleep longer, and smell worse— yes you can!
CANINE MOTIVATIONAL CD

a burning desire to achieve your goals, you are not easily swayed by negative comments or opposition from naysayers. Determination is the quality that enables you to keep calling until you close the sale. Commitment gives you the creative freedom to discover new tactics when your first efforts fail and to utilize new ideas until you find out what works.

All of these success elements are interdependent, but by using each one, you increase their collective power. Self-motivation is the only real and lasting motivation—and it's your responsibility to develop and use it consistently. Your company and leaders can provide a climate that encourages self-motivation, but even the most unfavorable environment cannot de-motivate you without your permission.

Success and the Wheel of Life

Organizations know that sales forces are essential to their success. However, they seldom pay much attention to what represents "success" for an individual. Success for salespeople is often measured only in terms of quotas and sales. This narrow view of success is responsible for destroying the self-confidence of untold numbers of salespeople.

We need to re-define success. Paul J. Meyer said, "*Success is the progressive realization of worthwhile, predetermined personal goals.*" This definition of success is especially applicable to salespeople, who may begin their careers with little training and no experience. It's encouraging to know that because success is progressive, you can be successful *immediately* just by choosing to pursue personal goals.

Many people fall into the same flawed thinking that organizations often follow in measuring success. Those worthwhile, predetermined goals must involve more than money and position, or any victory is likely to be hollow. Mike Singletary, former head coach for the San Francisco 49ers and pro bowl linebacker for the Chicago Bears, has spoken to youth groups all over the country. As a member of the NFL Hall of Fame and devoted husband and father to seven children, he has many great experiences from which we can learn. Mike encourages his young audiences to develop, not just in athletics or academics, but in all areas of life. Likewise, salespeople who concentrate only on career success and neglect other areas of life find their lives less fulfilled.

Money and position aren't all that matters. For this reason, you need to set goals in every area of life: health, education, personal, business, financial, and spiritual. Exhibit 7.4 pictures life as a wheel. If some aspects are missing or neglected, the ride will not go smoothly. Life will seem harsh, and you will feel dissatisfied and have a vague sense of uneasiness. When you have neglected areas in your life, they prevent enjoyment in other areas. Monetary success means little amid a broken home life, terminal illness, or lost friendships. You need all the aspects of the wheel to feel whole.

Find a product or service that you genuinely believe in, set personal goals, and your career can bring you so much satisfaction! Once you know what you want out of your job and dedicate yourself to achieving those goals, the responsibility for reaching success is in your hands. Just remember not to neglect the other areas of life in pursuit of career success.

Too many people confuse action with progress and effort with results. Trying hard does not guarantee success. Success comes as a result of determining the desired goals, finding out what activity is required to reach those goals, and then completing those actions based on a personal commitment to oneself.

Real success never comes by accident.

EXHIBIT 7.4 The Wheel of Life

When the wheel of life is *imbalanced*, the ride gets rough!

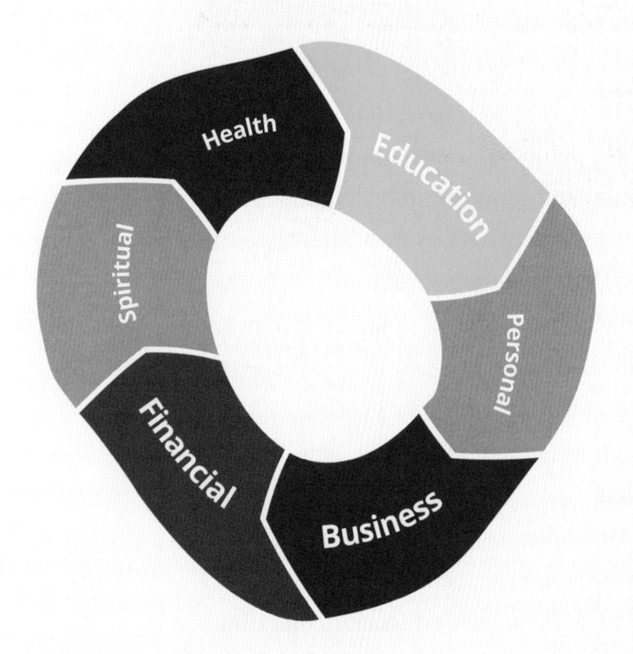

When the wheel of life is *balanced*, the ride is smooth.

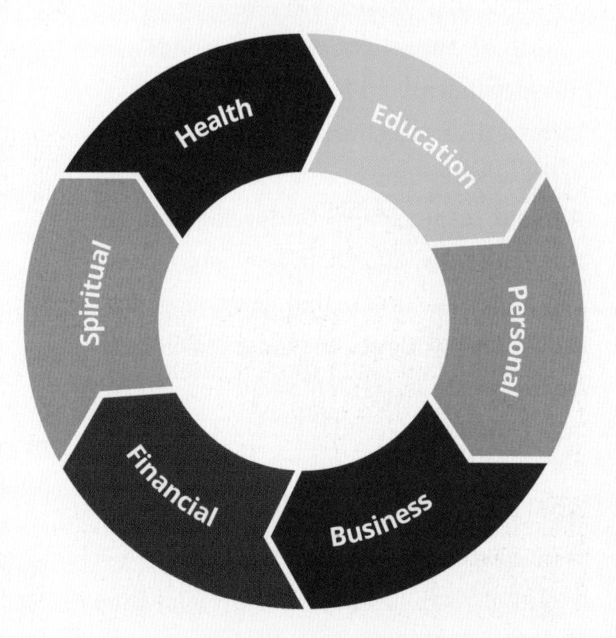

SUMMARY

Success in sales requires five areas of particular importance: the right knowledge, technology, networking, positioning, and motivation.

Product knowledge includes knowledge of the industry or field and specific knowledge about your product or service.

With web-based learning and the plethora of online learning options, there is no excuse for being untrained.

Salesforce automation tools increase your productivity, enhance communication, and enable greater efficiency.

Social media is an excellent way for salespeople and companies to build their brand and connect with their target audience.

Positioning refers to the place a product occupies in customers' minds relative to competing offerings.

Motivation comes from three sources: Fear, incentive, and attitude. Fear and incentives are limited, while attitude motivation is permanent.

Successful goal setting begins with crystallized thinking about what is important to you and then developing an action plan with deadlines.

Review Questions

1. What contributions can courses like this one make to success in selling? How much academic work do you need to guarantee success in professional selling?
2. Does your company carry any of the responsibility for preparing you for sales success? If so, what specific things are the company's responsibility?
3. Name four areas of product knowledge that are important for salespeople.
4. What advantage do you gain by knowing your competition?
5. How would you obtain product knowledge if you were hired to sell a highly technical product?
6. Salesforce automation can help increase your effectiveness in distinct ways. Discuss two of them and give an example for each to illustrate.
7. Name three popular social media sites. What are the primary uses of each? Which is best for business use?
8. Explain how fear and incentives can be sources of motivation. Give an example from your experience of both.
9. What limits the effectiveness of fear and incentives as motivating forces?
10. What are the advantages of using attitude as a basis of motivation?
11. Explain how goal setting affects self-motivation.
12. How do personal goals produce self-confidence?

IN-CLASS EXERCISES

The following in-class exercises help build teams, improve communication, and emphasize the real-world of selling. They are challenging, help you learn how to deal with problems that have more than one correct answer, and require skills beyond those employed in a typical review question. Read and complete each activity. Then in the next class, discuss and compare answers.

EXERCISE 7.1 Positioning Your College

Every organization—no matter the size or industry—must differentiate itself from its peers and competitors. Your college or university is no exception. The competition for students among higher education institutions is intense. After all, without the revenue supplied by a sufficient number of students through tuition and financial aid programs, many colleges and universities would have to close their doors. To appeal to enough students, colleges and universities must position themselves as superior to their competitors. In other words, they must communicate to prospective students how they are different from and superior to other schools in meeting their needs. Salespeople (and, yes, admissions officers for colleges and universities are salespeople) often overlook the importance of positioning in their quest for product knowledge.

Imagine that you are the Director of Admissions at your college or university. The Vice President of Enrollment Management has just asked for your professional estimate of the school's positioning strategy and your recommendations for changes. What do you say in your one-page report?

Be sure that your report draws upon your analysis of your college's website and marketing materials, and that you have at least looked at the sites of some of your college's closest competitors. How is your college presenting itself as distinctive? Does it work? Is there anything that you think should be changed in your college's current strategy? Bring your findings to class and be prepared to discuss them.

EXERCISE 7.2 How Much Product Knowledge is Enough?

For this exercise, you should pair up with another student in the class. Most people are aware that B2B (business to business) sales, especially for highly technical products, require a great deal of product knowledge and knowledge of the industry in general. But many assume that retail sales—where many salespersons get their start—is easy in that regard. After all, how much is there to learn about most retail products?

Select a retail product line and, with your partner, interview at least two salespeople who handle that line. Do your best to conduct your interviews when the stores are not busy or outside regular business hours since many retail reps work on commission. When they are talking to you, they can't make any money. The products might be smartphones, household appliances, furniture, upscale clothing, sports equipment—nearly anything at all.

Keeping in mind the various types of product knowledge presented in Chapter 7, ask the salespeople what sort of training their company provided to acquaint them with their products. Ask them how long it took until they felt comfortable presenting features and answering customers' questions about their products. Find out how much they need to know about their company's procedures, methods of getting their products into customers' hands, their company's history, financing or payment policies, etc. Finally, ask how often they have to update their product knowledge to remain on top of their game.

Summarize your findings in one or two pages and be prepared to discuss what you learned in class or online.

Case Studies

The following case studies present you with selling scenarios that require you to apply the critical skills discussed in the chapter and give you training through practical learning situations. They are meant to be both engaging and challenging, and like the exercises, don't have one right answer.

CASE 7.1—Motivation through Compensation

Dwayne Connors, regional vice president of sales at DirtCheap Corporation (an agricultural equipment manufacturer), didn't know where to turn next. Because of declining sales, his predecessor had been fired. The company had tried a fear-based policy of management that was approved at the highest levels. During those three years, the company had reduced the base pay of all salespeople whenever they failed to meet the month's quota. The rationale was, "If they don't sell, why should we pay them [their full base pay]?" As the company president put it, "Confronted with the fear of disaster, they'll perform."

Well, they didn't. Some salespeople resigned outright. Others failed to make quota month after month. As a district sales manager, Dwayne noticed the plunging morale and declining sales figures. He had promised a different approach that, he thought, would get better results.

So, for the past nine months, Dwayne had instituted a system of positive incentives. First on the list was a compensation structure that awarded salespeople a higher percentage commission the more they sold. For example, if a salesperson made quota, a 10 percent commission on total sales would be added. If a salesperson sold 150 percent of quota, a 25 percent commission would be paid, and so forth. Increased productivity would, therefore, be rewarded directly and immediately. Some salespeople had the potential to earn large sums, even surpassing Dwayne's fixed salary.

Also, Dwayne initiated a series of sales contests for lines of equipment that were overstocked. For four months, sales improved, and morale began to grow. Dwayne thought he had licked the problem by using carrots rather than sticks.

But now, after the last five months of stagnating results, Dwayne was stymied. Sales had slumped once again, although not alarmingly. He was beginning to receive caustically worded emails from his superiors at headquarters, wondering when his "new approach" would pay off. What to do?

Given what you have learned in Chapter 7 about attitude motivation or self-motivation, how would you advise Dwayne? What steps might he and his sales managers take to help the sales force to improve their motivation to succeed? If graduated commissions and sales contests didn't turn the tide permanently, what might?

CASE 7.2—Rescuing Greyhounds

After 35 years of a successful career in technical sales, Walt decided to give something back to his community during his retirement. He and his wife had rescued a couple of retired racing greyhounds in recent years and found them to be adorable, loving companions. So it seemed natural as a result for Walt to volunteer his services to the local greyhound adoption organization. Little did Walt know what he had gotten himself into!

Because of his background in sales, the organization's executive director decided that Walt should become the group's chief fundraiser. The job called for Walt to write grant proposals, visit philanthropic foundations to solicit financial support, and to make presentations on the organization's behalf to various community groups. In short, his job was to "sell" the organization to those who could provide financial and other resources.

From his experience selling air quality monitoring systems, Walt appreciated the value of product knowledge. Without it, a sales representative could not respond to a client's questions and concerns, could not position the product against the competition's offerings, and could never gain sufficient confidence to convince a client to buy. Walt put so much emphasis upon product knowledge that he assembled a team to keep him abreast of new developments. But what was the "product" in the case of the greyhound rescue organization? What did Walt need to know to sell this product effectively?

Based on the principles and categories of product knowledge presented in Chapter 7, describe the "product" of Walt's greyhound adoption agency and outline in a page or two what Walt needs to know about it in order to represent the agency effectively. This might require some research regarding retired racing greyhounds and the agencies that try to help them.

PART II

THE RELATIONSHIP SELLING CYCLE

Welcome to the heart of the book!
We will cover each step of the Relationship Selling Cycle in order to set you and your customers up to win.

The Relationship Selling Cycle provides you with the pieces to the puzzle you need to connect with qualified prospects in a way that benefits everyone. In our fast-paced world, relationships are more important than ever. Part II will guide you through every interaction with potential customers, from prospecting and pre-approach to the close, and extend to the actions needed after the sale. Follow-up that fosters loyalty is the key, with more competition emerging every year (and therefore more choices).

You never get a second chance to make a good first impression. Don't let good leads and willing would-be customers walk away. You often have just one chance to show them just how exceptional your offering is—and how important they are to you and your company! Let the Relationship Selling Cycle guide you through the steps it takes to form lasting, mutually beneficial relationships with customers that will benefit your company and your career for years to come.

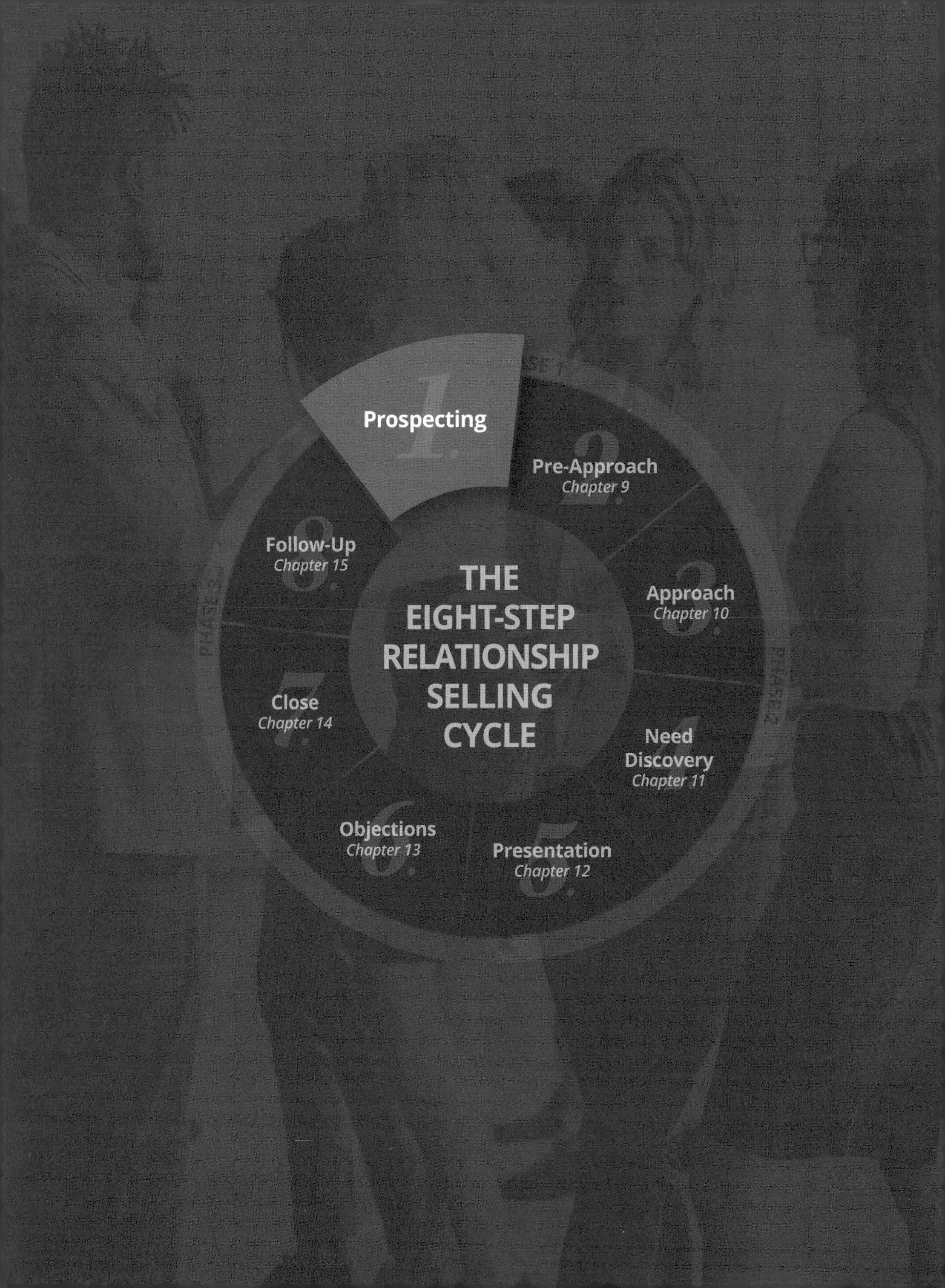

THE EIGHT-STEP RELATIONSHIP SELLING CYCLE

PHASE 1

1. Prospecting

2. Pre-Approach
Chapter 9

3. Approach
Chapter 10

PHASE 2

4. Need Discovery
Chapter 11

5. Presentation
Chapter 12

6. Objections
Chapter 13

PHASE 3

7. Close
Chapter 14

8. Follow-Up
Chapter 15

PROSPECTING: HOW TO FIND QUALIFIED PROSPECTS

OVERVIEW

Prospects are the lifeblood of professional sales. Without a regular stream of new sales opportunities, organizations would not survive. Every salesperson needs new prospects to excel—and this chapter discusses the procedures for locating and qualifying those prospects. As the saying goes, "I'd rather be a master prospector than a wizard of speech and have no one to tell my story to."

OBJECTIVES

- Understand the importance of prospecting.
- Find out who your prospects are.
- Learn the characteristics of a qualified prospect.
- Become familiar with a variety of prospecting methods, including referrals, centers of influence, and social media prospecting.
- Understand how to manage prospect information accurately.
- See the power and influence of analytics on your bottom line.

The Concept of Prospecting

Welcome to step one in the Relationship Selling Cycle. It all begins with prospecting. The reason is that a salesperson without prospects is as useful as a doctor without patients. Great salespeople ask smart questions, know how to close a deal, and have excellent follow-up techniques. The one trait they demonstrate more consistently than any other is constant prospecting, which is enhanced by creative approaches that build value and lasting relationships. They see opportunities everywhere, and they know it's not just the numbers—but the numbers still matter.[1] After all, you have to see more to sell more.

> **"Dig the well before you thirst."**
> *Confucius*

If your closing ratio is low, the problem may be that you don't have enough qualified prospects. If you see enough of the right people, sooner or later, you will sell to someone. To succeed in selling, locate qualified prospects in advance—before you need them. Develop multiple sources from which names of prospective customers continuously flow.

The marketing and sales departments need access to a central storehouse of all prospects and customers. It's a database where employees can track responses to marketing campaigns and look at the history of sales efforts. As the company interacts with that prospect or customer, every piece of communication and history needs to be in one spot. Call it a customer relationship management (CRM) system or a sales force automation (SFA) system. The key is to get marketing, sales, and, if possible, other departments to work from the same contact record.[2] Here are three principles to help you hold onto leads in a highly competitive market:

1. **Qualify leads.** Pay attention to lead qualification. Have a process in place

and the resources and skills to qualify those leads. Generating leads is akin to building a pipeline. Figure out how to construct the pipe and get oil flowing.

2. **Nurture leads.** There will likely be some leads that aren't ready for sales. A nurturing process, which should include phone calls, email, social media, and direct mail, is necessary to keep in touch with those prospects until they're ready.

3. **Add value.** The worst thing you can say is something like, "I'm just calling to find out if you've gotten that budget approval yet." Email case studies or relevant and insightful articles based on your research about them and their company. That way, you are not only checking in, but you are also contributing to their productivity.

The last principle may be the most critical part of prospecting. *All human behavior, at its root, is driven by the need to avoid pain and the desire to gain pleasure.* Even when we do something that appears to be painful, we do it because we associate pleasure with the action.

But what does this have to do with prospecting?

Everything! Most human beings have the same mental triggers that drive their actions.[3] If you want to influence and understand your customers, you need to know what those triggers are and how to utilize them during prospecting. You have to convey to leads, as quickly and effectively as possible, that you have an answer to one of their *pain points*, or specific problems they are facing.

Why is this so critical? Because the mind decides what to buy. So, if you know how the brain functions, you have more power to influence decisions. Of course, to influence someone, you need to know what already affects him or her. You find this out by getting clear on who your prospects are. This chapter will reveal how to get to the bottom of that important question by walking you through the process of turning "just another lead" into a qualified, eager prospect.

> **"I would rather be a master prospector than a wizard of speech and have no one to tell my story to."**
> *Paul J. Meyer*

Qualifying the Prospect

Establish a pattern for prospecting to avoid wasting a monumental amount of time calling on leads that are not prospects. When all you have is a name and email address, you have only the *possibility* of developing a qualified prospective customer. Exhibit 8.1 illustrates the process of moving a name from the status of lead to that of a qualified prospect.

Qualified prospects are those who are a fit for you because they possess the necessary characteristics that make them logical buyers for your offering. Apply a detailed screening

EXHIBIT 8.1 **How to Advance Leads into Qualified Prospects**

SALES LEAD
Research needs, history, ability to pay, authority to buy, etc.

PROSPECT
Evaluate information gained, add personal information.

process to each lead to increase your chances of completing a sale.[4] The best prospect can be defined this way:

> **A CLASS-A QUALIFIED PROSPECT** is a potential customer whose name you received from a person they respect, you have the sufficient personal information to make an exceptional presentation, and they have the authority to make a buying decision and pay for the product or service.[5]

There are few things as disheartening as going through the entire sales process only to discover that the person with whom you are speaking was never a real prospect. To avoid this, ensure that you have found a class A, qualified prospect before spending your valuable time trying to sell to someone who will never say yes.

One of the best ways to determine if you have a qualified class A prospect is to use the MADDEN Test. When you use The MADDEN Test to qualify prospects, you ensure that they have the Money to pay for your product, are Approachable, have a Desire to buy, have Decision-making ability, are Eligible, and have a Need you can satisfy. The next time you think you might have a class A prospect, use the MADDEN Test, which is detailed as follows:

Money

Separate the talkers from those who have the means to buy. You will save yourself from disappointment by determining a prospect's ability to pay before spending your time and energy on gaining a client who may quickly become more of a liability than an asset. It's not always easy to determine purchase capacity. However, there are ways to assess potential based on their purchase history of similar products, their status as a past customer, their profession, and their friends, colleagues, and social circles.

Approachable

Can you get an appointment? The president or CEO of a large company may grant an initial interview only to a senior-level executive in your company. Do not hesitate to ask for such help when there is a real possibility of gaining an important client. Some individual prospects are often approachable only if you are willing to adjust your schedule to fit their needs, so make sure you discover what works best for *them*, and then adjust your schedule accordingly.

Desire

Prospects may have no real interest in your company or what you have to offer. They may be happy with their current vendor or supplier. Is there anything you can discover about them or their company that would lead you to believe they will want what you have to offer? You can successfully reach prospects only if you create or discover a desire to satisfy a *pain point* in their business or personal lives, and how your offering is the solution. In other words, you have to help them find their *why*.

Decision Maker

Be sure the person you call on is the decision-maker. If you are unsure, then start with the head of the company. If you reach the CEO or COO, conducting business may be easier than you think. They earned the top spot by making tough calls and appreciate the challenging call you've just made. A survey of business-to-business (B2B) sales companies revealed that 63 percent of respondents found reaching the right decision-maker was the key to improved sales.[6] Salespeople spend a great deal of time talking to people who are not in a position to make a buying decision. After you have developed a level of comfort with the prospect, ask who else will be involved in making the decision and set up an appointment with all individuals at one time if possible.

Eligible

Determine whether the prospect is eligible to buy from you. Some prospects are already committed to a competitor and cannot buy. Others need a product with a greater or smaller capacity than you can offer, or require a service that is more or less extensive than yours. There is no sense in spending your valuable time calling on a prospect who is locked into a five-year contract with a competitor.

Need

Determine the need level for your product or service. To accomplish this, you must seek out the most up-to-date information about an individual's company and ask questions and listen carefully to determine what the prospect's buying motives are to uncover any specific needs. Then decide if your company has the products that effectively satisfy those needs. Ask yourself—is the business your company may gain worth the amount of time you must invest in getting it? This part of the qualifying process is meant to ensure that you have discovered a potential prospect's *why*—and whether your product or service is the answer.

> "Don't judge each day by the harvest you reap, but by the seeds you plant."
> *Robert Louis Stevenson*

The Social Media Connection

SOCIAL MEDIA OFFERS A BETTER WAY TO QUALIFY PROSPECTS

In the past, it wasn't always easy to pass a lead successfully through the MADDEN Test. How can you know things like a person's interest, ability to pay, or authority to decide before you even meet with the individual? Fortunately, social media has made qualifying prospects a little easier. Here are some helpful tips on how to use social media to seek out and discover qualified prospects:[7]

1. **Start at the top.** Get connected to executives first. Begin by tailoring your pitch to the company you are targeting, and then search for the CEO or top management on the social networks. Find the site where they are the most active and make your move.

2. **Know your competition.** Choose a target company and research it. Search their posts for information on promotions, purchases, acquisitions, and contracts. Take note when the company announces that they will be speaking at a particular conference and then search for a video from that conference. Once you have a clear idea of what your competitors provide, it is far easier to position yourself as the best solution.

3. **Make prospects come to you.** Perhaps the best social media tool for making your prospects come to you is a blog. Use Google's Keyword Planner to find out what people want to know about your industry and offer relevant content in a series of blogs and

e-books. Promote this content on social media and ask your employees and friends to share.

4. **Rotate your social networks.** When it comes to how many social media networks you join, just signing up isn't going to do you much good unless you stay active on it. To cast a wide net, you have to be systematic in covering as many as you can. Pick a single social network that is more niched, and for the next month, focus a portion of your prospecting efforts there. Go where everyone else isn't and start capturing all the under-served revenue sources.

Using social media networks for prospecting can be a profitable endeavor if you know what you are doing and do it well. These social media prospecting secrets can help get you on the right track toward generating more MADDEN-tested prospects.

Top Ten Prospecting Methods

While it may be true that practice makes perfect, this is only applicable to prospecting when you practice the correct methods. Incorrect practice on a musical instrument produces unpleasant sounds, and this idea applies to prospecting as well. Aimless, hit-or-miss prospecting generally leads to unpleasant outcomes. To streamline the job of prospecting and produce better results, learn multiple methods, and use the ones that work best.

Some companies provide leads to their sales forces. For the most part, however, the job of finding leads and qualifying rests squarely on your shoulders. The following is a list of ten prospecting techniques discussed in this chapter.

1. **Referrals**—The use of referrals is one of the most potent prospecting techniques available to sales professionals.
2. **Center of Influence**—This is a person who believes in what you are selling, influences others, and is willing to give you names and help to qualify them.
3. **Social Media**—Social media can aid prospecting efforts by helping you find and qualify prospects in a cost and time effective way.
4. **Group Prospecting**—This is when you bring people together for an organized event and capture their names and other information about them.
5. **Strategic Calling**—Strategic calling, once known as cold calling, is calling on a lead without an appointment or much knowledge about the contact.
6. **Email and Direct Mail**—The written word can be a powerful prospecting medium when you use a list of leads who appear to be at least partially qualified and send them communication that requests a reply.
7. **Current Customers**—A company's existing customer database can be a goldmine of new business.
8. **Business and Civic Groups**—Membership in civic groups such as your local Chamber of Commerce gives

you opportunities to meet people who may be qualified prospects.

9. **Networking**—In networking groups, salespeople from different businesses share information about the sales climate and exchange prospect information. At networking events, companies come together to target specific prospect demographic groups.
10. **Web**—All companies need a robust online presence and a modern, user-friendly website.

1. Referrals

A *referral* is a name from a customer, colleague, or prospect who didn't buy but trusts you. According to global information and measurement company Nielsen, people trust recommendations from business colleagues, friends, and family 92 percent of the time—far more than all other forms of marketing.[8]

Thus, the factor that makes this prospecting method valuable is its *leverage*. Until the proper time to use that leverage arrives, a referral is just a lead like any other.

Once you qualify a referred lead by securing all the information needed to show that this person fits your ideal customer profile, you are then ready to use the valuable leverage that is yours because of the referral. Those who provide referrals should be willing either to make initial contact for you or to allow you to use their names. Referrals work because people are naturally skeptical of strangers, especially those who try to persuade them to buy something. People accept you more readily if someone they know and respect has sent you.

Gain More Referred Leads. Salespeople do not have more referrals because they don't ask, or perhaps because they don't know how

to ask. There are two reasons why people do not immediately provide referrals. The first is that they find it difficult to think of names. They do not want to exert the mental effort to decide who might be interested.

The second reason is they consider themselves to be *conscientious objectors*—they claim they do not give referrals. Sales professionals estimate that 20 percent of clients won't give referrals, no matter how you ask. Another 20 percent of clients will always provide you with leads. It's the other 60 percent where a plan of action is essential.[9]

Exhibit 8.2 illustrates a step-by-step approach to use when you ask for referrals. Practice and rehearse it with your favorite clients or those who have given you referrals in the past. Your customers are professionals, and they deserve to buy from other professionals. Asking for referrals should

EXHIBIT 8.2 **How to Gain More Referral Leads**

1. **Ask with respect.** Open the dialogue with, "I have an important question I want to ask you." That statement will capture their attention and indicate to them just how significant this is to you.
2. **Ask for help.** Relax customers by saying, "I'm trying to build my business, and I would value and appreciate your help."
3. **Explain how i works.** Tell customers what will happen if they give you a referral, and also let them know that you will remain professional and report back to them.
4. **Get permission to explore.** You might give customers another softening statement: "I understand how you feel." Then you can go on to say, "I was wondering if we could agree on who you know who might also benefit from the products I have to offer. Are you comfortable with that?"
5. **Narrow their focus.** Once customers provide you with a few names, make a first step toward qualifying the leads. Ask your client, "If you were in my place, who would you see first?" Ask why. Then find out which one to contact next.
6. **Report back.** Whenever you receive referrals, be sure to report the result of your interviews with leads.
7. **Show your gratitude.** Always offer thanks for giving you referrals regardless of whether the prospect bought from you.

become an automatic part of every presentation you make.

What to Ask. The principal thing you ask for in a referral is for your client to make it easy for you to contact a new prospect. The variable in each situation is how to make contact. What to ask for depends upon your client's need for control:

- Some customers want to handle the communication themselves.
- Others want minimal involvement. They prefer that you initiate the contact for them.
- Other referral sources may have precise instructions on what they want you to do or say with the names they provide.

The best way to find out how much control your client wishes to have is to ask by using an alternate of choice type question: "Would you prefer that I call Mr. Evans, or would you want to call and talk to him on my behalf?" Here is a sample statement that can be used to make the client feel comfortable about giving you names:

"I'm not asking you to recommend me or my product. All I need is an introduction to a few people. It can even be through LinkedIn if that's easier for you! I will respectfully speak with them and give them an opportunity to learn about my company and me."

When to Ask. Make asking for referrals a part of the selling cycle. A logical time to ask for referrals is right after the close. A customer who buys is sold on you and likely to feel good about giving you names. Sometimes, however, a customer wants to use the product or service before providing referrals. Often, salespeople ask for referrals at the wrong time. They start asking for them before the ink on the contract is dry. You can't ask for recommendations; you must earn them. The best leads come from satisfaction, not a signature.

The Million-Dollar Referral

Michael Twining, the vice president of sales at a large distributor of agricultural products, used a smart way to secure more referrals when he was a sales rep in the field. Whenever he received a lead from an existing customer, he quickly mailed a handwritten thank-you note and included a lottery ticket with the message:

"Thanks a million for the referral. I hope you win a million!"

It cost him very little and always created a lot of goodwill and laughs on his next visit with that buyer. Michael said it almost always got him at least one more referral from every customer.[10]

2. Centers of Influence

This form of prospecting is a specific application of the referral method. In both, you begin with a satisfied customer or with a person whose interest has developed to the point of desiring to help you. The critical distinction between the two is that a *center of influence* can give you far more prospects and is both willing and able to provide new names continuously.

The best sales tool you have is a person who believes in what you are selling, is influential with many people who are potential customers, and is willing to give you the names of these people and help you qualify them. That is the essence of a center of influence. When you have several centers of influence, you always have plenty of prospects. People respect centers of influence to the extent that an introduction from them virtually assures you will get an appointment with the leads they provide. Cultivate their friendship, sell yourself, and ask centers of influence to help. Getting influencers on your team can open doors that would otherwise remain closed. Think about how you would react if such a person called you and said:

> *I had lunch this past week with Danielle Russell, a business associate of mine. I think she is a person you would like to meet, and I told her about you. She will be calling you this week; I hope you will meet her.*

Centers of influence are one of the most valuable assets you can have as a salesperson. Follow up on every lead they provide, and then report your results and thank them. Find a way to show your gratitude by being of service to them. After all, a mutually beneficial relationship is rewarding to both parties.

3. Social Media

As you read in the Social Media Connection earlier in the chapter, social media can be a powerful and useful prospecting method. Keep in mind, however, that being on social media and putting it to good use are two vastly different things. Prospects are not going to seek you out naturally—you've still got to work for them! Here are some tips for finding opportunities on your favorite social media sites quickly:

LinkedIn. LinkedIn is the most business-friendly social media channel. Still, it's also universally understood that many of its users are more wary about strangers connecting with them—that is, unless you've got the secret ingredient for finding leads and prospects on LinkedIn, which is groups. Over half of LinkedIn users join ten or more groups.[11] That makes it the best place to insert yourself into relevant conversations and provide useful advice, tips, and content to get you noticed and attract potential prospects to you and your business.

Facebook. Facebook, the number one social media network in the world, may seem pretty consumer-focused on the surface. For salespeople unsure of how to engage businesses and potential prospects via Facebook, it can be easy to identify the right prospects thanks to one of Facebook's search tools called Graph Search. What's unique about Graph Search is that it gives you search results based on precise search queries. Here is an excellent example of how specific your search can be, "Marketers in Boston looking for inbound marketing software." Because Graph Search pulls information from Facebook user profiles, it's a premier way to discover prospects who don't already live in your feed.[12]

Instagram. Instagram is now the second-most-popular social networking site behind Facebook. The platform surpassed a billion users in 2018, with a staggering 500 million people engaging with Instagram Stories daily.[13] There is a good chance that your target prospects are already on Instagram. No matter what you sell, there is likely a visual component to it. Putting images and videos on Instagram allows you to show off your product directly to your target audience, directly engage with potential customers, build a following, and enhance your reputation as an expert in your field.

Twitter. Twitter is a gold mine for prospecting.[14] It is both simple and easy to use Twitter's search function to attach industry-specific keywords to Twitter users who may be interested in what you're offering. It doesn't matter what you sell or your industry—anyone can use the search function and see quality results. You can even take your Twitter-mining one step further with HubSpot's Social Inbox. Social Inbox helps you track who is who in your Twitter list and searches by showing your contacts database of leads, opportunities, and customers, and merging it with your social media activity. Utilizing this tool means moving the most enticing prospects on Twitter right up to the top.

Social media prospecting is about *creating a context* with people so that your social interactions might eventually lead to a sale. Of course, social media can be noisy, busy, and filled with a lot of fluff—and sometimes, prospective customers get buried in a sea of look-alikes. But with a little effort and some strategizing, they will appear.

4. Group Prospecting

Many companies use group prospecting with great success. The idea is to bring together a group of people, from eight to 20 or more. The group may meet in a home, a hotel conference room, or an office. Your purpose is to inform prospects about your product or service.

Many reps in the financial services industry use group information sessions for gathering people together to offer free information about retirement, financial planning, or investing strategies. During the meeting, the professional has the opportunity (in front of a captive audience) to find and hone in on people's *pain points*. After such a session, it is always imperative to follow up with attendees and strike while the iron is hot.

A variation of this method is to attend or set up an exhibit at a networking meeting that targets a specific demographic. Yet another idea is to look for groups of potential prospects and offer to be a guest speaker. Members of civic clubs may be ideal prospects for you, and they are always looking for speakers who have beneficial information for their members. If you establish your credibility, you may be able to close your speech with a brief presentation. Meet as many audience members as possible, ask for business cards, and give them yours. If they were impressed enough to want you to call, you know you have a qualified prospect.

5. Strategic Calling

In the world of professional selling, cold calling has long been a dreaded part of a salesperson's day. But, if you dread it, you may not be doing it right. Calling on prospects without first gaining an appointment can be productive if you accept the reality of the situation. Call it *cold-calling* or *warm-calling*; it doesn't

"I'm not saying I believe in global warming, but have you noticed it's getting harder to make cold calls?"

matter. All that matters is your state of mind. For most salespeople, it is not meant to be their only source of leads. However, strategic calling on potential prospects who were not expecting your call can serve as an excellent supplement to other prospecting efforts.

The real issue with this prospecting technique rests in the message and how you communicate it. You must be able to communicate with prospects so that they understand and resonate with what you have to say. In short, planned prospecting is a communication skill—and like any communication skill, you can learn it and improve upon it.[15] You have a narrow window of opportunity on the phone or at a person's door to catch and engage your prospect. If you are not able to do that, the call ends without achieving your desired result. If you have the proper skills, however, it is possible to have productive conversations with prospects no matter how you choose to categorize them. Here are some other tips when making calls:

Use as a Supplement. Because this method of prospecting is designed to supplement your current prospect list, be careful that phone calls and in-person cold calling never take so much of your time that you neglect to call on qualified prospects and existing clients. Set aside a specific amount of time each week for making calls, but never at the expense of more profitable activity.

Always Preplan. Develop several effective icebreakers and interest-capturing statements and experiment until you find which ones work best for you. Your statement should be something relevant to them and their situation that causes prospects to remember you when you later call for an appointment to make your presentation.

Stay Enthusiastic. When you make calls, the person you want to talk to is almost certainly too busy to speak with you. If you remain enthusiastic in spite of such responses, you make a positive impression on the gatekeeper. You may even get enough information to qualify prospects without meeting them. Impress them with your professionalism, and you will find those doors to the buyers open more easily.

Golden Opportunities

Most salespeople would agree that calling without an appointment is the toughest part of selling. At the same time, however, the rewards can be significant. So, change your mindset by referring to them as *opportunity calls*—because that's what they are. Viewing a phone call as a golden opportunity gives you an even greater incentive for selling. Now go out and create some golden opportunities for yourself![16]

6. Email and Direct Mail

The ultimate success of email and direct mail prospecting depends upon the management of your mailing list. Some lists are better than others, and the best investment of your time and budget demands careful planning and analysis. The product or service you sell has a great deal to do with what kind of list you use. The goal is a list of people or businesses that are already at least partially qualified prospects.

Don't overlook online directories for developing your email and direct mail lists as a source of prospects. Some directories are useful in identifying possible opportunities, and others help you learn more about prospects to determine whether they have the potential to become customers. Exhibit 8.3 provides some suggestions for sources of email and direct mail lists. Keep in mind that much of the time, the best lists are not readily available to the general public.

The best lists are those that you have created over time through past prospecting and networking efforts. Be patient—and the list will come.

Develop a coding system to show which types of lists produce the highest percentage of responses—and then code the names of people who respond. You can easily track the open rates of your emails to see how effective your messages are at getting through. An *open rate* is a percentage measure of how many people on an email list open (or view) a particular email campaign.

EXHIBIT 8.3 Suggested Sources for Building Direct-Mail Lists

MEMBERSHIP ROSTERS

- Professional societies and trade associations
- College alumni lists
- Civic clubs such as Kiwanis, Lions, Civitan, and Optimist
- Special-interest groups
- Business groups such as the Chamber of Commerce

DIRECTORIES AND DATABASES

- People you have networked with in-person and online
- Professional online lists or purchased database lists
- People you have done business with in the past
- E-newsletter subscription field from your website

7. Current Customers

It would be a mistake not to mention one of a salesperson's most potent and ever-present sources of business—and that is the existing customer base. Every business needs new customers, but don't forget that your most accessible and most predictable source of new revenue is right under your nose:

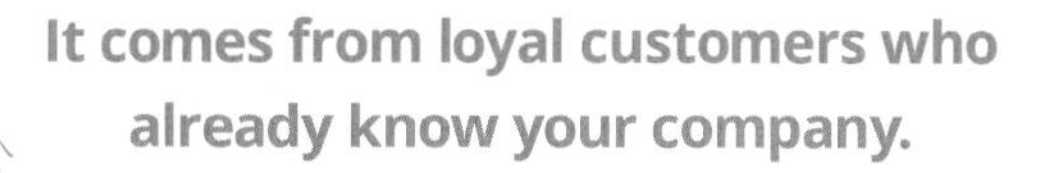

It comes from loyal customers who already know your company.

Acquiring new customers is expensive—five to ten times the cost of retaining an existing one—and the average spending of a repeat customer is a whopping 67 percent more than that of a new one.[17] So, put some energy into new prospecting methods and business development, but make sure you know that coming up with creative ways to sell more to your current customers is just as important.

8. Business and Civic Groups

Membership in civic groups can give you opportunities to meet people who are prospects for your product or service. Meetings provide you with regular times to reach more people and build relationships. Exhibit 8.4 lists tips for using membership in civic clubs as prospecting opportunities.

In selecting groups to join, consider the kinds of prospects you want to meet. It is also beneficial to choose organizations to which decision-makers belong. Set goals to reach a certain number of new people at each meeting and to reconnect, or establish stronger relationships, with a certain amount of others. Keep an updated file of the organization's members as you meet and learn about them. Avoid actively selling at meetings, but you may ask someone to tell you the best time to call to set up an appointment. Building relationships through

EXHIBIT 8.4 Tips for Prospecting in Groups

- Carefully select the groups you join.
- Assume leadership responsibilities to work for positive visibility.
- Set contact number goals for each meeting.
- Follow up with every contact.
- Maintain an information file on the contacts made in each organization.
- Use "re-meet" goals to help you develop closer relationships with people.
- Reach out to new members.

these contacts lays the groundwork for active selling in the future.

9. Networking

Networking refers to the active cooperation between business people to share information about the business climate, specific happenings in the business community, and prospects. It involves the three C's:

1. Connecting
2. Communicating
3. Cooperating

Sharing information and names of prospects makes sense. So, go ahead and mingle! As useful and handy as some of the newer, digital approaches to finding prospects are, good old networking should still be an essential part of your routine. Engage with people face-to-face, tell them about yourself, your business and your product, and ask about them. Exchange contact details, add them to your database, and keep in touch. There is another prospect waiting behind your next conversation if you make it your goal to discover not just what that person can do for you, but also how you can serve him or her.

10. Websites

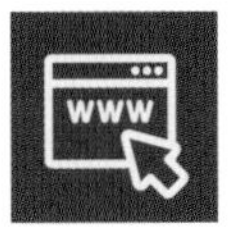

There is no excuse for not having a well-designed, user-friendly website, especially as more consumers shift to online tools as their primary means of contact. A website acts as the company's representative, so you want it to reflect your professionalism in terms of design and content quality. Exhibit 8.5 outlines the reasons you need a website working for you.[18]

Essential Site Components. A vast array of sales websites and blogs exists online, so yours or your company's site needs to stand out from the crowd. The most professional-looking sites remain relatively clean and minimalist. In other words, they know who they are marketing to and design the website for that audience. The best sites are also

EXHIBIT 8.5 What a Good Website Can Do

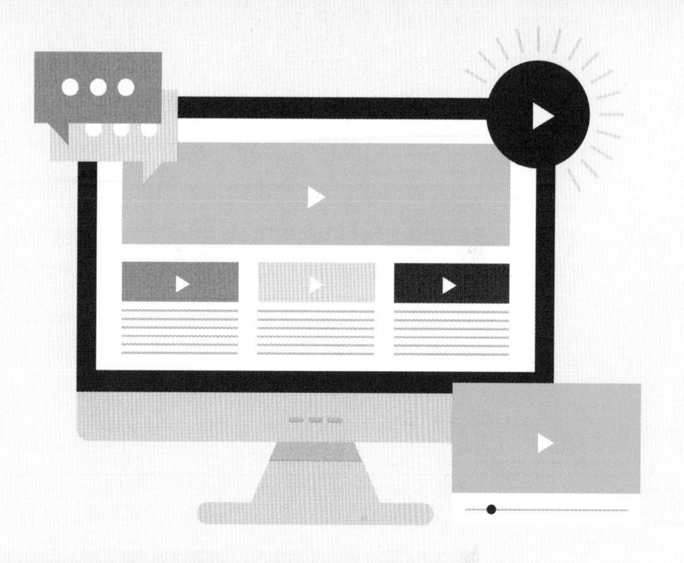

1. **Your site can prospect for new clients.** A search-engine-optimized site can attract customers who may not have even known about your business.
2. **Your site can offer 24/7 support.** Even when your office is closed, your website stays open, providing product and service information.
3. **Your site can cater to everyone.** Introverts aren't likely to pick up the phone until they have done their research. For these people, your website may be a valuable tool. Extroverts will also appreciate the information you share on your site.

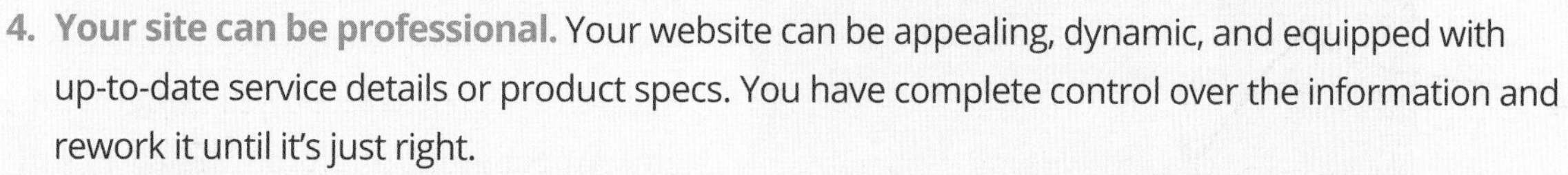

4. **Your site can be professional.** Your website can be appealing, dynamic, and equipped with up-to-date service details or product specs. You have complete control over the information and rework it until it's just right.
5. **Your site can build repeat business.** Keep your content compelling and fresh, giving visitors a reason to return and see what's new.
6. **Your site can gather information.** Your website might offer newsletter subscriptions, product sales, friend referrals, or marketing surveys. A visitor who interacts can give you contact details and become a lead.
7. **Your site can help you close.** Your site design should mimic your company's real-life strategy when it comes to closing a sale. If you are selling products, an online shopping cart is a great addition. If you are selling services, you might need an online signup or a contact form.
8. **Your site can make follow-up easier.** The sale should not be the end of the sales process. Design your website so that feedback is encouraged. Customer satisfaction surveys or short post-sales polls can give excellent feedback and help you to improve your sales strategy.

user-friendly, with easily navigable pages and links to relevant content. According to some experts, the websites with the most value, however, are often linked to blogs with more user interaction and high-quality content that is not a recycled product pitch; continuous updates and marketing efforts here are critical.[19]

Use Affiliate Program Marketing. You may want to offer ad space on your website or place ads on other affiliated sites. Google AdSense is the most popular affiliate marketing program and can earn your website some revenue. Google AdSense targets and customizes ads based on your website's content. You can choose how you would like your site to be paid for these ads, whether through user visits, earnings by user location, browser type, and referring source or by AdSense impressions, clicks, and revenue.[20] Alternately, if you are the advertiser, you can bid on premium ad space available on other websites. Of course, you should research other affiliate marketing programs and decide if you want to broker your ads or opt for a no-ad website, all based on your ideal prospect's profile.

On their own, each of these prospecting techniques is only mildly effective. However, when combined, they create a powerful prospecting arsenal. No matter what methods of prospecting you elect to use, your powers of observation provide many of your best prospects. The only way to get better at something is to practice. It stands to reason that if you want to become more skilled at recognizing qualified prospects among a sea of leads, you must learn what qualified prospects look and sound like and then plan how you will reach them.

Social media tools make observation more powerful and accessible than ever. By following Facebook pages and Twitter users, you'll be able to keep connected to your current clients at the same time that you track prospects who also follow them. Keep an eye on feeds for event notifications, announcements, birthday notices, and even changes in relationship status. Send a congratulatory note to a client on a new marriage or baby; send a personal message to a prospect who is launching a new store. Connect on LinkedIn, join a relevant group, and follow conversations on hot topics. Explore the public profiles of connected groups and individuals—you never know how or when a valuable connection could present itself.

Managing Prospect Information

Diligent prospecting is useless if you do not have a system for managing and using the information you find. Many contact management systems will help you organize your contacts and priorities, but be aware of how to classify and prioritize contacts so you can make the most of your prospecting time.

Initial Recording of Leads

The initial information you need about prospects depends a great deal upon the product or service you sell, but it will, in all likelihood, include these items:

1. **Prospect's full name and preferred name**
2. **Email address and business or home address**
3. **Direct phone number (cell phone is best)**
4. **Name of the company he or she works for**
5. **Position in company**
6. **Family information (spouse, children)**
7. **Personal data (club memberships, alma mater, hobbies)**
8. **Approximate income (if your offering is for individuals)**
9. **Source of prospect (referral, networking event, etc.)**

Prospect Classification

When you first find the name of an individual or company prospect, assign a classification. One classification system uses the letters A, B, and C:

CLASS A prospects are those about whom you have adequate information to make a presentation. You know they have the money to buy and the authority to make a decision. Ideally, you also have a referral from someone they respect.

CLASS B prospects are those about whom you have inadequate information to make the best possible presentation. You may not know enough to be sure they need your product or service. You may not know whether they have the authority to make a decision or whether they can afford to buy. You may not have a referral to help open the door. When one or more of these items is missing, the proper action is research rather than approach.

CLASS C prospects are people whose names you have found in some way, but about whom you have little or no information other than a name. They are leads, not prospects.

Prospecting activity involves not only finding new leads but also qualifying existing leads by adding information that allows you to move them up to class A status.

Scheduling Contacts

When you have classified a prospect as class A, determine when you will initiate contact, either by telephone, email, social media, personal visit, or direct mail, according to the method of approach you choose. Set up your calendar or contact management system to send reminders to ensure you take

the proper action on the date assigned. Once a prospect's name enters your database, it stays there permanently until you close a sale or determine that the person is not a qualified prospect and never will be. If you make a presentation and do not close, choose a time for a new attempt and schedule a time to contact the prospect again.

When you discover that a person is not a viable prospect for you and will probably not become one in the foreseeable future, then that person can still be a vital contact. The impression you give through your professionalism may cause that person to recommend you to a class A qualified prospect.

The Power of Analytics

The world of business analytics is a vast land of possibility, especially in the area of prospecting. With companies, data experts, and consultants all approaching analytics differently, it can also be overwhelming. In the simplest terms, there are two principal areas of analytics:

1. **Data and statistics-driven predictive modeling that enables prospect and client segmentation and opportunity identification.**
2. **Reporting and the software that allows you to retrieve information from a client or prospect database.**

Setting aside the complicated terminology and the latest buzzwords—such as big data, data mining, and donor intelligence—it boils down to performing and then utilizing data analysis, all driven by the need to sell in a more targeted and precise manner. In short:

It's about harnessing the power of information in a way that leads to more sales.

"Get all the information you can, we'll think of a use for it later!"

What does analyzing data mean? It can be summed up like this: *data analysis* is the process of extracting, compiling, and modeling raw data to obtain constructive information.[21] The pivotal word in that definition is "constructive." Data analysis is only valuable if it serves a purpose. Data analysis for its own sake is neither useful nor particularly insightful, and it is by no means a magic wand. But it can go a long way toward providing solutions for you if you:

- **Have a question that needs answering.**
- **Need to choose between different options.**
- **Believe that quantitatively showing information would increase clarity or motivate prospects to act.**

How can you take a collection of numbers and turn that into something useful—or in other words, something that allows you to segment leads and potential prospects in a way that helps you become more laser-focused in your marketing and approach methods? You have to have three things: 1) Accurate data (i.e., information) that can be quantified, 2) Tools to extract and compile the data, and 3) Ways to model the data so that it provides useful information. When you use it right, data analysis can provide helpful, intuitive knowledge. Proper use of analytics can answer questions like:

"Are my phone calls to potential prospects any more effective in the ***morning*** *or* ***after lunch****?"*

......

> *"What is our company's* ***second-largest*** *selling* ***month****?"*

> *"How well are we doing in increasing* ***year-over-year*** *sales?"*

With the right data, there is no limit to what you can discover through analytics because the answer to such questions will allow you to focus your time, energy, and resources where they will glean the biggest payoff. There is one important thing to note about the questions above: Note the words in bold.

Those words highlight the fact that there must be variables to study—at least two factors that can be measured or investigated to test how they are related—for data analysis to yield valuable results.

Using all the web tools available to you—whether through social media, e-newsletter campaigns, researching company websites, or purchasing data sets from data mining companies—there is no excuse for making a truly *cold* call anymore. Being as thorough as possible in your approach to prospecting goes a long way in securing new accounts and allows you to achieve the treasured personalized approach to selling. Put yourself in your clients' shoes, and you can offer your clients a real solution. That will accomplish more than merely establishing a solid rapport with prospects; it builds a relationship that will inevitably yield more significant success in the future.

SUMMARY

Prospecting is the skill that keeps salespeople flourishing. Qualify leads to determine whether they are viable prospective customers.

Class A, qualified prospects are those who pass the MADDEN test.

Two of the most effective prospecting methods are referrals and centers of influence.

Social media provides a compelling way to seek out, discover, and attract new qualified prospects.

Group prospecting is securing names of prospects at trade shows, meetings, or in any situation where you have the opportunity to meet people.

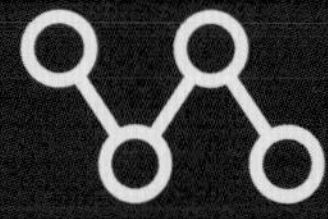

Networking is a valuable source of new prospects for salespeople who are willing to share information about their customers or clients.

A classification system will help you methodically catalog your prospects as class A, B, or C prospects. Such a system will save you time and frustration.

Use analytics to analyze your sales results to improve and determine where to spend more of your prospecting efforts.

Review Questions

1. How does your skill in prospecting exert a direct effect on your ability to close a sale?
2. What characteristics make a qualified prospect?
3. What are the ten prospecting techniques listed in this chapter, and which ones should you use most often?
4. What is a referral? How do you gain more of them?
5. What is the advantage of having referrals from your clients?
6. What is a center of influence?
7. What is one way to use Twitter to find new prospects?
8. How does networking work for salespeople?
9. How long should a prospect's name remain in your prospecting system?
10. What are the three things required to have data analysis provide you with useful, intuitive information?

IN-CLASS EXERCISES

The following exercises help build teams, improve communication, and emphasize the real-world side of selling. They are meant to be challenging, to help you learn how to deal with problems that have no single right answer, and to use a variety of skills beyond those employed in a typical review question. Read and complete each activity. Then in the next class, discuss and compare answers.

EXERCISE 8.1 Finding the Right CMP

For this assignment, you will work individually. Imagine that your company's vice president for sales and marketing has concluded that the company is dropping too many good sales leads because of the lack of a sound tracking system for contacts. At the quarterly sales meeting, the vice president asks the entire sales force to recommend a contact management program (CMP) that will allow anyone in the company to access contact information from anywhere, at any time. The vice president emphasizes that the application should be robust, well tested, and affordable. The salesperson who compiles the most complete and persuasive recommendation and whose choice is adopted by the company will receive a bonus and a chance for promotion. You want the bonus and promotion.

After conducting research online, select three acceptable CMPs, and recommend one as superior. Which criteria do you use in making your final recommendation? How do you respond to the suggestions of others in your class?

EXERCISE 8.2 Qualifying the Prospect

For this exercise, divide the class into four-person teams. One of the most important yet most difficult tasks of any salesperson is to qualify the prospect. Chapter 8 recommends the MADDEN approach to qualifying prospects. This approach identifies the information that salespeople need to consider a prospect or lead "qualified."

Nevertheless, asking for the necessary information (or finding it by other means) is often tricky. For example, it would be insensitive and counterproductive to ask, "Do you have the money or authorized budget to pay for this product?" Or again, imagine the response to the direct question, "Do you have the required authority to purchase this product?"

The MADDEN approach specifies what you need to know. The task for your team in this exercise is to think of how to obtain this information, to devise smart, inoffensive ways of soliciting needed information from prospects. In the first instance, confine your methods to what you might say or ask in a personal interview. If you have time, develop other research methods that might help you obtain the needed information.

Jot down your recommendations and the reasons for them, and be prepared to present and discuss them in class or online.

Case Studies

The following case studies present you with selling scenarios that require you to apply the critical skills discussed in the chapter and give you training through practical learning situations. They are meant to be both engaging and challenging, and like the exercises, don't have one right answer.

CASE 8.1—The Trade Show

Judy had just accepted a position as a sales representative with NewLine Papers, a manufacturer of high-quality specialty papers for businesses that use direct mail to promote their products and services. Typically, such companies must use paper that is attractive to look at and hold, that absorbs ink quickly because of high-speed printing, and that can stand up to the rigors of automatic folding equipment. For Judy to learn more about the business and to acquire good leads, her sales manager has sent her to the U.S. Postal Forum (USPF) annual meeting in Las Vegas.

Judy decided that for this trip to pay off in terms of generating solid leads, she needed to engage in careful planning. A quick check of USPF's website allowed her to compile a shortlist of attendees who might be interested in NewLine's latest product. About a week before the trade show, she phoned a couple of them to arrange an appointment. They

willingly agreed, so she flew to Las Vegas in the hope that she could snag an order, not just a couple of good leads. That would surely impress her manager!

After checking in at the convention hotel, Judy called Ned Harris, her first appointment for the next morning. Ned wasn't in, but she left a message indicating that she could meet him just off the lobby at 10:00 a.m. Her second appointment, Anita Scoby, answered on the second ring. She and Judy agreed to meet tomorrow afternoon at 2:30 following the keynote speech by the head of the U.S. Environmental Protection Agency. Everything was all set.

Ned arrived for their meeting the next morning a couple of minutes late, explaining that he was not a morning person and needed a second cup of coffee. They moved to the hotel's coffee bar and settled at a small table. Judy brightened when Ned reported that his company had done business with NewLine some years before. Immediately, Judy pulled out a couple of samples from her briefcase and launched into her presentation of the outstanding features of the new product. Ned listened attentively, sipping his coffee, and sitting with arms folded. When Judy finished her spiel, she asked if he had any questions. He didn't. She then asked whether Ned's company would be interested in placing a trial order. He replied, rather curtly, that he didn't know and would have to get back to her on that. He added that he was late for another meeting. With that, he picked up his newspaper and left, leaving Judy to reflect on what had happened.

Her meeting that afternoon with Anita Scoby was even briefer. Before Judy could begin to describe the samples, Anita cut her off, explaining that she had no authority to engage in such discussions. She added that while she was interested in Judy's product, her role was in sales for her company and that she was attending the trade show merely to network with other clients. She wished Judy luck and promised to pass along Judy's information to more appropriate people at her firm.

As Judy flew home the next morning, she wondered what she had done wrong. She had researched attendees of the trade show and had obtained appointments, but she was returning home with no orders and, worse, no real leads.

Where do you think Judy went wrong? What would she need to do to become a "master prospector?"

If you were sent to the trade show by your manager, what would you have done? What would have been your objectives? Which tactics would you have employed to fulfill those objectives?

CASE 8.2—The Over-Eager Realtor

Sherry Huffman had just moved with her husband to San Diego from upstate New York, where she had lived for her entire life. At age 30 and having worked in real estate for seven years, Sherry had no intention of giving up her career. She, therefore, joined a real estate company in San Diego and began searching for prospects. Sherry realized that being a real estate agent in San Diego was going to be more challenging than in small-town New York, where nearly everyone in the area already knew her. In her new, larger city, she would have to cultivate a new sphere of influence if she wanted to build up a web of satisfied clients who could subsequently help generate new business. In other words, Sherry realized, she would have to network aggressively (among other tactics) to succeed.

There was only one problem: networking, in the sense of meeting and cultivating new acquaintances, was new to Sherry. In New York, she was already networked; she didn't have to work at it or meet new people. Now, however, she would have to get to know new people to the point where they could begin to trust her.

Sherry's first foray into networking was to join the local Chamber of Commerce. What better source of new prospects, she thought, than successful, established businesspersons from a variety of fields? In typical fashion, she approached the task enthusiastically.

At the first meeting of the Chamber that Sherry attended, she introduced herself to the president and proceeded to work the room. As small groups of people carried on sometimes animated conversation during the cocktail hour, Sherry went from one group to another, introducing herself, distributing her business cards to all, and saying, "Hi! I'm Sherry Huffman. I just joined Golden Bear Real Estate. Here's my card. If any of you are in the market to buy or sell real estate, please give me a call." Generally, people looked at her a little quizzically, politely took her card, and returned to their conversation. Sherry began to get the feeling that something was wrong.

After dinner, the Chamber president approached Sherry. "I couldn't help noticing how you managed to introduce yourself to everyone before dinner. Very impressive! But I think it would be wise for you to slow down a little. This isn't a real estate open house, you know."

The president's words stung. On the way home, Sherry's eyes welled up, and she pounded the steering wheel in frustration. What had she done wrong? How could she rectify the situation? What changes would you recommend to Sherry to turn her into a master prospector through networking?

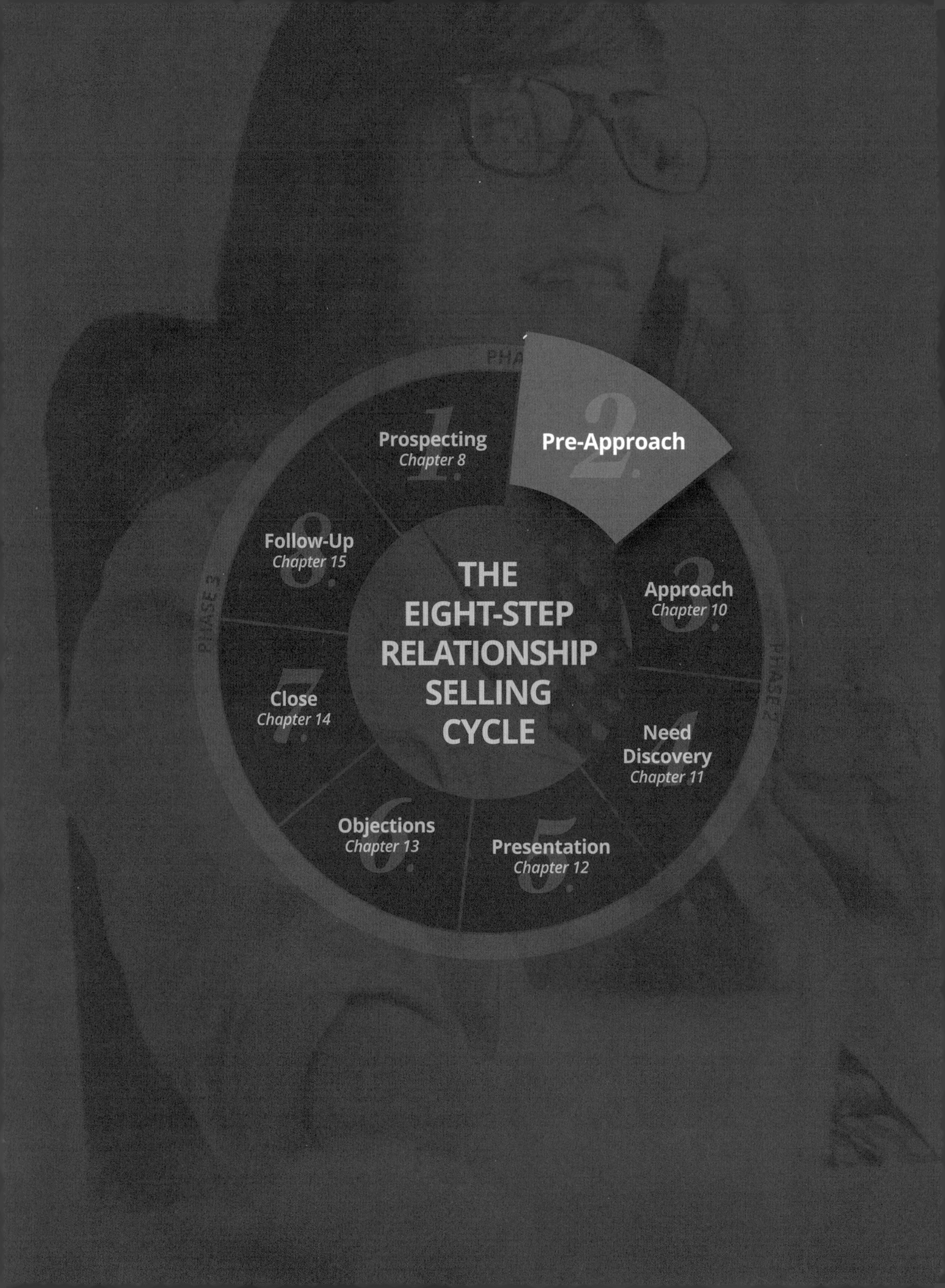

PHASE 1

PHASE 2

PHASE 3

THE EIGHT-STEP RELATIONSHIP SELLING CYCLE

1. Prospecting
Chapter 8

2. Pre-Approach

3. Approach
Chapter 10

4. Need Discovery
Chapter 11

5. Presentation
Chapter 12

6. Objections
Chapter 13

7. Close
Chapter 14

8. Follow-Up
Chapter 15

THE PRE-APPROACH: WHAT TO DO BEFORE YOU MEET

OVERVIEW

In step one of the Relationship Selling Cycle, you prospected for qualified leads. In this chapter, you will learn what kinds of information you should work to discover about leads to help you get the most out of your prospecting efforts. We will discuss the process of gathering pre-approach information and present telephone techniques that will help you have more success in scheduling that critical first appointment with a prospect.

OBJECTIVES

- Learn the goals of the pre-approach and the planning needed to make it useful.
- Study how to prepare for an effective pre-approach.
- Understand how the pre-approach functions as an extension of prospecting.
- Realize the power of social media in pre-approach.
- Discover effective methods for telephone calls that are successful in leading to face-to-face meetings.
- Understand the six-step telephone track and how to use it to make appointments.
- Learn some of the best ways to follow up with prospects after the initial call.

Finding the Right Prospects

See enough people. See the right people. See them at the right time. That course of action sounds logical enough—but the pivotal part of this advice is the "right people." How can you be sure that you are investing your time in calling on qualified prospects? The answer lies in your diligence in collecting information about the leads you record in your prospecting system. This information-gathering process is step two in the Relationship Selling Cycle.

Collecting the right information takes time and effort, but with practice, it will become a regular part of your daily life as a salesperson. For example, as soon as someone gives you a referral, ask questions to learn what you need to know about that prospect. Research the prospect's business or industry and the company itself. Find that person on social media and see what his or her profiles reveal about the individual's personality, tastes, and tendencies. Discover information that will help you know what kind of social style to expect.

The various activities that provide this necessary personal and business information are called presale planning, or *pre-approach.* The pre-approach is the planning and preparation you do before contact with prospects. In gathering such information, you learn who to call, why, when, and where. Seemingly insignificant details might be the key to the approach that spells the difference between a sale and disappointment. Leave nothing to chance.

The sales cycle is a continuous process with no clear pause between one phase and the next. In practice, you cannot separate the prospecting, pre-approach, approach, and need discovery elements into different segments. Instead, they blend and become one. However, the exact point where one phase ends, and the next begins, will likely never be the same.

Exhibit 9.1 illustrates the absence of clear dividing lines between the steps in the Relationship Selling Cycle, and it also shows that it is possible to discover that your lead is a qualified prospect at any point in time during the process.

Industries and sales positions vary so widely that it's difficult to make any broad generalizations about the type and amount of pre-approach information to gather. Depending on what you sell and your target demographic, the pre-approach will differ considerably. At times, the only opportunity to qualify prospects is during the approach and need discovery process by asking questions, observing, listening, and interpreting communication signals.

EXHIBIT 9.1 Qualify Leads at Many Points in the Cycle

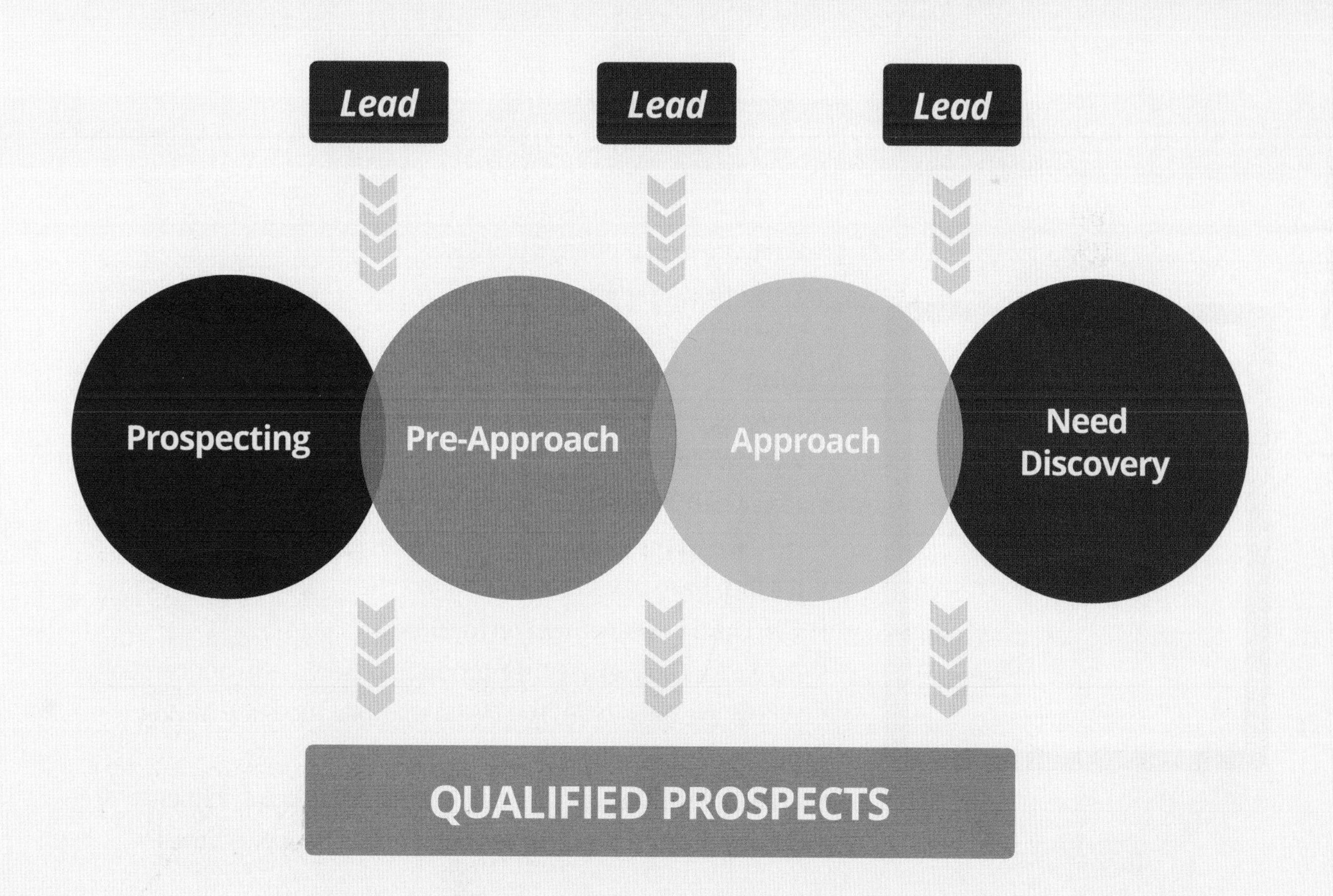

Preparing to Win

During step two of the Relationship Selling Cycle, the pre-approach phase, you must analyze all the information you have about a prospect to understand present needs for what you sell, current use of competing products, and feelings about the competition.

You must identify decision-makers, review account history, assess product needs, plan a sales presentation to address identified concerns, and set call objectives. You also develop a preliminary strategy for the sales process during this phase, keeping in mind that you may need to refine the procedure as you learn more about each prospect.[1]

The quality of information uncovered during the pre-approach is vital. Just like some students dislike homework, many adults have an aversion to pre-approach groundwork and prefer to skip to the "real work." However, the preliminary steps are a must. Successful sales professionals rarely even make a cold call without some preparation.[2] When they are ready for a formal sales call, expert salespeople have studied and analyzed the prospect's personality, company, operations, needs, and financial position.

One of the best ways to prepare is to develop a checklist of questions to answer before you make a sales call. Exhibit 9.2 presents a list designed to help gather the essential sales information you need before you are face-to-face with a prospect.

EXHIBIT 9.2 Pre-Approach Information Checklist

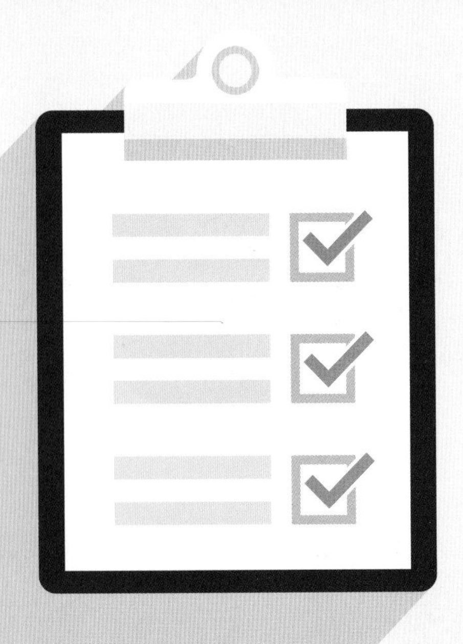

- What are the company's products?
- Who are its primary customers?
- In what industry does the company compete, and where does it rank?
- How big is the company (is that large enough to make a call worthwhile)?
- How often does this company buy my type of product or service?
- How well is the company satisfied with its present supplier?
- Do they have plans that could affect their need for my product?
- Can I help educate them on my product's uses?
- Do we (or can we) use their products or services in our company?
- Who is the decision-maker? Who else influences the buying decision?
- What are the background and interests of decision influencers?
- Do any of our top executives know any of their executives?

Prep for the Presentation

Do your research to find out about the prospect and develop a purpose for the call that is linked to a potential client benefit. Set a goal for each contact with a prospect, know what you want to accomplish, and how you plan to do it. There is much more to preparation than merely gathering and reviewing information. Rehearsal eliminates the stammering, nervous speech habits, and repetition that often result from a lack of preparation.

Allow time in your daily schedule to prepare the sales approach and presentation you will use in each call. Decide how you can make the best possible use of sales literature and tools provided by your company. Review the social profiles and company websites of your contacts. Plan how to incorporate visual aids into your approach and presentation for maximum effectiveness.

When preparing for a presentation, making a video allows you to see how you look. Webcams and phones make self-assessment easy and convenient. Video also allows you to note whether you use filler words such as *um, uh, like,* and *you know.* Here are some rehearsal tips:

- Practice your presentation with specific customers in mind.
- Film presentations to reveal verbal and nonverbal strengths and weaknesses.
- Make large, exaggerated motions until you feel comfortable making more natural gestures.

Visualize Successful Selling

Salespeople can learn a great deal from the training habits of world-class athletes. Olympians use visualization techniques to help them focus on a specific event. An integral part of their training consists of *mental toughening sessions.* They run a race over and over in their minds. Over ten years from 1977 to 1987, Edwin Moses won 107 consecutive races in the 400-meter hurdles. His power of visualization became so acute that when he mentally visualized hitting a hurdle, he felt the physical pain in his leg.[3]

To further illustrate how powerful visualization can be, consider this incredible example. Captain Jack Sands was an American POW who was captured during the Vietnam War and spent seven years in Hanoi's Hỏa Lò Prison, the same camp where Senator John McCain was once imprisoned.

Captain Sands lived in a small, solitary cell, with no interaction and no physical

activity. One day, he decided he would recreate, in his mind, the most beautiful and perfect golf course imaginable. Each day, Captain Sands would play that course, stroke by stroke. He closed his eyes to swing his imaginary club. He imagined the wind rustling his hair and the sun in his eyes.

Every single day, in his five-by-five-foot cell, he played a perfect round of golf.

Before he was imprisoned, Captain Sands was an average golfer, always shooting around 100. After seven long years, when he was finally released and sent home, that was no longer the case. His first time on the course, he scored a 74—and he hadn't actually played golf or even held a club in over eight years![4]

The mind is that powerful, which is why you can't allow it to limit you from achieving greatness in your profession. As Earl Nightingale said, "Whatever we plant in our subconscious mind and nourish with repetition and emotion will one day become a reality."

You can practice this same type of mental exercise. Positively affirm the feeling you want to create and visualize the outcomes you wish to obtain. Think about what you will say and anticipate the prospect's responses. Create a mental image of the desired results, and then live it over and over in your mind. Practice out loud; your brain believes the sound of your voice. Remember, your mind cannot separate a real experience from an imagined one.

Sources of Pre-Approach Information

When you know what information you need, you can identify how to obtain it. The information you gather will help you gain access to make a presentation, as well as guide you in preparing a strategy for the interview itself. For example, you can ask colleagues on your sales team for information they have on particular prospects. Current customers are also excellent sources of information, and they may be happy to share what they know. One of the most convenient ways to gain knowledge is to use search engines, industry websites, and social media profiles.

In most cases, there is nothing wrong with calling on prospects without an appointment. At the very least, a cold call allows you to learn something that validates them as partially qualified prospects. You cannot predict the most beneficial sources of information, so keep your eyes and ears open so you won't miss a great opportunity![5]

Read magazines and newsletters that are related to your customer's industry. You likely read publications that are pertinent in your field, so your clients probably also read material that is relevant to their areas. You can also subscribe to newsletters and updates from companies and organizations in your client's industry. That is a great way to uncover ideas to serve their needs better. However, reading is not enough. You must know what to look for as you read and research.[6] Here are six items to consider that may give you valuable information:

1. **Mergers.** Will new alliances give you better opportunities to see companies that have dismissed you in the past?
2. **Personnel changes.** Watch for new positions accepted by your customers, prospects, and competitors.
3. **Changes in product lines.** Companies that drop or add products may be suggesting a new priority that gives you a reason to call.
4. **Advertising campaigns.** Have your competitors or customers changed advertising agencies or created a new approach to product promotion? New advertising campaigns or revamped

websites may signal a change that affects their need for your offering.

5. **Ad content.** The images and points of emphasis in online ads, TV commercials, and print ads are invaluable clues.

6. **Sales training.** The media may highlight new training endeavors. Is your prospective customer's company developing a sales training program of which you can make use?

Excellence in selling requires a keen awareness that the most challenging work often takes place during the pre-approach. However, all that work is what leads to the desired result—a yes. You must be prepared to answer the questions in the minds of new prospects. Exhibit 9.3 lists ten questions that prospective customers have, although they don't often volunteer to ask you these questions.

EXHIBIT 9.3 Ten Questions Your Prospects Are Wondering

1. What are you selling?
2. Why do I need it?
3. Who is your company, and are they reputable?
4. How much will it cost?
5. Who else is using it, and are they satisfied?
6. What kind of a person are you?
7. Is your price genuinely competitive?
8. How does your solution compare to the alternatives?
9. Why do I need it now?
10. What is your record for support and service?

Building Self-Confidence

A beneficial feature of doing pre-approach planning is that it builds self-confidence. Preparation gives you an added measure of confidence that is transmitted to the prospect. The opposite of this confidence is fear—and fear in selling comes from a lack and knowledge and preparation.

A specific plan for each prospect means you are more likely to be accepted. A purchasing agent for an international food processing plant who sees many salespeople described his reactions like this:

> *"I turn away salespeople every day who stumble in here like lost sheep. They hope that somehow they'll trip into an order. I*

"My self-esteem was so low, I just followed her around everywhere she would go."

get the impression that they figure I'll do the selling for them. I haven't got time for people like that."

Salespeople call on professionals whose job is to make sound decisions for their companies. These professionals expect to interact with another professional, not an incompetent amateur. If you walk confidently into a prospect's office and get down to business immediately without wasting the prospect's time with unnecessary questions, you increase the likelihood of a successful close. By emitting an air of self-confidence, you add to your perceived value.[7]

Setting Up the Sales Meeting

Pre-approach involves doing research, studying a company's online presence, and discovering other companies with whom they do business. It also encompasses the methods used to set up the face-to-face interview itself. There is more to consider than merely picking a day and time. Here are two factors to address that ensure you walk into an ideal situation when you meet with a prospect.

Timing

With a little research, you can determine the best time to call a prospect you have not previously met. For example, Powell Kenney, former vice-president of Clampitt Paper Company in Fort Worth, would see salespeople only between 5:30 and 8:30 a.m. He did not want his regular work routine disrupted by sales presentations.

Ordinarily, you can schedule sales calls for almost any time during the business day. Like Mr. Kenney, however, many prospects have a particular time when they will be more receptive to your presentation. Some like to see salespeople first thing in the morning. Others prefer to handle routine matters first. Fortunately, prospects have different preferences to the extent that salespeople can fill the workday with appointments.

If every buyer insisted on appointments before 8:30 a.m., you'd be in serious trouble. If a prospect does not seem to have a preference for a time of day to meet, try to discover when most salespeople call on this prospect. If it's the morning, schedule your call for late in the afternoon. Many executives work past 5:00 p.m. and will see you—and they may well appreciate your diligent work ethic.

Gaining Entry

Before you can arrange a face-to-face meeting, you must choose a way to contact the prospect and set up the interview. Appointments can be set up in several fundamental ways. You may send an email requesting an appointment, make contact through social media, call on the company in person, or call the prospect and schedule the interview. Sending an email to set an appointment may not produce a response, or it may require several back-and-forths to arrange a mutually convenient time. Unscheduled visits have a low probability of finding the prospect available for an interview.[8] Often, it involves a combination of several methods to land a face-to-face meeting.

Since email, texting, and social media contact continue to prevail as the desired forms of communication, it's easy to assume that phone calls don't work anymore.[9] That is not true. In fact, since picking up the phone and calling a person is becoming rarer, you can stand out by doing so. You may have to wade through an automated system, but eventually, you will get through to someone. After you make contact, in many cases, a few minutes are all you need to make an appointment.

Using the telephone successfully requires the same selling skills as a face-to-face call, plus some additional skills to meet the unique challenges of telephone use. Finding a prospect in a bad mood or under a time constraint, the surprise element of a call, and the lack of visual contact are some of the aspects that may prevent you from feeling as comfortable on the phone as you do face-to-face.

Gatekeepers. In an ideal world, you could pick up the phone or drop by a prospect's office and reach the decision-maker right away. That's not how it works in real life. There is often something standing in your way—or more like *someone*. You find yourself talking to a gatekeeper, someone who is trained to screen out unwanted sales calls or anything else that would waste a decision-maker's precious time.

Some salespeople think they need to "soften up" gatekeepers to get past them. However, a friendly smile and a little charm will only get you so far. For many gatekeepers, engaging them in small talk is the kiss of death. It signals that you're attempting to distract them, and they quickly shut you down.

You've got to give gatekeepers the credit they deserve. Statistics show that the majority of them have significant influence over the purchase of products and services. That is why it is a mistake to view them as barriers to overcome. In reality, they could be your greatest allies. Exhibit 9.4 outlines six ways to build rapport with gatekeepers.[10]

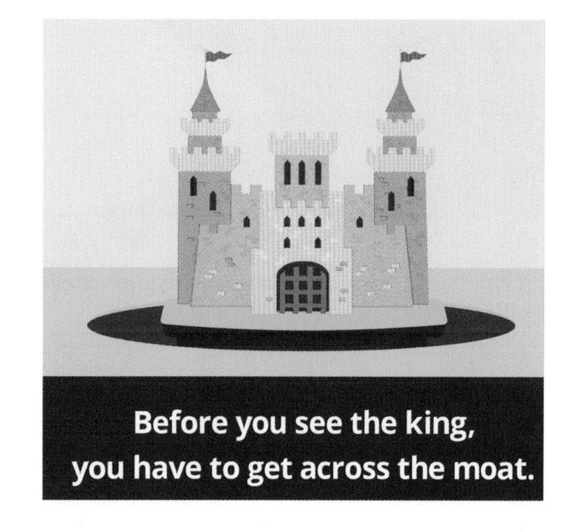
Before you see the king, you have to get across the moat.

Being charming and friendly with gatekeepers isn't enough. You need *substance.* Don't assume that a gatekeeper doesn't want to hear or wouldn't be able to understand

EXHIBIT 9.4 Build Rapport with Gatekeepers

1. **Adjust your attitude.** Gatekeepers appreciate respect, and they can recognize insincerity.
2. **Honesty is the best policy.** Don't lie to increase your chances of seeing their boss. Gatekeepers will inevitably discover your falsehoods, and once this happens, you have no chance of making a sale.
3. **Sell to the gatekeeper.** Gatekeepers influence buying decisions. If you show them how their company can benefit by using your product or service, the chances of you making the sale increase.
4. **Question gatekeepers.** Ask them what the needs and goals of their company are, and they might be willing to tell you.
5. **Be thoughtful.** Thank gatekeepers for their help, and also remember special occasions such as birthdays and holidays. Don't go overboard or use gifts as bribes.
6. **Be patient.** It may take longer than you expect to get through the door, but if you stay patient, your persistence will be rewarded.

what you have to say. Treat them as equals and send the message that you respect them. Who knows? They may even do some of the work for you and make your case in front of their boss.

Pre-Approach and Social Networking

There is no doubt that social media plays an influential role in business—but increasing your social media presence by no means guarantees results. To use your social networking accounts as viable sources of pre-approach information, you must ensure that potentially qualified prospects are among your friends, networks, and followers. Use these tips for maximizing the reach of the effectiveness of LinkedIn, Twitter, Facebook, and other sites to boost your pre-approach efforts.

Get Selectively LinkedIn

LinkedIn is the largest professional network in the world, and there is a great benefit to be had when used correctly. If you wish to get the pre-approach benefits of LinkedIn, you must be able to count on all of the people in your network. In other words, the people in your network matter (as opposed to those who merely like your Facebook page). Sometimes, that means turning down invitations to connect on LinkedIn, which is an unappealing thought to many people. Quality over quantity matters, especially on LinkedIn. When it comes to deciding whom to include in your LinkedIn network, here's a good rule of thumb:

If you wouldn't pick up the phone and call a person, do not add that person to your LinkedIn network.

LinkedIn has a wealth of information for researching potential clients. It's like a giant qualified prospect database. The information on prospects' profiles (and the people in their networks) can provide you with valuable clues on how best to appeal to them. You can also use this social network to determine who in your company's sphere of influence can introduce you to a prospect.[11]

So, know who you are connecting with rather than blindly accepting all requests, and steer clear of the automated requests that send a generic invitation like: "Sally Smith would like to connect with you on LinkedIn." It's much more effective to send a personal note along with the invitation.

Get to the Point on Twitter

Twitter can do some great things for salespeople who take the time to understand what it can and cannot do. Twitter was created as a way to share short messages as a "micro-blog," a mini-posting of useful information that is limited to 280 characters. The platform gives people a way to keep in touch with essential ideas, people, and companies without having to read overwhelming amounts of text.

"Do the people on Twitter really care how many times you went to the bathroom today?"

Do not be quick to equate the sheer number of Twitter followers to success. Do you have the *right* followers? Services like Klout.com measure influence not only by how many followers you have but whether those followers interact with you.[12] Do they re-tweet your messages? Or are they just following you in the hopes you'll follow them, so their numbers look significant to *their* audiences? Look for followers who talk about things that are relevant to your business or some other real connection, and those are the connections worth having.

Inspire Through Your Facebook Page

One of the most common barriers to getting the most out of Facebook is setting up the wrong type of account. If you don't get it right the first time, you'll find yourself writing a mass post later asking all your hard-earned followers to trail you as you switch accounts. If you join Facebook for the first time, you will initially set up an individual account. Once you're registered, you can then set up a group or page. Facebook Groups have some beneficial features, such as allowing you to email all members and make the group private. With Pages, anyone can like a page to show their support, and anyone can read posts with or without being a fan or liking your page.[13]

Work the characteristics of each of these sites to your advantage by approaching new contacts on LinkedIn, for example, via previously established professional connections in your industry and by interacting on a more informal basis with prospects through Twitter and Facebook. Once you build rapport, you can carry interactions over from one social site to another.

As with approaching potential customers in person, on the telephone, or through email, preemptive research and self-confidence can go a long way toward showing people that you understand their needs and that you are offering a valuable product or service.

Telephone Techniques

Smartphones are less about their actual call-making abilities anymore and more about, well, everything else. However, knowing how to make impactful phone calls is imperative for salespeople. Direct marketing expert Bob Stone defines telemarketing in this way:

> **TELEMARKETING** utilizes sophisticated telecommunications and information systems, combined with personal selling and servicing skills, to help companies keep in close contact with present and potential customers, increase sales, and enhance productivity.

It is a marketing discipline that uses telecommunications technology as part of a planned, organized, and managed marketing program that prominently features the use of personal selling, using non-face-to-face contacts.

Proper telephone usage helps you qualify prospects, budget time, and save money. Excellent telephone techniques also enhance your image and pre-condition prospects to receive you favorably. Phoning for an appointment implies that you are courteous and considerate of the prospect's time. The initial phone call helps to create a favorable selling situation because, just by agreeing to see you, the prospect indirectly indicates interest.

The use of the phone to set appointments is a genuine sales activity, not a necessary evil. Just remember what you are selling over the phone—and it's not your product. You are selling the prospect on the idea of granting you an appointment. You can call that your initial "mini-sale."

You can make multiple calls in a fraction of the time it takes to make personal visits. You will find that when you set an appointment over the phone, the in-person meeting will be far more positive and productive.

Making First Impressions

The quality, hesitation, volume, and strength of your voice all convey an image to people. The goal is to come across as sincere, honest, confident, knowledgeable, and likable. If you sound weak and tentative or use words like *well*, *sort-of*, *maybe*, or *perhaps*, that says to the prospect, "I'm not sure about what I'm doing, and this will probably be a waste of your time." Some salespeople even include phrases like, "Well, to be honest with you," which implies that they aren't always honest.

The #1 Mistake. Even more common than using weak words is another mistake. It's the most common mistake salespeople make over the phone and in person: Making it all about them and not the prospect. Consider how you would react to this type of phone call:

> *Hi, I'm Leonard, and I was born and raised on Long Island. I've been working here for almost ten years, and these guys are like my second family. Before I worked here, I lived abroad for a few years, which, as you can imagine, was amazing! But I knew I couldn't start a family over there, so I came back here and started my own company before I abandoned that dream and began pursuing...yadda, yadda, yadda."*

We are hard-wired to seek out people who are interested in us. Your prospects are no exception to this. So, when you start the call with who you are and what you do, it triggers their flight response, and they will be scheming for ways to end the call as soon as possible.

The #2 Mistake. Cold calling is *not* solely a numbers game. When you "smile and dial" someone about whom you know absolutely nothing, you've probably just blown a potential sale. If possible, don't make a phone call to someone with zero information. Use all of the pre-approach tools available to you: websites, press releases, social media, other customers, and anything and everything else!

The #3 Mistake. Don't improvise your calls. *You need a script.* It takes skill to disarm someone in 15 seconds or less, so you have to prepare and practice, so it doesn't sound scripted.

People buy from the people they like. Remember, you're projecting your personality over the phone.[14] How you speak can be as important as what you say. Put a smile in your voice, and the prospect can hear it. The most successful salespeople project positive voice qualities such as sincerity, courtesy, and confidence.

Evaluate Your Telephone Voice

Your voice makes an immediate impression that can portray you as friendly vs. distant, confident vs. timid, spontaneous vs. mechanical, and relaxed vs. nervous. How do you come across over the phone? If you aren't sure, record yourself on a phone call and evaluate these attributes:

Pitch. In ordinary speech, the pitch varies. These variations are known as inflection. The more *inflection* you use, the more enjoyable your tone of voice generally becomes. The tone of your voice is a gauge of confidence

and poise. Keep in mind that when you are under emotional stress, the pitch of your voice may rise and become shrill or strained.

Volume. Check the volume or loudness of your voice. You may even get a friend to help you determine your volume. Is it too soft or too loud? When people are tired or upset, their voices may fade, making it hard for others to hear them. Speak loudly enough to be heard, but not so powerfully that you sound excessively forceful.

Rate. If you speak too slowly, you'll lose the attention of the listener. Conversely, your listener won't be able to follow you if you speak too rapidly. In either case, your message won't get through.

Quality. The quality of your voice is its most distinctive and individual characteristic. It's where the essence of warmth, understanding, and likability come into play. Smiling as you speak enhances your vocal quality. Being angry, upset, or in a hurry negatively affects your vocal quality.

Articulation. The price of poor articulation is high, particularly in business. You must enunciate your words very clearly, or your listeners will misinterpret what you say. Faulty diction and incorrect word pronunciation give your listener the impression that you are sloppy, careless, and uninformed.

The telephone is one of the most powerful, efficient, and cost-effective business tools you have at your disposal. Telephone manners and etiquette are critical components of a professional image. Through experience, you'll develop your unique telephone style.

Organizing the Call

Inadequate preparation reduces the effectiveness of your phone delivery. Ask yourself these four questions to help you stay on track:[15]

1. **Why am I calling?** Is the goal of the phone call to set an appointment, upsell, follow-up, or respond to an inquiry?
2. **What is my proposal?** Your plan for the call should have two parts: 1. What you want from the person you are calling, and 2. What commitment you will make to that person.
3. **What would make this person grant my request?** Before calling, determine why the person you are calling would do what you are asking.
4. **How does my script sound?** Identify keywords or phrases in your sales call that you can emphasize to make your message more convincing and sincere.

Before you pick up the phone, go through a mental checklist to ensure that you are fully prepared. Exhibit 9.5 presents ten strategic checkpoints to consider when using the telephone to make appointments.

Dealing with Voicemail

Voicemail is a big part of selling. Prospects are often away from their desks and not able to answer the phone. When you get their voicemail, be prepared to leave a message. Don't give too much information that will allow prospects to make up their mind about you or what you are selling on the spot. Have a call to action in your message and give them a specific, compelling reason to call back, or to answer when you call again. Here are a few other tips for leaving voicemails:[16]

EXHIBIT 9.5 Secrets to Becoming a Telephone Superstar

1. Arrange a specific time each day to make calls and determine a particular number of calls to make during that time.
2. Arrange for privacy to avoid interruptions and make as many calls as you can in the allotted time.
3. Develop a well-written, structured script so that you know what to say before you call, but never make a canned spiel. You can avoid sounding canned through practice!
4. Verify that you are talking to the person that you intended to call. Be sure you have the correct pronunciation of the name and use it during the call.
5. Tell the prospect just enough to get the appointment. Just pique interest so that the prospect agrees to a meeting.
6. Convey excitement and enthusiasm with your voice. Give your voice the emotional feel of shaking hands over the telephone and smile. You can even try placing a mirror by the phone to watch your expression.
7. Never argue, but politely ask for the appointment. Always offer a choice of times so prospects can choose a time that is convenient for them.
8. Sell your name. Ask the prospect to write it down, so he or she remembers you when you arrive for the appointment.
9. Be courteous. Say thank you and begin sentences with phrases like, "May I ask" and "If I may."
10. Watch your language. Choose your words carefully for a more significant impact. Repetition of non-functional, filler expressions like, "I see," "uh-huh," "you know," and "awesome" are irritating and unprofessional.

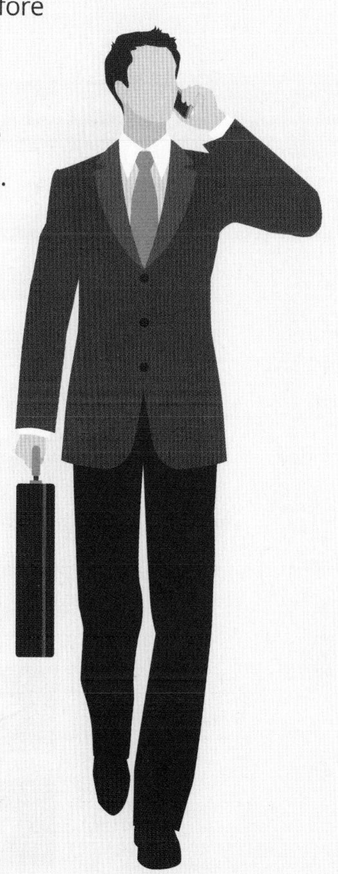

1. Give your number twice. If the listener doesn't write it down the first time, he or she gets a second chance without having to repeat the message.
2. Try to avoid leaving messages on a Friday afternoon, because messages left at that time are the least likely to be returned.
3. Monday mornings can also be ineffective times to leave a message as higher priorities demand attention, and your call may not be one of them.
4. Two of the best time windows in which to leave voicemails are 7:00 to 8:00 am and 4:30 to 6:30 pm.

The Six-Step Telephone Track

The key to using the telephone effectively is to engineer conversations that sound like typical dialogue. They should be two-sided, but simultaneously help people to sell themselves on seeing you. When you try to set an appointment by phone, you don't have the advantage of being able to show what a great product you offer or to communicate nonverbally. Instead, you need a careful strategy that allows the prospect to take an interest in what you're saying and agree to meet with you face-to-face. Use the six-step outline shown in Exhibit 9.6 to plan your appointment-setting calls so that the

EXHIBIT 9.6 **The Six-Step Telephone Track**

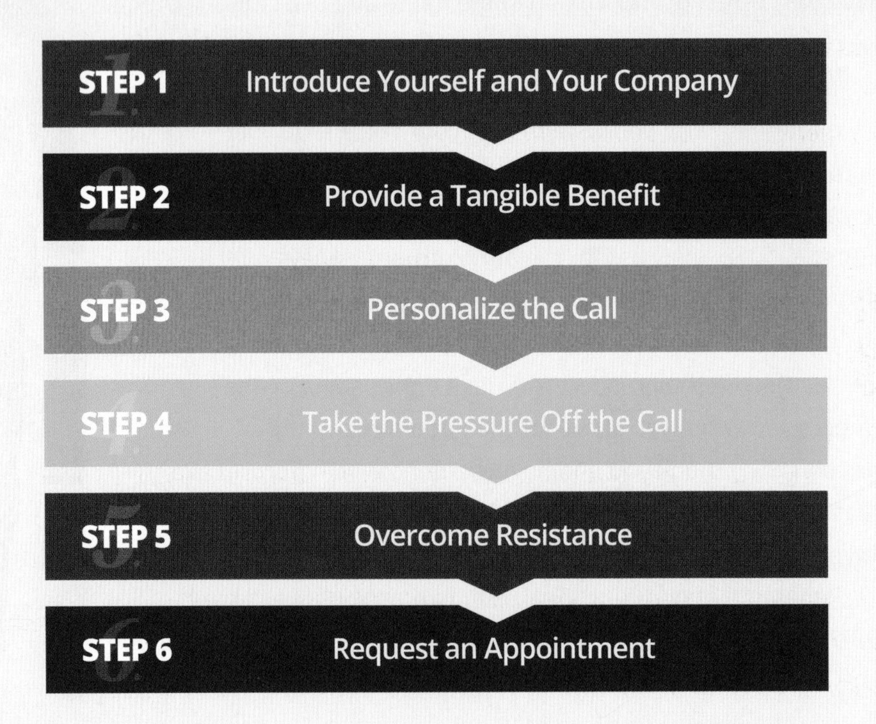
STEP 1 Introduce Yourself and Your Company
STEP 2 Provide a Tangible Benefit
STEP 3 Personalize the Call
STEP 4 Take the Pressure Off the Call
STEP 5 Overcome Resistance
STEP 6 Request an Appointment

next time you talk to prospects, you're sitting face-to-face with them.

STEP 1 Introduce Yourself and Your Company

The success of sales connections depends heavily on first impressions. When you place a call, the prospect will most likely make a judgment about you after your first 12 words.[17] How you introduce yourself, therefore, and what you say immediately after that is critically important. A weak or tentative opening puts you at a severe disadvantage throughout the rest of the call. Your opening words should be simple and to the point. They should tell who you are, who you represent, and confirm that you are speaking to the correct person:

Good morning, I'm George Costanza with Vandelay Industries. Is this Jay Peterman? Good!

Smile as you speak so that you transmit a warm, friendly personality. Watch the rate at which you speak. Prospects instinctively pay more attention to someone who speaks at a moderate and energetic rate.

STEP 2 Provide a Tangible Benefit

A phone call is an interruption of your prospect's day. To sell people on the idea of granting you an appointment, you must detach their attention from what they were doing or thinking when the phone rang and attract it to what you are saying. You've got to give them a real reason to stop and listen. Follow your introduction with a brief

"I don't have any sales experience, but I think I'd be very good at making cold calls!"

but hard-hitting benefit. Give just enough to capture the prospect's attention and avoid describing full details of any benefits you may present later in person:

I'm calling because we've recently helped several shipping companies, including Titan Transport, decrease their packing costs by as much as 20 percent.

In this statement, George mentioned another client and a fellow competitor in the international shipping business, Titan Transport. Mentioning a competitor will help bring the prospect into the conversation by introducing the thought, "Oh, that company is working with this person..." Just make sure you know that the prospect is familiar with the person or company you mention.

If you were calling someone because of a referral, this would be a good time to mention the person who referred you to this prospect. A respected referral source is often enough to get the prospective customer to hear you out politely. Then you must generate enough interest to motivate the prospect to agree to an appointment. Here is an example of how to use a referral in this step:

> *We recently started working with Reynolds International, and we were able to reduce their outbound freight costs by 22 percent last month. Their CEO, Murphy Reynolds, was so thrilled with the results that she asked me to get in touch with you and see whether we might also be able to help you.*

STEP 3 Personalize the Call

The next step is where all of that pre-approach you have done comes to good use! You now personalize the call by using information from your pre-approach research. In this example, George learned about the prospective company's margin pressures from an article in an industry-specific magazine. According to the article, a sudden spike in air cargo volume on Asia-to-U.S. routes in the last quarter placed a significant burden on international shipping businesses. The demand forced companies to drastically increase volumes at lower profitability rates to keep their heads above water. George now needs to present this information in a way that converts *attention* into *interest* and lets the prospect know that he is aware of their company's situation (and that this isn't just another cold call):

> *I know that at your company and others, there is tremendous pressure on margins these days, especially in the last quarter.*

The inclusion of this impactful, concise fact answers the all-important and unspoken question in the mind of every single one of your prospects: *"What's in it for me?"*[18] After you have established a legitimate purpose for the call, you are ready for the next step.

STEP 4

Take the Pressure off the Call

George has done an excellent job of making compelling and personalized statements, but the work is not over yet. Now it's time to take the pressure off the call and getting permission to continue. Never assume that it's okay to forge ahead. Make it simple and to the point:

> *May I ask you a few questions to see if there's any chance we could assist your company as well?*

Ultimately, the critical point that George successfully conveyed is that he is looking for a problem he *might* be able to solve. George disarmed his prospect by letting the prospective customer know that George only wanted to "see if there's any chance" that what he had to say could help their business.

Overcome Resistance

Using the telephone to set up appointments gives rise to two types of objections: An objection to receiving the telephone call and an objection to granting an interview. A prospect who was engaged in an activity before you called may feel irritated and wish to resume that activity. This prospect's goal is to get you off the phone by refusing to become interested in what you have to say.

If a prospect offers an objection at this point, remind them that there is no pressure to make any decision and that what you have to say may not even interest them—but it doesn't hurt to check! Here are two examples of how to word such a statement:

> *Not every company is right for our product. But my clients always tell*

me they're glad I checked. Do you have a minute for us to figure out whether or not it's worth our time to meet in person?

It may or may not be right for your company. When it is a fit, it saves most of my customers close to 20 percent on their shipping costs and increases their margins. May I ask you a couple of questions to see if this is worth looking into further?

Prospects who do not want to grant an interview often fear that they cannot successfully defend their ideas or decisions against an experienced salesperson. They are afraid that they *will* buy. Admitting that your product or service is not right for everyone can overcome this obstacle. Convey to your prospect that you want to find out *together* whether or not you can help him or her—and if you can't, then the conversation is over.

STEP 6 Request an Appointment

Remember that your goal is to secure an appointment with the prospect so that you can make a complete presentation later. If you launch into a full performance, the prospect can easily say, "I'm not interested" over the phone—and then you have nowhere to go. The conclusion could be much different when you give an excellent presentation in person. So, try the K.I.S.S. approach to setting the appointment: ***Keep It Simple, Salesperson!*** The telephone itself encourages brevity, so ask for the appointment confidently and directly.

After you ask another question or two to ensure that the prospect has some interest and saw value in your benefit statement, add this:

Most of my clients agree that it's best to go over the details in person. To make it easier for you, I can stop by next Monday or Tuesday in the morning for a few minutes. Which one works better for your calendar?

If those days don't work, but the prospect genuinely wants to meet with you, he or she will offer an alternative. If the prospective customer is not interested in meeting with you at all, you can try one more time to gain interest. Circle briefly back to any pain points you discovered through your pre-approach efforts (such as the profit margin pinch that George's prospect is experiencing). If they are still unwilling to meet, then you are on to the next call!

> **"Everything should be made as simple as possible, but not simpler."**
> *Albert Einstein*

When you combine the six-step telephone approach with confidence and friendliness, you are likely to find yourself getting face to face with receptive prospects. A well-written phone script should take three to four minutes at the most, and that's only if the prospect offers multiple objections, or in a better scenario, shows interest! With the proper pre-approach, each call can take a unique twist and keep you from sounding canned. You will hear, "I'm not interested," but you will also hear, "I'd like to meet with you." Persistence is the key—so keep smiling and dialing.

After the Call

One of two things will happen on a phone call: A prospect will either say yes or no to meeting with you. Either way, immediate action is required once you hang up the phone. Reach out within the next one to two business days to thank them for their time, regardless of whether you set an appointment. You may even ask more about their business needs to find out how you can share leads and help each other's businesses grow.

If the prospect agreed to meet: Confirm the date and time and send an invitation to confirm the meeting. You can also slip something in the mail—brochures and handwritten thank-you notes are useful items to send to prospects who agreed to meet with you. If the appointment is a week or more away, there's a higher chance the prospect will cancel on you as the conversation's details and reasons for meeting with you fade from their minds. Keep your ears and eyes out for ways to stay top of mind via mail, email, or social media.

If a prospect did not agree to meet: You could still send something to entice them to get on your email list or a flyer about a special promotion. If the conversation was pleasant enough, that "no" may become a "yes" someday with the right follow-up. Here are some great ways to turn a refusal on the phone into a customer down the road:

1. **Add them to your database.** Add anyone you speak with to your database (if appropriate) and make sure they get an email notice within a week or so. Do not add them to a mass email list unless they verbally agree to receive it or opt-in online.
2. **Make a creative impression.** If a highly qualified prospect will not agree to meet with you, drop by promotional products with your card, or send them in the mail. Make sure your promotional products stand out from your competition and are unique or memorable. However, this can be time-consuming, so reserve this type of activity for significant prospects.
3. **Systematize your follow-up.** Sort your database according to prospect classification (such as A, B, or C

prospects) and also by where you got the lead (such as at a networking event, via social media, or by referral) so that you can schedule personalized future communications. Send a direct mail piece to everyone in your database quarterly, and email them monthly at a minimum.[19]

Sometimes, the best thing you can do is drop a handwritten note in the mail from time to time. Whether or not a prospect has agreed to meet with you, this simple follow-up can add class and a personal touch. Notes are often more likely to get through to the person than an email, phone call, or a direct message on social media.

The Social Media Connection

CAN YOU USE SOCIAL MEDIA TO FOLLOW UP AFTER THE CALL?

After you connect with a new prospect on the phone, it's crucial to start deepening the relationship as quickly as possible. Social media is the perfect venue to accomplish this. After a successful (or unsuccessful) call, it's helpful for your prospects to be able to put a face with the voice they just heard on the phone.

Engaging with a new prospect on social media after an initial connection strikes a nice balance. Come on too strong with your sales pitch and a hard sell, and your prospects will go running. Engage too little by only following or visiting their profiles, and they'll feel like you are just doing reconnaissance.

The easiest way to find this balance is to focus on *delivering value*. Social media is not the appropriate medium to close a sale, but it is certainly the right place to start or continue one. By providing advice and helpful content, you can open a dialogue and establish yourself as a trusted resource.[20]

SUMMARY

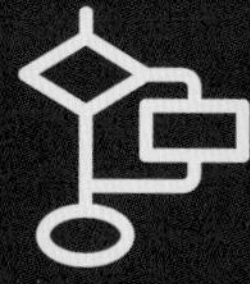

Planning and preparation are essential to securing an appointment for an in-person sales presentation.

Pre-approach is the various activities that provide the necessary personal and business information required to make productive contact with prospects.

Use pre-approach information during appointment-setting calls and also in email and online introductions.

Always use a telephone script but practice so that you internalize it to the point where it sounds natural.

The purpose of an initial phone call is to sell the prospect on the idea of granting an interview, not buying your product.

On the six-step telephone track, it's essential to customize the script based on the pre-approach you gathered before the call.

Take the pressure off phone calls by asking permission to continue and indicating that your offering may or may not be a fit.

After the call, follow up with both prospects who agreed to an appointment and those who did not.

Review Questions

1. What are the steps to follow in pre-approach planning?
2. What information do you need about a prospect before you call to request an appointment for a sales interview?
3. What are the ideal sources for obtaining information about a prospect?
4. In what way may a telephone call to request an appointment serve to qualify the prospect?
5. What advantages and disadvantages does calling for an appointment present regarding the first impression you make on the prospect?
6. What is the six-step framework for making a telephone presentation?
7. If the prospect asks you to describe your proposition over the telephone, how would you handle the situation?
8. Who should be in control of the flow of the pre-approach telephone call? How do you make sure leverage is in the proper hands?
9. How can a salesperson use social media in the pre-approach process?
10. Suppose that you call to make an appointment with a prospect. When the assistant answers, you say, "Mr. Steele, please, Joan Gray calling." If the secretary responds, "May I ask why you are calling?" what answer would you give? If you give your answer and then hear, "He's busy," what do you say then?

IN-CLASS EXERCISES

The following exercises help build teams, improve communication, and emphasize the real-world side of selling. They are meant to be challenging, to help you learn how to deal with problems that have no single right answer, and to use a variety of skills beyond those employed in a typical review question. Read and complete each activity. Then in the next class, discuss and compare answers.

EXERCISE 9.1 Phone Script

Divide the class into four-person teams. The primary objective is for each team to write a telephone script for a salesperson who aims to secure an appointment. Each team should share their script with the rest of the class either during a regular class session or online to receive constructive criticism. Each script should include the following features:

- Description of the caller's business and product or service offered.
- Pre-approach analysis of target's business, need for product/service, and person to whom the call is directed.
- Use of the six-step telephone track to structure the script.
- Use of the ten buyer questions (Exhibit 9.3) to structure anticipated objections.

Each team's script should be directed toward one of the following situations:

1. Arrange an appointment to meet with a new prospect for the first time.
2. Arrange an appointment to meet with an existing, dissatisfied customer.
3. Arrange an appointment to meet with an existing customer whose order for the product/ service is due for renewal.

The next class session, or a portion thereof, should be devoted to team discussion of their project and how they want to address it. The actual production of the script should be done outside of class and in a way that team members can consult with one another. A subsequent class session, or portion thereof, should be devoted to critiquing selected scripts.

EXERCISE 9.2 Screening Prospects

For this exercise, pair up with another student. Often, the degree and nature of pre-approach planning vary by the general business field. Your task in this role play is for you and your partner to interview a salesperson in financial services (financial planning, insurance, brokerage firm, bank, etc.). Your objective is to learn how this salesperson goes about gathering and using information about prospects before approaching them. What information do they seek to discover? How? How do they use the information to prepare for an initial approach?

If this salesperson claims never to gather information before calling on prospects, that, too, is vital information for you! Your next question should be, "Why not?" Jot down the results of your interview and be prepared to report and discuss them in class or online.

Case Studies

The following case studies present you with selling scenarios that require you to apply the critical skills discussed in the chapter and give you training through practical learning situations. They are meant to be both engaging and challenging, and like the exercises, don't have one right answer.

CASE 9.1—Crossing the Moat

Rich Cohen sells paint. Although his job might not sound glamorous to some, he enjoys the challenge since it involves his skills as a chemical engineer as well as a marketer. The problem is that Rich isn't selling as much paint as he used to. And the company's owner is becoming disturbed by the falloff in business. As he recently remarked to Rich, "We need more new business. We can't subsist merely on our existing base since many of them have cut back because of the recession."

From his extensive preparatory research about prospective clients, Rich knows that many could use his company's product, especially the recently developed exterior paints that stand up to northeastern winters much better. But over the past several months, Rich has developed a rather long list of potential clients with whom he has been unable to arrange an appointment. Once he gets an appointment, Rich is capable, but getting the meeting is another matter.

Recently, over drinks after a tough week, Rich confided in one of his buddies at the company, Millard, who seems to have an easier time generating new business in his territory.

"I don't get it, Millard. Why won't these guys see me? If I get 20 minutes, I can show 'em how to cut down on their do-overs and save themselves a ton of money."

"Well, Rich. I've always said, 'Before you can see the king, you have to get across the moat.'"

"What does that mean?"

"It means that you have to deal with the person who controls the drawbridge. If that person doesn't lower the bridge, you never get to speak to the king."

"And how do I do that? Whenever I call, I can hear the grumpiness on the other end of the phone. They always bluntly tell me that their boss isn't accepting calls, is busy, is out of the office, blah, blah, blah."

"Then sell the bridge-keeper, Rich. Once

you help that person with their problem, they'll escort you across that bridge and right into the throne room!"

As he drove home, Rich began to develop a plan of action that depended on asking gatekeepers ("bridge keepers") about their problems. Rich figured that if he could make their life a little easier, a little more pleasant, his chances of seeing their boss would improve.

What do you think Rich should include in his plan? What sort of questions should he ask the next administrative assistant who answers his call? How much and what kind of information should Rich provide the assistant? How can Rich demonstrate genuine empathy without offending the all-important bridge-keeper?

CASE 9.2—Gossip or Useful Information?

"Hey! Guess what I heard?" Running to catch up with Nancy, Hank was out of breath.

"What?" Nancy replied, wishing that Hank would dial it back a little.

"Long Meadow is merging with LD Mobile Homes! Do you know what that means?" Hank exclaimed.

"Well, it means that one of our clients is disappearing," Nancy answered. "What else?"

"No, no! You don't get it!" yelled Hank. He was becoming annoying. "We'll now have a shot at LD's business. We've never been able even to get an appointment before."

"What makes you think they'll see us now?" Nancy asked evenly. But her mind was turning. Her insurance company was, perhaps, about to lose a client; instead, she saw an opportunity to gain an even larger account. She wasn't sure how Hank knew about the merger, and she didn't want to know. Now, however, presuming that Hank's outburst was reliable, she needed a plan to turn his gossip into reliable information that would elicit an appointment.

What information does Nancy need to gather? Presuming that the merger is still a secret, how should she go about obtaining the necessary information to approach LD Mobile Homes? What strategies should Nancy employ? And when should she make her initial approach?

THE EIGHT-STEP RELATIONSHIP SELLING CYCLE

PHASE 1

1. Prospecting
Chapter 8

2. Pre-Approach
Chapter 9

3. **Approach**

4. Need Discovery
Chapter 11

5. Presentation
Chapter 12

6. Objections
Chapter 13

7. Close
Chapter 14

PHASE 3

8. Follow-Up
Chapter 15

THE APPROACH: MAKE THE RIGHT FIRST IMPRESSION

OVERVIEW

This chapter focuses on step three of the Relationship Selling Cycle. This step includes what are perhaps the most crucial elements of your face-to-face time with prospects, which are the first few minutes (even seconds) of your encounter. You will learn how to introduce yourself in a way that builds trust and credibility as we continue to focus on growing your reputation as an expert in your field. You've only got one chance to make a great first impression, and the approach is your chance to let prospects know that you and your solution is the right choice.

OBJECTIVES

- Discover the purpose of the approach.
- Learn the importance of first impressions and ways to control them as a means of improving your sales performance.
- Understand how nonverbal language affects your ability to establish rapport with a prospect.
- Examine the elements of the greeting and how to control them.
- Discover ways to get the attention and capture the interest of the prospect.
- Explore different types of approaches and the best circumstances in which to use each one.

Setting the Mood

You did your homework, and your prospecting and pre-approach efforts uncovered potential customers. You have successfully arranged a personal meeting with a prospect. So, now what? What happens during the opening of the face-to-face encounter profoundly affects the success of the entire presentation and your ability to get a commitment to buy.

The *approach* is step three of the Relationship Selling Cycle, and it represents the first moments of face-to-face contact with a prospect. More importantly, it is the salesperson's opportunity to set the mood of the presentation and the relationship with the customer.

The approach is the point of the selling process where the sales professional meets the prospect, begins to establish rapport, and asks questions to learn more about the prospect and his or her needs.[1] The approach is crucial because it determines the character of your relationship with a prospective customer, including how receptive the prospect will be to your presentation and whether the close will be challenging or natural.

Although the overall success of the interview depends on more than the approach, an effective approach creates a favorable sales environment. Although we will discuss the approach in the context of the first call on a new prospect, every meeting with a prospect or customer technically includes an approach, or a chance to make a good impression.

Salespeople often overlook the importance of the approach or take it for granted. They tend to use the same approach over and over, but prospects and situations are not the same. Instead, salespeople should practice using various types of approaches that fit the needs of a specific situation, whether calling on new prospects or established customers. An effective approach achieves four key objectives:

1. To make a favorable or positive impression.
2. To gain the prospect's undivided attention.
3. To develop a real interest in your proposition.
4. To lead smoothly into the need discovery step.

The Right First Impression

In his book, *Contact: The First Four Minutes*, Leonard Zunin says that the first four minutes of initial contact with a prospect is crucial. He suggests that four minutes is the average time a prospect takes to decide whether to buy from you. Others say it takes even less time than that. However long it takes, one thing is sure: prospects start judging you the moment you walk into the meeting.[2] So, impress them with your polite manners, good diction, and professional attire. When you look and act like a professional, prospects begin to trust you.

People make quick decisions based on feelings, emotions, or hunches. The more positive their feelings, the more they hear and accept what you say. The opening moments of the approach must be designed to create an atmosphere of trust. The first ten words you speak will reveal volumes about you.[3]

The initial impression you make on a new prospect is much like a homebuyer who looks at a potential home for the first time. Sellers and their real estate agents go to great lengths to present the house in the best light possible through a process called *staging*. Staging things as seemingly insignificant as the optimal location of the furniture and other items in the seller's home can make a difference between a sale or no sale.[4] Remember that this is a business meeting, not a personal lunch with a close friend. You must put your best foot forward from the beginning to ensure that prospects haven't mentally said "no" before they ever hear your presentation.

Successful salespeople know how to make other people feel important. It does not matter how knowledgeable they are about their product lines or how many closing techniques they have memorized. Unless they earn their prospect's trust and confidence, they are not going to make the sale—period.

If you want to make sincere connections with prospects and customers, you must be able to work effectively, even in the presence of a personality clash. You also have to temper the first impressions you make about others.

Spend some time and look further before making an unalterable judgment.

There's something about an excellent initial person-to-person contact that instinctively leads to more sales.

Prospects watch and evaluate virtually every personal characteristic you have, so your approach must be impeccable.[5] Positive first impressions count. Here are some guidelines for making the first impression a favorable one. *After all, you never get a second chance to make a good first impression.*[6]

Visual Factors

- Correct visible distractions (ragged briefcase, a messy car, inappropriate attire or grooming).
- Pay attention to your body language.
- Don't wear items that advertise your membership in an organization that may not be admired by some people.

Professional Habits

- Be prompt, or even early.
- State the purpose of your call right away.
- Make it clear that you are not going to waste the prospect's time.

Building Rapport

- Pronounce names correctly. A person's name is their unique identifier; mispronouncing it takes away some of their status.
- If you pay the prospect a compliment, make it specific and sincere.
- Look for common ground like mutual friends, membership in the same groups, or similar hobbies.

Physical Actions

- Shake hands; maintain eye contact; use the prospect's name.
- Refrain from smoking, chewing gum, or using offensive language.
- Respect the prospect's personal space.

Although first impressions may be reasonably reliable guideposts for the feelings you leave with a prospect, first impressions do have some weaknesses:

1. They are likely to be based on feelings and emotions.
2. All behavior traits do not show up at once, and an initial short interview may not provide enough time for all characteristics (either favorable or unfavorable) to surface.

3. The prospect may deliberately control behavior and allow you to see only certain personality traits.
4. An event immediately preceding the interview may strongly influence the prospect's current behavior.

Be willing to wait before you conclude that you and a prospect are experiencing a personality conflict that you cannot overcome. Your job is to establish rapport, build confidence, and make the prospect feel comfortable. Do everything in your power to satisfy the needs of your prospects and refuse to allow first impressions to prevent a mutually beneficial sales experience.

Nonverbal Language

Nonverbal language includes the various aspects—grooming, clothing, accessories, posture, tone of voice, and time and space aspects—that vitally affect first impressions. Although nonverbal factors provide limited or shallow insight into the actual person, people use them every day to make snap judgments about others.

Salespeople must be sure the statements they make with their nonverbal language are favorable since impressions formed during the first few minutes of an encounter last indefinitely. Successful salespeople increase the odds in their favor by taking advantage of the power of first impressions. *Visual impressions* almost always come first. Fortunately, you can do a lot to shape the visual impact you make when a prospect first sees you.

Projecting an Image

You want your clothes to command respect, inspire credibility, and create trust. You must come across as the authority on the product or service you offer.[7] Your clothes speak volumes about you, your company, your work, and how you relate to customers.

When you dress appropriately, you feel good about yourself. When you are confident, prospects unconsciously interpret that confidence as trustworthiness.[8] Appearance is also significant because a prospect's initial attention is focused on you rather than your product. If you want to *be* successful, you must *look* successful. A salesperson who wears an ill-fitting, wrinkled suit, for example, creates a negative impression and sets up this line of thinking in the mind of the prospect:

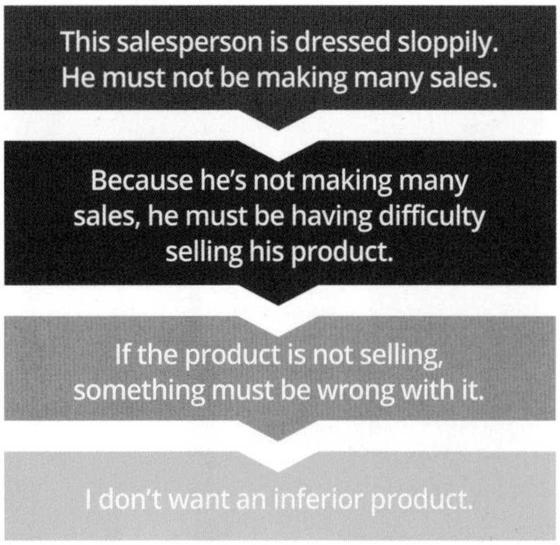

This salesperson is dressed sloppily. He must not be making many sales.

Because he's not making many sales, he must be having difficulty selling his product.

If the product is not selling, something must be wrong with it.

I don't want an inferior product.

Look The Part. You must look the part of a professional to be viewed as one. Lois Frankel, author of the bestselling *Nice Girls Don't Get the Corner Office*, says that research shows about 60 percent of our credibility comes from how we look.[9] Personal appearance and behavior are the most accessible areas to address on the road to greater success. Yet, all too often, sales professionals choose to ignore these aspects.

Unspoken rules for appropriate dress extend into every aspect of professional life. When you go to the doctor, you want the doctor to be dressed in a manner that projects his authority and knowledge. You wouldn't trust a surgeon to operate on you who is wearing flip-flops and a tank top. Then how can you expect a prospect to buy your product or service if you don't look the part? Dress in such a way that commands respect and credibility.

Your objective is to focus the prospect's attention on the benefits of buying your product or service. Anything that detracts from that focus works against you. Whether you are meeting at the prospect's office, your office, a neutral location, or the prospect's home, always look professional. Pay attention to the crispness and cleanliness of your clothing, and ensure that you do not look sloppy.

There are two sets of guidelines for appropriate attire that fits many situations. The first is *business casual*, which is a style of clothing that is less formal than traditional business wear but is still intended to give a professional and businesslike impression.[10] The second is *dressy casual*, which is often confused with business casual. Dressy casual clothing is not all that different from what is typically described as business casual but has a bit more informality.

For men, the look is very similar, although the clothing might be more conservative for a business casual event. Women's clothing tends to be a little more dressed up; a modest top and skirt might be worn instead of a suit, for example. A woman might also wear more jewelry than she would for business casual. Always consider the nature of the meeting or event when choosing an outfit from the following guidelines:

Business Casual for Men:

- Sport coat or blazer with slacks or khakis, professionally laundered and pressed
- Professionally laundered and pressed collared shirt, optional tie
- Laundered and pressed polo or golf shirt
- Loafers or Oxford-style shoes with dress socks and matching belt

Business Casual for Women:

- Knee-length or longer skirt, khakis or pants
- Modest top or sweater
- Conservative dress
- Dress shoes or heels (no flip flops)

Dressy Casual for Men:

- Seasonal sport coat or blazer, and slacks
- Dress shirt, casual button-down shirt, open-collar or polo shirt
- Optional tie

Dressy Casual for Women:

- Dress
- Skirt and dressy top
- Dressy pants outfit
- Suit with dressy top

Business casual style is not intended to convey a lack of professionalism, just a more comfortable, perhaps less dull way of projecting one's best. "Professional" is the keyword to remember when dressing business casual. Do not dress too casually. Instead, make sure your clothes reflect your position and the message you wish to convey to your clients.

People feel comfortable dealing with those who appear to fit into their lifestyle. If your clothes are too formal, you may cause the prospect to feel intimidated. Conversely, if you dress too casually, wear distracting clothing or jewelry, or look disheveled, such actions may cause prospective customers to sense that you do not consider this meeting to be important.

We all have a million things on our minds. For you, one of the dominating thoughts is, "How can I grow my business and my customer base?" For your prospects, they want to know, *"Why should I do business with you when there are ten salespeople in line right behind you?"* Hopefully, you are ready to answer that question with passion and conviction. But also remember this:

You are the ambassador of your company. No matter how much you may believe your offering sells itself, your appearance is what sells it first.

The Handshake

Your voice inflection and pronunciation and how you shake hands are as important as what you say. Make sure not to inflect your voice up at the end of each sentence. You must project yourself as a leader, not as insecure or apologetic. Confidence signals to the prospect that you believe in what you sell. Do you stand behind what you sell, or are you just trying to pay the bills?

> "Leadership has less to do with position than it has with disposition."
> *John Maxwell*

When combined with your tone of voice and facial expression, your handshake reveals to a prospect your mood. The business handshake is an essential selling technique to make a positive lasting impression. When the first handshake with a prospect is a firm one, it forms a solid foundation for a strong business relationship.[11] Here are some guidelines for effective handshakes:

"Of course I remember you. You're the salesman with the firm handshake."

The Proper Greeting

To increase the odds of making a good impression during the meet-and-greet, use the business etiquette "Rule of Ten." The first ten words you speak should include a form of thanks, as in, "Good morning, Mrs. Robertson. Thank you for agreeing to see me," or "Good afternoon, Ernie. It's a pleasure to meet you."

Shaking Hands Like a Pro

- Maintain eye contact for the duration of the handshake.
- You may wait for the prospect to initiate the handshake since some people have germ phobias or prefer not to be touched.
- If your palm tends to be damp, carry a small handkerchief with powder and pat your hand several times just before entering the meeting.
- Apply firm, consistent pressure on the hand and avoid limp-wristed, wet-fish, or bone-crusher handshakes.
- Hands should meet at an equal distance between you and the prospect in a vertical position. If your hand is over the prospect's, you are signaling dominant intentions. If your hand is on the bottom, you are indicating a submissive nature.

Casual questions like "How are you?" have lost all semblance of meaning. How does the prospect respond? They will always say, "Great" or "Fine," but what if the person is not feeling great, and what if the business is not doing well? If a prospect covers up real feelings with a conventional answer, a vague sense of uneasiness may result from the untruth.

When a prospect asks, "How are you doing?" come up with a different response delivered with a smile on your face and enthusiasm in your voice. For example, instead of responding with the typical "Fine," you can say, "Fantastic!" Your prospects will appreciate your positive attitude—and enthusiasm is an excellent catalyst for making sales.

A proper greeting is not just about a friendly face or the appropriate words. Appealing surroundings also help make a positive impression. Sometimes the location is out of your control, especially if you are meeting at their office. However, if you have the opportunity to select the meeting location, find a spot that is warm and inviting, and one in which you will not have to shout. Salespeople often meet clients at coffee shops. These are great neutral locations that have free Wi-Fi, which comes in handy if you need to access a web-based presentation. You may want to avoid coffee shops around the busiest times of the day (early morning and lunch), or

The Social Media Connection

HOW INSTAGRAM AND FACEBOOK CAN MAKE THE FIRST MEETING BETTER

People love posting pictures online. There is no limit to the kinds of images people post, from pictures of their family activities to pets, hobbies, favorite destinations, and more. Luckily for a salesperson, these online pictures can be a significant clue as to how the prospect presents himself or herself. They provide you with an excellent opportunity to see how a person dresses and what type of attire is most comfortable for him or her.

Keep in mind that casual pictures with family don't tell the whole story. Instead, look for pictures of the prospect at work or work-related functions.

People also love to tag their locations when they post. These location tags can be great clues as to where a prospect likes to have coffee or lunch. If the initial meeting is at a neutral location, it may be wise to pick a place that you know the prospect enjoys. Social media comments and photos may give you a clue as to some of the best places to meet.

outside distractions could diminish any good impression you attempt to make.[12]

Use the Prospect's Name

People do not like to have their names forgotten, misspelled, or mispronounced. Typically, when we meet someone, we hear our name, but we may or may not hear the other person's name. If we forget a name or mispronounce it, we send out this message: "I care more about me than I do about you."

Imagine how a prospect would feel if you said, *"So, Mrs., uh, excuse me (look down at the calendar reminder on the phone), uh, Mr. Hill, I mean, Mr. Lill."* The prospect would probably stiffen, the environment turn frosty, and you may well walk out without an order.[13] Now recall how pleased you were when someone remembered your name after a casual meeting several weeks ago. You would stand in line to do business with such a person.

Improving your memory is not as difficult as it may seem. Plenty of resources are available to help you devise a method to correct a careless memory for names. Exhibit 10.1 gives some suggestions for remembering names.

> **"Remember that a person's name is to that person the sweetest and most important sound in any language."**
>
> *Dale Carnegie*

"You're a pretty good salesman; except for the nine times you called me Wallet instead of Walter."

Small Talk or Get Down to Business

In the initial face-to-face meeting, both parties may experience some *relationship tension.* Prospects fear being sold something they do not want, and salespeople face the fear of being rejected. The opening few minutes of conversation are designed to find a comfort level for both parties so that you can quickly establish rapport. The purpose of small talk at the opening of the interview is to set a positive tone that breaks the ice and eases tensions. Small talk could be a discussion of topics entirely unrelated to what you are selling. Still, it's not just an idle conversation—it's *chit-chat with a purpose.* Here are some basic questions

EXHIBIT 10.1 **How to Remember Customers' Names**

When someone you just met remembers your name the next time you see each other again, it's a special feeling. Give your donors the gift of hearing their names, pronounced correctly, over and over again.

LEARN.
Ask to have the name repeated, even spelled. It will impress the person.

CONCENTRATE.
Look for characteristics that distinguish this person from others.

ASSOCIATE.
Relate a characteristic with some gimmick to help you recall the name.

OBSERVE.
Study people regularly to strengthen your ability to see characteristics and practice your imagination.

REPEAT.
Use the prospect's name numerous times during the interview.

that are non-threatening, easy to answer, and objective:

1. Are you a native of this area?
2. Where did you go to school?
3. What are your favorite weekend activities?

This socializing at the beginning of the interview eases tension and may give you some insight into your prospect's behavioral style. It warms up a cold environment and has the side benefit of providing additional information about the prospective customer. If the prospect seems withdrawn or even hostile, this warm-up conversation helps you determine whether that is the person's real personality or whether you have arrived on an especially bad day.

Speaker and author James Malinchak teaches a simple rhyme to remember before approaching a new prospect: "*When you meet someone new, they don't want to talk about you.*" People love to tell you about what they do on the weekends, their accomplishments, or their families. So, memorize this rhyme, and it will remind you to let your prospects and customers talk about themselves or their interests.

This non-selling conversation is essential. An ideal topic for chit-chat is one that relaxes the prospect, is of personal importance, and relates, if possible, to your objective so that you can move smoothly into the attention getter and then into need discovery.[14]

People have no confidence in salespeople who are only interested in themselves, who seek to use their customers instead of being useful to their customers.

Getting Their Attention

Getting a prospect's attention is more than a gimmick. Prospects may still be thinking, "What does this person want? Why should I allow my work to be interrupted?" Unless prospects want to listen, they won't—so give them a reason. Much like magazines use attention-grabbing headlines, work to develop an attention-getting opening that breaks through their preoccupation, and focuses prospects' attention on you. You can use two basic methods of getting attention: *Appealing to the senses and introducing a benefit.*

Appeal to the Senses. An appeal to the senses gets the prospect involved in the presentation. Be sure to use a little dramatization. Show something they can see; hand them something to hold.

Introduce a Benefit. Introduce a benefit through a statement that relates to the prospect's need for your product or service.

Highlight the value of the product or service, especially in terms of how it may save prospects their most valuable resources—time and money. If you can modify the product to suit your prospect's particular needs, also be sure to outline this option.

Suit the Approach to the Person

Most people have more work than they can hope to complete during regular working hours. Individual consumers, purchasing agents, engineers—anyone a sales rep might contact—feel time pressure and naturally regard you as an intruder. Prospects may react with resentment toward anyone who appears intent upon "stealing" precious time to engage in small talk. How much or how little time you give to small talk or chit-chat depends on the prospect's behavioral style, the circumstances of the moment, and the nature of your visit. If you sense that the prospect wants to get on with the interview, move on to your presentation.

An effective attention-getting statement requires preparation. If you have done your homework and gathered pre-approach information, you already have some idea about the needs and behavioral style of the prospect. If you spend a few minutes in small-talk, you gain further clues to confirm or adjust your information. Use what you know to plan a capable attention-getting device to introduce the heart of your presentation. Exhibit 10.2 suggests ways to gain prospects' attention by appealing to their behavioral styles during your initial exchange.[15]

EXHIBIT 10.2 Using Behavioral Styles to Choose the Right Approach

EXPRESSIVE: **Open in terms of long-range goals or implications.**
I would like to show you how our innovative service will help your department reach its long-term potential.

ANALYTICAL: **Open in precise terms.**
I would like to give you a brief background on our service. Then we'll discuss how it will reduce your overhead, increase your productivity, and improve your profit margin by 10 percent.

AMIABLE: **Open in supportive, people-oriented terms.**
I am aware of some of the pressing concerns you must be facing at this time, and I believe our service will help you and your people overcome some of these problems.

DRIVER: **Open in results-oriented terms.**
Our automated-calling software could increase your sales by 15 percent in just six months. Are you interested? (Be prepared to prove your statement.)

"*Trust me.* You don't want that little, inexpensive, easy-to-use gadget. What you want is *this*."

Build a Foundation of Trust

As the business world grows more complex and information becomes more accessible and more overwhelming, buyers aren't looking for someone with fact-sheet-style knowledge. No one has time for salespeople like that anymore. They want someone who they can trust to lead them through unfamiliar territory.

You have the product and company knowledge you need. Still, when it comes to gaining attention, and more importantly, *earning trust* during the initial meeting or meetings, it can be a tricky situation. Buyers know that you're there to make a sale. So, how can you convey that you are there to serve *their* interests first instead of your own? To answer that question (and discover the secret ingredient for building trust), let's read about Annie:

Annie sells a sophisticated line of cloud computing solutions to small and medium-sized enterprises. At her first appointment of the day, her prospect Doug cuts to the chase. "Look, Annie, I'll be the first to tell you that I don't know much about this technology. All this cloud stuff is kind of over my head, pardon the pun."

Annie chuckles (it's not the first time she's heard that one) as Doug continues. "You're the sixth or seventh tech salesperson I've had in here, and so far, everyone seems to be good at telling me what their stuff can do. But what I need to know is what I should do."

Doug wants someone to tell him what he needs. He doesn't need another lesson on how to convert to cloud servers. How can

Annie convince Doug that he can trust her to tell him what to do without him even fully understanding the product?

What is the primary thing standing in the way of Doug trusting Annie (and of your buyers trusting you)? Let's examine this differently: There is a personal stylist named Katrina, who works in an upscale department store selling designer suits to men. Katrina has already made almost double what the other stylists have made so far this year. We are going to listen in during one of her sessions to find out how she's doing it:

> *Her new customer John just arrived and is contemplating which suit to try on first. As he picks out one of the most expensive suits and holds it up, Katrina touches his arm. She slowly and deliberately looks around to make sure no one is listening. She whispers, "My supervisor would fire me if he heard me telling you this, but the only advantage you'll be getting with that suit is the brand name. That designer recently changed manufacturers, and the quality isn't what it used to be." Then she carefully checks for prying eyes again before suggesting a much less expensive alternative.*

What did she do? She gave a signal (albeit a manipulative one) to John that she's looking out for his best interests with no thought to her now-diminished commissions.

All prospects are worried about being *taken*. Katrina used this fact to her advantage by suggesting something that appeared to contradict her desire for financial gain. By doing this at the beginning, she has influenced how John will view every recommendation that she gives him from that point on. So, when she suggests the most expensive ties, the most expensive shoes, the most costly belts, and the unnecessary wallet, he assumes she is still looking out for him.

Is Katrina looking out for John? In Katrina's case, she sent a *false signal.* If John comes back and sees Katrina go into her "I

could get fired for this" act, he'll know he got taken. Maybe she won't care because she got her commission. But sooner or later, clients will catch on to her game.

What's the difference between Katrina's tactics and sincerely putting the buyer's needs first? It's the secret ingredient for gaining trust: *integrity*. Integrity is not a short-term gimmick. It's a long-term commitment that builds your authority over the long haul. Let's see what happens when Annie puts Doug's interests first:

> *Annie has a wide range of cloud capabilities, and one of them is a starter package with the basic functionality that fits most of her clients' needs. She also has the "bells and whistles" package, complete with the high price tag and high margins. Doug asks about that package first because they are expanding, and he thinks they'll need the capabilities soon.*
>
> *Annie shoots him straight. "That package requires a fully staffed IT department, and I remember you saying your IT department is a one-person team. Let's review your current IT capabilities —we may find that the starter package fits you better right now. You can always upgrade later."*

Did Annie talk herself out of a big commission? No. She knows the most expensive package won't work for him, given his current situation. Doug could make it work, but it would mean incurring some unbudgeted IT costs. She tells Doug the truth and boosts her credibility—and proves the weight of her integrity.

Doug may go with the basic package after she goes through her presentation, or he may decide to ramp things up now. Whatever he decides, it will be a choice made with all the facts because his trusted advisor Annie has his best interests at heart.

Types of Approaches

Because every prospect and every selling situation is different, you must have several approach methods available to use the one that best fits the particular circumstance. Learn the principles of each of the different types of approaches so that you can use the one that is most appropriate for a specific situation. How many approach techniques are enough? The answer is simple—you cannot have too many. Different social styles, current moods, and more necessitate that you prepare an opening for every situation. If you sense that a prospect is having a bad day, for

example, you may have to deviate from the opening and presentation you had planned.

Before launching into any approach before your presentation, make sure you have established a sufficient level of rapport. Here are eight possible approaches to consider:

1. Relevant Benefit Approach

This approach is useful when you already know a specific "pain point" based on a prospect's answers to your questions or your pre-approach efforts. *Pain* is a reminder that unless your prospect needs to solve a problem, they are not going to buy a product or service. The benefit statement should be unique and appeal to the prospect's dominant buying motive. It should be sincere and must never sound like a gimmick. Something new and different about your product or service that paves the way for the rest of the interview is a sound choice.

> *Thank you again, Ms. Robinson, for agreeing to see me today. Based on our discussion so far, I believe our product will provide you with increased IT capacities without you having to hire additional IT employees.*

Because salespeople want to offer tangible value to their customers, presenting this benefit statement may well cause the prospect to seek more information. Such a statement often sparks questions from the prospective customer that lead directly into the presentation. It also shows that you have been listening to what the prospect has been saying.

2. Curiosity Approach

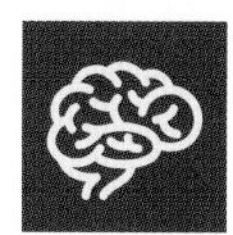

The curiosity approach works best when you know something about the prospect's needs and why they agreed to meet with you in the first place. Some behavioral styles, particularly analyticals and drivers, may find this approach unappealing (they may think it sounds "gimmicky"). Used sensibly, however, this approach is a compelling presentation opener. Suppose you are selling a telecommuting software package so a sales force can get up-to-date information on their laptops when they are out in the field selling. You might say something like this:

> *Mr. Sherrill, have you ever been in a meeting, and someone brings you a hard copy of a report analyzing a new competitive product? Do you know how much time you are losing by having to scan and email that report to share with your sales team?*

3. Question Approach

The question approach quickly establishes two-way communication. It enables you to investigate the prospect's needs and apply the benefits of your product or service to those expressed needs. This type of approach suggests your interest in the prospect's problems and draws attention to the need to identify problems.

You may frame a leading question designed to obtain a mental commitment from the prospect and at the same time, show a significant benefit. Here are two examples of how you can do this:

Mr. Dyer, would you like to have distinctive-looking, quality-driven reports, and the most up-to-date pricing information to share with your customers?

••••••

Do you feel you could get more accomplished in meetings if you had complete and current information at your fingertips? Wouldn't you also like the capability to edit that information quickly, thus enabling you to provide your customers with the best support possible?

4. Qualifying Question Approach

This variation of the question approach seeks a commitment from the prospect. The qualifying question approach asks potential customers to consider buying the product. It can help determine whether you have a candidate who feels cold, lukewarm, or red hot about your opportunity. Here are two illustrations of this technique:

Jordan, if I can satisfactorily demonstrate to you that our service will save you at least $5,000 within the next three months, would you do business with us?

••••••

Will, I am looking for individuals who have the discretionary funds to invest in an opportunity that will produce a return on their investment of at least 15 percent. If I can show you the evidence to support this claim, would you be willing to invest with us?

These may seem like bold questions, but if the prospect says yes, you have a sale—provided, you can back up your statement with valid proof.

5. Compliment Approach

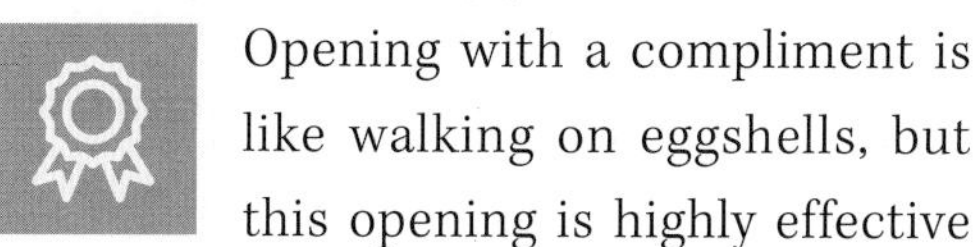

Opening with a compliment is like walking on eggshells, but this opening is highly effective if used properly. Follow the same guidelines you would use in any situation: *Offer compliments with warmth and sincerity*. The purpose is to signal your sincere interest in the prospect. Sources of information for the praise will vary. You can discover a trait that you genuinely admire about a prospective customer via a referral source, social media, or article about the person or their business. You can also see hints in the company office as you arrive or see an item in the prospect's private office that suggests a potential basis for a compliment.

Camco Inc., with international headquarters in Houston, sells gas-lift equipment, well-completion systems, safety systems, and wireline tools and units to the oil industry. At a time when the oil industry is experiencing some instability, a Camco salesperson would be out of line to compliment a prospect on the company's prosperity. Instead, a compliment should center on some other commendable factor:

> *I have been impressed with your continuous emphasis on safety on your offshore drilling rigs. I noticed the recent announcement that your company ranked first in safety ratings last year. You must be proud of that achievement.*

This type of compliment not only builds rapport but also directs the prospect's train of thought toward safety and the related products that Camco has to sell. Whenever you use a compliment as an opener, it must be *specific*, *of genuine interest* to the prospect, and sincere.

6. Referral Approach

The referral approach is especially useful because it helps you establish leverage by borrowing the influence of someone the prospect trusts and respects. This approach enhances your credibility and increases the likelihood that the prospect will give you full attention. Here are two good examples:

Miss Reid, your former partner Rob Hibray has recently completed one of our courses in personal leadership. He told me that you are also interested in growing as a person and in becoming a better leader, and suggested that you would like to hear about what our company has to offer.

......

Rita Dadosky, who recently purchased an inventory software package from us, suggested that I contact you, Mr. Parker. She thought you would like to have an opportunity to consider whether our technology solutions and cost-saving features could also be of benefit to you.

7. Educational Approach

The educational approach reflects the trend toward relationship selling. Here, salespeople research the field so thoroughly, they can present new information to the prospect by becoming an authority not just on the product, but on the industry or market the product serves. The presentation becomes less of a sales pitch and more of an educational lesson for the prospect.

This approach places control in the hands of the person doing the educating. This shift in the dynamic is especially useful in a virtual meeting, where it can be more difficult to establish credibility. Here is how this approach could work:[16]

> *Sarah, we've done some studies and found out that in your industry, five things make companies fail, and five things make them succeed. I'm going to be sharing this information with [name their competitors here], and I wondered if you were interested in seeing this same data.*

8. Hands-On Approach

This approach is useful when meeting with visual, outgoing, and overtly friendly prospects open to active involvement in the discussion. This approach consists of handing the product or some physical representation of it to a prospect to produce a positive reaction. This approach should focus on the uniqueness of the product and, as far as possible, allow the product to tell its own story.

Bringing the product to the prospect stirs interest, naturally leads to a demonstration, makes a multiple sense appeal, and promotes a feeling of commitment to listen and to participate actively in the presentation. For example, a medical device salesperson might say:

> *Mr. Stone, chances are, your busy nursing staff would love to have tools that make their lives easier. Our new wireless, handheld bedside devices allow them to assist their patients from the nurses' station or even from another patient's room! Here, take a look.*

Sometimes you cannot bring the actual product with you because of size or other constraints. You can use different devices to simulate the actual product. It could be a piece of literature, a sample of the machine output, a small working model, an animation, or a picture—any visual tool that helps focus the prospect's attention. If you are selling a service, such as a time-management program, hand the prospect a letter from a satisfied client that identifies specific benefits of the program.

The Transition from the Approach

Whatever approach you decide to use, it should be directly related to your plan for beginning the need discovery phase of the presentation. The exchange of conversation in the approach phase allows you to move smoothly into the questions you plan to ask to discover the needs of the prospect. If your opening has involved "chit-chat with a purpose," the transition is relatively simple.

Any *compliment* you offer should relate to the general area of your product or service so that the presentation grows naturally from the opening. A *relevant benefit* opening leads directly into more in-depth need discovery. A *product approach* immediately gets the prospect involved in examining your offering. The *referral approach* focuses on the approval of someone whom the prospective customer respects and emphasizes the referral source's belief that the prospect will be interested in the product.

Because the presentation should never begin until the prospect agrees to need what you offer, do whatever you can to make need discovery feel natural. The degree of rapport established between you and the prospect during the approach determines how willing the prospective customer will be to answer your questions and accept your buying recommendation.

SUMMARY

What you do and say in the initial moments of a meeting has a profound effect on overall outcomes. The first ten words out of your mouth are crucial.

Be aware of the power of first impressions. You never get a second chance to make a good one.

Proper dress and grooming give the prospect the feeling that you are competent and professional.

Appropriate choices in clothing and grooming let the prospect focus on your sales message instead of on your physical appearance.

Use the prospect's name often and begin with some purposeful small talk to feel out moods and behavioral styles.

Use a firm handshake, maintain eye contact, and make use of voice properties that reflect confidence.

Confirm or modify your impressions of the prospect's behavioral style and adapt your plans for the presentation accordingly.

A planned approach forms a natural transition into the need discovery phase of the Relationship Selling Cycle.

Review Questions

1. What are the four objectives of an effective approach?
2. What nonverbal language most directly affects first impressions?
3. Should you plan your greeting ahead of time, or should you depend mainly on the inspiration of the moment? Justify your choice.
4. Under what conditions would you change the approach you had planned when you arrive for an interview?
5. What would you consider to be appropriate attire for calling on an insurance executive? What about a manager of a health and fitness facility?
6. List some guidelines for making a good first impression.
7. What are some weaknesses in evaluating a prospect totally on first impressions?
8. What can you learn about a prospect from a handshake?
9. What is the purpose of small talk? How can you use it to your advantage? In what kind of situation is small talk a negative?
10. Name and explain the eight types of approaches discussed in the chapter. Why does a salesperson need to master multiple approach strategies?

IN-CLASS EXERCISES

The following role-play exercises help build teams, improve communication, and emphasize the real-world side of selling. They are meant to challenge, help you learn how to deal with problems that have more than one right answer, and use a variety of skills beyond those required in a typical review question. Read and complete each activity. Then in the next class, discuss and compare answers.

EXERCISE 10.1 Dress for Success!

Come to class dressed for the role of a salesperson who represents an organization in a field in which you would like to work. You should attend to the details of your attire and appearance to make a good first impression. Also, be prepared to role-play greeting your prospective customer for the first time through the first words of your approach. Your instructor will invite other members of the class to critique your appearance and your initial greeting or exchange.

Alternatively, you can dress for a job interview with the company or organization for which you would like to work. You should prepare to role-play your greeting and your approach through your response to the typical interview question, "So, tell me about yourself." Again, your colleagues will be invited to critique your appearance and your initial greeting or exchange.

EXERCISE 10.2 First Impressions

For this exercise, pair up with another student. In this role play, one of you will play the part of a B2B customer, while your partner will play the part of the salesperson. You may select the product or service you want to sell.

According to Chapter 10, every salesperson has approximately four minutes to make a strong first impression. Much depends on how quickly the salesperson can evaluate the personality or social style of the prospect so that the approach can be adjusted to fit the prospect's behavioral traits.

For this role play, work together outside of class to develop two brief scripts. For the prospect, you should select one of the basic social styles (review these if necessary). For that social style, create a script for both the prospect and salesperson that is unlikely to work. Create another script that you think is likely to succeed. Rehearse both scripts and be prepared to role-play them in class.

Case Studies

The following case studies present you with selling scenarios that require you to apply the critical skills discussed in the chapter and give you training through practical learning situations. They are meant to be both engaging and challenging, and like the role-play exercises, they don't have one right answer.

CASE 10.1 – A Referral Gone Wrong

Rita Thurber represents a small publisher, Coastal Maine Publishing Co., that markets a shortlist of poetry books, travel magazines, children's books, and good, but relatively unknown, fiction authors. Rita is opening up new territory on Maryland's Eastern Shore. She is meeting the owner of an independent bookshop, Sam Wetherington, for the first time. Since the store is located in an upscale village to which the wealthy escape from Washington, D.C., and where tourists moor their sailboats, Rita guesses that the store's clientele would be a perfect match for her company's offerings.

Rita has prepared carefully for this interview. She is dressed stylishly in a navy blue blazer, gray slacks, a pink striped blouse, and low heels. She has researched Mr. Wetherington's online merchandise, and she comes armed with a referral from one of her authors. The bell tinkles as she steps through the front door, and she immediately spots Mr. Wetherington sitting at a desk behind the counter.

"Hi. Mr. Wetherington? I'm Rita Thurber from Coastal Maine Publishing. It's nice to meet you," Rita says as she strides across the room, her hand extended in greeting. "Thanks for agreeing to meet with me."

"Welcome to my shop," replies Wetherington, shaking her hand. "Please call me Sam."

"You have a lovely store here, just like Milton Stokes described it. In fact, Milton is the main reason I'm here. As you may recall, we feature his books of poetry."

"Oh, yes. Milton. We hosted a book signing for him once. Big mistake. He teaches at the local college part-time, and we thought it might get some new customers here from the college people and their families. But it never worked out. Milton's a terrible poet, and his stuff doesn't sell. I took a large shipment of his latest volume but had to return nearly all of it to your company. What a terrible experience."

"Oh, I'm sorry," Rita responded. Sam's negative criticism threw her for a loop. Using Milton's name clearly got things off on the wrong foot. What could she say to turn things around—and quickly?

CASE 10.2 – Grasping the Relay Baton

Jamie couldn't believe her good luck. Just after accepting a sales position with OfficeDecor, Inc. (a company that sells office furnishings to medium-sized companies and offices), Jamie learned that she would be assigned a different territory. In her new territory, she'd have sole responsibility for managing all new and existing accounts. Her predecessor Sally left the company under something of a cloud (Jamie hasn't been told what the problem was); sales in the region had declined during the past year as well. Still, Jamie was excited when Pete, her manager, called her in for a meeting. This was her big chance!

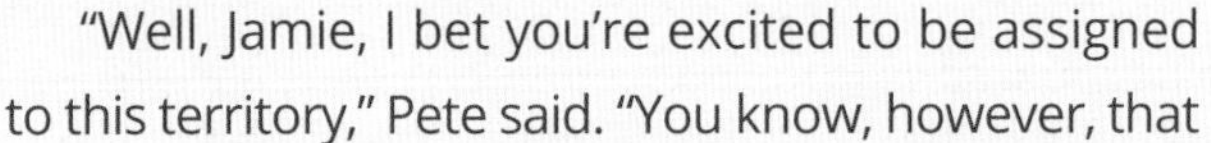

"Well, Jamie, I bet you're excited to be assigned to this territory," Pete said. "You know, however, that you're walking into a difficult situation. The territory has a lot of potential, but taking over from someone else under these circumstances can be challenging."

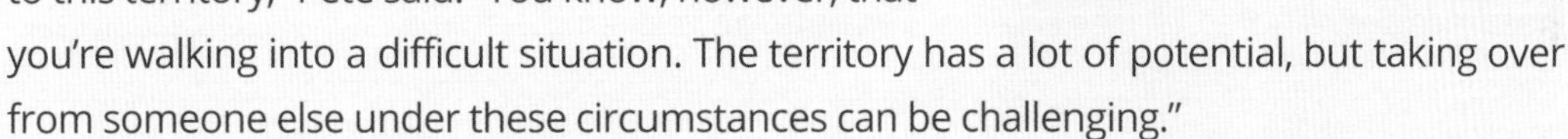

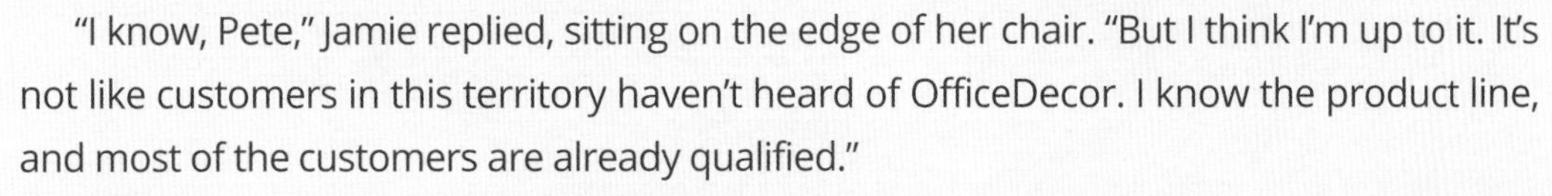

"I know, Pete," Jamie replied, sitting on the edge of her chair. "But I think I'm up to it. It's not like customers in this territory haven't heard of OfficeDecor. I know the product line, and most of the customers are already qualified."

"That's true," Pete agreed. "And I'm sure that you can break the ice with new prospects just fine. But Sally left some of her customers with a bad experience by overpromising delivery schedules. You're going to have some fence-mending to do, and I want you to think carefully about how you're going to approach these people."

"Well, I'm not going to make the same mistake that Sally did," promised Jamie. "But you're right: I've never had to deal with this sort of situation before. Introducing myself, getting their attention, reassuring them that I understand their needs and problems, and so forth will be a big challenge initially."

"Exactly," said Pete. "It's like running a close relay race when you're a couple of paces behind the leader. You can't afford to drop the baton. We're counting on you. Let me know what you come up with."

Recognizing that every situation is a little different, Jamie realized that she needed to develop a basic script that would launch her approach. She decided to consider basic sales approaches and to combine two or three that would help her to achieve her initial goals.

What should Jamie include in her script? Which approach(es) would offer the greatest promise in this situation? Why? Write out a one-paragraph script for Jamie and be prepared to explain your reasoning.

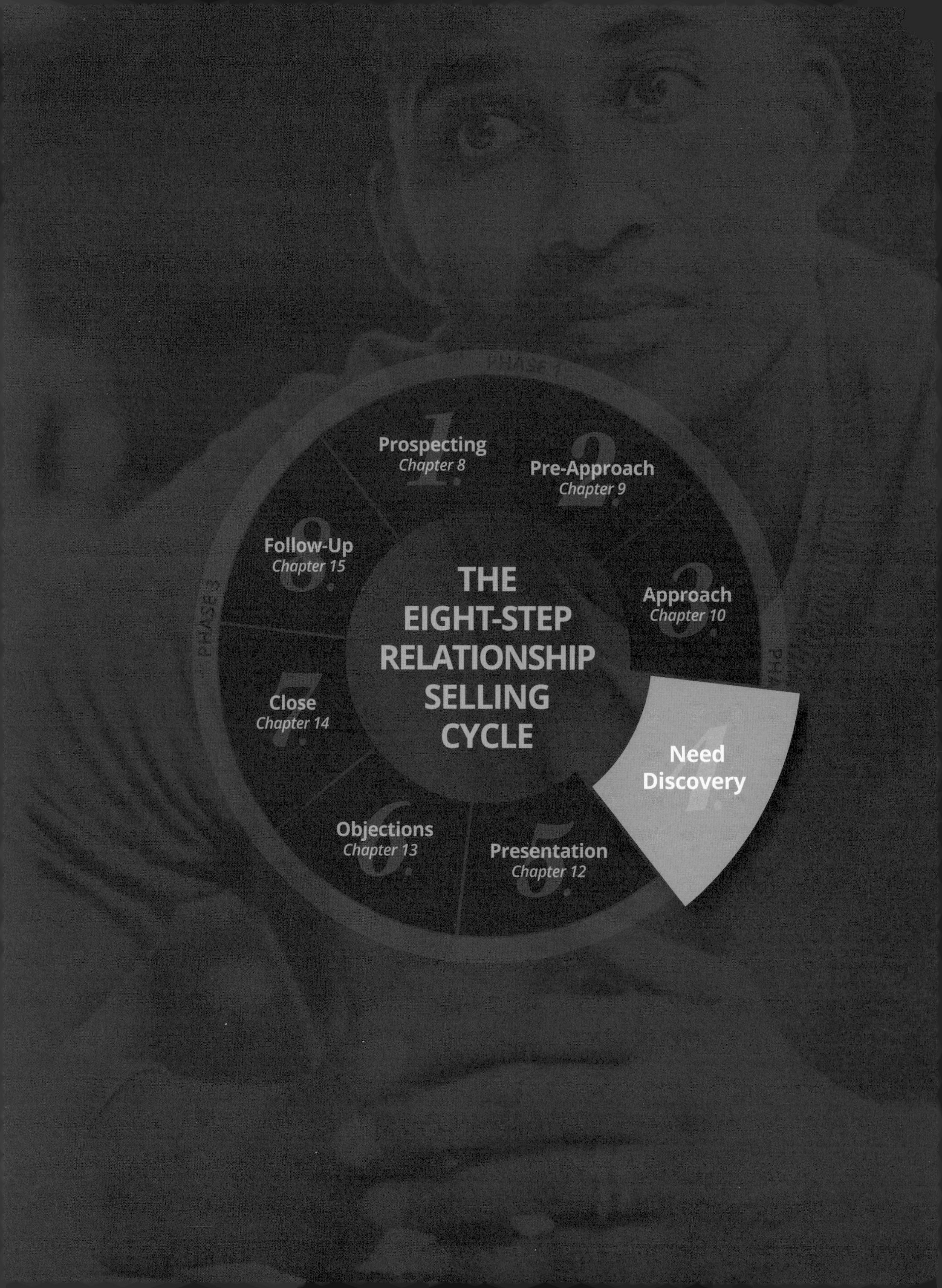

PHASE 1

PHASE 3

1\. Prospecting
Chapter 8

2\. Pre-Approach
Chapter 9

3\. Approach
Chapter 10

4\. Need Discovery

5\. Presentation
Chapter 12

6\. Objections
Chapter 13

7\. Close
Chapter 14

8\. Follow-Up
Chapter 15

THE EIGHT-STEP RELATIONSHIP SELLING CYCLE

NEED DISCOVERY: HOW TO QUESTION AND LISTEN EFFECTIVELY

OVERVIEW

This chapter is devoted to step four of the Relationship Selling Cycle, need discovery. Need discovery is all about asking the right questions and listening effectively. You will learn critical questioning and listening skills to help carry you through the entire sales process to the close and beyond. This step is a vital part of the cycle because successful salespeople don't ask their way into a sale; they listen their way into a sale. Chapter 11 also explains and dramatizes the legendary SPIN® Selling technique through a practical example.

OBJECTIVES

- Understand the purpose of asking questions.
- Study several specific questioning techniques.
- Learn how to select the most appropriate questioning tactics.
- Examine SPIN® Selling and its applications.
- Understand the functions served by various types of questions.
- Discover and appreciate the importance of listening in selling.
- Become more familiar with techniques for improving listening skills.

The Key to Winning in Sales

What lies at the heart of selling? Some may say selling is filling a need, while others say it's solving a problem. Some people say it's closing the deal as quickly as possible and by any means necessary.

The problem is, none of those definitions work. Selling is ultimately asking people what they do, and how, when, where, for who, and why. Only after knowing the answer to all of those pieces can you help them do it even better.[1] You can't talk your way into a sale. You have to learn what motivates your prospects into action.

**Telling isn't selling.
Asking is selling.**

The idea that "talking equals selling" creates the misconception that every prospect uses a product or service for the same purposes. In actuality, each prospect has unique needs. Of the many benefits you have to offer, only a few will be the key motivators for a specific prospective customer.[2] The challenge is to determine each prospect's buying criteria before your presentation and then use only the precise benefits that address their unique situation.[3]

If you went to your doctor complaining of back pain and the physician prescribed medicine without asking any questions, that would be a serious red flag. How could the doctor make an accurate diagnosis and prescribe the appropriate medication without making a thorough examination and asking some probing questions about the problem?

You would expect the doctor to understand your issue (not the subject of back pain in general) before prescribing treatment. "Doctors of selling" follow a similar process: they diagnose potential buyers fully to uncover any needs they may have. Strive to become a *doctor of selling*, because your prospects have the right to demand personalized, professional attention.

The Heart of the Cycle

Relationship selling is focused on building genuine connections. This relationship-centric approach requires the need discovery step to play a unique role in the sales cycle.[4] Exhibit 11.1 on the next page shows the relationship between need discovery and the other stages in the face-to-face phase of the process. In many ways, need discovery is the heart of the cycle. As such, more time should be spent building rapport, asking questions, and listening than anything else. It is during need discovery—not in the close—that the sale is most often lost.

Need discovery is the foundation upon which a successful sale is built.

Telling prospects what they need is a mistake. Asking questions that allow them to discover their own needs and share those needs positions you as a sounding board for the solutions they "discover" during their time with you. Prospects are more receptive when they feel that the solution is their idea. That is why successful sales interviews contain more requests for opinions and suggestions and fewer statements of disagreement and tension.

In successful meetings, salespeople control the direction of the conversation by the way they ask questions.[5] However, while salespeople must retain control of the discussion, it is not through endless talking, but through guided directing and listening.

EXHIBIT 11.1 Need Discovery's Central Role

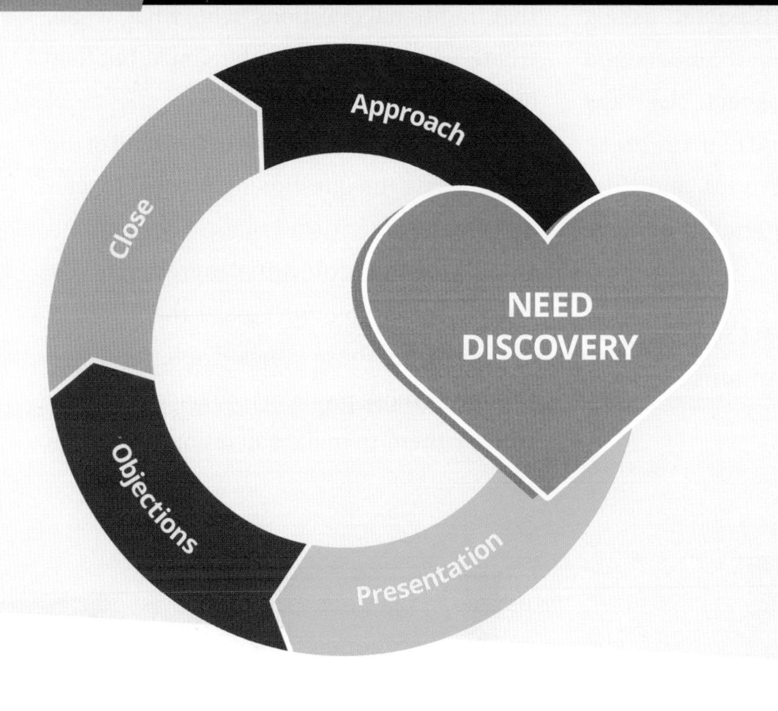

THE RELATIONSHIP SELLING CYCLE WON'T WORK WITHOUT ITS HEART.

Because the entire process must be focused on the customer, need discovery is the critical step! It's there for you to ask questions and get to know your customers so that you can discover what matters most to them.

People are often unaware of a problem until you ask them more about it. Here is an example: An insurance agent sold a life insurance policy to a seemingly uninterested prospect by asking a straightforward question followed by an observation. The agent asked, "How much life insurance coverage do you have as a safeguard for your family's future?"

When the prospect replied that he had $75,000, the insurance agent remarked, "Wow, I guess you don't plan to be dead for very long."

This statement could catch someone off guard or perhaps even offend a few people.

In this case, it caused the prospect to notice the disparity between his coverage and the amount that would be sufficient to allow his family to maintain their current lifestyle if something happened to him.

Salespeople don't convince prospects. They help prospects recognize that they already have a need.

Strategic Question Planning

Asking the right questions is a skill all too often neglected. In sales, it isn't about asking just *any* questions. It's about asking the *right* questions that help to understand the perspective of the prospect, clear any misunderstanding, strengthen or break assumptions, lead to discoveries, and close the sale.[6] Your questions should achieve four objectives:

1. **Discover the prospect's "hot button" or dominant buying motive.**
2. **Establish the purchase criteria or specifications.**
3. **Agree on a time frame for completion of negotiations.**
4. **Gain agreement on the problem(s) before making the presentation.**

The traditional questions are simple but powerful. Decide in advance what you need to know, and then plan what questions will elicit that information most quickly and efficiently and in a manner that is consistent with the prospect's social style. Remember that traditional questions (who, what, when, where, why, and how) may be simple, but they are also powerful.

Because the sale is made in the mind of the buyer, using the questioning process to gain agreement on critical issues is paramount. Once you have obtained agreement on crucial issues, you must assist the prospect in prioritizing those issues. Then, you agree to address those problems or concerns before you ask them to make a decision. Prospects

are more likely to buy if you establish points on which you both agree early in the process.

Some salespeople hesitate to ask questions because they are afraid the prospect will refuse to answer. However, prospects that refuse to cooperate during need discovery are also unlikely to cooperate during the close. Communication is a two-way street that demands participation by both parties. If you want to involve prospects in the sales process, you must be prepared to ask questions that maximize engagement.

Strategic Question Suggestions

It is not difficult to ask effective questions if you follow a few simple guidelines. As you select specific questioning methods, keep these three tactics in mind:[7]

Avoid Confusing Language. Your clients are not impressed by your industry jargon. For example, an account executive selling ad space in a trade magazine should avoid terms such as kerning, Bodoni extra bold, mistral fonts, or page bleed. Unless, of course, he is confident that the prospect is familiar with all of those terms and expects them to be used. In the same way, using company stock numbers, codes, or abbreviations may confuse clients. Your goal is to promote understanding, not to demonstrate how smart you are.

Establish a Clear Agenda. Chapter 10 presented four objectives of the approach: To make a favorable first impression, to gain attention, to create interest, and to serve as a transition into need discovery. This transition into need discovery requires that you tell the prospect exactly what you intend to accomplish during the interview session. You should provide a clear agenda for the presentation. Always let the prospect know what you want to achieve. You can set up the desired atmosphere by requesting permission to ask questions. Here are two practical permissive questions:

> *I believe I can offer you a valuable service. But to be sure, and to discover a little more about your particular situation, may I ask you a few questions?*

> *The only way for us to know how my company can best serve your needs is for me to ask a few questions. Will that be alright with you? Oh, and is it okay if I take a few notes while we talk?*

Give Each Question a Purpose. An ambiguous question or one with multiple interpretations creates misunderstanding. Proceed logically, one topic at a time. Anything that can be misunderstood will be misunderstood. So, be as clear as possible. Conciseness matters, too. Phrase each question in a way that will produce the maximum amount of information with the least amount of overall questions required.[8]

Five Key Questions That Build Relationships

If you listen more than you talk, you are taking a positive step in the right direction. But are you listening out for key pieces of information? In the world of professional selling, the questions you ask are just as important, if not more so, than the fact that you are taking the time to ask them. That means that you need to ask the questions that give you the answers you need to move smoothly into the presentation. Asking the *right* questions, in the *best* way, changes the sales process in significant ways, to the benefit of both parties.

There is a series of specific questions that work well for salespeople who use them correctly. They are questions that invite a dialog between prospect and salesperson that goes a long way toward establishing trust and placing them on the same wavelength. The following five questions encompass the key things to ask:

1. The Motivation Question: "Why are you passionate about this product/service?"

This question spotlights prospect motivations. Their motivations might be personal and driven by their needs, or they may be business-related. Prospects may feel pressured by their managers to increase profit margins or improve a business process. Every person has his or her motivations for buying, and if you aren't sure what those motives are, ask!

2. The Success Question: "What do you want to achieve?"

This question is known as the Success Question because it highlights what constitutes *success* for your prospects. This short, simple question can keep prospects talking for hours. The beauty is in its simplicity. There are so many directions your prospective customers can take with their answers. Here are some variations on this question:

What inspired you to agree to this appointment today?

......

What products or services are most likely to get your attention?

......

What do you want this meeting to accomplish?

......

If we left this meeting today with a plan for incorporating this product into your company, would that make you happy?

3. The Frustration Question: "What do you want to avoid?"

This question will give you an even more complete picture of the prospect when it is paired with the Success Question. It allows you to see both sides of prospect motivation—the things that motivate them to find solutions and the things they want to avoid when it comes to buying. Here are some variations of this question that may fit your needs:

What is it about [issue, problem, need] that is affecting your business/life? How important is it to address this need?

......

When you think of your current suppliers/vendors, what would you change about your interactions with them or their products/services?

......

What do you dread might happen if [issue, problem, need] is not resolved? Why is that important to you?

4. The Right Fit Question: "What helps you decide which products to buy?"

This question can work wonders. It can reveal a prospect's expectations, or in other words, what they expect in return for buying what you are offering (i.e., the "what's in

it for me" of relationship selling). Here are some variations:

How do you choose what companies to do business with?

......

What do you have to know about a product/company for you to make a **yes** *decision?*

......

What would a company need to show you, after you've committed, to convince you that you've made a wise investment?

......

When you think about vendors you've done business with previously that sell similar products/services, what did you like best about them? Why was that important to you?

You must be as diplomatic as possible when asking the "right fit" questions to engage the prospect's trust and not be disparaging of another company or a competitor.

5. The Commitment Question: "How involved do you want to be in incorporating this change?"

Some prospects want to sign the contract and never think about the purchase again. Others wish to have significantly more involvement and follow-up. Learning your prospects' perspectives can help you assess their desired level of engagement or follow up after the contract has been signed.

Asking these questions won't guarantee a sale. Still, they comprise the first critical step in building deep, authentic relationships over the long haul with your best potential customers. With the insight that these questions provide, you can quickly determine whether the prospect merits the significant investment of your time and attention. The questions don't just help you—they help the prospect convey to you, in the most direct way, how to add them to your growing client base. Not

to mention, utilizing these questions toward the beginning of your meeting with a new prospect will reveal the best course of action to take for the remainder of your interactions and in the presentation itself.

The SPIN® Selling Technique

Neil Rackham is the founder and former president of Huthwaite Inc. and the author of the book, *SPIN® Selling.* His corporation's 12-year, million-dollar research into effective sales performance resulted in the formulation of a unique sales strategy called the SPIN® Selling method. The SPIN® technique utilizes Situation, Problem, Implication, and Need-payoff questions. Successful salespeople don't ask random questions. The four types of questions represent how relationship salespeople explore and are meant to serve as a flexible guide rather than a rigid formula.

There is a distinct pattern in a successful call. You can use the answers you hear during need discovery to underscore the benefits you choose to present during the presentation. The questions provide a road map for you, guiding the sales call until you have a distinct list of stated needs. People don't appreciate having to expend extra brainpower, and they certainly don't want to admit that their problems are readily apparent.[9] The SPIN® Selling technique allows prospects to discover for themselves the issues they have.

SPIN® Selling in Action

Let's look at a specific example to demonstrate the SPIN® method. Transworld Systems Inc. (TSI) is one of the largest flat-fee collection agencies in the country. TSI helps over 60,000 clients recover their slow-paying and delinquent accounts without having to pay up to 50 percent of the collection charged by traditional percentage-based agencies.

A business with overdue accounts has three options for collecting: it can hire a percentage-based agency, hire a flat-fee agency, or handle the collections internally. Many clients have found the TSI system to be the only economical method for obtaining reliable third-party collections. TSI pays the money they collect directly to the customer. The client maintains control of their accounts, and they do not have to pay a percentage. TSI has a low flat-fee that enables clients to assign their accounts to TSI in the early stages of delinquency, thus providing the best opportunity for a successful recovery.[10]

The following helps explain how the SPIN® technique can help companies like TSI connect with their prospects and discover needs in a valuable way:

S **Situation Questions.** Situation questions are designed to find out about the customer's current condition. These are data-gathering questions that ask about the prospect's general state of affairs or circumstances as it relates to what TSI offers. They help TSI salespeople get to know their prospects and obtain some initial information and a general understanding of the prospect's needs. The sample questions below play a critical fact-finding role, are non-threatening, and help to build an atmosphere of trust and cooperation:

How many active accounts do you bill each month?

Do you have out-of-state accounts?

What percentage of your customers do not pay their bills on time?

Do you do all the collection of overdue accounts internally?

Do you use a collection agency?

Are the billing and follow-up conducted in this office?

Are you responsible for making the purchasing decision?

SITUATION QUESTIONS ARE FACT-CENTERED.
They uncover current conditions and circumstances that help determine the level of need for your offering.

P **Problem Questions.** Once a TSI sales rep has sufficient general knowledge about a buyer's situation, he or she moves to the second type of questioning. These questions explore needs, any difficulties prospects may be having, and dissatisfactions in areas where TSI's service could be the solution. The goal is to have the prospect realize and then acknowledge, "I have a problem with the collection of my accounts receivables."

TSI wants to determine specific needs and uncover a prospect's primary *hot button*, or the one thing that would drive them to say yes if TSI could address it and fix it. Remember, the sale is made in the mind of the buyer, not in the mind of the salesperson.

Whatever customers say is always right—but when you say it, they may doubt it! Customers don't want to be told they have a problem. The best salespeople allow them to discover it for themselves. If you can uncover problems your service can solve, then you're providing the buyer with something useful. The goal is to uncover areas where TSI can solve a specific dilemma. So, the agent would ask these kinds of problem questions:

At what point do you consider an account to be a problem?

Do you know how much it costs to handle your collections internally?

Do you ever get mail returned or emails bounced back because of the wrong address?

How often do you get checks or online payments rejected?

Do you have a service to help recover checks or declined credit card payments? Is it a guaranteed service?

PROBLEM QUESTIONS ARE DISCOVERY-CENTERED. They determine specific needs and uncover a prospect's primary pain points.

Implication Questions. Implication questions build up the magnitude of the problem so that prospects see it as a serious issue that needs a speedy resolution. The phrasing of implication questions is critical because you want the prospect to discuss the problem and how it might be improved. Implication questions are the language of decision-makers, and if you can speak their language, you'll influence them.

Attach a bottom-line figure to implication questions. It is imperative for the prospect to agree that the company's problems are causing significant issues in the forms of lost revenue, negative customer perception, and more. Prospects must see that the problem is severe enough to outweigh the cost of the solution. In this case, that means using TSI's services. So, a TSI salesperson might ask these questions:

Do you know most collection agencies deposit the money they collect into their bank account and hold it up to 60 days?

In the last five years, we collected over $2.4 billion for our clients, and the money was paid directly to them. Would it help if the collections were paid directly to you?

Is it crucial to recover your delinquent accounts more quickly than a conventional collection agency could and put the money directly into your hands?

Is it safe to say that you would like to collect delinquent accounts quickly, without disturbing ongoing relationships with customers?

IMPLICATION QUESTIONS ARE PROBLEM-CENTERED. They build up the magnitude of the problem to create a sense of urgency to find a solution.

Need-Payoff Questions. Finally, the salesperson uses need-payoff questions to build the value of the solution they offer. These questions help you build up the value of your proposed solution in the customer's mind. They are designed to prompt the customer to tell you the benefits that your solution offers. In essence, prospects explain to you why your offering is the best solution for them! You want to focus the customer's attention on the solution rather than on the problem, and that, in turn, creates a positive problem-solving atmosphere.

In the words of an eight-year-old, "Implication questions are always sad; need-payoff questions are always happy." That's because implication questions are problem-centered, while need-payoff questions are solution-centered. Here are some examples of useful need-payoff questions that a TSI salesperson might ask a prospect:[11]

Would it be useful to speed up the rate of collection, and at the same time, be guaranteed that you will recover at least twice as much as you pay for our service?

......

If you could create the perfect collection agency, what would you want them to do for you?

......

We automatically send regular reports detailing the status of each account assigned for collection. Does this sound like something that would interest you?

......

Do you want the account handled sensitively or rigorously? We have a division that handles more intensive collection problems. Would you like to have that option?

......

Would you like us to send a thank you card to debtors after an account has been paid?

SPIN® selling is not a magic formula for success. However, its systematic approach to asking questions is field-tested and proven to yield tremendous results. If you are interested in using the SPIN® technique in your next sales meeting, prepare your Situation, Problem,

NEED-PAYOFF QUESTIONS ARE SOLUTION-CENTERED. They allow the prospect to convince themselves that your answer is the right one.

Implication, and Need-payoff questions, and then experiment to see how they work.

Common Questioning Techniques

When it comes to asking questions, you've probably never thought about what category of question you are asking. However, question categories are relevant because certain types of queries are designed to produce specific responses that move the sales process forward.

Exhibit 11.2 summarizes the most notable questioning techniques, which are generally classified by the type of answers required and their intended purpose. You may wish to begin the questioning process with closed-end or fact-finding questions that are easy to answer and, therefore, not threatening to a new prospect. If the first few questions are easy, the prospect begins to gain confidence and feel comfortable with the process. Subsequent questions, although gradually more challenging, will seem more natural.

EXHIBIT 11.2 Types of Questions and Asking Techniques

TWO QUESTION TYPES

1. **Closed-ended questions** provide a precise list of responses from which the prospect can select. They are easy to answer, elicit feedback, and can be used to get a commitment.
2. **Open-ended questions** identify a topic to discuss but do not provide structured alternatives for responses. They often begin with 'how' or 'what,' can't be answered with a 'yes' or 'no,' and are designed to stimulate thinking.

THREE QUESTIONING TECHNIQUES

1. **Amplification questions** ask the prospect to expand on an answer. Do not direct thoughts but encourage the prospect to continue talking.
2. **Internal summary questions** assimilate information, put it in perspective, and check to see that interpretation is correct. You may even repeat all of the prospect's last response in the form of a question.
3. **Agreement questions** are meant to achieve agreement. Restate the problem, get the prospect to agree, and attempt to get a commitment before continuing.

Closed-Ended Questions. These are direct, fact-finding questions that are designed to reveal background information about the prospect's business or family. They ask an either/or question or request a choice from a series of suggested responses. Closed-ended questions are usually answered with a brief response, often a single word. They often ask for a yes or no response or a choice between two alternatives. They are directive questions for which you want specific answers:

How many employees do you have on the day-shift?

What accounting software have you used in the past?

Is crash-test safety reporting critical to you?

Does your company pay the full cost of employee health insurance or only a portion?

You may also phrase closed-ended questions to get feedback or to gain commitment:

Would you like deliveries to be on Fridays, or are Mondays better?

Are you responsible for deciding to purchase from us, or will there be others involved?

Do you know what your customers do with your product after buying it?

Do you prefer to pay upfront, or would you like to arrange a monthly payment plan?

Do you realize I'll get fired if you don't buy something? Can you live with yourself if the bank takes my house and my children have to sell their toys on Ebay? How will you feel when our poodle starts eating people to survive?

CHARLIE BECAME THE TOP SALESMAN IN HIS COMPANY ONCE HE LEARNED THE POWER OF EFFECTIVE QUESTIONS!

You may use closed-ended questions as a substitute for telling the prospect something. A question can sometimes make a point more tellingly than a statement because the prospect must think to answer it, and thinking makes a stronger impression than hearing. Consider these two ways to impart the same message:

Our procedure will eliminate waste in your welding operations.

VS.

How much savings would you have if you used a procedure that eliminates waste from your welding operations?

The first method tells the prospect something. The salesperson hopes the prospect is impressed, but that may not be the case. If you don't encourage prospective customers to speak, they will bury their skepticism until it manifests in the close as a vague objection like, "We're not thinking of making any changes right now."

Using the question method, however, gains attention because the prospect has to think about an answer. Disbelief surfaces, and you can deal with it now instead of encountering it during the close. Here are the primary purposes served by asking closed-ended questions:

1. **They uncover specific facts.**
2. **They reduce prospect tension because they are easy questions to answer.**
3. **They check for understanding and receive feedback.**
4. **They maintain control by directing the flow of conversation.**
5. **They reinforce prospect commitment to a specific position.**

Open-Ended Questions. These broadly phrased questions allow prospects plenty of room to answer as they wish. They call for explanations. Open-ended questions encourage prospects to discuss their needs by explaining their preferences, expectations, or judgments. Open questions tend to be general rather than specific. Use them when you want the prospect to talk freely. You can encourage the prospect to verbalize feelings by asking questions that begin with phrases like, "What do you think" or "How do you feel." Thinking out loud often helps people clarify and organize their thoughts. Real feelings are often revealed when they are vocalized.[12]

Open-ended questions help you and the prospect sort out ideas and begin to make decisions. Here are some examples of questions that give prospects the freedom and responsibility to express their thoughts and use their information in the decision-making process:

What options would you want on your new Mercedes?

How do you think I might be able to help you?

In a perfect world, what would you like to see us deliver?

What are five unique characteristics of your business?

What benefits would you expect to receive from our ten-week, self-paced time-management program?

Open-ended questions reveal attitudes that a salesperson must be aware of for a successful sale. You cannot easily ask a prospect, "Does pride motivate you?" but you can ask open-ended questions designed to detect this motivator. You then have the answer to the direct question you cannot ask. Open-ended questions often begin with "how" or "what." Here are the primary purposes served by asking open-ended questions:

1. **They allow the prospect to move in any direction.**
2. **They cannot be answered with a simple "yes" or "no."**
3. **They are designed to stimulate thinking and increase dialogue.**
4. **They help determine dominant buying motives (rational or emotional).**
5. **They help uncover the social or behavioral style of the prospect.**

Classification of Questioning Techniques

The best way to classify questions is according to the purpose they are intended to perform. Here are three basic classes of questions: amplification, internal summary or reflective, and questions to gain agreement on a problem. Both open-ended and closed-ended questions may be asked for any of these purposes, depending upon the situation. If one question does not provide all of the needed information, you can use another questioning technique to elicit a more thorough response and a better understanding.

Relationship selling is more than a process in which two people sit together in a room and take turns talking. As the salesperson, you must be sure that the prospect knows what you are talking about and understands it. You must also be sure that you know the prospect's needs and are confident you can satisfy them.

You need feedback. Asking questions is the best way to receive the feedback you need.

Be careful how you phrase the questions you ask. Place the responsibility for not understanding on yourself rather than on the prospect. "Do you understand what I said?" or "Did you get that?" or "Are you with me?" seems to imply that the prospect may not be too bright. You must take responsibility for any possible misunderstanding by asking, "Have I explained this well enough? Is there some part I need to clarify or go over again?"

Amplification Questions

Amplification questioning techniques encourage prospects to continue to provide enlightening information and also encourage them to explain the meaning of a statement made. Amplification questions help both salespeople and prospects. At times, prospects may not make themselves clear; they may wander off the subject or may stop talking before you can fully understand their position. Subtly, these techniques ask the prospect to expand on or clarify the meaning of a statement and help identify the frame of reference used. There are four types of amplification questions:

1. **Double-Check Question.** A double-check question is a means of giving feedback to the prospect. It involves taking the information the prospective customer has provided, rephrasing it, and handing it right back. A prospect might tell a motor freight salesperson, "Every Tuesday and Thursday, the whole yard is backed up with trucks for the entire afternoon." The salesperson might offer feedback by saying, "As I understand it, you find that your loading platforms get badly jammed at peak hours." This statement functions

as a question because it evokes an answer. It serves the dual purpose of clarifying the salesperson's impression of the situation and solidifying the prospect's opinion.

2. **Nonverbal Gestures.** Visual cues such as head nodding and leaning forward show that you are listening, that you believe the prospect, and that you understand what he or she is saying. You may also inject appropriate words or phrases to encourage the prospect to continue, such as, "Is that right?" or "That's interesting!" You may imply a question by the nonverbal choice of silence accompanied by a slightly raised eyebrow or furrowed brow.

3. **Silence.** Silence is a powerful sales tool. When prospects avoid telling you the whole truth, the knowledge that they are less than honest makes them uncomfortable. Your silence convinces them to go ahead and tell you the entire story. Silence allows you to slow down and relax the pace of questions. Take their social style into account—some prospects want to think and contemplate longer than others before responding to your questions. Give people time to reply at their own pace. Silence also gives you valuable time to formulate your next question or comment.

4. **Continuation Questions.** Continuation questions encourage prospects

to keep on talking by making an affirmative request for more information. Such questions do not push for a particular response or agreement; they encourage more communication from the prospect. Here are two examples:

What additional thoughts or questions do you have regarding our shipping policies?

······

Could you tell me in more detail why you feel that way?

There are several advantages to using amplification questions:

- **These techniques encourage the prospect to reveal information.**
- **They also allow the salesperson to rephrase what the prospect appears to have intended.**
- **Amplification questions can invite the prospect to expand or clarify any point of disagreement.**
- **They can serve to narrow down generalizations and eliminate ambiguities.**

Internal Summary Questions

Probes designed to get prospects to think, see, and consider your interpretation of the situation may be called *internal summary* or *reflective* questions. Summarize what you understood the prospect to mean. You want to assimilate the information provided, place it in the perspective that suits your purpose, and ask if the interpretation is correct.

You achieve this by repeating all or part of the prospect's last response in the form of a question or by rephrasing the entire idea expressed by the prospective customer, feeding it back in a slightly different way, and asking for confirmation. Consider the following example in which a company president explains why the firm may not be able to sponsor an in-house blood drive. Note how the salesperson empathizes and rewords or echoes the president's remarks but suggests the process can be accomplished without disruption:

PROSPECT (company president): *My company has always felt the need to support the charitable activities of organizations like yours. But where do we draw the line? I am besieged continuously with requests for my company's time. We have only so many hours a day.*

SALESPERSON (fundraiser): *I certainly understand how you feel. If I were in your position, I'm sure I'd feel the same. I sense that the blood donor program is something you fully endorse. But with only so many hours in the working day, humanitarian concerns take a back seat to the realities of business. However, if you could accomplish a drive with a minimal time commitment, and you felt your employees wanted to do it, we could make it happen. May I tell you how?*

These types of questions are useful throughout the interview. Successful salespeople know it's smart to summarize key benefits just before asking for the order. For example, you could say, "We've agreed that a new organic line, with these special features and price points, will produce the margin increase you need. Am I right about that?" Such summary techniques help lead to a successful close.

The summary question may be used to underscore points on which you already agree. An occasional summary of points the prospect has previously agreed on will fix those points firmly in the prospect's mind and show how much you two already agree on about the issue.

Agreement Questions

In his book, *Open the Mind, Close the Sale*, John Wilson says that the salesperson's failure to confirm the problem is one of the biggest mistakes in selling. The underlying purpose of asking questions is to determine whether the prospect has a problem or need that you are capable of solving. State the problem in your own words and get the prospect to agree, "Yes, that's it."

Never begin the actual presentation until the problem has been well established on both sides. Begin the formal statement of the problem by using such phrases as these:

> *Let me attempt to summarize what we have been saying...*

As I understand it, here is (are) the problem(s) we must solve...

Based on your answers to my questions, I see the problem as...

After you pinpoint the problem, you must seek confirmation. Get the prospect to agree by following your summary of the problem with questions such as:[13]

If I show you some comparisons demonstrating that my company can save you money without sacrificing quality, would you commit to our program?

Is that a fair statement of the current situation?

If I can adequately demonstrate a solution to your concerns, would it be enough to earn your business?

If the prospect agrees with the problem statement, you are ready to present the specific benefits of your product or service that can solve the problem. Even if the prospect disagrees with your summary of the problem, you have both learned by sharing information.

The Social Media Connection

ASKING THE RIGHT QUESTIONS ON SOCIAL MEDIA

Research shows that one-quarter of social media and online discussion mentions a product, service, or brand. The opportunity to engage with and listen to potential prospects via social media is clear, and more companies are finding it *essential* rather than *optional*.

Enhance your sales efforts by combining listening and asking with researching. One success story demonstrates how social media was used to reshape a baby diaper campaign. Traditional survey results (not conducted on social media) showed that the majority of consumers believed that "environmentally friendly" was the most important product attribute.

But in online conversations that were allowed to progress between users on social media, results indicated that "organic" and "avoiding diaper rash" were the most important product features. The social media analysis revealed a more accurate picture of consumer sentiment around product desires. That led to a new campaign theme centered on "Caring," which produced phenomenal results for the brand.[14]

How do you ask the right questions on social media? First, decide what kind of answer you want. Are you looking for short answers with no room for discussion, or are you trying to create dialogue? Closed-ended questions on social media assume answers that can be given in a few words or result in yes or no choices. Open-ended questions usually require more deliberation and quickly lead to secondary questions and answers that flesh out a concept or opinion or provide critical problem-solving information.

Social media can be an outstanding aid to your organization's strategic marketing plans, as long as you ask the right questions and listen to the responses.

Become a Master Listener

Everybody wants the secret to closing more sales, but it's no secret. If you're not closing deals, you're not listening to the customer. Salespeople are busy telling their prospects all the incredible things their offering can do instead of letting prospects tell them what they need.[15] Prospective customers are not patiently sitting at their desks waiting for you to call so they can buy your product. Buyers are shrewd and discerning, which is why you must do more than mechanically go through your script. Prospects can sense insincerity, and they will know if you are not listening and giving only scripted generic responses.

If you listen carefully, your prospects will reveal their needs and show you how you can help them.

Eighty percent of waking hours are spent communicating, and about half of that time is spent listening. Active listening is not just hearing what the prospect is saying but also looking for clues about their real needs and concerns. If you fail to listen, you will fail to understand what motivates your demographic. Research indicates that 60 percent of misunderstandings in business situations are due to poor listening.[16] Fortunately, you can learn how to listen well. Actively listening to prospects not only increases the effectiveness of the interaction but it also dramatically increases the chance of making a sale.[17]

To succeed in professional selling, you must be able to offer a product or service that satisfies the buyer's needs. Presenting features and benefits is not always enough. You have to listen so that you understand what features and benefits mean something to your prospects! Unfortunately, excellent

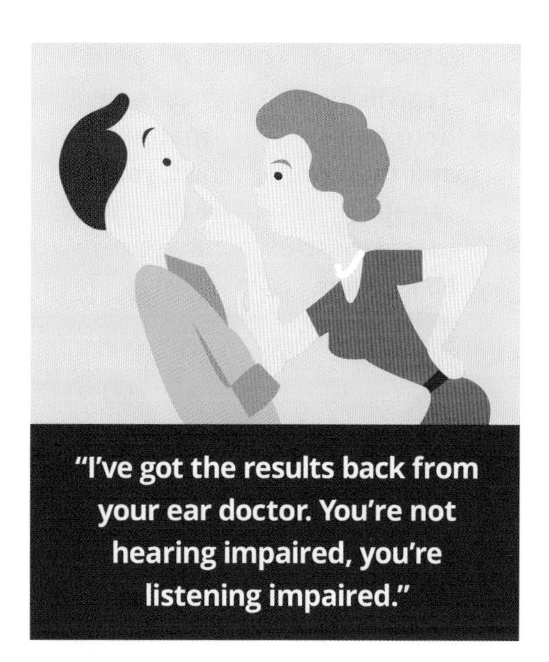

"I've got the results back from your ear doctor. You're not hearing impaired, you're listening impaired."

listening skills usually require a change in our behavior, which is why it can be so hard for salespeople to become good listeners.[18]

Psychologists claim that listening uses only about 25 percent of our brain. The other 75 percent either thinks about what to say next or stops listening if the conversation is boring or of no interest. To improve your listening skills, practice these five mental activities as you listen:

1. **Avoid prejudgment.** If you want to make real connections with others, do not cut people off in mid-sentence to respond. Additionally, wait until you have heard the entire message before judging it. Making value judgments colors your thinking, creating emotional blind spots that can block your ability to make a solid buying recommendation. Jumping to conclusions is a common fault of poor listeners. Assuming you know what is coming next can seriously damage your understanding of the actual meaning intended.

2. **Be patient.** Listen more and give nonverbal and verbal nods of encouragement. Such action allows speakers plenty of time to answer questions and encourages them to express their ideas. Speak at the same speed as the other person, since matching speed is a rapport builder. Also, find the person's mental rate of speed and then adjust or modify your thinking to that rate. Even though the speaker may be saying something exciting, wait until the message is complete, and make sure you understand before you contribute your thoughts.

3. **Take notes.** Remembering everything a person says is difficult. Open your tablet or phone and take notes (or use old-fashioned pen and paper). Be sure to include the prospect's thoughts as well as your thoughts on how to meet needs, requirements, or desires. The mere physical action of writing down keywords reinforces your memory and understanding. You can go back to the prospect's words to help you show your product's applicability to the problem.[19]

4. **Reinforce.** Anchor the prospects' most essential points in their mind through the use of reinforcing responses. If the prospect says a vehicle's average miles per gallon (MPG) is a significant concern, respond, "Yes, that is very

important." Later, state the MPG of the car that the prospect is most interested in buying. If the prospect says, "Our administrators spend too much time making copies," respond, "That has to be a problem." Then later emphasize (and show, if possible) how your copier significantly cuts copy time.

5. **Capitalize on the speed of thought.** We can process about 600 words a minute, but even a fast talker gets out only 100 to 150 words in one minute.[20] Thus, you can think about four times as fast as the average prospect talks. All that spare time is valuable. The poor listener uses it to fidget impatiently, to think about what happened earlier in the day or what will happen later, or to plan what to say as soon as the prospect pauses. Successful salespeople have a plan to follow for using this time profitably:

    - **Anticipate where the prospect is going.** If you guess right, it reinforces the direction you have chosen. If you are wrong, compare your thoughts with the prospect's points and work harder to get on the same wavelength.
    - **Mentally summarize the message.** Pinpoint problems, misconceptions, attitudes, objections, or misunderstandings. What you learn can be an excellent guide to the topics that should be stressed in the presentation and at the close.

    - **Formulate a response.** Be careful not to formulate a response before you hear everything the prospect wants to say. Listen, understand, and then turn the prospect's words to your advantage.
    - **Listen between the lines.** Nonverbal messages are as important as verbal ones. Watch facial expressions, body movement, and position; listen to the tone of voice and volume changes.

Listening is the key to finding ways to offer benefits that enhance the possibility of a close. Effective listening helps sales professionals catch verbal and nonverbal signals indicating a prospect who is interested in buying their product or service. If you leave too many meetings without a sale, listen harder to hear what customers are saying beyond just their words.

SUMMARY

Asking questions is the relationship salesperson's primary tool for identifying problems.

When you ask the right questions, prospects clarify problems in their minds and yours.

There is no universally applicable set of questions. The offering, pre-approach information, and behavioral styles help determine the best questions.

Questions may be closed-ended or open-ended. A closed-ended question asks for a simple response, while open-ended questions ask for more.

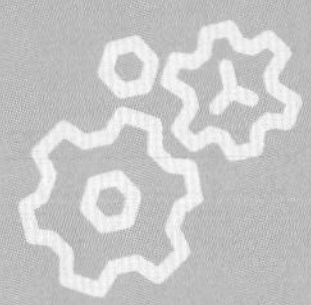

Ask questions according to their structure: amplification, internal summary, and agreement questions.

Listening is one of the most neglected skills in any training program.

Taking notes focuses your attention on what the prospect is saying and avoids prejudgment.

People can think at a rate much faster than they talk. Actively listen so you can anticipate, mentally summarize, plan a response, and refine the message.

Review Questions

1. What factors determine a salesperson's ability to formulate the right questions?
2. What is the difference between manipulation and consultation? Which is the most useful, and why?
3. What kinds of questions allow a salesperson to discover the prospect's behavioral style? How does this information help the salesperson?
4. What tactic is useful as a transition from the approach to need discovery?
5. Who should control the questioning step of the cycle? How is control maintained?
6. What is the purpose of open-ended questions? Formulate an open-ended question that might be used to sell a piece of investment property.
7. Briefly describe the previous training you have had in school, at home, or elsewhere on listening skills.
8. In what situations do you find it hardest to listen? Easiest? What makes the difference?
9. Is listening easier if there is a visual component? For example, do you prefer to talk to someone in person or on the phone when the matter is serious?
10. Educators say effective learning involves more than one of the senses. Explain how this applies to listening and taking notes, to simultaneously listening and looking at visual aids, and to listening to music versus watching television.

IN-CLASS EXERCISES

The following exercises help build teams, improve communication, and emphasize the real-world side of selling. They are meant to challenge you, help you learn how to deal with problems with no single right answer, and use a variety of skills beyond those required in a typical review question. Read and complete each activity. Then in the next class, discuss and compare answers.

EXERCISE 11.1 Ten Questions

Pair up in class with another student as directed by your instructor. Imagine that you two are seated next to one another on a flight from Hawaii to San Francisco. You represent a company that supplies electronics components for jet engine controls, while your seatmate is a procurement officer for a company that manufactures jet engines. Since your companies are well known to one another, you are aware that your flight companion's company is not a client of your company. It is a once-in-a-career chance: you are determined to gain an appointment with the other company to make a full-scale presentation.

On the spur of the moment, compile a list of no more than ten questions along with anticipated responses that you can ask your seatmate that will secure the appointment.

Next, role-play your questions. Did they succeed? What type of questions did you ask (your partner can help categorize the questions)? Would other questions have been more successful? If you role-play your questions in front of other class members, what do they think of your effort?

EXERCISE 11.2 A Need for Questions?

For this exercise, divide the class into four-person teams. On each team, two people will undertake the following role-play: Select a technical device you have on hand, such as a smartphone. One person, acting as a sales rep, will sell the phone to the other, but without asking any questions. This process should take no more than five minutes. Whether the sale is closed successfully does not matter. The other two members of the team will observe.

Then, the remaining two members of the team will undertake the same exercise, but this time the salesperson will conduct the sale by asking questions to determine the customer's needs. The two nonparticipants will observe.

After both role-plays, the team will discuss and critique both. Which role play—without questions or with questions—seemed to go more smoothly? Which felt better or more natural to the participants? To the observers? Why? If you were employed to sell this product, which approach would you use, and why?

Case Studies

The following case studies present you with selling scenarios that require you to apply the critical skills discussed in the chapter and give you training through practical learning situations. They are meant to be both engaging and challenging, and like the in-class exercises, they don't have one right answer.

CASE 11.1—Clanging Pots and Pans

Jack Lund couldn't figure out what had happened. As a representative for WearStrong Restaurant Supplies, he had been supplying equipment to Midwest Diners for the past 15 years. Midwest ran a string of 88 Greek diners in ten major metro areas from Detroit through Indianapolis and Des Moines. They had been one of Jack's first major clients, and he counted the owner, Mark Antonopoulos, a friend. He and Mark had attended trade shows together and on many occasions, had golfed together whenever Jack was in the Chicago area. From the time that Mark had opened his first diner, Jack had come through with a good deal as Mark expanded his business one location at a time. That's why the phone conversation just a few minutes ago was so disturbing.

Jack had just called Mark to let him know that it was time once again to begin his regular replacement rotation. Every five years, Mark's diners had to replace their aluminum cookware. Although sturdy and capable of being scrubbed to a mirror finish, WearStrong's top-of-the-line, heavy aluminum pots and pans could withstand only so much abuse. The replacement schedule called for replacing every pot and pan in each kitchen every five years, but stretching the process out over three years for all 88 stores. When Jack mentioned to Mark that another replacement round was near, he was met with a long silence.

"Jack, I just don't think we're going to do that this time," Mark finally sighed. "You see, we've decided to go with a three-ply line offered by one of your competitors. They have a durable, non-stick finish with a copper lining underneath. It can save us cleanup time and still provide even heat."

"I don't get it, Mark. You know that WearStrong manufactures the same sort of item, but you never expressed any interest in it. You said that our aluminum pan had been a workhorse for you, and you saw no reason to change."

"I know. I know. But do you remember, Jack, when you met last with our operations people here in Chicago? They mentioned that they were interested in saving time in cleanup costs, among other things."

"I think I recall something along those lines, Mark, but since you didn't say anything, I figured everything was all right the way it was," replied Jack.

"Well, it wasn't. You need to pay closer attention, Jack." Mark paused. "Tell you what. The deal isn't done yet. In light of our long-term association, I'll give you one more shot. You can meet with our people next Tuesday, but bring your 'A' game." With that, Mark clicked off.

What do you think had gone wrong? What can Jack do to save the situation? If you were advising Jack, how would you suggest that he prepare for next Tuesday's meeting? Precisely how should he approach Midwest Diner's operations executives? What sort of questions should Jack be prepared to ask next Tuesday?

CASE 11.2—Smothering the Sale

Kurt Edwards had just landed on his feet. After working for fifteen years as a regional manager for a major moving and storage company, he was laid off when the housing bubble burst. People couldn't afford to sell their homes for a loss to move, and Kurt's company had to downsize. Kurt's supervisory responsibilities had included maintaining the company's fleet of moving vans in good working order. Now, however, he had been hired in sales by a major truck parts distributor in the Northwest. Kurt was poised to make more money than he ever had in his previous management position. After all, he knew firsthand what his new clients would need.

As part of his training, Kurt accompanied his district manager in the field. Today, they were calling on the WashMont Hauling Co., a major carrier in Washington and Montana. As they got out of their car, Kurt's manager told him, "After I introduce you, you're on your own. You know the product line. I'm just going to sit back and watch. Go ahead as if I'm not there."

"Okay," Kurt replied, eager to show his manager that he knew his stuff.

Once inside, they proceeded to the office of Bruce Olds, fleet operations manager. After the usual pleasantries had been exchanged, Kurt turned the conversation to the purpose of their visit.

"As we get started, Bruce, I want to assure you that, with me, you will be dealing with someone who understands your situation. I managed a fleet of moving vans for 15 years, so you can be confident that I know what you're facing these days."

"Well, I'm glad to hear that," Bruce replied. "You see..."

"I'll bet your chief problem is delivery of spare parts on time, especially those that wear out more quickly," Kurt interrupted. "That's always the way it was for me. But our company has solved that problem so that you'll never have to worry about having portions of your fleet stranded for lack of parts."

"That's wonderful," Bruce said, "but, you know..."

"And for a large account like yours," Kurt continued, "we can warehouse the parts for you for daily delivery. The large volume allows us to absorb that cost for you. Would you like to solve your major problem today for the next six months?"

"Well, Kurt, I'm not sure that I'm ready to go there just yet. Perhaps you could call back once I've got a better handle on just what our needs are," Bruce said, standing and extending his hand.

Back in the car, Kurt's manager exploded, "What was that about? You don't know the first thing about sales! You smothered the guy!"

"What do you mean?" asked Kurt. "I solved his problem for him. He just wasn't ready."

Based on what you've learned from Chapter 11, what happened here? Why was Kurt's manager so angry? Why didn't Kurt's knowledge and connection with Bruce produce better results? What do you think Kurt's manager should recommend in terms of additional training for Kurt?

PHASE 1

1. Prospecting
Chapter 8

2. Pre-Approach
Chapter 9

3. Approach
Chapter 10

PHASE 2

4. Need Discovery
Chapter 11

5. Presentation

6. Objections
Chapter 13

7. Close
Chapter 14

PHASE 3

8. Follow-Up
Chapter 15

THE EIGHT-STEP RELATIONSHIP SELLING CYCLE

THE PRESENTATION: HOW TO BE ENGAGING AND COMPELLING

OVERVIEW

This chapter details step five of the Relationship Selling Cycle, which includes techniques to use during the presentation to continue building on the connection and rapport you previously established. At this point in the process, you have studied your prospects and discovered more about what drives them to buy. Now you are ready to make your presentation so they can fully see the benefits of becoming customers. You will learn the key elements that comprise units of conviction—the building blocks upon which to build a meaningful sales presentation.

OBJECTIVES

- Understand how to make a presentation.
- Learn how units of conviction help prospects reach a buying decision.
- Discover effective tactics for making a sales presentation.
- Study different methods for involving the prospect in the presentation.
- Understand the importance of demonstrations and other tools.
- Examine the different types of sales aids available.
- Recognize the value of using technology in making presentations.

Presenting Value

"Want to buy? There's an app for that." Perhaps in another few years, that's all salespeople will have to say to their customers. With the proliferation of technology and the ease with which we can access information any time, anywhere, it's tempting to presume that face-to-face selling is on the road to extinction.

Nothing could be further from the truth.

Future-focused salespeople leverage developments in technology to more accurately identify prospects in advance, and then use that data to drive face-to-face visits and stimulate sales. Granted, the future of person-to-person interactions will look different from classic sales. Still, personal prospect engagement will continue to be the driving force in professional selling. It is the technology tools themselves that will enable in-person selling to remain an affordable approach to build relationships effectively and increase sales.

Relationship salespeople will continue to prosper if they understand one simple concept: There is a vast difference between presenting data and presenting valuable information. It is easy to fall into the trap of creating a *data-dense presentation*, one that is filled with facts and figures that complicate a presentation. No matter how important you think something might be, your prospects may not agree. They may not even be listening! Here are some surprising facts:[1]

- **The typical salesperson presents six to eight benefits during a presentation. Just 24 hours later, the average prospect remembers one benefit.**
- **In 39 percent of those cases, they remember that one benefit incorrectly.**
- **In 49 percent of the cases, they remember something that wasn't mentioned at all.**

These days, we're all so busy and preoccupied with technology and other interruptions that we would welcome the opportunity to engage in an effective, efficient, and beneficial presentation. In those moments, we don't want to hear facts. We want to hear tangible pieces of useful and targeted information that will remind us why we need to listen to this presentation in the first place.

In short, data and numbers are important —but data is *not* what stimulates sales. Customers say yes when they see that what you have to offer will solve a problem or fill a pressing need, not when you impress their intellects. The future of professional relationship selling will be based on how well sales professionals become trusted advisors who provide value and guide clients to solutions to their problems. The future belongs to those who can present their knowledge, offer wisdom, and create value in tangible ways.

Strive for Passion, Not Perfection

More often than not, customers buy because of rapport established with a trusted salesperson or company over time. Selling is all about relationship building. There are hundreds of competitors vying for the same customers, which is why it comes down to the way you present yourself and your offering, as well as the value you create. Sales presentations must be listener centered. People want to have their problems solved. In his book, *What They Don't Teach You at the Harvard Business School*, Mark McCormack says there are three fundamental selling truths:

TRUTH #1:
If you don't know your product, people will resent your efforts to sell it.

TRUTH #2:
If you don't believe in your product, no amount of personality or technique will cover that fact.

TRUTH #3:
If you can't sell your product with enthusiasm, the absence of it will be infectious.

No one wants to buy from a dispassionate seller. In other words, if you don't believe in the product, no one else will. The more enthusiasm you display and the more options you create for the prospect, the higher the chance for a sale.[2] Don't worry about making the perfect presentation. No such thing exists. Prospects are looking to you for knowledge about your offering and how it can help them solve a problem or become more successful.

You must genuinely believe in what you're selling and show some passion when doing it—and that is far more important than perfection.

Get Creative with Regular Customers

If you are calling on the same customers regularly, you may tend to give the same presentation or skip the performance entirely and ask, "What do you need today?" If you are unwilling to put in some real work and are content to be an order taker for the duration of your career, your best opportunity for financial success is to win the lottery! Vary your presentation. Provide new ideas to help your customers make money, save time, or increase efficiency. Plan to use concepts like these:

- **Give customers new advertising or merchandising design ideas.**
- **Help customers develop a marketing plan for improving their business.**
- **Educate loyal customers on new product features.**
- **Share a piece of industry or trade news that affects their interests.**

Begin with Planning

All essential tasks in life begin with planning. Successful salespeople learn to dutifully focus, segment, and measure inputs, outputs, and performance. The Nielsen Corporation has built a multibillion-dollar business on gathering and distributing sales data to analyze and report their compelling findings.

Consumers and organizations love this kind of analysis, and some even refer to this research as a *science.*[3] That may seem like an overstatement. Still, effective planning based on statistics and research has become highly methodological and scientific in its approach.

Random, haphazard action never leads to success in any worthwhile effort. In this respect, selling is no different from any other undertaking. How well you plan what takes place during the sales interview plays a significant role in the success you achieve when closing time arrives.

Here's a good rule of thumb to follow when developing a new sales talk: spend one hour of preparation time for each minute of presentation. For example, if you plan to present for 20 minutes, you should invest 20 hours in research, development, organizing, outlining, and rehearsing your presentation. It sounds like a lot of time—and it is—but it's necessary if you want to deliver a dynamic presentation. If you invest the time in constructing a superb, researched performance, you'll be able to bring your best to every sales presentation consistently. You will need to tweak each presentation based on each prospect's unique needs. But, as Dr. Norman Vincent Peale once said, *"I give the same mashed potatoes for each speech, I just change the gravy."*

The Call Objective

The most successful salespeople have specific objectives for each meeting. In many instances, the call objective is to present your product or service and complete the sale. In others, you endeavor to dig more deeply to discover the prospect's needs so that you may prepare a proposal for later consideration. Other times, you may meet to prompt one of the decision-makers to allow you to set up a meeting to present to a buying center. In these latter instances, you will probably plan several interviews that, taken together, contain all the elements that may be considered parts of the presentation. The difference is that you present in multiple interviews rather than in a single meeting.

Whether you intend to complete the presentation and the close in a single call or multiple calls depends upon what you sell and the size or complexity of the expected order. The single-call close is appropriate for sales situations with a sole decision-maker. If a buying center is involved, it may require multiple calls.

When Tanis Cornell was the global enterprise manager for NetApp, Inc., she managed many of their top accounts, including AT&T. Tanis had a team of 25 people and was

required to navigate the team through each complex sales process for the giant data storage company. Her approach to selling a major account involved an elaborate, multistep process. Here is the system she used:

1. **Initial Call.** Develop rapport and establish a need. Judge how far to go by how quickly a relationship is established. Take notes all along to help build trust by remembering key details.
2. **Survey Call.** Interview all principal decision-makers to get information. The decision is ultimately based on three factors: cost, quality, and service. Discover which one is most important to this client.
3. **Proposal Call.** Present a buying recommendation. Recognize the fact that this is a joint or buying center decision, and give each person what that individual needs to decide. Use trial closes.
4. **Closing Call.** Get a verbal commitment and then a written one.
5. **Follow-Up Calls.** Continue meeting with executives, managers, and department heads until a solution is reached. Consider each meeting as a mini contract negotiation.

Tanis knew that she or a team member could close the sale at any one of the calls, but often it required more than four appointments to reach the closing meeting. For more extensive deals with multiple calls involved, the complete sales cycle could take up to a year. If you sell something with a complex buying process, it's critical to have a system in place so that you know what to expect.

Sales Call Planning

Many companies (especially those whose product or service requires extensive research into customer needs) require their salespeople

"Great plan! **Could we get some more details?"**

to prepare a formal presentation plan. Such a plan serves numerous purposes. It reveals areas of incomplete information, helps ensure that suggested solutions meet customer needs, and provides an overview of the entire situation. Planning for sales calls can be done low tech—on a sheet of paper—or done on a device with CRM access.

Using the latest technology for call planning will produce added benefits. The Professional Selling Skills® Call Planner, for instance, plugs into Salesforce CRM and is designed to maximize productivity by tracking the sales cycle for complex, multi-tiered sales. It stores and shares best practices in call planning and execution and helps the team gain insights into the sales process.[4]

Using a call-planning system can enhance your sales efforts substantially. Whatever sales call tools you use, you will need to gather key pieces of information to make them useful. Exhibit 12.1 shows the kind of information you need to create the best sales call planning sheet possible.[5]

Product-Analysis Worksheet

Prospects don't know as much about your product or service or why they need it as you do. That's why you're here! You must not only know all the facts about your product but also be able to relate your knowledge directly to the specific needs of the prospect. If you can

EXHIBIT 12.1 Sales Call Planning Information

1. Company name and industry
2. Website and mailing address
3. Buyer profile(s) including position, background, best times to call, and preferred communication method
4. Major competitors and their area sales reps
5. The objective for the particular call
6. Expressed needs or problems to address during this call
7. Strategies and tactics useful for the situation such as:
    a. The best approach to use
    a. Specific, fact-finding questions
    a. Features and benefits to stress
    a. Anticipated objections and how to answer them
    a. Closing techniques to use
8. Sales tools/resources to take along
9. Results of the meeting
10. Next steps (email, call, meeting, order fulfillment, etc.)

quote prices, catalog numbers, shipping dates, delivery schedules, and credit terms but have no convincing evidence of the product's value to offer to prospects, you may be afflicted with what is called the *salesperson's curse*: You know your product better than you know how your clients can use it.[6]

A sales rep who suffers from the salesperson's curse is in the same league as a math student who can recite all the formulas in the geometry book but never knows which one to use. Before you can expect a signed contract, you must figure out how to use the information you have to discover the best solution to your prospect's problems.

THE SALESPERSON'S CURSE: You know your product better than you know how your clients can use it.

You can do this by preparing units of conviction.

Units of Conviction

Units of conviction are concise, carefully prepared "mini-presentations" used as building blocks to construct the information you present. You combine individual units of conviction to form a *product-analysis worksheet.* Making a product-analysis worksheet helps you evaluate the various characteristics of your offering so that you are better able to present it to prospects. When you prepare units of conviction and add them to your reserve of available options, they become a permanent part of your selling arsenal. A unit of conviction consists of five elements:

1. **A feature of your product or service**
2. **A transitional phrase**
3. **The benefits the feature provides**
4. **Evidence to support your claims**
5. **A tie-down to gain the prospect's agreement**

Features. *Features* are the tangible and intangible qualities of the product or service you sell. They are facts that are the same no matter who uses the product or service. Tangible features include observable factors such as color, size, capacity, performance, and base material.[7] Intangible features include customer service, price, delivery, service availability, and the support that you personally promise to provide.

Transitional Phrase. The ability to translate features into benefits—the value or worth that

the user derives from the product or service—is one of the strengths of a relationship salesperson. Even if you know which feature can fulfill the buying motive, you cannot expect the prospect to make the connection automatically. You must make the verbal transition. Prospective customers do not know your product as well as you know it, so help them by connecting features to benefits via a transitional phrase. Some salespeople call this connection between a feature and its benefits a *bridge*.[8] While the words may vary, bridges are designed to accomplish the same purpose: to join the features to their benefits. These phrases serve the purpose of answering the prospect's question, "What's in it for me?" Some common transitional phrases are:

"This is beneficial to you because . . ."

"This allows you to . . ."

"This prevents the issue of . . ."

"What this means to you is . . ."

Begin preparing units of conviction by listing in writing all the features of your product or service. If you sell more than one primary product, make separate lists for each one. Then go back and list all the ways the first feature can benefit your prospect. If you neglect this preliminary step, you will find yourself facing prospects who listen to features and ask, "So what?" and you will have no suitable answers. When you prepare units of conviction in advance, finding the right one is like reaching into your briefcase and pulling out a sample. You know what's in there, and all of it is ready the moment you need it.

Benefits. Every feature of your product has numerous benefits. Of the multiple benefits a product or service has to offer, only four or five will be key motivators to a prospect.[9] Your task is to find out which ones are the chief motivators. For example, what are the benefits of a 600-horsepower engine in a luxury car? They could include a smoother ride, plenty of power to quickly pass a car, swift acceleration away from a road hazard, the feeling of being in charge, slower wear and tear, and higher resale value, among other things. The point is that one feature does not equal one benefit.

List your product's top ten characteristics, and then come up with at least three different benefits for each feature. Remember, features may justify the price, but benefits are what warrant the purchase. The benefits provide you with multiple ways to close more sales.

Exhibit 12.2 illustrates a features-and-benefits analysis for the Apple iPhone. In the left column, you will find one feature of the phone, and in the right column, the numerous benefits of that single feature. If a potential customer is trying to decide between an Apple iPhone and a Samsung Galaxy or a Google Pixel, such an analysis may tip the scales in the favor of an iPhone.

EXHIBIT 12.2 Features and Benefits of the Apple iPhone

Feature	Benefits
Universal Interface	The iPhone ensures all apps and functions perform the way Apple intended them to perform, which allows for a simple user experience. Every iPhone works the same, and its functionality is identical to iPads and other Apple devices, creating a shorter learning curve. Thanks to the Apple iCloud, all of your important photos and information syncs seamlessly across every platform.
Accessory Options	With the popularity of the Apple Watch, Air Pods, and so many Bluetooth devices that pair seamlessly with the iPhone, plentiful accessory options create a wealth of variety and possibility. Apple's Health app pairs with every major fitness tracker brand and makes getting healthy easier.

Apple Store	Apple Stores are everywhere, so finding one is easy. Their simple approach to solving any problem with your Apple product makes troubleshooting a no-brainer. You can make an appointment to ensure prompt service and never have to wait in line since every employee is equipped to complete purchases from where they stand.
Apple Pay	No more carrying your wallet into the coffee shop or thousands of other businesses. Just pay with your iPhone using Face ID in stores, within apps, and on the web. This makes purchasing safe, fast, and easy. You can even send and receive money in Messages from the couch or bed.
Enhanced Security	Malicious content has been known to access millions of non-Apple phones, corrupting them and stealing important information. Many users have huge charges on their bill, following a virus attack on their phone. iPhones are the safest on the market, with the fewest security breaches, so you can feel safe.
Dual 12MP Ultra-Wide and Wide Cameras	The new cameras on the iPhone will take professional quality photos from any distance with 5x zoom. Use Portrait mode to take studio-level photos to capture special moments. There is even six portrait lighting effects to choose from, ensuring you get the perfect shot every time. If you want to shoot a pic at night without that trademark "flash" look, just use night mode to make your night shot look like it was shot in the daytime.

Evidence To Support Claims. You present benefits to avert the prospect's question, "So what?" and you present evidence to support any claims you make to prevent the concerns, "Can you prove it?" and "Who says?" Even if you have been successful in establishing credibility, you are unlikely to be considered an all-knowing sage whose answers are accepted without question. You must be prepared to back up what you say with:

1. **Facts and Statistics.** Numbers matter, which means you need to utilize quantifiable results. If a percentage or figure helps back up what you just said, share it.

2. **Testimonials.** The best possible recommendation for your product or service is for one of your satisfied customers to provide a testimonial. This person can express his or her satisfaction with you and the product, which predisposes the prospect to accept what you say.

3. **Demonstrations.** Show your product in action. Demonstrations are more useful if you have a tangible item that can be touched and seen. You can also show a video demonstration if it's not possible to bring the display with you.

4. **Samples.** Samples are intended to provide an appeal to one or more of the five senses. A salesperson for a company that supplies mosquito nets, for example, may bring one along.

5. **Case Histories.** The use of examples or case histories is another way to show a prospect how you helped other people or companies. Tell the prospect about other customers who faced similar circumstances before you helped solve their problems. Use details from their cases (get permission from those customers first). Use these guidelines when planning to use this type of evidence:

   a. The case history must be authentic.
   b. Use details to indicate you are personally familiar with the situation.
   c. Back up the example with pictures, letters, articles, and other evidence.

d. Relate it directly to a prospect's stated areas of need.

The evidence used to back up the features and benefits you present must be carefully tailored to the needs, problems, and personality of the prospect. For example, use cost-saving statistics with a prospective customer especially interested in cost-effectiveness. Use testimonials from prominent people with a potential customer who is motivated by the desire for status. Use everything you know about the prospect's social style as input for each step in the sales process.

Tie-Down. The *tie-down* is an essential step in building units of conviction, although it usually consists of no more than a single question that asks for the prospect's agreement. Your goal is to translate *features* into *benefits*, to provide the necessary *evidence* to prove your points and gain a *commitment*. Here are some examples of tie-down questions:

Considering these facts, wouldn't you agree that this is a safe tire, Ms. Cooper?

I believe you will agree with me, Don, that this is a better way to handle the process (nod your head to encourage the prospect to nod if he agrees as well).

I think you can see the enormous advantage you will have with unlimited data, right, Ms. Grimmett?

The tie-down is vital throughout the presentation to check on understanding and agreement and to make sure the prospect is ready to proceed to the next point. One of the functions of the tie-down is to incite a series of yes responses throughout the presentation. Therefore, when you attempt a close, the prospect is used to saying yes and may more readily say yes again.

Suppose, however, that you ask a tie-down question, and the prospect says, "No, I don't agree with you." Although it may not feel like it at that moment, this is a good thing. Had you not asked the tie-down question, you would have pushed on to the close, only to hear "no" and not know why. Now you are aware of a disconnect and can go back to find its source. Then you can correct it, ask another tie-down, and move forward when you reach an agreement.

Exhibit 12.3 is one complete unit of conviction for a wireless phone company's unlimited data plan. Notice the tie-down at the end—the question that leads the prospect into an agreement and moves the sales process forward.

EXHIBIT 12.3 Unit of Conviction: Cell Phone Carrier Data Plan

Feature	While many wireless providers still offer plans based on data used per month, we offer unlimited data (and of course, unlimited talk and text) for as low as $60 per month.
Transition	What this means is...
Benefit	... if you like to stream video and are always online, you never have to worry about overage charges again. You don't even need to make sure you are connected to Wi-Fi!
Evidence	Let's say you love to binge-watch on Netflix, but you aren't always connected to Wi-Fi when you're watching. Watching movies or shows on Netflix uses about 1 GB of data per hour for each stream of standard definition video, and up to 3 GB per hour for each stream of HD video. That means that after a few movies or one weekend of binge-watching, on other plans, you could already be over your data limit! That could amount to hundreds of extra dollars in data charges per month.
Tie-Down	Wouldn't you agree that unlimited data is a necessity for your wireless plan, Jesse?

Crafting Your Presentation Style

Once you have discovered critical motivators during the previous sales cycle steps, set call goals, and planned your units of conviction, it's time to choose your presentation style. The choice includes determining how well-rehearsed you will be. There is much more to preparation than merely gathering and reviewing information. Rehearsal eliminates the stammering, nervous speech habits, and repetition that can result from a lack of preparation.

When you rehearse and internalize your presentation, you allow the passion for your product to shine.

But how much should salespeople rehearse? Controversy has long raged over the effectiveness of "canned" presentations. Opponents claim that performances that are memorized and delivered robotically are likely to produce disengaged, bored listeners. Supporters of memorized presentations point to the many advantages of knowing what you will say and when.

The issue lies more with the presenter than with the delivery method. In short, it's a personal choice. If you thrive on being prepared or have little to no experience, then you may do well with a memorized presentation. In deciding how you will deliver your message, consider the unique features of the three basic choices: memorized, outline, and impromptu.

Memorized Presentation

Even though you may learn a presentation, it should never *sound* memorized. Instead, internalize it to the point that you can deliver a personalized message with a relaxed but warm tone. Use a memorized presentation as a guide to expertly lead you and your prospect through the process. Because every prospect has different needs, using a word-for-word presentation from start to finish would be a mistake. However, planning out portions of your performance offers some advantages, especially to new salespeople. Using units of conviction that have worked well for other successful salespeople means that those units are reliable and proven. Also, memorizing portions of a presentation can be a confidence builder for those who are brand-new to selling.

Memorizing your presentation as well as answers to the most commonly asked questions and objections prevents you from committing pitfalls from which you may never recover. No one expects you to know every last detail about your offering, but starting a response with, "Um, I think..." is not an option.[10] You must be confident in your answer, even if that answer is, "I'll get back to you on that." By memorizing your presentation and learning the answers to common concerns, you can display confidence and set yourself apart.

Outline Presentation

With this technique, you do not plan exact words in full detail. You know what content you will present but are confident enough in both knowledge and skill levels to believe that the right words will come as needed. Outlined presentations are the common choice of experienced public speakers. Using an outline presentation successfully depends upon developing and internalizing numerous units of conviction. You then build the outline using those units and by considering all the information you have gathered about the prospect. Most salespeople who use an outline method follow the same general outline for most presentations. They may, however, have multiple approaches, numerous units of conviction, and plenty of evidence—all of which can be blended to meet the needs of a specific prospect.

Procter & Gamble is one company that recommends its sales reps follow an outline plan for presentations. Exhibit 12.4 is an outline for a presentation written by one of Procter & Gamble's sales managers.

EXHIBIT 12.4 Procter & Gamble Sales Plan

Purpose of the Sales Call: Sell 40 cases of Folger's new line of fair-trade ground coffee bags for display at the front of the Foodrite grocery store.

Background of the Account: Foodrite is a natural grocery store with 40 locations throughout the Southeast. Each store is allowed to select their own store displays in addition to ones required by corporate. This particular Foodrite location has a $100,000 weekly volume, and they need to increase dollar volume per customer transaction. This location also has a back stock of eight cases of canister creamers that we may be able to help them move.

Summarize the Situation: The store manager told me that he wants to increase the volume per customer by 7 percent over the next three months by increasing the average amount of each transaction. I plan to suggest our new fair trade coffee line to help achieve this goal.

State the Idea: My idea is for the store to display our eye-catching, newly designed line with their already-stocked canister creamers from the store's backstock.

Explain How It Works: Last year's records show that the store displayed 30 cases of Folger's one-pound coffee during this time, and it sold out quickly at regular shelf price. Now in the cold months, coffee consumption is the number one dry grocery item, and fair-trade coffee is trending in the coffee world. Capitalize on customer appeal of the Folger's name, combined with more responsibly sourced coffee beans (which is relevant to natural food shoppers), and enhance it with an appealing display with the canister creamers. The store now moves ten cases weekly, and a unique exhibition will move 40 cases quickly. Offer to help build the display, which will save time and labor for the store.

Reinforce Key Benefits: Show calculations of the contribution this display can make to help reach the percent increase desired: which is approximately $8,400 in sales. Add a quality image created by Folger's advertising. The related item display will increase movement on the creamers that are now sitting in backstock. The result is an increase in the average per-customer sale, which is the goal.

Suggest a Natural Next Step: Ask for a decision on which truck to send the 40 cases of Folger's and suggest a specific day, say next Tuesday.

Impromptu Presentation

Some highly successful salespeople, particularly those who have many years of experience, may say that they don't prepare for their presentations. Their preparation time is distributed in a different way than that of the less experienced sales reps—but they do prepare. The impromptu presentation follows the same principles that any other presentation would. Still, those who use an ad-libbed approach are master people watchers. They understand people; they ask questions and listen. They know their product so thoroughly that they can seize almost mysteriously upon the one thing that will best appeal to a specific prospect. They possess such charisma that the air of trust and credibility they create makes objections nonexistent and painlessly turn prospects into customers.

As a result, these master salespeople spend most of their "preparation time" in gathering additional information about the prospect rather than spending time in consciously matching features and benefits to individual prospects.

Effective Presentation Tactics

You have the option of telling your story to prospects using a variety of sales tactics. Which tactics you select will depend upon what you learned about the prospect during the pre-approach, what you observed in the opening minutes, and what kind of environment you find in the meeting location. The only limit to the number of presentation tactics is your creative imagination.

The most common tactics are presented here, and you will likely use all of them at some point in your career as they fit into your sales activity. Over time, you will find yourself developing a unique mixture of tactics—a blend that suits your personality, your product, and your prospects' needs.

Participation

Every presentation, no matter how it is organized or delivered, must get the prospect involved. When prospects are shut out of the presentation process or choose to say nothing and contribute nothing, they also buy nothing. The prime tactic for getting prospective customers to participate is to ask questions and listen attentively so that the remainder of your presentation is highly individualized and based on their responses.

Beyond asking questions, you should encourage prospects to ask their own questions about a product benefit or any factor involved in its application. Their stated concerns and questions will go a long way toward preventing misunderstanding and allow you to address the problem or need that is most relevant to them.

Demonstration

Showmanship is highly effective if you keep it professional and not over-the-top. There is a big difference between *showmanship* and *show-off-manship*. A well-timed dramatic touch can seize and hold the prospect's attention like nothing else. A demonstration can add showmanship to the presentation and while helping you more effectively present features and benefits. A well timed and executed demonstration enables you to:[11]

1. Catch the buyer's interest
2. Strengthen your selling points
3. Help visually-oriented prospects better understand
4. Reduce the number of objections
5. Help you close the sale

The value of a demonstration is that it involves more than one of the senses. Remember these three points when determining how you will deliver your message to the prospect:[12]

- If you rely solely on talking about your product, you only engage the *auditory* sense. If you add a demonstration, you include the *visual* sense.
- If you involve the prospect in the demonstration, you add the sense of *touch*. The more senses you engage, the more quickly your audience absorbs the information that could lead to a sale.
- People remember 20 percent of what they hear and 20 percent of what they see, but they remember 50 percent of what they see and hear. By mapping your information out visually, you increase how much your prospective clients retain.

Here are four principles for you to follow when using demonstrations in your sales presentation:

1. Concentrate their attention. The CEO of a large corporation once called a meeting in his office. When his employees came in, he was juggling tennis balls. After they were all seated, he tossed aside all but one and said, "We all have many things on our minds—like these tennis balls. But we must put them aside and concentrate on one problem at a time, or we'll waste energy and time trying to juggle them all."

The same thing can be said about your presentations. You must do everything in your power to focus a prospect's attention on one thing: what you are saying. A planned demonstration is an excellent tool for accomplishing this purpose.

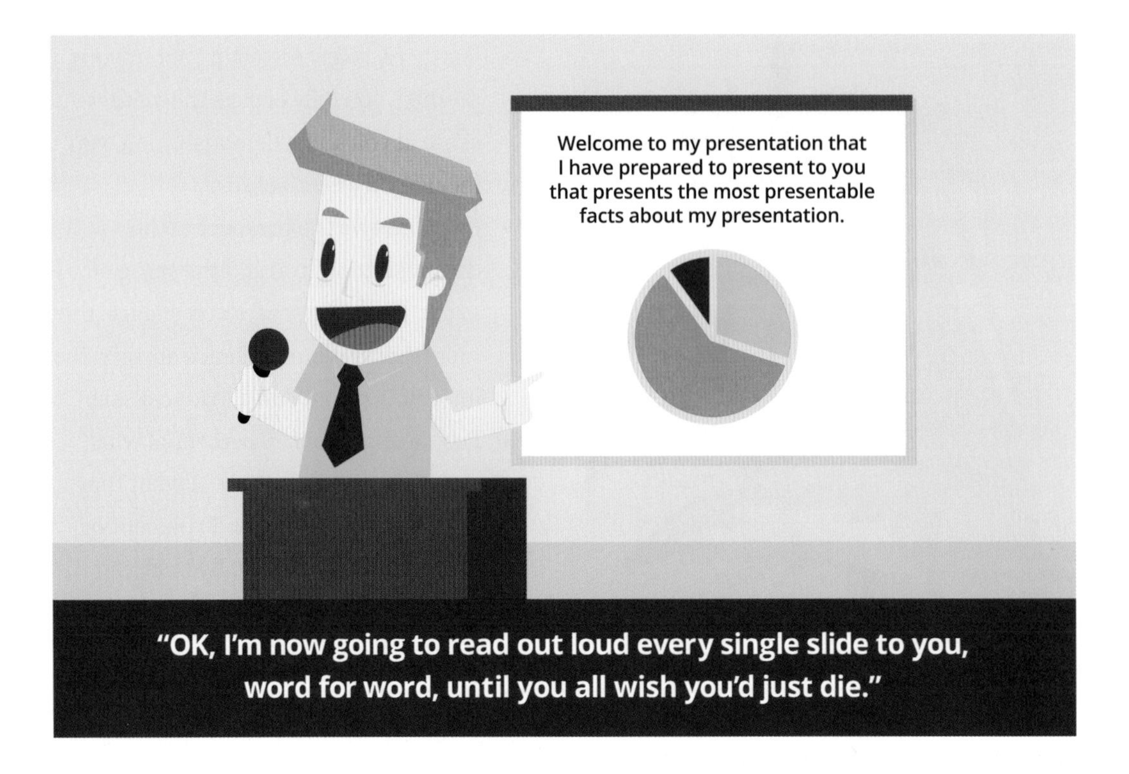

When you fill prospects in on the agenda and key points in your introduction, you send a signal as to what "files" your audience should open in their minds. When you cover those points in your presentation, you place the data you want them to remember in those open mental files. Then, when you repeat the most significant points just before or during the close, it's like you are hitting the "save" button and reinforcing the critical data.

Remember that your prospect can't re-read relevant passages from your oral presentation. So, make their lives easier by reminding them of the essential points and adding a visual component to make those points even more memorable.

2. Get prospects into the act. Invite the prospect to operate the device, taste the food, smell the fragrance, feel the depth of the tread on the tires, or listen to the quiet sound of the machine in operation. If you are selling an intangible product, show the prospect a few photos, charts, or a prospectus. Get as many senses involved as possible.

The Gulf Coast Regional Blood Center in Houston once asked prospects to put a 30-letter word puzzle together. The sales representative would hand the prospect a small box full of letters that, when properly arranged, spelled: **"WILL YOU HAVE BLOOD WHEN YOU NEED IT?"** This demonstration was designed to dramatically illustrate how critical a company-sponsored blood drive is to the community.

3. Keep prospects glued to the screen. Since selling is a mobile profession, salespeople often need to engage in virtual meetings—sometimes called *webinars*—through Cisco,

Skype, Zoom, or other web-based applications. A webinar can be mutually beneficial for prospects when meeting face-to-face is time or cost prohibitive. However, virtual meetings do have some pitfalls. The average person has an attention span of just five to eight seconds, and it continues to decrease as we integrate technology further into our daily lives. Think of all the ways your prospect could be distracted by what's on their screen. That means it's your job to ensure that your presentations are riveting.

4. Paint a picture with metaphors. Metaphors imply comparisons between otherwise dissimilar things without using the words "like" or "as," often creating a dramatic visual image. Remember this motto: "Facts tell, but stories sell." Painting a mental picture is a hook that grabs prospects, reels them in, and keeps them interested in hearing more and asking questions. Here is an example of a creative metaphor:

> *Picture yourself in a desert without a canteen. In the distance, you see a well. There's a bucket with a rope nearby. Now, would you jump into the water headfirst, or would you use the bucket and rope to fetch the water? My company supplies you with the bucket and rope—the tools required to get what you want in the most efficient way.*

Metaphors, analogies, and similes can breathe life into dull sales presentations. These are effective ways to reinforce concepts while building rapport and showing people the value you provide.[13]

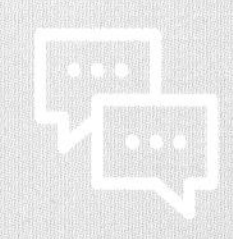

The Social Media Connection

CREATING A BACKCHANNEL TO ENHANCE YOUR PRESENTATIONS

More salespeople are using social media to engage their prospects and extend their reach. Twitter, Facebook, and numerous custom online tools allow presenters to create a *backchannel*—an online conversation about a presentation or the presenter—for their prospects' ideas and feedback. This two-way engagement can enrich understanding as well as the presentation's effectiveness. Here are some tips for improving your presentations with social media:[14]

1. **Engage before the presentation.** Before you meet a prospect, you can lay the groundwork for making your presentation. Listen to your prospects' tweets and use them as trigger points for building your presentation. Look for trends in their posts. Are they launching new products? Buying new companies? Expanding to a new market? If any of those announcements could be a trigger for something you sell, mention the update or tweet during the presentation, and ask them how that issue is affecting their business.
2. **Create a separate hashtag.** Make it easy for your prospects to talk about your company or your presentation on social media by creating a unique hashtag to isolate it. Because Twitter hashtags expire, create an archive to ensure the Twitter backchannel will be available later.
3. **Welcome the backchannel.** Make sure to make readily available your Twitter username, other social media handles, and the hashtags for your presentation. That provides a visual cue that you welcome the backchannel from the start, and it will give your presentation a highly interactive and customized feel.
4. **Make key points tweetable.** Make your presentation social media-friendly by expressing each of your main points as a tweetbite, which is a soundbite that will get picked up and tweeted. Ensure your bites are easily re-tweetable by allowing space for your username. If you're using slides, display your bites. You can also program PowerPoint and Keynote to publish tweets using add-ins like Slide Tweet for PowerPoint and Keynote Tweet for Keynote.
5. **Learn from the backchannel.** Enrich your future presentations by analyzing the blow-by-blow account of how your performance was received. The feedback is likely to be more genuine and detailed than a typical evaluation form. In your next presentation, stop what fell flat, clarify areas of confusion, and capitalize on what resonated most with your prospects.

Presentation Sales Tools

Sales aids fall mainly into the *audio*, *visual*, or *audiovisual* categories. Many people are visually oriented. That's why exciting, illustrative slides and tech-driven programs are useful presentation tools. Sales aids are used to help the prospect visualize the benefits of the product or service, or to help you organize the presentation so that your prospect receives a compelling, memorable performance. Low-tech tools like flip charts can be simple but effective ways to engage prospects. Still, with technology as ubiquitous as it is today, the sky is the limit with the use of presentation tools.

Tablets and Flip Charts

Companies may provide salespeople with tablets or laptops for presenting. Some companies use flip charts or binders, especially when presenting to clients who may need to summarize what you say to other decision-makers or a buying center. These non-tech tools are also helpful if the meeting environment is not conducive to a web-based or slide presentation.

Having an organized presentation that is ready at the click of a button provides an engaging experience for the prospect, and it also reminds you what to cover next and keeps the meeting on track. A well-designed presentation via a low-tech or tech-based device has these characteristics:

1. **It emphasizes user benefits since most visual presentations are structured around units of conviction.**
2. **It fosters two-way communication because you can listen rather than worry about what to say next.**
3. **It increases your success rate by leading naturally into the close.**
4. **It helps you tell your complete story in less time.**
5. **It helps the interview get back on track after an interruption.**

Although a company-prepared organizer is a useful beginning tool, most successful salespeople develop visuals that work for their unique style of selling. You may choose

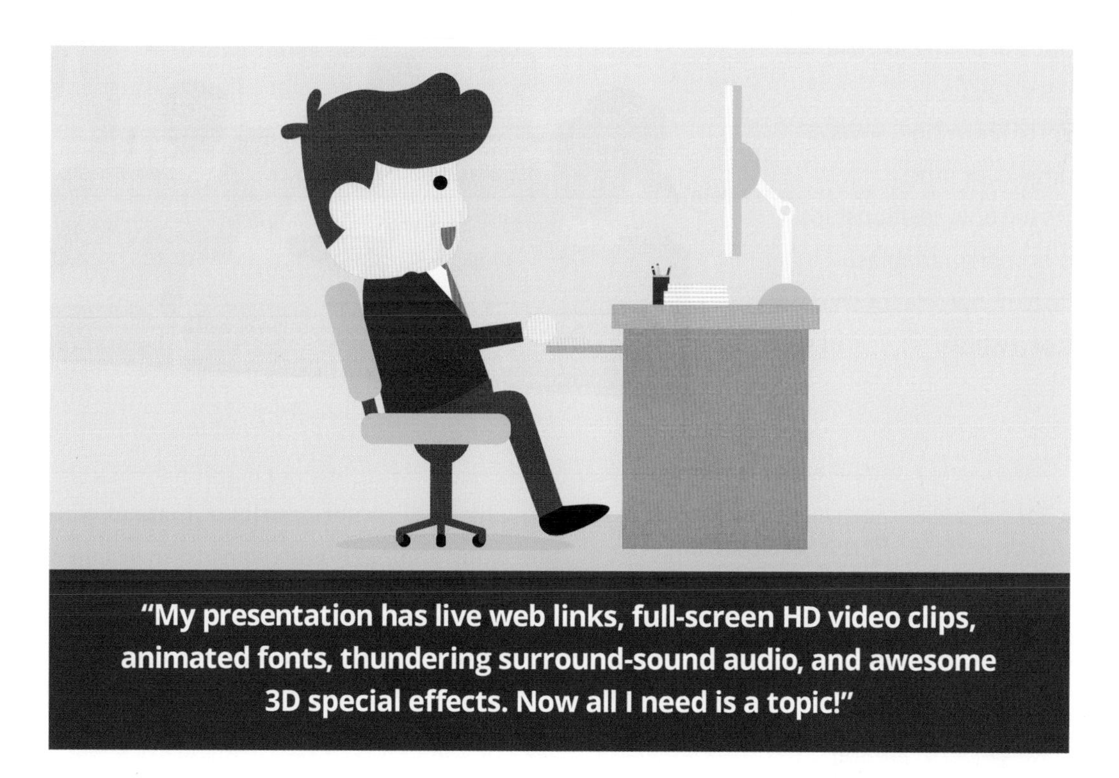

"My presentation has live web links, full-screen HD video clips, animated fonts, thundering surround-sound audio, and awesome 3D special effects. Now all I need is a topic!"

to include letters from existing satisfied customers praising the product, the company, or your service. You can also post pictures of clients utilizing the product or service on social media and show those during the presentation.

Visual aids are especially helpful when presenting to a group or when needing to explain complicated equipment or processes. Exhibit 12.5 presents some useful guidelines to follow when preparing visuals.[15]

EXHIBIT 12.5 **Guidelines for Preparing Visuals**

- Keep your visuals simple.
- The text should be in short phrases, not complete sentences.
- Leave plenty of white space and follow a consistent format.
- Use functional colors that are easy on the eyes (use red sparingly).
- Never put the entire presentation on a slide and read it.
- Only use complex data when prospects have the time and knowledge to study the numbers carefully.
- Present one idea at a time to ensure a clear understanding.
- Use line charts to show how several variables change over time.
- Use bar charts to show relationships between two or more variables.
- Use pie charts to show relationships among parts of a whole.

Audiovisual Presentations

There is no reason why any salesperson should not have an up-to-date, creative, and engaging presentation. Microsoft PowerPoint may not always be the answer in terms of quality and professionalism. Instead, you or your company may want to invest in a professional, designer-quality presentation program. These are often compatible with your CRM system so that you can track the dates of presentations, presenters, and other variables. Web or cloud-based presentations are common because they eliminate the possibility of system crashes. If you've got a reliable Wi-Fi connection, you've got the capacity for an excellent presentation.

> **"The world is but a canvas to the imagination."**
> *Henry David Thoreau*

Situational Selling

Master salespeople have a plan for every sales interview, but they never feel bound by that plan. Relationship selling requires you to be flexible and versatile. No matter how much you learn about a prospect before a sales meeting, you can never be sure what kind of situation to expect when you arrive. Instead of finding a calm, receptive person who is ready to listen and evaluate your product, you may find someone who is angry, tired, or stressed. If you plan and prepare, you can shift gears and make a different kind of presentation, switch to another purpose for the meeting, or even delay the presentation until a better time.

Salespeople find their Wi-Fi enabled devices ideal when making sales calls. With those tools in hand, you don't walk into a buyer's office lugging a briefcase or folder. Instead, you can be prepared to take an order, calculate totals, present add-ons, and make changes quickly and efficiently.[16]

The ability to exercise flexibility in a sales meeting or presentation is called *situational selling*. When you practice situational selling, you adapt smoothly to any situation. You also learn how to make every interaction with prospects as useful as possible in achieving your ultimate goals of providing value and building relationships.

The Setting

Where the sales interview takes place is a vital factor in determining its success. The prospect's office is often the best place if you can control interruptions such as office drop-ins and phone calls. The prospect feels at ease and in control in familiar surroundings and doesn't resent having to leave the office to meet with you. You are a guest and automatically a person to be treated politely.

If you discovered during pre-approach planning or initial phone call that a prospect likes to be in control at meetings, it might be better to meet at a neutral location. Some salespeople make effective use of a *power*

lunch. Inviting the prospect to lunch at a carefully selected restaurant allows you to present your product or service with several advantages:

- The atmosphere is non-threatening.
- You are away from an office where interruptions may occur.
- You are the host, and the prospect, as your guest, feels inclined to listen politely.
- Relaxing over the meal relieves some of the stress of making a decision.

Interruptions

No matter how carefully you schedule an interview, your best-laid plans often go astray. Asking the prospect at the beginning of the meeting if an administrator could hold all routine calls until later can prevent many interruptions. This request tells the prospect that you believe the conversation is more important than routine matters, but that you know some critical issues could take precedence over the interview.

If you encounter an interruption but decide to continue, quickly summarize any significant points you already covered. If you and the prospect have discovered some pain points, seek agreement on those again, and move ahead. Be sure the prospect is back on track with you and is following your planned path of reasoning.

You may decide that the interruption warrants a return visit. If the interruption is caused by a genuine crisis that demands the prospect's immediate attention, leave quickly, but make concrete plans to return.

When you do come back, begin the presentation again. You can safely assume that the interruption completely erased any effect you had built. Preface points with phrases like, "You will remember that we discussed," "As I told you the other day," and "I believe you told me that." Scatter your remarks in with questions that verify what the prospect remembers, and you can quickly discover what information needs a more thorough review.

When your pre-approach information indicates that a prospect does not have a private office or access to a conference room, consider arranging the interview away from that environment. When an interruption does occur, your sense of timing will tell you whether the discussion can be resumed or whether scheduling a later interview would be better for everyone.

> **"Creativity is thinking up new things. Innovation is doing new things."**
> *Theodore Levitt*

SUMMARY

Despite advances in technology and the popularity of online buying, face-to-face interaction is the driving force in professional selling.

Use a sales call planning sheet to get the most out of every meeting and blaze the path toward the close.

Develop units of conviction as the foundation of your presentation, which include a feature, transition, benefits, evidence, and tie-down.

You can memorize a presentation, use an outline, or make an impromptu performance based on your level of pre-approach and experience.

Personalize each presentation to the needs of the prospect. One of the most useful tactics is prospect participation.

Sales aids include visuals and audiovisuals. Many people are visually oriented, which is why sharp graphics are useful.

Interruptions represent anything that distracts the prospect's attention from your message.

Practice situational selling by being flexible with environmental issues including interruptions.

Review Questions

1. Why must the prospect become involved in the selling process?
2. Define the "salesperson's curse." Why is it a problem?
3. How does a salesperson learn to personalize units of conviction? Why is this important?
4. Distinguish between a feature and a benefit. Why is it important to know both?
5. What is a tie-down, and why is it an essential part of the sales presentation?
6. Describe the types of evidence that may be used to back up a claim.
7. How can a novice salesperson prevent a memorized sales presentation from sounding memorized?
8. What are the pros and cons of using a well-designed organizer as an integral part of your sales presentation?
9. What visuals could a salesperson selling a landscaping service use?
10. How can a salesperson get back on track after an interruption?

IN-CLASS EXERCISES

The following in-class exercises help build teams, improve communication, and emphasize the real-world side of selling. They are meant to challenge you, help you learn to deal with problems that have no one right answer, and use skills beyond those employed in a typical review question. Read and complete each activity. Then in the next class, discuss and compare answers.

EXERCISE 12.1 Presentation Planning

Divide the class into four-person teams. This role play requires your team to plan (not deliver) a presentation of MimioPad™, a product in the MimioClassroom™ family of products from DYMO™/Mimio® ITT. This major sales presentation is to be delivered to the buying center of a community college so that the product will be placed in the hands of every full-time faculty member. Each member of the sales team should produce a portion of the presentation plan in one of these areas:

- Presentation style, including persuasive reasons for the recommended method.
- Product analysis, including features and benefits, proof of claims, and a tie-down question for each unit of conviction.
- Presentation tactics.
- Presentation sales tools.

The team should discuss and modify each section as necessary and present everything in a unified document. Each team's presentation plan should be shared with other teams online or via email. In a subsequent class session, the discussion will focus on differences among the methods, the reasons for such differences, and which planning features are optimal.

EXERCISE 12.2 Features and Benefits

For this exercise, you will work independently. Select a product of your choosing. After conducting appropriate research (online or otherwise), prepare a "features and benefits chart" for the product (see discussion in Chapter 12, including the iPhone example in Exhibit 12.2). Make the chart as complete as possible, and for every feature, list at least one customer benefit (bear in mind that each feature can have more than one benefit).

Once the chart is complete, write out a one-page summary of a sales presentation approach in which you structure at least two units of conviction (see discussion in Chapter 12). Be prepared to share and discuss your chart and sales presentation approach in class or online.

Case Studies

The following case studies present you with selling scenarios that require you to apply the critical skills discussed in the chapter and give you training through practical learning situations. They are meant to be both engaging and challenging, and like the in-class exercises, they don't have one right answer.

CASE 12.1—Teaching is Selling!

Dave Casper's dean was not happy. From the moment that Dave walked into the dean's office, he knew that this would not be a pleasant meeting. Peering over the top of his reading glasses as Dave sat on the edge of the sofa, the dean asked, "Have you had a chance to review your student evaluations from last semester? They're substandard once again."

"I know, Dean Farber. You'll notice, however, that I get high marks for knowing the material and for being prepared for class. I just don't know what to do about the rest," Dave replied.

"Well, you're going to have to figure it out," the dean retorted. "Too many students are withdrawing from this course. Since macroeconomics is required for business majors, we can't have that because it delays completion of their program. If you can't solve the problem, I'll have to find someone else who can get the job done."

Dave realized that defending his teaching approach and arguing with the dean was not the right strategy. "Do you have any suggestions? I'm not above trying something different."

"I'm not an economics professor. But your colleague, Martha Oakshott, has stellar reviews. Moreover, her average assigned grade is a C+, so she's clearly not bribing the students with high grades. Go talk to her and see if you can learn something useful." With that, the meeting was over.

When Dave knocked on Martha's office door, she greeted him warmly. "Hi, Dave! What brings you here today?"

"Dean Farber suggested that I talk with you. My student evaluations are low again, and he thought you might have some suggestions for me."

"OK. Tell me what you're doing now," said Martha.

"As you know, I have a reputation for thoroughness and organization. I always get through the required material, and I'm extremely organized in class. For years, I have copied a detailed outline of my lecture on the board, and then I go over each point in order, embellishing whenever I can. I've refined my system so that I always finish on time. You know how students hate to be late getting out of class."

"Wow! You sure are organized," she said, struggling somewhat unsuccessfully not to wince.

"I can never stick to the material that well. But tell me, what exactly are you selling?"

"Selling? I don't know. I never thought of teaching as selling anything."

"Oh, but we're all selling something," said Martha with a twinkle. "Just for starters, aren't you trying to convince your students that macroeconomics is important for them as individuals? That what happens on a macroeconomic level will affect their careers directly and that they should, therefore, pay attention to national and international economic developments?"

"I guess so. But how do you sell an idea like that? It's so abstract."

Martha then proceeded to explain in some detail what she meant by selling an idea. What do you think she told Dave? What sort of strategies did she advise him to try? How could Dave improve his classroom presentation to engage his students more effectively? Do or should selling techniques as outlined in Chapter 12 play any role at all in Dave's approach to teaching?

CASE 12.2—Dorothy's Debut

The president of Dorothy Strong's company, SurgiMax, decided that it was time to make a splash. The company had just developed a new, high-intensity fiber-optic light and lens system, called a laparoscope, for surgical use. The new laparoscope was much smaller but could generate a higher resolution image for viewing on a monitor. This would allow surgeons to perform noninvasive microsurgery in places that were impossible before. Since there were already hundreds of thousands of older laparoscopes already in use, surgeons would need to be convinced of the advantages of the new model before significant sales could be generated.

A convention of West Coast surgeons was coming up in San Francisco, and SurgiMax was on the program. The president himself usually made these presentations. Still, this time, the president thought he would call on Dorothy, his new vice president for sales and marketing, to do the honors. It would be an impressive way to introduce the new product: Dorothy was energetic, passionate about improving health care, and incredibly successful as a salesperson in her own right. There was only one catch: there would be over 1,200 surgeons in the audience, and Dorothy had never addressed such a large group. While Dorothy was an expert at relationship selling, she had never had to anticipate the needs of so many people in a situation where no interaction was possible.

As Dorothy planned her presentation, she realized that she needed to accomplish three primary objectives: 1) seize and hold the attention of 1,200 surgeons who were typically skeptical and jaded for at least 30 minutes, 2) present the features and benefits of the new laparoscope without appearing to be a medical authority, and 3) convince as many in the audience as possible to contact her or SurgiMax for more information.

How would you advise Dorothy regarding the following questions or issues pertaining to her big day?

- Should she memorize her presentation, or should she use an outline approach?
- What sort of visual or audio/visual aids should she use, and how much?
- Should she use technical jargon and medical terms in describing the laparoscope's features?
- What sort of evidence should she introduce to back up her claims that surgeons would find convincing?
- As she moves through the presentation, what sort of tie-down questions should she introduce (even if no immediate responses are possible)? Or should she just forget about tie-down questions in this situation?
- How should she end her presentation so that her audience desires more information?

THE EIGHT-STEP RELATIONSHIP SELLING CYCLE

PHASE 1

1. Prospecting
Chapter 8

2. Pre-Approach
Chapter 9

PHASE 2

3. Approach
Chapter 10

4. Need Discovery
Chapter 11

5. Presentation
Chapter 12

PHASE 3

6. Objections

7. Close
Chapter 14

8. Follow-Up
Chapter 15

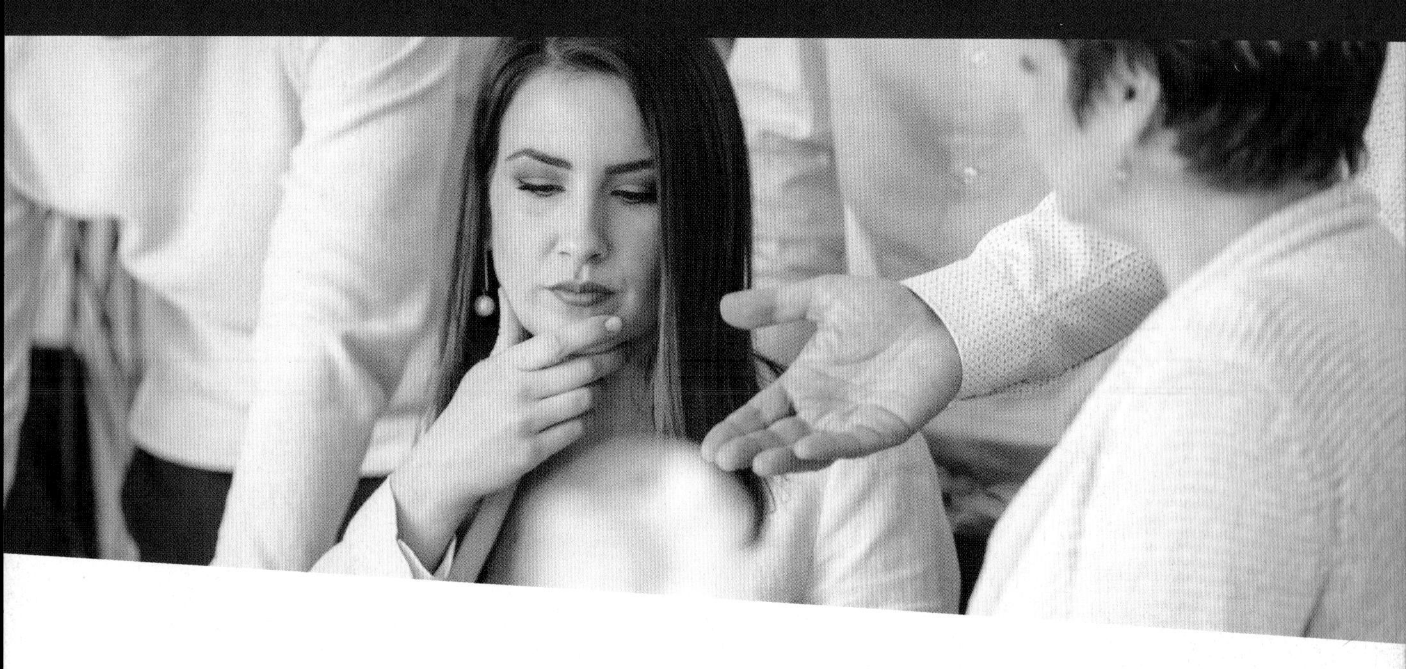

HANDLING OBJECTIONS: TURN HESITATION INTO COMMITMENT

OVERVIEW

This chapter invites you to take a different approach to objections from potential customers by welcoming resistance into the sales process. You will learn how prospects' objections are often signs of interest. You will also discover the various types of objections you will encounter and the best ways to overcome them.

OBJECTIVES

- Develop a positive attitude toward objections.
- Understand why prospects have sales resistance.
- Learn how to uncover hidden concerns or questions.
- Know the primary strategies for overcoming sales resistance.
- Learn specific techniques to overcome objections.
- Study the six-step plan for dealing with sales resistance.
- Discover tactics to handle price concerns.

Redefining Objections

We have reached the sixth step in the Relationship Selling Cycle, which is handling objections. No salesperson loves the idea of nearing the end of the presentation or heading into the close and hearing doubt or concern. However, it's time for an attitude shift regarding objections. We need them! If your product or service sold itself, there would be no need for salespeople. So, as we move into a discussion of how to handle objections from prospects, let's consider them in a more positive light.

By definition, an *objection* is an expression from a potential buyer that becomes an obstacle to the smooth completion of a sale. That sounds simple enough. However, it's not quite that easy to explain because an objection (also called *sales resistance*) contains elements of both logic and emotion. When people want something, logic often takes a back seat to feelings. But that is not always the case, especially when it comes to complex business transactions. Regardless of how much emotion is involved, objections are a natural part of almost every conversation.[1] People want their opinions and concerns to be heard.

Research suggests prospects will say no an average of five times before they say yes.[2] This could be because every purchasing decision involves some *risk*. People face the risk of having to make a decision, the risk of trying something new, and the risk of buying something that does not solve their problem. To ease the fear of uncertainty, people raise concerns and ask questions to get answers that will convince them that they are making the right decision.

The first task in answering an objection is to calm the prospect's emotions through empathy. Pause before responding, and then acknowledge that you respect the prospect's opinion and are glad to consider the concern. People are open to changing their opinions and attitudes when you convince them that

others value their views and grant them the right to those opinions.

Debating with prospects is one of the most disastrous mistakes you can make.[3] The negotiation process is not a battle. Instead, it is a place of cooperation and mutual benefit. Never try to force a prospect into making a decision. Prospects are more likely to be satisfied and remain loyal if the decision to buy was their idea.

Objections Reveal Interest

The problem with the word *objection* is that it brings to mind some clash between salesperson and prospect where someone wins, and someone loses. However, what many people fail to understand is hearing "no" and hearing an objection are two different things. Objections move prospects nearer to the close and reveal their concerns. In short, objections often signal that you are on the right track!

Some sales trainers refer to objections as the real beginning of the sales process. Zig Ziglar, one of the most well-known and respected sales experts of all time, said we should view an objection not as an obstacle, but as an encouragement.[4] For fully qualified prospects, objections are *buying signals*. Offering an objection is another way for qualified prospects to tell you, "Here are my conditions for buying," or "I will say yes as soon as you answer a few more questions."

Welcome objections! They are verbal and nonverbal signs that give you the chance to discover what the prospect is thinking. Objections later become leverage for closing the sale. Successful sales presentations often have twice as many objections as unsuccessful ones.[5] Prospects will not raise objections when they have no interest. They will quietly wait—and then say no.

Types of Objections

The difficulty with objections is that they tend to *sound* like blocks that will unquestionably stop the sale. When the prospect objects, you must understand what type of sales resistance it is before you can handle it effectively. There are four categories of sales resistance: *stalls or put-offs, searcher objections, hidden objections, and stoppers.*

Stalls or Put-Offs

A *stall* is an objection designed to do as its name suggests, which is to stall for more time. If you hear a stall, it could mean that you have not presented a compelling enough reason to buy. Prospects do not fully believe that your product or service will solve their problem.[6]

When prospects seem to be stalling, look for the true meaning behind their words. Often, prospective customers are trying to avoid making a decision.[7] Other times, you may not have convinced prospects that your offering will help their bottom line.[8] However, you should rarely hear stalls when you take the time to qualify prospects before presenting to them.

A stall is a sale killer unless you can build on the rapport you established with the prospect. If you hear a stall, confirm your understanding, ask a related question, and digest the response. You are much more likely to work through the stall if you ask questions, uncover genuine concerns, and focus on the relationship, not the sale. Here are some examples of stalls and suggestions for responding to them:[9]

I have to leave in 15 minutes for an important meeting.

I understand, and I certainly don't want to keep you from your work. I will call you again next week to briefly get your opinion on a few recent changes that are negatively affecting your industry. Then we'll know whether or not we could help you navigate these changes.

......

Just leave your material with my assistant. I will look it over and call you.

I'd love to leave some material. I think you will find we've covered a lot of it already. I apologize—I must not have made myself clear at some point. Would you tell me which areas require a better explanation?

I need to talk this over with my spouse/business partner.

I can certainly understand wanting to involve your partner in a decision like this. Can we ask him to join us now, or should we set up a meeting that works for everyone's schedule?

How you handle a stall is a test of your *attitude*. If you believe you have a qualified prospect whose needs will be satisfied with your product, then you do not allow a put-off to put *you* off or deter you. Do your best to uncover the real reason behind the stall.

Searcher Objections

The second type of objection is called a *searcher*, which is a cryptic request for additional information.[10] Some prospects object as a way to get more info even though they have already mentally decided they want to buy or not buy. The customer wants to be convinced that buying is the right thing to do. Here are some suggested responses for handling the four most common searcher objections:

I'm not interested.

I understand. There is no reason why you should be interested until I've explained how we help people like you to pay their bills when they are unable to work. Are you aware of how much a three-day stay in the hospital costs, even with major medical coverage?

I don't have the money for this.

If you did have the money, would you want it? Good! What is it about the product that is so appealing to you?

We are satisfied with what we have now.

It's nice to talk to satisfied customers! Tell you what: I'd still like to understand what you love and what you'd change about your current equipment, so that next year, perhaps you'll remember us as you assess your needs for upgrades. Now, if you could change one thing about your current process, what would it be?

I like your competitor's product.

I'm not surprised to hear you say that. Their product has some attractive features. Allow me to show you how what we are doing is cutting edge and can't be directly compared to their efforts.

Hidden Objections

The third type of sales resistance is called the *hidden objection.* This kind of resistance is often more challenging to overcome. The prospect keeps the real reason hidden. Perhaps the reason is personal, so the prospect prefers not to reveal it or doesn't know how to explain it. *A hidden objection is like an iceberg.* The spoken issues show only the tip of what's lurking beneath the surface.

You know the prospect has a hidden objection when the reasons for objecting to the sale are not logical. That means the prospect likely has other grounds for opposing that are not directly related to something in your presentation. For example, a prospective customer may not feel comfortable revealing these genuine objections:

Circumstances have changed since we first spoke. Recent health issues have caused severe financial difficulties, and I no longer have the money to pay for your product.

I don't like you, but I am not blunt enough to tell you.

I am not in the market for your product, but you seem nice.

I want to say no, but I'm not too fond of confrontation.

I don't know what my concern is. It just doesn't feel right.

Your product looks cheap and ordinary.

Stopper Objections

Prospects often have legitimate reasons for not buying. This fourth type of objection is called a *stopper.*[11] The stopper is an objection to which you can find no satisfactory solution. For instance, if you can promise delivery no sooner than six months from now, but the prospect must have the order in three months, you cannot (and should not) make that sale.

Not every prospect is a fit for your product or service. That is inevitable, and if you encounter a poor fit, thank those prospects for their time and move on to class-A qualified candidates with a genuine need for what you sell and the ability to buy.

The Heart of Resistance

Relationship salespeople must get to the heart of objections before they can overcome them. To make logical responses to customer resistance, you must know the underlying circumstances.[12] If you spent sufficient time establishing rapport and building trust, the process is much more straightforward.

Most objections you will hear are not original. If you have been selling for any length of time, your chance of encountering a new objection is remote. Research estimates that 80 percent of buyers give the same five or six objections. You should, therefore, be ready in advance and practice how you will respond to the standard objections.[13]

To deal effectively with objections, categorize them and the answers you will use. Write your responses word for word, commit them to memory, and practice delivering them. Polish and refine your replies and keep a record of how they are received. You will eventually be able to choose the best responses from your prepared list for each situation you encounter. Exhibit 13.1 lists five categories of buyer resistance with examples of what potential customers might say or think.

EXHIBIT 13.1 Categories of Buyer Objections

PRODUCT OR SERVICE OBJECTIONS

- The product is of poor quality and probably won't last long.
- Your service has the same features as your competitor but costs more.
- Your maintenance and delivery policies don't meet our needs.

COMPANY OBJECTIONS

- Your company is too new. I only work with established companies.
- I've never heard of your company or know anyone who has.
- Didn't your organization get some bad press recently?

SALESPERSON OBJECTIONS
(Possibly Hidden)

- You're not listening to me.
- You're too aggressive.
- You are not prepared.

PRICE OBJECTIONS
(Possibly Hiding True Objection)

- I can't afford it.
- Your pricing structure is ridiculous.
- I'm going to wait until prices come down.

DECISION-MAKING STALLS

- We are happy with what we have.
- Check back with me later.
- I want to think about it.

When To Answer Objections

There is plenty of information available on *how* to answer objections. What is not as readily available is information about *when* to answer them. Your response timing is just as crucial as your actual response.[14] You must consider factors such as the type of objection, the prospect's current mood and social style, the timing of the objection itself, and much more.

Timing is vital in any negotiation. Prospects introduce an objection at a time that favors their position. So why shouldn't you choose to handle it when the timing supports *your* position? There are four logical times for responding to a buyer's concerns:

1. Anticipate and forestall objections.
2. Answer an objection immediately.
3. Postpone the answer.
4. Do not answer an excuse.

Anticipate and Forestall Objections

Every product or service has its strengths and weaknesses. Because no product is perfect, a prospect may identify a negative feature or shortcoming in what you sell. It's fruitless to hope that a prospect will fail to notice any negative points. Instead of waiting for the prospect to bring something up, anticipate and *forestall* or answer it before it surfaces.[15]

Weave answers to anticipated objections into the presentation. Anticipating objections requires a planned presentation delivered from the prospect's point of view and focused on value. Don't just identify potential roadblocks—spell out how to overcome. The more obstacles removed in advance, the easier it is for prospects to welcome suggestions.[16]

Just as companies strive to stay ahead of the product development curve, you must strive to stay ahead of the "objection curve."

A good strategy for anticipating and overcoming objections is to do your homework. Before you meet, make sure that your prospect matches your ideal customer profile. When you call on a prospect who is not a good match for your offering, you make things needlessly complicated. Such leads don't need or want what you have to offer—so naturally, they have objections.[17]

Highlighting a common objection does not guarantee that you won't hear it later. However, doing so has two advantages:

- The objection has much less impact the second time.
- You may repeat the original answer, expand upon it, and then move on into a close or back into the presentation if necessary.

Answer Immediately

If you feel the hesitation is valid, then it should be handled immediately. Answering an objection prevents it from lingering in your prospect's mind and blocking out vital information in your presentation. Never reply until you are

"That objection wasn't covered in my sales training... so, let's just skip it and stick to my script, OK?"

sure of the real concern, but once you confirm the objection, answer it in 30 seconds or less. Reply briefly and honestly, and be friendly and clear.[18] A sincere, immediate response conveys professionalism, respect for the prospect's point of view, empathy, and excellent listening skills. The right answer helps remove resistance and promote the sale.

Postpone the Answer

Sometimes, the best action is to postpone the answer to an objection. This tactic is logical when you are planning to cover the point later. To answer too soon might disrupt the presentation and make the answer less effective.

For example, the prospect may be wondering about price and ask, "How much is this going to cost me?" That often occurs before you have had the chance to establish the value of your product. If you answer immediately, the price may seem too high because the prospect has not learned enough about the product to make a value judgment. The final cost may depend upon options selected, and in that case, you cannot even quote an accurate price. You may need to build a better foundation first.[19] You can postpone answering an objection by saying something like:

I appreciate that you would be interested in that, and I assure you we will discuss it thoroughly. Before we consider that issue, I want to be sure that my service can satisfy your needs. Would that be all right?

......

Shannon, your concern about the price is understandable. The amount paid for the product, however, will depend upon the options you select. Let's consider the price after we establish the features you will require. Is that fair?

> **"Nothing will ever be attempted if all possible objections must be first overcome."**
> *Samuel Johnson*

The price question should be answered near the end of the presentation after you discuss the need, value, and benefit. For the most part, however, postponing your answer to a prospect's question should be done infrequently.

Do Not Answer an Excuse

A final alternative is not to answer an excuse. Some issues do not have a good answer. Prospects may raise concerns that have nothing to do with your discussion and say things that have no relevance to the points you are trying to make. In reality, they are offering excuses for not buying rather than actual resistance.

By acknowledging excuses, you may inadvertently turn them into real objections. If you must reply to excuses, suggest to the prospect that you will answer them at the end of the presentation. If the question is a serious objection, the prospect will repeat it later. Exhibit 13.2 summarizes the four timing options for answering objections.

EXHIBIT 13.2 Timing Considerations for Objections

ANTICIPATE THE OBJECTION

- Highlight a common objection only when you are sure that the prospect will mention it.
- Anticipating the objection prevents a future confrontation and shows your objectivity.

ANSWER IMMEDIATELY

- Answer immediately so the prospect can concentrate.
- Answering prospects quickly conveys respect.
- A direct answer prevents prospects from inferring that you don't know the answer or aren't listening to them.

POSTPONE THE ANSWER

- Postponing allows you to present more benefits that could reduce or eliminate the concern.
- Postponing allows you to maintain control of the interview.
- Postponing gives you time to think about how to respond.

DO NOT ANSWER EXCUSES

- Not acknowledging an objection may reveal it was an excuse and not a real opposition. Prospects will repeat serious misgivings.
- By not answering, you suggest that the excuse is not relevant.

"The 'No Excuses Sales Seminar' is this weekend...but I'm going to try to get out of it."

Six Techniques for Navigating Objections

Six techniques can help you smoothly transition from an objection back into your presentation or close. These techniques do not establish trust and credibility because that is your job! They are merely vehicles for organizing your responses. When you take the time to form genuine connections and provide value, objections become a small hiccup in an otherwise smooth-running career.

Relationship-focused salespeople do not rely on gimmicks to make sales. Rest assured that these "techniques" are not crafty tricks but rather proven ways to help qualified prospects make the best possible decision. After you clarify and classify an objection, you are in an excellent position to respond to the concern by using one or more of the following:

Feel, Felt, Found

This technique has been around for ages and is a traditional way to overcome a stall or personal concern. It can offset prospect hostility, appease an unhappy customer, and inform someone who does not understand the value of your product or service. Answer an objection with this language:

> *I can understand how you feel. Other customers felt the same way until they found that...*

This approach shows prospects that you understand their concerns, and it reassures them that this kind of hesitation is common. Now the stage is set to introduce information that can change their thinking. The technique asserts that other customers had similar misgivings but changed their minds after they discovered new information. These new facts allow prospects to reevaluate your proposition. The following example illustrates how a financial consultant might use this technique with an unhappy client:

> **CONSULTANT:** *"Good afternoon, Mr. Reznor. I'm Porter Andrews with Green Leaf Financial. I have been assigned to your account and would like to—" (suddenly interrupted)*
>
> **CLIENT:** *"So your company is playing musical chairs with its reps again! It took Lily Allen six months to learn my business needs, and now I have to train someone new. Why can't you give me someone who will stick around?"*

CONSULTANT: *"I understand. Some of Lily's other clients felt the same frustration. The good news is that Lily is still with us! She's so talented that leadership thought someone with her experience would be an invaluable asset in our specialty loans division. I should mention that I work with numerous firms in your industry (name them and offer to provide testimonial letters). After an account review and conversations with Lily, I feel I have a solid understanding of your operation, and I will only need to ask a few questions for clarification. Does that sound good to you?"*

The "feel, felt, found" technique is used in many industries. If you are dealing with seasoned professionals, they may recognize that you are using this approach and get annoyed. Then again, such prospects might appreciate what you are trying to accomplish.[20] Here is an example of how to rearrange your words slightly in those situations:

> *"Denise, I do understand how you must feel. Frankly, lots of my customers had felt the same way when they heard about our new program. But what they found after speaking with me was the benefits heavily outweighed the limitations."*

Compensation or Counterbalance Method

At times, prospects may buy in spite of valid objections. That is, as long as you can show them that while what they are saying is correct, the pros still outweigh the cons. Admit that your product does have the disadvantage the prospect noticed and then immediately point out how other benefits overshadow the objection. Your job is to assure the prospect that the compensating benefits provide enough value to outweigh the disadvantages. By admitting the objection, you impress the prospect with your honesty. Then you can select the best strengths of your offering to offset the prospect's negative feelings.

An excellent way to accomplish this is to offer compelling statistical evidence, third-party endorsements, or case histories of satisfied customers who had similar misgivings. This method works because you approach the prospect positively with an acknowledgment of their concerns, and then provide them with logical, compensating benefits to counterbalance the stated objection.

Ask Why or a Specific Question

This method is helpful not only for separating excuses from real objections but also for overcoming objections in general. You can use questions to narrow a generic opposition down to specific points that are easier to handle. If the prospect says, "I don't want to do business with your company," ask, "I'm sorry to hear that. What is it that you don't like about us?"

The answer may reveal a past misunderstanding that you can dispel. If the prospect states, "I don't like the look of your product," ask, "Why do you object to its appearance?" The objection could be based on a minor aspect that can be changed or is no longer valid.

Remove a Misconception

One way to address resistance is to suggest that the prospect has received some misinformation. Either they misunderstood a portion of the presentation, or someone previously provided incorrect information. Use this technique with caution, or it could alienate prospects. Point out the misunderstanding thoughtfully. Listen attentively to the buyer's concern, and then begin by saying:

"Would you mind explaining the issue to me so that I can better understand it? I want to make sure I can fully resolve this for you."

This response allows the potential buyer time to cool down emotionally. It also allows you to regain your composure. After the prospect repeats the incorrect information, respond in this manner:

"If I gave you that impression, I apologize. I must have stated my position poorly. Please let me correct it for you."

Your attitude is critical when using this technique. Your goal is to earn the prospect's respect and avoid an adverse reaction. However, you do want the prospect to know that you will not be intimidated—and sometimes a direct denial is your only option.

Boomerang Method

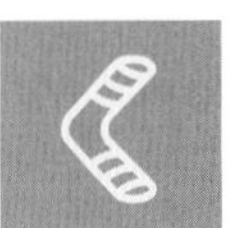

The boomerang method allows you to agree with prospects, yet show them that their objections do not need to prevent a purchase. You may use this method in a situation where the prospect is objecting to something that is actually a reason to buy. The boomerang method involves agreeing with the objection and then making another statement that translates the objection into a buying incentive. For example, a sales representative for Blue Bell Ice Cream might hear:

"Blue Bell is too new to this area. My customers will not buy something they have never heard of before."

Then turn the objection into a sales point:

"There is no question that our ice cream is new around here. That's why we're eager to build consumer awareness. We plan to spend over $100,000 this quarter alone to tell your customers about us. If you agree to carry our products, we will generate customer demand and increase store traffic for you."

The boomerang method works well when the prospect lacks complete information or perceives a drawback that may not exist. Be careful of the image you project with this technique. If prospects feel that you are directly challenging them or patronizing them, they may respond negatively.

Curiosity Method

Prospects are most comfortable when you get to know them and address their specific needs. The curiosity method works well with this relationship-driven approach. Since you should already be asking your prospects questions, it will be natural for you to answer an objection with another question. Consider the following scenario in which a software salesperson is trying to close a sale:

> **PROSPECT:** *"I don't think my clients will readily accept such a complex electronic billing system."*
>
> **SALESPERSON:** *"Interesting. Why do you think that is?"*

Notice the salesperson did not merely say "why," which doesn't reflect an active listening attitude. Instead, the salesperson demonstrated genuine curiosity about the prospect's objection. This curiosity allows for exploration and identification of specific needs. The salesperson can then more meaningfully explain the value of the product features.

The effectiveness of these objection-handling techniques depends on factors such as the category of the objection, the personality of the prospect, and the level of prospect knowledge you have. Practice each one and see which techniques fit best with your style.

Follow Up Your Response With Visuals. One great way to move back into the presentation after an objection is to use a visual. For example, you can use infographics (visual representations of data), images of the product, or letters from satisfied customers to take the focus off the resistance and put it back on the presentation. This idea works well with prospects who are visually oriented, and it works exceptionally well with the younger generations. That is one of the reasons why Instagram (which is all about visuals) is the fastest growing social network. This chapter's Social Media Connection provides you with five ways to make the most of visual sharing on Instagram.

GETTING THE MOST OUT OF INSTAGRAM

Instagram is a social media site owned by Facebook that allows you to share photos and short videos with your followers. But since 90 percent of its users are younger than 35, it is beneficial for salespeople? The experts say yes! Every day, more people are trying Instagram and love its simplicity and visual emphasis. Here are some ideas for getting the most out of Instagram.[21]

1. **Use it to report live.** Use Instagram to capture moments in real-time through photos and videos in the field or at product launches. Always include a short caption.

2. **Share screenshots of photos (a.k.a. re-gram).** Using the screenshot function on your smartphone, you can add images to your phone's photo library that you later share on Instagram. Create screenshots of your photos or of branded images that you have posted on other social networks and then share them on Instagram.
3. **Add hashtags to captions.** Users that consistently use hashtags on Instagram have twice as many followers as those that don't. Instagram users regularly monitor hashtags, thus enabling you to gain more exposure to potential new followers. In addition to product or company-specific hashtags, you should also follow and use the hashtags that are most popular on Instagram.
4. **Use third-party Instagram apps.** There are several third-party Instagram apps worth trying. In addition to Slidagram and Flipagram, explore Statigram for tracking your Instagram analytics and Copygram, which allows you to print your Instagram photos.
5. **Share daily.** To gain followers, you must be active. If possible, post once in the morning and once in the afternoon or evening. Instagram images and videos have peak activity during the first four hours after sharing, so to be consistently active, strive to post twice daily.

A Six-Step Plan for Handling Objections

Let's review the pieces to the objection puzzle we have covered so far:

1. We redefined objections as signs of interest.
2. We covered the four main categories of objections.
3. We addressed timing considerations for handling objections.
4. We presented six techniques for dealing with objections.

Now we are going to put all the pieces together. You can handle prospects' objections successfully by identifying them and then placing them in the proper perspective. When you do that effectively, objections become useful sales aids. To treat them skillfully, you need a defined strategy so that you react naturally to concerns. Exhibit 13.3 displays the six-step plan for overcoming objections that we cover over the next few pages. Knowing that you have a strategy gives you confidence. It allows you to welcome objections instead of shuddering at the thought that a prospect may object at any moment.

EXHIBIT 13.3 **A Plan for Overcoming Prospect Concerns**

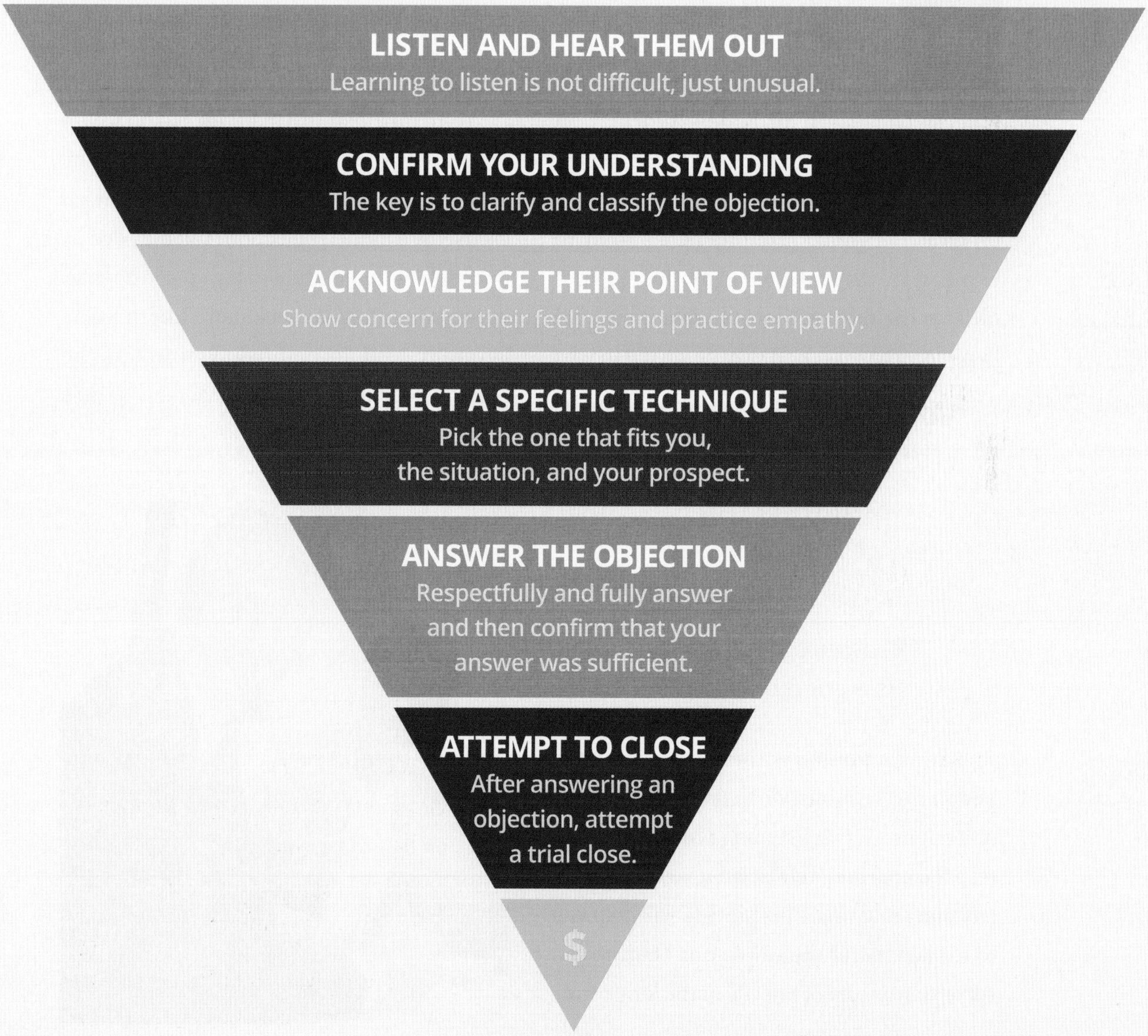

LISTEN AND HEAR THEM OUT
Learning to listen is not difficult, just unusual.

CONFIRM YOUR UNDERSTANDING
The key is to clarify and classify the objection.

ACKNOWLEDGE THEIR POINT OF VIEW
Show concern for their feelings and practice empathy.

SELECT A SPECIFIC TECHNIQUE
Pick the one that fits you, the situation, and your prospect.

ANSWER THE OBJECTION
Respectfully and fully answer and then confirm that your answer was sufficient.

ATTEMPT TO CLOSE
After answering an objection, attempt a trial close.

$

Why do salespeople need a specific plan to handle objections? The answer rests in maintaining control. If you allow a prospect to derail you from your presentation with every question or comment, you lose control of the conversation. When this happens, your perceived value decreases—and so do your chances for making the sale.[22] The following steps are part of the six-step plan that you can use to overcome objections.

STEP 1 *Listen and Hear Them Out*

Be happy when the prospect objects because it provides information you need to understand them better. Never interrupt a prospect who is expressing an opinion. Recognize the prospect's right to express views and concerns. Listen and observe the prospect's verbal and nonverbal behavior. The objection may be saying to you:

"Give me more information."

"Go over that service agreement again."

"Reassure me that this is a good decision."

Paying attention is the first step toward becoming responsive to your prospect's objections. Active listening will help you to respond appropriately to what your potential customer is saying. This process will help you to explain better the ways your offering can serve your prospect's needs in the long term.

STEP 2 *Confirm Your Understanding*

Restate the prospect's objection aloud to ensure you understand it so that you can more accurately classify it. Repeating it also gives you time to formulate an answer. Say, "As I understand it, your position is...," and then explain the prospect's position in your own words. When you prove you understand, the prospect is ready to listen to you.

Restating the objection in a thoughtful manner dissolves the prospect's defensiveness.

Your purpose in this step is to isolate the stated concern. Determine whether the expressed reason is the real reason, a stall, an excuse, or a hidden objection. You may decide to answer immediately, delay your response, not answer at all, or seek more information. Several questions can help you isolate the issue and confirm your understanding.[23] These questions include:

Other than that, is there any other reason that would prevent you from joining our family of clients?

......

I am glad you brought that out into the open. Is this your only concern?

......

If we can work together to find a solution to this critical concern, would that help you make a decision?

It may help to ask the prospect to explain the objection. Explaining it again may help clarify the issue for you and the prospect.

STEP 3 Acknowledge Their Point of View

People want to be heard. For example, if the prospect tells you about a horrible experience with your company or your predecessor, believe it and take responsibility. Potential customers feel they have good reasons for not buying, and you must respect and address those reasons. Instead of debating, say something like this:

I can certainly understand how you feel, Todd. Other customers had the same feeling when I first presented the concept to them. Here's what's interesting... (then provide a plausible explanation).

......

I appreciate your concern, and you have a relevant point, Wyatt. Thank you for bringing it to my attention.

STEP 4 Select a Technique

It's time to select one of the six techniques for addressing objections. Not all of them work all the time. When deciding which method to use, consider these factors:

- The prospect's behavioral style
- The type of objection (searcher, excuse, stall, stopper)
- The stage of the sales cycle process in which you heard the objection
- The mood (confrontational or receptive) of the prospect
- The number of times the prospect raised the objection

Decide quickly on the technique you will use and avoid showing if an objection has rattled you. Ultimately, keep in mind that far too many variables operate in any given selling situation to guarantee that you will answer every objection satisfactorily.

STEP 5 Answer the Objection

Negotiation is persuasion, not manipulation. Avoid explanations that cloud the issue and cause prospects to feel pressured. Present just enough information to gain the prospect's cooperation and commitment. Minimize the objection by not dwelling on it. Be honest and factual, and do not promise anything that you and your company cannot deliver.

Consider the prospect's ego and help the prospect win. Your answer should include a benefit and be shaped to fit the behavioral style of that prospect. Finally, confirm that your answer satisfied the prospect. Gain agreement by suggesting, "Have I have completely satisfied you regarding this concern?"

Attempt to Close

Closing opportunities exist throughout the negotiation process. When you have successfully answered a significant objection, this creates a chance to close, especially if you are near the end of the presentation. Attempt a *trial close* to gauge a prospect's reaction without exerting undue pressure. Trial closes may be used at any point in the presentation to test the waters and determine whether you have presented enough information for the prospect to decide. Typical trial closes begin with phrases like, "If you were to buy..." "In your opinion..." and "How do you feel about..."

If you receive positive buying signals from the prospect, you can attempt to close. If the close proves unsuccessful, continue the presentation until another closing opportunity presents itself.

Demystifying Price Objections

The *price objection* surfaces so frequently that it requires individual analysis. Your prospects and customers want as much for their money as they can get. While that's not surprising, you can't provide value-added service at reasonable prices if you give up too much.

To overcome it, you must see the price objection for what it is. However, the price objection is difficult to pin down because it can mean many different things. The final price paid depends on available discounts and promotions, service costs, trial periods, warranties, sales support service, delivery charges, and many other cost-related variables.

"How can I learn more about your company's needs if you keep interrupting me?"

Beyond all of those variables, a prospect may object to the price to hide the real reason for hesitating. Often the buyer's concerns or questions about price represent an incomplete sales job. When prospects say, "I can't afford it" or "Your prices are too high," they may be saying, "You have not convinced me that the value I will receive is worth the price I have to pay."

Never be afraid to ask the full value for your offering, but be prepared to justify the price. Do not be defensive or apologetic. You need to know that the price you are quoting is fair and provides excellent value. If your product has exclusive features that are not obvious, convert them to benefits and sell those benefits.

People do not mind spending money when you successfully establish the quality and value of the purchase.

Four Methods for Vanquishing the Price Question

You will not always have the lowest-priced offering. Competitors may be able to undersell you because they cut corners with lower quality, service, or delivery standards. Additionally, your product may have hidden attributes, and a prospect may not fully appreciate them until you point them out. Understand and apply the differential competitive advantages you have in the product, source, personnel, or service.[24] Several negotiation tactics can also help you overcome the price obstacle. Respond to the price question by using one of the following four methods:

Do a Price Breakdown. If the prospect objects to the total price, then break the overall cost down. An intimidating amount often becomes more comfortable to consider when you break it down into payments and compare it to how the customer typically spends extra money. Here is an example of how you might use this technique with a physician:

> *"I'm glad you mentioned the price, and I can certainly appreciate your concern. The upfront investment does seem substantial on the surface. However, I know that you understand how essential a professional graphics suite is for your practice. My company recognizes this and recently implemented an easy payment plan. For the monthly price of a waiting room magazine subscription, your staff will now have access to the best software on the market."*

Compare the one-time price of your product to the amount of money the prospect will save after using it for a specified length of time. The clearer you make the connection of what they pay to the value they receive, the easier it will be for them to recognize your offering's worth. Your job is to establish value, not price.[25] Talk about both the initial price and ultimate costs. Look at the price-cost-value comparison from two perspectives: *the price* represents the initial amount paid for the product, while *the cost* is the amount the buyer pays over time.

Use the Presumption of Exclusivity. What can you do when your price is higher than your competitor's? Stress features that are exclusive to your offering, highlight extras that only come from you, and sell the exclusivity (your product's uniqueness) and differential features. What does your product have that the competition doesn't offer? Analyze your competitor's offering to see why it has a lower price. If your analysis indicates that you are offering more, then drive home those exclusive features.

Identify the advantages your product has and explain why prospects need these features. In other words, justify the price with unique and notable facts. This process is known as using the *presumption of exclusivity*. Concentrate on exclusive features until prospects feel that only you can fulfill their needs. Consider this example of how one salesperson's lack of unique product knowledge stopped a sale:

Tim was unfamiliar with Ron's new product line and was reluctant to change suppliers. With every question Tim asked, it became evident that Tim knew more about the competition's options and pricing than Ron did.

"Really?" Ron would say, "That's their new angle, huh?"

After every question, Ron went into a huddle with his boss, who appeared equally clueless. Tim thanked Ron for

his time, and, as the hapless duo left his office, Tim wondered how their company ever made any sales at all.

Tim had the upper hand because Ron did not use the presumption of exclusivity. In contrast, relationship-focused salespeople are highly aware of how their offering compares to their competition. Then they present their product's unique features in such a way that the price objection never even surfaces.[26]

If a prospect gives you a hard time about price, stop selling the price. Instead, show what the price buys. Make the cost seem unimportant in comparison to the value received. You may try something like:

"I know that my competitor has a lower price, but it may not be the best buy for you, Jamie. Let's consider the quality of our product and why the investment is more on the front end. We pay our employees generously, purchase superior-grade materials, and have a warranty period that exceeds our closest competitor's warranty by ten years."

"I can understand your concern about the amount. The good news is our price includes in-house training, convenient auto-shipments for spare parts, and our 100 percent money-back guarantee. And we fix issues with no questions asked, because our customers are always right! Don't you agree?"

Sell quality and exclusivity when the prospect debates the price. If you sell the exclusive features appropriately, the prospect will not be fixated on the price by the end of the presentation.

Perform a Comparison. Be prepared to present logical reasons for the price you ask. One technique is to compare the quality of your product to that of the prospect's company. For example, you could stress that both companies sell superior products:

> *"Marcel, I know that your company makes superior products that command a high price—and rightly so. Your tools deserve their outstanding reputation because of the top-quality materials used to make them. Our high-viscosity, high-grade motor oil is naturally suited for your machines. You can buy less expensive brands, but I don't believe you will be satisfied with their performance."*

It makes sense to acknowledge the exceptional nature of your prospect's product and suggest that the prospect's company and your company are two of a kind. This approach elevates your product to the same level of pride that the prospect has in his company's offering.

If you make comparisons, be sure you have facts to substantiate your claims. Case histories and testimonials are useful for this purpose. For example, Curtis Randolph sells x-ray equipment to hospitals by focusing on company performance and referrals to build trust. "My customers are more concerned about what happens after they sign a purchase order than the actual price," says Randolph.

To reduce their fear of feeling *buyer's remorse*, he provides prospects with a list of current customers, and he encourages prospects to contact all of the names on the list. Randolph uses his company's reputation to build trust and justify their higher prices.[27]

Sell Down. All prospects have a buying range, and if you've done your research, you should have some idea of what that range is before you make a presentation. Prepare a variety of options or benefits available for your offering and present the best, most comprehensive package first. Doing so accomplishes two things: First, your prospects will know the extent of the available features. Second, it allows you to reduce the price by removing elements or presenting different levels of options.

As an added benefit, it gives prospects a sense of control over the buying process without placing you in a position of devaluing the product or service offered. Here is how you can present the sell-down when a prospect objects to the price:

> *"Although I believe that our premium package is the best option, I am confident that we can still meet your needs with a lower-priced alternative."*

Your prospects know it is unwise to pay too much, but it is sometimes even worse to pay too little. Your customers may spend too much and lose a little money. But when they get too much of a "bargain," they could lose everything when they discover the inferior version doesn't meet their needs. If all else fails, be patient with your prospects and focus on the benefits if they still seem fixated on price.

SUMMARY

Success in handling objections depends on your attitude. Without objections, you'd be out of a job.

Regard an objection as a sign of interest and an open invitation to continue negotiating.

Offering objections enables prospects to avoid the risk of making a decision.

Many objections are valid and indicate either a logical reason for not buying or a need to hear additional information.

Classify and clarify objections according to their category and apply the appropriate plan to overcome them.

Study the most common objections and develop logical answers to use for each.

The six-step strategic plan for handling objections allows you to manage whatever opposition you encounter positively.

You will not always have the lowest price. Stress your competitive advantages, break the price down, and use comparisons.

Review Questions

1. How can an objection be considered a buying signal?
2. In what phases of the Relationship Selling Cycle might you hear an objection?
3. What are some underlying causes of psychological sales resistance?
4. In deciding when to answer an objection, what factors would lead you to choose to answer before it arises, postpone the answer, respond immediately, or elect not to answer at all?
5. Why might a prospect raise objections even when that prospect has already mentally decided to buy?
6. Is there any way to prevent an objection before it happens? How?
7. Who is responsible if prospects misunderstand part of the presentation or are not convinced that the product applies to their needs? Give examples of how objections reflecting these conditions may sound.
8. If you are showing homes in the $500,000 to $750,000 price range, how would you anticipate and forestall price objections?
9. List the six steps in the strategic plan for handling objections.
10. Discuss several strategies for coping with price objections.

IN-CLASS EXERCISES

The following in-class exercises help build teams, improve communication, and emphasize the real-world side of selling. They are meant to challenge you, help you learn how to deal with problems with no single right answer, and use a variety of skills beyond those employed in a typical review question. Read and complete each activity. Then in the next class, discuss and compare answers.

EXERCISE 13.1 Anticipating Objections

Working with the same team of which you were a member for Exercise 12.1 in the previous chapter, review your presentation plan. This time, try to anticipate objections that your buying center counterparts might raise to various points in your presentation. For each objection that you identify, classify it according to the category of objection (see Exhibit 13.1). Next, decide on when you intend to answer each objection and why. Finally, describe the approach you would take toward answering each objection. In the case of price objections, be especially careful to explain how you would handle them. Be prepared to discuss the results in class.

EXERCISE 13.2 Which Objections Are True Stoppers?

For this exercise, divide the class into as many teams as possible of two people. In categorizing objections, Chapter 13 mentions that there is one type, the stopper, that calls a halt to the selling process because it cannot be answered successfully.

In class, team A (a two-person team) identifies a product or service and begins to present its features and benefits to team B. During the presentation, team B interrupts with an objection. Team A then consults briefly and responds appropriately to the opposition. The presentation continues, and team B poses another objection to which team A has an opportunity to respond. Whenever a stopper objection is raised—that is, an objection to which no appropriate response is possible—the presentation is over. Then, the teams reverse roles so that team B presents a product to team A, and team A raises objections. The duo that responds appropriately to the most objections wins.

Case Studies

The following case studies present you with selling scenarios that require you to apply the critical skills discussed in the chapter and give you training through practical learning situations. They are meant to be both engaging and challenging, and like the in-class exercises, they don't have one right answer.

CASE 13.1—Don't Let the Bedbugs Bite

Research shows that people hate purchasing mattresses more than any other item for the home. There are good reasons for that. A mattress showroom is intimidating: all of the mattresses are laid out in rows, and they all seem to look alike. Moreover, there are thousands of brands, types, models, and price points, making it almost impossible to compare one store's mattress directly to another. Finally, there is no way for an ordinary customer to "look under the hood" to check independently the features built into each mattress. All customers can do is lie on the mattresses to test their comfort. But even that doesn't work well, because mattresses begin to feel the same after a while. No wonder people hate the process, and no wonder bedding salespersons encounter multiple objections!

Bob Driscoll's store, Mattress Mavens, carries only mattresses on the medium to the high end of the pricing scale—$3,500 to $8,000—on the theory that customer satisfaction will be better. That not only cuts down on complaints and returns, but it also improves word-of-mouth marketing. Still, Mattress Mavens faces stiff competition from Doug's Discounts. Doug's produces many TV ads that blare, "Why pay more for just a name? Come on down to Doug's for a quality night's sleep at a fraction of the cost!"

The ads drive Bob nuts because prospects who come into his store don't know what they are looking at or for. They don't have a clue about the shoddy materials that go into Doug's no-name bedding or, worse, about what a $500 mattress will do to their spine over time. Professional ethics prevents Bob from trashing the competition. Still, he has become frustrated at dealing with pricing objections day in and day out.

When Bob approaches his manager about the problem, he receives some outstanding support (pun intended!). The manager says that he has just requested some cutaway displays from StarCrest, the store's high-end vendor so that customers can see and feel the superior construction. These will be displayed on the showroom floor, along with a few cutaways of disgustingly cheap mattresses for comparison. Also, the company is sending videos that show the construction process, from the harvesting of wood and production of the memory steel coils to the creation of foam and cotton layers and the stitching and packaging. Mattress Maven will play the videos in an endless loop on six monitors at various locations in the store. "But," says the manager, "when it comes to handling pricing objections directly, Bob, you're on your own!"

With all of the above support, what should Bob be prepared to do? How can he handle the pricing objections creatively and effectively? What strategies should he employ?

CASE 13.2—The Spouse Objection

Charlie Brandon has been selling home furnishings for eight years. He's worked for high-end companies and discount outlets. Throughout his career, he has encountered more objections than even he had thought possible. Some people wouldn't buy leather furniture because they thought it felt hot. Others thought it felt cold (the truth is that leather always conforms to room temperature). Charlie had worked out responses to most objections. It didn't mean that all the customers bought. Still, Charlie never blamed himself for being unable to help most customers make a buying decision in their best interest. But there was one objection that stumped Charlie nearly every time, and that was some variation of, "I must check with my spouse."

There were, in Charlie's experience, two problems with this objection. First, it could often be used to mask a more important yet hidden objection. Second, by invoking the privacy of the marital bond, a customer could thwart probing questions that might be

considered offensive. Moreover, whenever this objection surfaced, Charlie knew that a customer rarely returned with the spouse. Even if they did return together, the second spouse was often grumpy and usually found some pretext to veto a purchase. The merchandise was always "the wrong color," "the wrong size," or "too expensive." It just never worked.

Now that Charlie had accepted a new position with a mid-level retailer, he thought he would attempt to address the problem again. Perhaps Tanya, his new manager, could shed some light on how to handle the spousal objection.

Having explained his previous difficulty with this objection, Charlie complained, "I just don't know what to do, Tanya. Now, every time a customer raises this objection, I freeze."

"Well, Charlie, I have two suggestions for you," Tanya replied. "First, you need to qualify your customers more carefully and earlier in the process. When a person comes in alone, find ways to ask who the merchandise is for and who is involved in the selection process. If another person will need to weigh in, present just enough to keep the customer interested. Then, press for a follow-up appointment with the spouse present."

"What's the second suggestion?" asked Charlie.

"The second suggestion applies later in the process when you're attempting to close after having made a presentation. Perhaps you couldn't qualify the customer for some reason. But now, you need to probe whether this is a real objection on its face or whether it masks some other concern," answered Tanya. "You need to come up with a list of gently probing, inoffensive questions."

"Okay, I'll try," Charlie responded, somewhat apprehensively.

Knowing what you've learned from Chapter 13, what sort of questions should Charlie ask? When should he stop, and why?

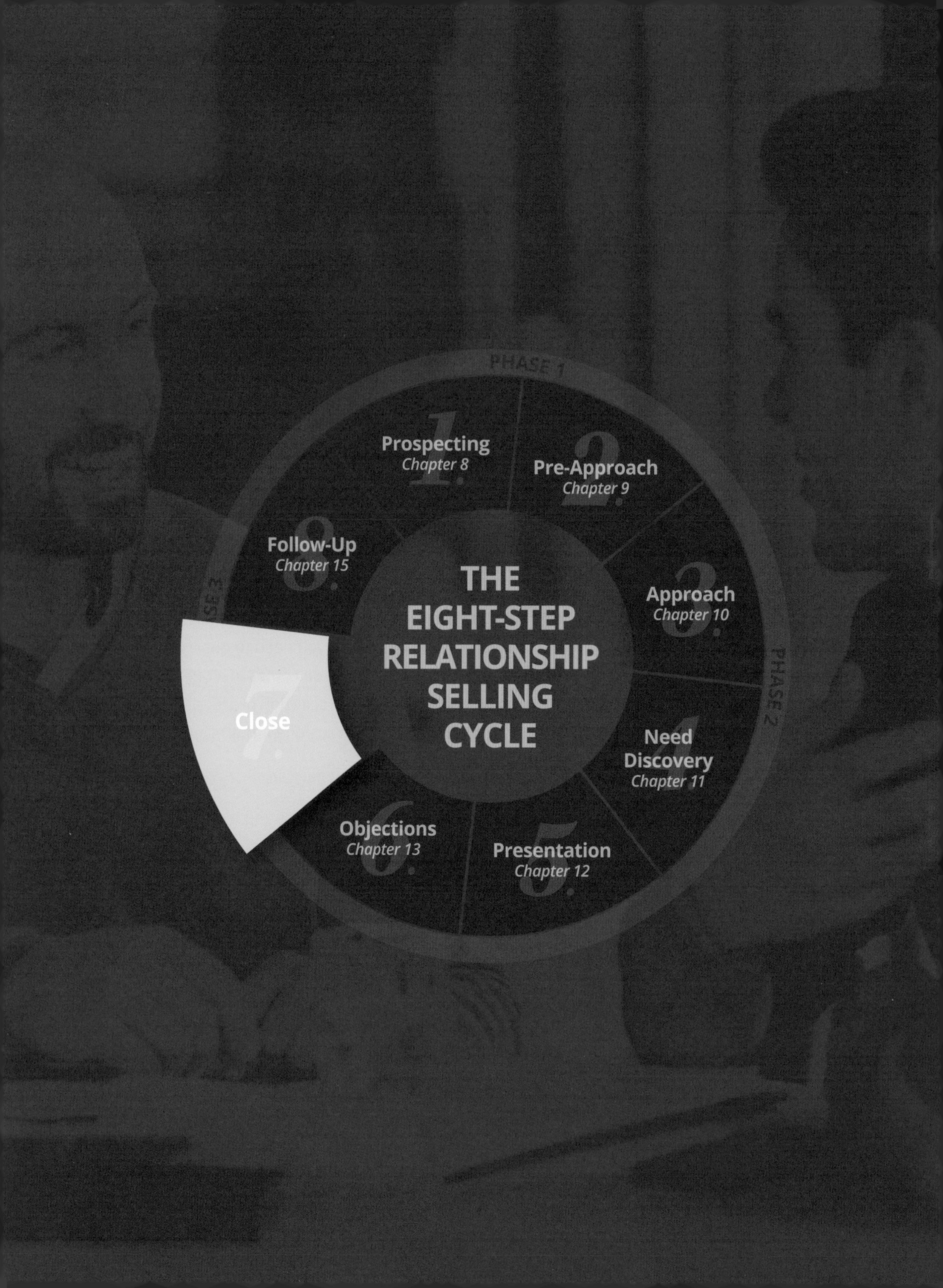

PHASE 1

PHASE 2

PHASE 3

THE EIGHT-STEP RELATIONSHIP SELLING CYCLE

1. Prospecting
Chapter 8

2. Pre-Approach
Chapter 9

3. Approach
Chapter 10

4. Need Discovery
Chapter 11

5. Presentation
Chapter 12

6. Objections
Chapter 13

7. Close

8. Follow-Up
Chapter 15

THE CLOSE: HOW TO CONFIRM THE SALE

OVERVIEW

Even though many salespeople dread this step of the Relationship Selling Cycle, the close should be a natural conclusion to a successful presentation with a qualified prospect. In this chapter, we will discuss how to face the close with confidence, how to recognize signals that reveal a prospect's readiness to buy, and how to use specific techniques during the close. No matter how intimidating it may be, the only way to get more sales is to ask for more sales.

OBJECTIVES

- Develop productive attitudes and perspectives toward closing.
- Discover the importance of reassuring the prospect.
- Understand how to deal with rejection.
- Appreciate the value of persistence in sales.
- Develop a sense of timing in knowing when to close.
- Recognize buying signals that indicate closing opportunities.
- Study the various types of closes available.

A Closing Frame of Mind

Finding new prospects, successfully making appointments, establishing trust, and adequately explaining features and benefits is stressful enough. When it comes time to perform step seven in the Relationship Sales Cycle, it can be even more difficult. Not to mention, an unsuccessful close can crush even the most seasoned sales practitioner. However, closing the sale should not be difficult for a salesperson who conducts professional sales interviews with qualified prospects under favorable conditions.

> **"Many of life's failures are people who did not realize how close they were to success when they gave up."**
> *Thomas Edison*

A ***close*** is a question asked or an action taken by a salesperson designed to cause a favorable buying decision.[1] Although closing a sale is natural, many salespeople have adopted such a distorted view of the close that they dread it. Salespeople fail to ask for the prospect's business 62 percent of the time.[2] That is absurd considering that the close is what secures sales for them and solves problems for their customers. They do a phenomenal job up until that moment, but then they lose their confidence. The scenario may go something like this:

> *"Well, that concludes my presentation. Do you have any questions? Okay, so I guess I'll call you in a few weeks. Have a good day."*

Then the salesperson stands outside the prospect's office, wondering, "I thought for sure I had that order. What did I do wrong?" The fact is the salesperson did not do anything wrong. The salesperson did not do *anything*.

Closing is not an unspoken step of the sales process that naturally takes place without any conscious effort on your part. It's also not supposed to be a separate event you tack onto the end of a sales interview. It is a tone that you actively foster throughout your face-to-face interactions.

Closing might be easier to understand if it had a better name. The word itself suggests something that occurs at the end of a process, which is why most salespeople view it as an isolated event. In reality, the opportunity to close may appear at any time. By meeting the prospect's expectations and desires from the start, the close should occur without having to force it. You simply need to be aware enough to take advantage of every closing opportunity.

Always Be Closing

Closing essentially begins the moment you speak the first word to a prospect and continues until you have the order. You close on many points in the sales cycle. For example, a prospect agrees to meet with you, you and a potential customer agree on the existence of a need, your prospect permits you to ask questions, and much more. In this way, the sale has been made long before the time arrives to sign an official agreement. The final step should be a formality—a necessary step, but not one that requires weighty decisions.

The concept is simple: ***always be closing***. However, don't confuse this idea with a *hard sell* because a cutthroat approach will only alienate potential customers. Instead, explain your agenda. Tell prospective customers precisely what you're selling and how it can benefit their business. Be upfront about your intentions to promote an honest, mutually respectful, and rewarding discussion that paves the way to a smooth close.[3]

If you fail to prospect, qualify, research, or ask useful questions, you decrease the odds of a successful close. Without the right pre-approach activities and need discovery, your presentation will focus on features and benefits that may or may not matter.

In short, a prospect's failure to buy does not automatically brand you a weak closer. Your closing rate is no more an indicator of success than is the final putt that lands a golf ball in the hole. That may be the last shot that wins the championship, but all the other great strokes up until that shot made the win possible.

Functions of the Close

Even when all the steps leading to the close go well, the prospect may still hesitate. Logically, prospects want superior products or services at fair prices, and if that is what you offer, why would anyone wait? It goes back to risk. The moment of decision is awkward because of the inherent risks in buying that include:

- The risk of regretting the purchase.
- The risk of unsuccessfully justifying the purchase to someone else.

- The risk of the financial burden the purchase creates.
- The risk of negatively impacting productivity or profitability.

Salespeople may also feel the strain at the moment of decision. You may ask yourself questions like, "Did I tell the prospect enough? Have I uncovered the driving need? Did I read the verbal and nonverbal clues correctly? Is this the best moment to close? What if the answer is no?"

The salesperson-prospect relationship is much like a doctor-patient relationship. A doctor urges his patients to follow a treatment that will help solve their health issues. Likewise, a salesperson advises prospects to make buying decisions that will address their stated needs.[4]

Be Their Reassurance

Consider how prospective buyers must feel at the close. Do you remember the first time you jumped off a diving board? You may have thought, "What if I can't swim in the deep end? What if I swallow water?" But then a friend in the water encouraged you to try. "The water is fine," your friend reassured you. When you finally jumped, you discovered that the water was fine, just as your friend had said.

At the close, *you* are that friend in the water. You know how the prospect feels, and you offer the needed reassurance, "You'll be glad you jumped in, and I'm here to help if you need me." However, you must respect prospects and their decisions, whether or not they decide to leap. Reassure them until

they make a decision and then support that decision, whatever it may be. The next time you advise them, they will trust your recommendations more readily.

Once prospects agree that they can benefit from using your product or service, your responsibility is to guide them to a close. Do not be discouraged when the buyer hesitates or initially says no. People do not like to make decisions. Without assistance and reassurance, some cannot make decisions at all.

If you believe that a sale is an exchange of mutual benefits, then a no should cause you to think, "The prospect is asking me to explain once more that this decision is the right one. So, I will continue to reassure and close." Be the trusted advisor who helps calm their fears enough to commit.

A Closing Consciousness

The x-factor in successfully closing a sale is not having the lowest price or the best product. Your attitude is the x-factor. You must have an absolute belief in what you are selling and expect to be successful. If you assume that you will close the sale, the prospect interprets your confidence as belief in the product. Your positive attitude makes a difficult decision much more comfortable. All they have to do is say, "Yes, you're right" when you recommend that they buy.

Confidence is contagious—it inspires prospects, draws them to your side, and allows you to ask for the order directly. Here is an example of a confident, self-assured close:

> *Mr. Eastwood, we have agreed on the functions of the printer, its speed capabilities, and the cost of ongoing supplies, and we have clarified your questions regarding the service contract. We could significantly speed up the process if we could settle now on a date for delivery. Does next Friday work well for you?*

Closing is only frustrating if you have not identified customer needs, displayed a positive attitude, made a compelling presentation, and worked to solve problems.[5] If you and the prospect have together defined the need and determined a solution, then the final question is nothing more than the next step in a sequence.

Self-Confidence

When you display confidence and believe in your product, you create an atmosphere within which you can easily handle rejection. In their book, *Go for No*, co-authors Richard Fenton and Andrea Waltz reveal how to shake off the shackles of rejection. They teach that while *yes* is the destination, *no* is the path to get there.[6]

When prospects fail to follow your buying advice, their rejection of you is not personal. It is merely a reflection of their different opinions. You have lost nothing but a little of your time, and if you have set up the relationship correctly, you will be able to call on them again in the future. Celebrate both the successes and the failures, because we need both to shape our lives and careers. Be confident in the person that those experiences make you.[7]

Persistence

When it comes to the appropriate level of persistence in sales, Jim Duerr, a former sales rep for Chris-More, Inc., says, "You should push, but never be pushy." Duerr called on Nashville commercial builders to sell his company's line of plumbing supplies. Jim says

that persistence is what made the difference between a good career and a great career. He shared his secret to making persistence work for him. "Make repeated, meaningful calls to demonstrate to prospects that you are not going to give up. *The idea is to be graciously tenacious—without being obnoxious.*"[8]

Successful salespeople never take no for an answer unless it is in everyone's interest to do so. If the business is worth having, it is worth going after repeatedly—with multiple attempts to close during a single call as long as the atmosphere remains positive and productive. The extra effort often spells the difference between success and failure.

Gerhard Gschwandtner, founder and CEO of *Selling Power* magazine, says, "When you are at the point where you think it's not worth it—that's when you need to redouble your efforts. Customers are looking for someone dependable, who is persistent, and who will do what it takes to get the best solution implemented within the customer's organization."

When sales are slow, and you feel like every step is an uphill battle, that's when you should not quit. Salespeople who redouble their efforts will be rewarded. "The pain goes away the minute you are victorious," Gschwandtner says, "but if you give up, the pain will persist for the rest of your life."[9]

How often should you ask prospects for their business? The best answer is "one more time." Studies have shown that only about 2 percent of sales close at the first meeting.[10] That means the only way to make your time worthwhile is to follow up with prospects. Selling should be a side-by-side, step-by-step process in which the salesperson *earns* the right to close.

There could be any number of issues that would keep someone from saying yes at the first meeting. Five is the average number of calls it takes to close a major account.[11] Giving up after one or two calls means you did not even reach the halfway mark to success!

When you work to understand priorities, ask questions, watch for buying signals, and choose a close that fits their unique style, your chances of a successful close skyrocket. Recognize opportunities to close, persist, and ask for the order.

> **"Ambition is the path to success. Persistence is the vehicle you arrive in."**
> *Bill Bradley*

Dealing with Rejection

Many would-be salespeople leave the profession because of their inability to cope with the rejection they experience. They interpret a prospect's refusal to buy as a message that says, "You are worthless." Eleanor Roosevelt once said, "No one can make you feel inferior without your permission." This concept is especially vital for sales reps.

Sales professionals must learn to deal with rejection by keeping a positive attitude about themselves and their careers. They may feel disappointed if they fail to close. Still, successful salespeople focus on the sense of accomplishment they feel when they *do* close a sale.[12] Accept the fact that rejection exists and never make the mistake of allowing it to serve as a measure of your self-worth.

Professional baseball players who average .300 (that's just three hits for every ten times at bat) or more for a full season are considered wildly successful players. Consider some of the great names in baseball history and their successes compared to their extensive failures:

- Babe Ruth hit 714 career home runs but struck out 1,330 times.
- Cy Young won 515 games but lost 313.
- Ty Cobb stole 96 bases one year but was caught stealing 38 times.

What is a good "batting average" in selling? Imagine failing to get a yes 70 percent of the time. Would you continue to persist and work not to internalize those setbacks? A true professional thinks, "I may have failed, but that does not mean I am a failure."[13]

A salesperson who never hears a no is not a salesperson, but an *order taker*. Rejection is as much a part of selling as muscle fatigue is a part of lifting weights. Do not take rejection personally and refuse to let anyone else make you feel like a failure. Here are nine tactics for coping with rejection.[14]

1. **Remind yourself that you are not alone.** How many rejections have exceptional salespeople faced on their journey to success? You see, you are not alone!
2. **Forgive yourself.** Mistakes are great learning experiences, but to benefit from them, you have to keep moving forward.
3. **Give yourself a pep talk.** Replace negative thoughts with positive ones such as, "I'm a great salesperson who delivers value to my customers!"
4. **Refuse to give up.** Remind yourself that persistence is key to success, and that rejection may not be pleasant, but you won't let it stop you.
5. **Be you, not your title.** Remind yourself that you are valuable because of who you are, not what you do.
6. **Engage in positive self-talk.** Separate your ego from the sale and say to yourself, "This prospect doesn't even know me. This refusal is about the product, not me."
7. **Positively anticipate rejection.** Expect it, but don't create it. Think in advance what your response to rejection will be.
8. **Your definition of success.** Instead of looking at outcomes, look at success as getting out there in the first place.
9. **Keep your pipeline full.** Commit to attracting more customers than you need. Rejection stings less when you have a steady flow of prospects.

> **"My great concern is not whether you have failed, but whether you are content with your failure."**
> *Abraham Lincoln*

When to Close

Most of the sales you make will not close themselves. Many factors go into a successful closing, from timing to presenting, and more.[15] The closing curve in Exhibit 14.1 illustrates how the closing process works. As the bell shape suggests, a small percentage of prospects will say yes early (bottom left of the bell), while some prospects will never say yes (bottom right of the bell). Most of your prospects will decide to buy somewhere in between the two extremes.

The vertical line down the middle of the graph called the *will-buy-line* (WBL) demonstrates the point during your presentation when the majority of prospects are most likely to say yes. The WBL is not a fixed place, and you can reach it at almost any time. Still, in the majority of cases, you can successfully close when interest has peaked after you adequately establish needs and present relevant features and benefits. The farther you go past the WBL, the harder the close becomes.

The key is recognizing the spots at which a close can be made—or when the buyer gives a *buying signal*. The appearance of a buying signal is the critical moment during the presentation when a successful close is more likely.

EXHIBIT 14.1 **The Closing Curve**

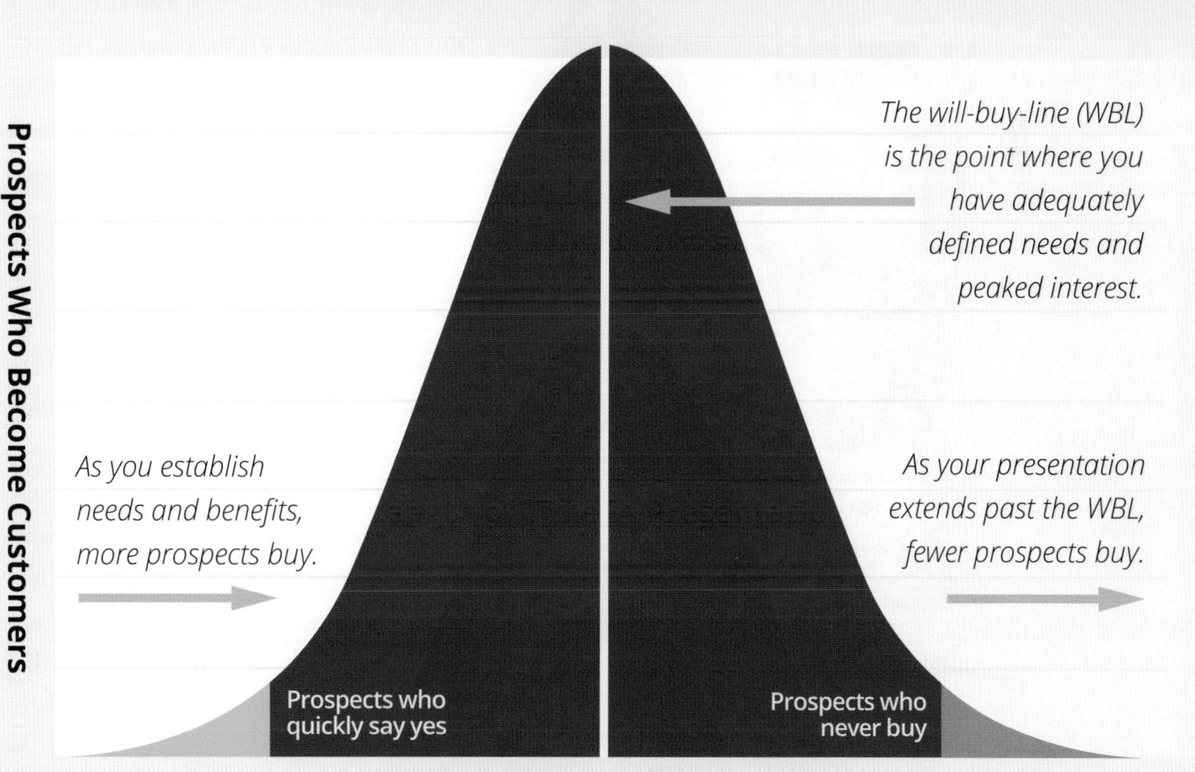
Prospects Who Become Customers
The will-buy-line (WBL) is the point where you have adequately defined needs and peaked interest.
As you establish needs and benefits, more prospects buy.
As your presentation extends past the WBL, fewer prospects buy.
Prospects who quickly say yes
Prospects who never buy
Length of Time in Presentation

When you sense the psychological moment to close, do so immediately.[16] If you fail to recognize these critical moments in which the prospect is ready to make a buying decision and talk past them, the close becomes steadily more complicated. After the crucial point passes, you must work hard to regain the prospect's readiness. In other words, you must once again convince the prospect that buying is the proper decision. Talking too much and *overselling* is a much greater danger than *underselling*. Frequent attempts to close eliminate the possibility of going past the point at which the prospect is ready to buy.

The best psychological moment for closing may occur at any time during the presentation. When it does come, prospects signal in some way that you have convinced them, and they are ready to buy.[17] You never have only one possible moment to close.

Recognizing Buying Signals

As you communicate with prospects, you must learn not only what to ask, but also when to ask by watching for buying signals.[18] A *buying signal* is anything the prospect does or says that indicates a readiness to buy. Buying signals are all around us if we learn to recognize them.[19] Unfortunately, it's all too easy to become so focused on your presentation that you overlook these signals. Buying signals occur quickly and may be verbal or nonverbal. Genuine buying signals show that the prospect has moved from evaluating your proposal to deciding about it.

A buying signal may come in the form of a question. A prospect may ask you to repeat some point or benefit previously discussed or stop you right in the middle of the presentation to ask how long delivery will take. Take advantage of any buying signal by attempting a trial close or close immediately. Always remember that when the prospect is ready to buy, you will receive a signal. Here are three of the most common nonverbal buying signals:[20]

1. **Nodding.** In conversation, people nod so often that it might come as a surprise that constant nodding is a nonverbal buying signal. If you see your prospects nodding frequently, it is a sign that they are listening and engaged. However, it can also be a sign that they might already be familiar with the ground that you're covering. Be sure to ask the prospects questions to keep them engaged when they are sending out this nonverbal buying signal.

2. **Fidgeting with documents or other materials.** Handling the product and rifling through the supporting documentation are clear nonverbal buying signals. Such motions are a subconscious way of imagining owning the product or receiving the service. That is why many top salespeople encourage prospects to touch, handle, and examine things before the close. Once a prospect exhibits this nonverbal buying signal, the yes could be next.

3. **Consistent eye contact.** Steady eye contact is a classic nonverbal buying signal. The person is engaged in the conversation and interested in your presentation. The prospect also likely feels comfortable with you, which has to happen before a deal can close.

   To understand how important eye contact is as a nonverbal buying signal, think about past transactions that you've closed. The chances are that in every instance, consistent eye contact was present.

To know when to close, look for at least two nonverbal buying signals. Other nonverbal buying signals include smiling, changes in posture, and rubbing chins or noses, which indicates rational thinking. By being aware of nonverbal buying signals (which sometimes contradict simultaneous verbal buying signals), you can improve your closing ratio. Avoid the temptation to oversell and let nonverbal buying signals indicate when its time to close.

With the traditional method of selling, salespeople were taught to close, close, close.

They were told to spend most of their time closing the deal. Trainers taught salespeople fancy closes to handle and overcome objections. Over the years, a new school of thought has evolved: *The school of possibility*. Imagine what would be possible if you could defuse all the objections you typically hear at the close during your presentation.[21]

Work daily to create an atmosphere in which trust naturally manifests. People like to buy from people who understand them and take the time to get to know their unique situation.

The Trial Close

Instead of watching passively for signs of interest, you must create situations in which you can generate and detect interest. One way is through the use of a trial close, which we discussed briefly in the presentation and objection steps. A *trial close* asks for an opinion, while a *closing question* asks for a decision. A trial close serves as a thermometer that tells you whether the prospect is warm, hot, or cold to your proposition. It is designed to help you read the prospect's feelings and predict probable reactions.

In chapter 12, we discussed the *tie-down question* as one element in a unit of conviction. The tie-down and the trial close serve primarily the same purpose. When prospects agree with you throughout the presentation, they are much more likely to agree with you when you ask the formal closing question. You want to be careful not to talk past the sale.

During every sales call, there will be several opportunities to close the sale. How do you know the proper time? When in doubt, test the prospect with trial closes such as:[22]

How do you feel about what we have discussed so far?

What do you think about the solution I've shared with you?

How does what we've talked about sound to you?

······

Based on what you've heard so far, what are your questions?

······

If you had your way, what changes would you make to the proposal?

Notice these are all open-ended questions. You need to ask a trial closing question that will get the prospect talking so you can learn about where you are in the sales process and when is the right time to ask for the sale.

The trial close is used to reveal how far along the prospect is in the decision-making process. The time to ask for the order is when the prospect is fully ready to buy. You can, however, ask for an *opinion* at any time.

A Closing Question. A closing question, in contrast to the trial close, is designed to produce an answer that confirms the fact that the prospect has bought. Look at these two examples:

Would it be better for you to receive the shipment of a full month's supply right away, or would you prefer to receive half at the end of this week and the other half in about ten days?

······

We can have the product delivered to your warehouse next week. Is Monday a convenient delivery day for you?

Your Most Powerful Closing Tool

What is the most potent thing you bring to the table when it comes to the close? Salespeople are often taught to provide a *reason* when they ask for something since people may be more likely to agree to a request if a reason accompanies it. But is this true in all cases—and especially in cases involving price?

You have probably heard the idea that you have to give something to get something. For example, if you want to get a referral, you have to offer your customers some reason for providing you with a name. There's a study that allegedly proves this idea:

A group of experimenters went around a college campus asking to cut in line to make copies. When they gave no reason for wanting to cut ahead, 60 percent agreed to the cut. When they gave a reason for needing to cut, 93 percent agreed. However, the "reason" the experimenters gave was, "Because I have to make a copy."

They concluded that saying "because..." after a request is what made people more agreeable, not the reason itself. But

interestingly, once they told people they wanted to jump ahead because they needed to make *multiple* copies, only 24 percent agreed, reason or no reason.[23]

Justifications may help you get agreement on issues in the beginning or during the presentation. However, when you are involved in price negotiation, adding an explanation can work against you. In your mind, you may think you are reinforcing value, but as you list all that value after the price, prospects won't hear any of those justifications. They will only be thinking of reasons to object to the amount.

What should you say after you ask a closing question or present the price? The most powerful thing to say after the close is *nothing*. For example, let's say you close with a question like:

"Would it be better for you to receive the shipment of a full month's supply right away, or would you prefer to receive the order in two shipments?"

Then after you ask, say *nothing* until the prospect answers. The pressure of silence is enormous. If you remain silent after asking the closing question, two outcomes are possible: 1) The prospect says yes or 2) the prospect gives you a reason for not wanting to buy.[24] In either instance, you are better off than you were before. If the answer is *yes*, you have a sale. If the prospect gives you a reason for not buying, you can use that concern to identify points to revisit and then attempt to close again.

Never miss the opportunity *not* to say something.

Eleven Useful Closing Strategies

There is a multitude of closing techniques, and your best strategy is to have numerous methods for different occasions and prospects. Include closing ideas in your sales call plan that fit with the presentation you expect to deliver. However, just as circumstances often dictate some changes in your performance, they also may necessitate shifts in your closing plans.

Let's say an insurance agent prepared a comprehensive insurance program to present to a client. Upon arrival, the agent finds an enthusiastic prospect who says he just found out that he and his wife are expecting triplets. He tells the insurance agent to present the best plan for his growing family. The presentation instantly becomes a work session to devise a new program. That means that the planned close may also no longer fit. With a full arsenal of closes at his disposal, the salesperson chooses one that fits the revised situation and continues.

The closing methods described on the following pages will be useful depending on your unique personality, your product, and your prospects. Learn the principles behind these techniques and adapt them to your needs:

1. The Assumptive Close

In a way, every close is *assumptive.* When you enter a sales interview with a positive expectation of success, you are assuming that the prospect will buy. Your attitude throughout the interview is assumptive. Say, "*When* you use this product," and "*As* your program progresses." Avoid words like *if* and *should* because they are conditional and block closing action. Throughout the presentation, assuming that the prospect will buy allows him or her to make the decision more easily by presenting opportunities to make smaller or easier choices.

To further promote an assumptive environment, you can act as if they already purchased. Talk about your product and how prospects will use it. Discuss how it already fits into their lives. Do not talk about whether they are ready to buy but act as if it has always been theirs.[25] Here are some examples:

Have you decided where you will put your new furniture?

······

What will your manager say about your next-gen upgrade?

······

What do you think you'll like most about your new software?

······

How will you use the cash payment from your accident policy?

An assumptive approach to closing establishes a positive environment in which the prospect can more easily say yes. This

The assumptive close is about having a positive attitude.

close works well with indecisive buyers who are nervous about making a final decision. Present them with minor choices that allow them to appear decisive in a small matter while they are painlessly making the big decision at the same time.

2. The Continuous Yes Close

By asking a series of questions with *yes* answers, it becomes more difficult for buyers to say *no* when they have said *yes* several times. That is why you must get agreement on minor points before you ask for the order. These questions begin in the need discovery phase. For example: "I'd like to ask you a few questions that help me understand your particular needs. Would that be okay with you?" *Yes.*

Then continue these questions during the presentation: "Do you like the idea of our same-day, free repair service?" *Yes.* During the closing phase, you may ask: "Are you satisfied with the comprehensive guarantee that we offer?" *Yes.* "Do the financing terms seem fair to you?" *Yes.* "Then, it seems we can go ahead with our plans to begin the installation process?" *Yes.* These are all closed-ended questions, so you must be confident that you will receive an affirmative response before you ask them. And, when you ask the final closing question, the prospect will be inclined to keep agreeing with you.

The continuous yes close makes 'yes' the natural reply.

3. Let Your Actions Speak (Physical Action Close)

Without directly asking for the order, begin taking some action that assumes you completed the sale. For example, start filling out paperwork and ask the prospect for a signature when you finish. Ask a series of questions and write the answers on the contract or agreement form. You might ask, "Do you use your middle name or just an initial?" Continue to fill out the information and then ask for a signature:

> *Now that we have reached an agreement, I know you will want to expedite delivery. Just indicate your approval by placing your name right here.*

If the prospect does not object or stop your action, you just made a sale. An action

The physical action close lets your actions do the talking.

close won't do all of the work for you, but it nonverbally signals to the buyer that the deal is moving forward.

4. Be Clear and Ask (Direct Close)

Once you have covered the features and benefits of your product and matched them with dominant buying motives, you can ask, "May I have your business?" This type of close is common when selling to industrial buyers who appreciate a no-nonsense approach. Of course, be mindful of the buyer's behavioral style. Amiables, for example, might find this approach threatening.

Be sure to keep the direct close positive. Avoid the word, *don't.* "Why don't we begin next week?" and "Why don't you try the product for a while and see what happens?" are open invitations to objections. Negative words may implant doubt where none existed. Use positive statements like these:

So, I will schedule the delivery for next Tuesday?

Each workstation will come with either laptops or desktops. I suggest you assign the laptops to the sales team.

Let's run your first ad beginning on Friday of this week. Sound good?

The direct close requires you to ask for their business directly.

When you use this type of closing statement, then you and your customer can make concrete plans together.

5. Provide Options (Alternative Choice Close)

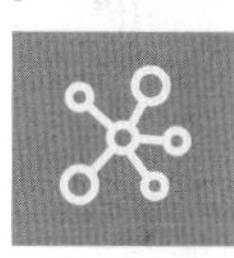

People like to exercise their freedom of choice, and salespeople want to lead their buyers toward an agreement. So, give the prospect a choice between two positive alternatives. Here are some suggestions:

Should I schedule the delivery for Thursday, or would you prefer Friday?

Do you prefer to pay upfront, or is our monthly payment plan a better fit?

The alternative choice close leads prospects to the close through options.

Where would you like the order sent—directly to your warehouse or the main office?

The idea is to offer the prospect a choice between choosing door #1 or #2 instead of opening *no* door at all. The question is not, "Will you buy?" but "Which one?" or "How much?"

Exhibit 14.2 is a whimsical example of the power of options in a close. It's also an excellent example of the power of persistence!

6. Summarize Major Points (Summary Close)

A summary gives the prospect and you an opportunity to reconsider information from the presentation. Summarizing the major selling points is especially useful when the prospect must later defend a purchase to someone else. Allow the prospect to agree that the summary is correct.

Concentrate on those items that were of most interest to the prospect and that related directly to the dominant buying motives.[27] For example, a sales rep selling advertising space in an industrial magazine might use the summary close like this:

EXHIBIT 14.2 In a Box or on a Fox?

One of the best examples of persistence is a story you probably loved as a child—*Green Eggs and Ham*. This Dr. Seuss classic describes the attempt of the "salesman," Sam I Am, to induce a wary "prospect" to try a meal of green eggs and ham.

When his first straightforward offer is rejected, Sam I Am tries one assumptive close after another: "Do you want them here or there? Would you like them in a box or with a fox? Do you want them in a house or with a mouse?"

Finally, the "prospect" tries green eggs and ham and is surprised to find them delicious. His refusals seemingly never registered with the persistent Sam I Am. If you have not read *Green Eggs and Ham* lately, visit the children's section of the library and re-learn the story's important lesson about persistence and the persuasive power of options.[26]

Let's review the major points on which we have agreed:

1. *A national ad in our magazine will give you the circulation you need to reach an additional 10,000 target leads each month.*
2. *Your ads will have a guaranteed readership rate of 37 percent.*
3. *Businesses like yours have had great success advertising with us (refer to case histories used during the presentation).*
4. *Our marketing staff will help you develop ads for both online and magazine use.*
5. *You'll receive complimentary design work and layout assistance included in the price.*

Bring up additional points only if the summary fails, and you need the extra ammunition to answer new objections. Once you both agree, the prospect is in a positive frame of mind, and the time is ripe to close. You can then combine the summary with a question like:

With all of these significant benefits, you can see that advertising with us is a sound investment. Do you want to run your first ad on October 15th, or would November 1st work better for your holiday promotion?

The summary close highlights selling points related to key buying motives.

7. Give a Reason to Act (Impending Event Close)

This tactic promotes a sense of urgency by suggesting that an approaching event may affect some aspects of the buying process. Always base this close on truth, and do not be manipulative. The most common incentives are prices increases or resources that will soon be in short supply:

My company has announced that prices on this product will increase by 5 percent next month because of an uptick in supplier costs. If I receive your order this week, you can stock up before the price increase goes into effect.

Whatever the upcoming change or event, it must be genuine. You must also know that it is indeed in the prospect's best interest to order now. When you have useful information to work with, you can prevent a customer from running short on inventory or facing an unexpected surge in the cost of materials. The positive side effect of this is you will gain the appreciation and the loyalty of the customer.

The impending event close stresses a legitimate urgency to act now.

8. Offer a Trial (Trial Order Close)

This technique involves asking the prospect for a trial order with no obligation. Prospects like it because their risk is low. This is also

known as the *puppy dog close*. How could you ever return a puppy to the pet store and get your money back after the children have played with it for a week? By then, everyone is in love with it.

Suppose you are selling Dave Ramsey's Financial Peace University™ program to financial planners. A prospect says, "I've never used a program like this in my planning activities. Let me think about it." Respond with:

> *I can certainly appreciate that. One thing that might be helpful to you is to try the program for one month, risk-free. That gives you time to work with the material and see if it is something that would be useful in your career consulting sessions. We encourage you to view the introductory videos, read the manual, and try it out with some clients.*
>
> *After 30 days, if you believe you will benefit from using it, keep using it, and we will bill you the following month. If you find it's not suitable for your situation, let us know and return the hard-copy materials. You'll never be charged a penny. Is that fair enough?*

The trial order close offers a "no obligation" way to say yes.

9. Build a Balance Sheet (Balance Sheet Close)

A balance sheet format is familiar to most prospects, and they will feel comfortable with you using it to help them decide. This tactic involves using either paper or a device with a stylus pen.

Draw a line down the center to form two columns. In the first column, list all the reasons for saying yes (the assets). Then list all the questions or concerns about a buying decision (the liabilities). Make sure the prospect can see as you write. The closing process is an analysis of the two columns to show the prospect that the reasons for buying outweigh the reasons for not buying. You can begin like this:

> *The decision you are about to make is important. I know you want to be sure you are making the right choice. Let's look at all the reasons in favor of buying as well as any questions or concerns. You can then determine which side weighs more and make your decision accordingly. Let's begin with ideas that support a favorable decision today.*

List the reasons for buying and avoid the word *objection*. Instead of talking about the prospect's objections to buying, state them as concerns or questions to be answered, as in, "You expressed concern about delivery schedules." When you use the word objection, you are setting up the prospect and yourself as adversaries—and if you are adversaries, one of you must win, and the other must lose.

The balance sheet close lists the pros and cons of buying.

10. Make a Comparison (Cost of Ownership Close)

Rather than talking about price, you may want to focus on the total cost of ownership. Then total these costs and compare them to the prices offered by your competition. This tactic works by comparing costs over time rather than only up-front payments. Here is an example:

> *The competition's product may seem less expensive. However, when you take into account our complimentary installation, free maintenance for life, and the lifetime guarantee, we are about half the price.*

Because people often focus on the price due now, they miss the long-term costs and

savings. This comparison works by revealing costs and value over time rather than up-front payments alone. Lower service costs mean that you should be offering a more reliable product, and it helps to have evidence of your product's superior quality.

The cost of ownership close emphasizes long-term value rather than up-front costs.

11. Come Back Again (Call-Back Close)

Sales opportunities are lost every day because salespeople take a prospect's decision not to buy as permanent. However, many accounts require five or more calls and closes to win. Each time you return, you must present new information that will stimulate the prospect to buy. If you walk into the prospect's office and say, "Have you thought it over?" the prospect's natural tendency will probably be to restate the original objection. Then you won't be any better off than before. Here is an effective plan for a call-back situation:

1. **Approach.** Start by stating a reason for calling back. For example, you could say, "After I left last week, I realized that there is some information we did not cover that has a real impact on your business." Be sure you do have something different to present—new data, additional evidence in the form of testimonials, or anything else that may be compelling or pertinent.
2. **Review.** Next, review the whole presentation. Begin with, "Let's review items we talked about last time." The last meeting may be fresh in your mind, but the prospect will remember only a fraction (maybe 10 percent) of what you presented. Use phrases like, "As you remember," "You will recall," and "We said that" to suggest points of agreement from the previous meeting.

These new approaches may not always work, but you know that you cannot sell to most customers without face-to-face contact. Being there gives you the only opportunity you will ever have to make the sale.

The call-back close relies on persistence and a desire to help qualified prospects who didn't buy.

After the Close

We've talked a lot about learning to read the sales situation and selling when the time is right! Let's say you've done that, and a *prospect* just became a *customer*. That is undoubtedly an exciting time in any salesperson's career—but it may not be time for the celebration yet. Some customers may still have unfinished business, and if you ignore it, you could find that your sale wasn't complete. Here's an example of what that might look like:

Jordan worked hard to close this deal with Rita. After months of meetings, presentations, negotiations, and follow up, he finally got the 'yes' he was after. Rita tells him to come by the next day to complete the paperwork. They are both satisfied and eager to make things official as he leaves. Jordan is so happy that he takes his wife out to celebrate.

The next morning, he goes to see Rita and hands her the papers. Her look puzzles him as she takes the contract and sets it aside. She draws in a deep breath and says, "Okay, Jordan, here's the thing..."

Jordan thought it was a done deal—so what could have happened overnight? It turns out that Jordan had stopped selling just a little too soon. Rita had felt good about her decision because her current vendor's quality had been suffering for months. When she'd call to complain about it, things would get better for a while, but then the quality would start slipping again. That's why, when Jordan initially contacted her, she was open to hearing what he had to offer.

When it came time for the "break up call" to her current vendor after Jordan left, the vendor wasn't going to give up easily. He reminded Rita of how long they'd been working together. The vendor also made her doubt Jordan's capabilities and ability to understand her needs. Finally, he promised her that the problems would be fixed and asked her to give them 30 days, free of charge, to prove it.

Jordan hadn't won the sale—and now he was facing an entrenched competitor who had the upper hand again. He could have avoided all of this by using the *"after the close" close*. Here's how it works: when a customer

"Sorry, but pinky swear doesn't cut it anymore. My attorney has a few documents for you to sign."

tells you that they are ready to sign, rather than celebrate, secure the deal by saying:

> *Rita, I'm excited about working with you, and thanks for the opportunity. I'm sure that your current vendor will not want to lose your account. What are you planning to say to him?*

This statement allows your customer to consider the possibility that a phone call to the current vendor or supplier may not be easy. If a customer has never thought about that next step before now, this gives you the chance to walk them through it as you reinforce in their mind the reasons for switching in the first place.

You may not use this technique every time. Still, it could be an invaluable reinforcement when you are not sure whether a sale is complete. As a bonus, this technique is ideal for *amiables* and *expressives* who may have a harder time letting a current vendor go. So, make sure you've done an excellent job of reading your prospect.

The Social Media Connection

USING SOCIAL MEDIA TO MAINTAIN TOP OF MIND AWARENESS

TOMA, which stands for top of mind awareness, is an important acronym in today's business world. Customers make buying decisions every day based on one factor: who comes to mind first. Brands who maintain top of mind awareness qualify under one of three conditions:[28]

1. A perennial favorite: The only way to increase your chances of getting in under this condition is to provide exceptional products and customer service to all customers consistently.
2. A lingering bad taste: You've heard the phrase, "I don't know what I want, but I know what I don't want." If the thing they don't want is your product, this is top of mind, but not in a good way.
3. The right exposure: This is your chance for an advantageous top of mind awareness, and it is within your control.

Let's say a prospect was qualified, but for reasons beyond your control, they were unable to commit. They are finally ready to make a purchase six months later. Will they remember you and buy from you? Or will they forget about you and buy from one of your competitors?

Take steps to ensure they remember you. Social media can help you do this, especially in conjunction with blogging and other forms of content marketing, including *content curation*—which is the process of sorting through the vast amounts of content on the web and presenting it in a meaningful and organized way around a specific theme.[29]

It's rare to close a sale through social media. Still, you can drive traffic from your social media pages to other marketing channels. For example, when you post a new entry on your blog, announce it through your social media outlets. (Include a link to your article, of course.)

If you do video marketing, you should post links to your YouTube videos on social media. Present a compelling bit of content that arouses curiosity and makes people eager to check out the video. On your YouTube page, include your website's URL. On your Facebook fan page or LinkedIn business page, add a signup form for your email list.

Those are just a few of the ways to retain top of mind awareness among your prospects. When the time is right to buy, they may think of you!

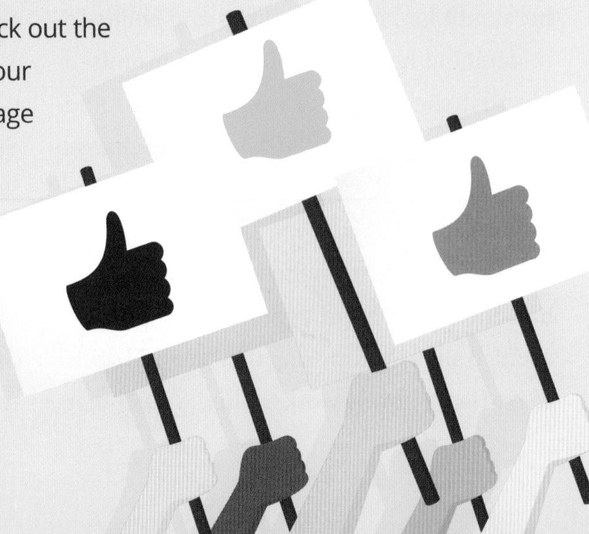

SUMMARY

Closing the sale is a natural conclusion to a carefully prepared and well-conducted presentation to a qualified prospect.

Learn to recognize buying signals. These enable you to close at the earliest possible point in the presentation.

The most threatening element in the sale is often the fear of rejection. Develop a plan for dealing with rejection.

Both verbal and nonverbal clues point to the prospect's readiness to buy. The buying signals often suggest the type of close that would be appropriate. Close when the prospect is ready to buy.

One effective tactic is a trial close that asks for an opinion rather than a commitment; this allows the salesperson to determine just how ready the prospect is to say yes!

Use words like *when* or *as* during the close. Avoid words such as *if* and *should* because they are conditional and block closing action.

Use a summary during the close to restate significant selling points made in the presentation. This repetition overcomes the prospect's tendency to forget or neglect main points.

It may be helpful to present a balance sheet during the close in a pro and con format. Analytical and amiables respond well to this technique.

Review Questions

1. Discuss some strategies for handling the rejection that salespeople experience from missing a sale.
2. Why do many prospects naturally say no at the close?
3. Why do many salespeople dread the close? Is this fear unfounded?
4. When should a salesperson decide how to close? Why?
5. Should a pre-planned close ever be changed in the middle of the meeting? Why or why not?
6. Timing is crucial in closing. Is attempting a close before the prospect is ready more harmful than trying to close past the critical point? Why or why not?
7. Distinguish between a trial close and a closing question. When is each appropriate?
8. What is the purpose of reassurance in connection with the close?
9. How many times in one interview should a salesperson ask for the order? How many times should you call on the same prospect to ask for an order?
10. What is the difference between persistence and pushiness?
11. Describe some typical verbal and nonverbal buying signals.

IN-CLASS EXERCISES

The following exercises help build teams, improve communication, and emphasize the real-world side of selling. They are meant to challenge you, help you learn how to deal with problems with no one right answer, and use a variety of skills beyond those employed in a typical review question. Read and complete each activity. Then in the next class, discuss and compare answers.

EXERCISE 14.1 Planning Closes

This is the final planning exercise for your team. Therefore, you should use the same team that worked with for role plays 12.1 and 13.1. Review your presentation plan as amended by your approach to handling objections. Now you need to insert appropriate closing attempts. Although you are dealing with a buying center, your experience as the chief decision-maker should allow you to identify personality types (driver, expressive, amiable, analytical). With all of the other information about the buying center's needs and concerns that you have developed, insert closing opportunities into your plan. Specifically, note the following points:

- When will you introduce trial closes (calls for opinion), and why? Which type of trial closes will you use?
- What sorts of nonverbal buying signals will you look for throughout your presentation?
- What type of final close (call for decision) will you attempt? Why? When?
- What will be the objective of your final close, your call to action (sale, trial order, call back, etc.), and why?

EXERCISE 14.2 A Sign of True Love?

For this exercise, the class should be divided into teams of four. Beginning salespeople often have difficulty remembering and noticing verbal and nonverbal buying signals. But put them in a social situation in which they are trying to attract the romantic attentions of someone they admire, and they notice every little twitch and nuance!

As a team, you should brainstorm subtle verbal and nonverbal cues that indicate personal attraction. Exclude any overt verbal expressions of love or affection, or nonverbal expressions such as touching, hugging, or kissing. As you create your list, also think in each case of a corresponding or analogous buying signal, verbal or nonverbal, based on what you know about body language. The team with the highest number of legitimate pairings (as determined by your instructor) wins.

Case Studies

The following case studies present you with selling scenarios that require you to apply the critical skills discussed in the chapter and give you training through practical learning situations. They are meant to be both engaging and challenging, and like the in-class exercises, they don't have one right answer.

CASE 14.1—"Don't Tell Me No Lies!"

Harold was not feeling good about his last sales presentation. A customer who was somewhat interested in purchasing an entire season's worth of lawn care and landscape maintenance service had proved in the end to be indecisive. Harold had gone through all of the benefits of his company's service. He told the prospect how it would save him time and effort, how his lawn and shrubs would recover quickly after a harsh winter, and how his plants would better withstand drought. Still, the customer wouldn't pull the trigger.

Acquiring new customers was becoming difficult for McPhee's Landscaping Service thanks to the increased level of competition (especially from two large home improvement centers that had just opened). So, the company sent Harold to Atlanta for intense sales training. The trainers emphasized hard, aggressive selling that was designed to close the deal in one visit. Allowing a customer to think things over, they said, was the same as handing your business to your competitors. The trainers emphasized closing techniques as the heart of the entire sales process. When Harold returned home to Cleveland, he told his boss that he was ready to try the new methods.

The Atlanta trainers had emphasized using physical action (like filling out an order form before hearing an actual *yes*) as particularly effective when dealing with indecisive amiable or analytical types. Harold's latest customer seemed to fit that mold perfectly. However, he didn't respond to the technique at all. So, Harold turned to his last trick and told the customer that if he didn't purchase the contract today, the price would go up by 25 percent. He explained that the lower price was only available for those who signed on the dotted line in advance of needing the service. The customer signed and wrote out a check for the full, discounted amount. Harold thought to himself that this is like shooting fish in a barrel. It would be a good year.

Two weeks later, Harold's boss angrily reported that the customer had called to cancel the contract and demand a full refund. The customer had learned from friends who had purchased later after the lawn-mowing season had begun, that no price increase had occurred. At least one person had waited ten days before signing a contract for the same price that Harold's customer got! The customer canceled because Harold had lied to him.

Should Harold have been surprised by this turn of events? What was the matter with Harold's attitude toward selling? Which closing techniques should he have used that would have been more effective, and that would not have involved deception?

CASE 14.2—Always Be Closing Means What?

James Arnold sells airplanes, big ones. He heads a large team of salespersons, financial experts, contract attorneys, and aviation engineers that sells fleets of planes to major airlines around the world. In the current global economy and with the reality of financial difficulties in the industry, his team has had to become more aggressive and focused on closing business. When James broke into sales at his father's auto dealership, the mantra, "Always Be Closing," was drummed into his head. Now, 30 years later, he realizes that his team needs to learn the same motto. But what can "always" mean for a sales cycle that can take as long as seven to 12 months? To get a handle on what this might mean for the team, James calls a meeting of the primary team leaders.

"How can we keep ourselves and our clients directed toward completing the final transaction?" he asked. "What might 'Always Be Closing' mean for our respective roles?"

"Well, I know one thing," said Sherm Atkins, the chief engineer on the team. "If we have to persuade anyone to buy our planes, we've already lost the sale. As we work out answers to problems and questions, some of which come from our clients, it must be one seamless process, in fact, a process of ceaseless assent."

"Very well put, Sherm," James answered. "But how do we make sure that happens?"

"I think the answer to that is simple," interjected Marian, the lead attorney. "We all work in very disparate areas and on long-term, complicated negotiations. However, at the end of every meeting with our airline counterparts, we must agree on the next steps. Whether that is merely to keep working on the same problem or to move on to something new, we need to get a commitment to keep moving forward. Every time. Without fail. If we do that, signing the final contracts will be a mere formality."

"I think you're onto something, Marian," said Jim. "Let's try to unpack that a little."

What do you think? Given what you've learned from Chapter 14 about different types of and strategies for closing successfully, have Sherm and Marian captured what their team should be doing? Do you have any additional suggestions to refine or correct their approach?

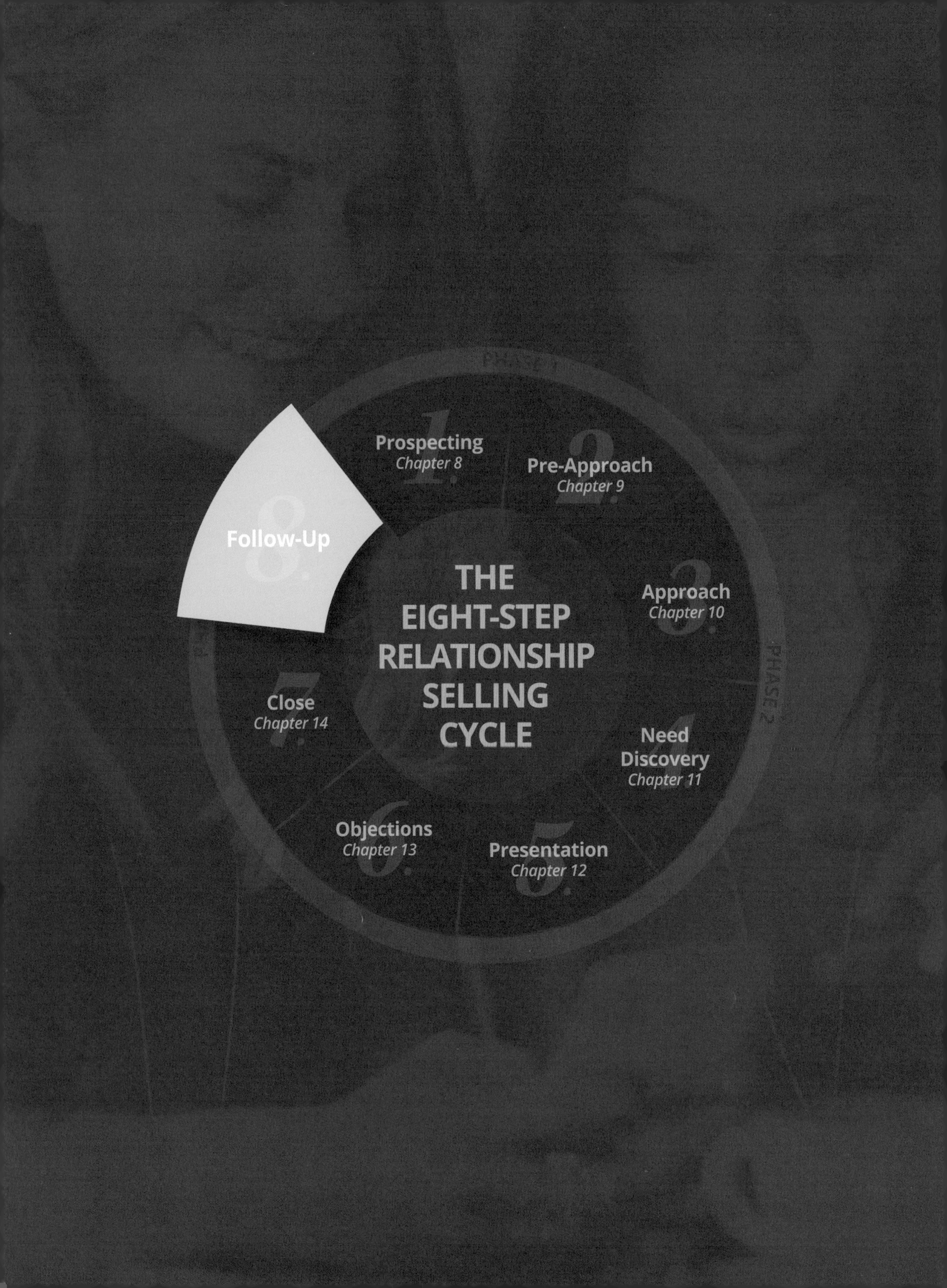

THE EIGHT-STEP RELATIONSHIP SELLING CYCLE

PHASE 1

PHASE 2

1. Prospecting
Chapter 8

2. Pre-Approach
Chapter 9

3. Approach
Chapter 10

4. Need Discovery
Chapter 11

5. Presentation
Chapter 12

6. Objections
Chapter 13

7. Close
Chapter 14

8. Follow-Up

AFTER THE SALE: BUILD ENDURING LOYALTY

OVERVIEW

The way you follow up with customers after the sale is complete can be as significant, or even more significant, than the sale itself. Keeping current customers happy and regaining lost clients is the focus of our last step in the Relationship Selling Cycle. The customer defines quality in every transaction, and they ultimately determine the success of your organization. So you must learn how to make them feel as valuable as they are. Great salespeople don't *talk* customer service—they *live* exemplary service.

OBJECTIVES

- Examine the purpose of follow-through when it comes to customer service.
- Determine what constitutes adding value for your customers.
- Know when and how to service your customer base.
- Understand the salesperson's role in servicing clients.
- Appreciate how to upgrade and cross-sell current customers.
- Develop a system for your follow-up to ensure you stay top of mind.

The Profound Role of Service

Customer service after the sale may be the eighth and final step in the Relationship Selling Cycle, and but it's certainly not the least important. You have probably had a terrible customer service experience in the past that made you wish you'd never given that company a dime of your money. Hopefully, you've also had a magical customer service experience that not only solved your problem but also restored your faith in humanity. The right customer service can move mountains. Below are some customer service statistics that prove this point.[1]

Excellent customer service is essential for your clients and you. While it's true that most companies say that their customers are their top priority, how many of them walk the walk? You can have the most exceptional products and salespeople in the world. Still, if you're losing customers through poor customer service, the company's bottom line and your compensation will suffer.

Every salesperson and company should realize that long-term sustainability depends on the ability to generate consistent excellent service that keeps customers satisfied. The cost of acquiring new customers far outweighs that of retaining existing customers. No salesperson would willingly choose cold calling over reaching out to a happy customer for an additional sale. That is why you must do everything in your power to keep more of the customers you already have.

Despite this common-sense idea, salespeople get so caught up in chasing leads or assuming that all their customers want is the lowest price. Studies show that customers are

Customer Service Statistics

1. A customer is four times more likely to defect to a competitor if the problem is service-related rather than price or product-related.
2. The probability of selling to a new prospect is 5 to 20 percent. The likelihood of selling to an existing customer is 60 to 70 percent.
3. For every customer complaint, 26 unhappy customers have remained silent.
4. An estimated 96 percent of unhappy customers don't complain, but 91 percent of them will eventually leave and never return.
5. Approximately 70 percent of buying experiences are based on how customers feel about their treatment, not on price or product.
6. Over half (55 percent) of a polled customer base would pay extra to guarantee better service.

willing to pay more for improved customer experiences.[2] Your clients want you to do what you promise and prove your worth. You must follow through and support your customers in any way you can after the purchase. As Benjamin Franklin once remarked:

"Well done is better than well said."

Customers expect excellent service, and most will not tolerate you sidelining them after you have their money. Consequently, they are more likely to move to the vendors who provide the highest-quality service. Your company's job is to create and keep a customer, and your job is the same. The best way to increase your value is to build a loyal customer base through first-class customer service. The buyer defines quality in every transaction. Don't talk customer service—live perfect service.

> **"A lot of people have fancy things to say about customer service, but it's just a day-in, day-out, ongoing, never-ending, unremitting, persevering, compassionate type of activity."**
> *Leon Gorman, L.L. Bean*

Standing Out From the Crowd

With today's stiff competition, consumers often find it difficult to differentiate one product from another, which means that the

differentiators are the buying experience and customer service. You can start practicing excellent service by treating the people in your company well. Do you treat other team members the way you want to be treated? Here are some questions from the National Association of Sales Professionals (NASP) that you and your sales team can ask to determine how you can stand out from the crowd:[3]

- **Where do you want to be?** What do you want your customers to be saying about you, your team, your brand, and your company? Come up with some potential statements you'd want them to say if you asked them.
- **What needs to happen?** Looking closely at the statements you'd want others to say about you, think about what sort of changes you'd need to make to ensure these statements come true. If you can't get there right away, prioritize one new activity at a time.

- **Where are you now?** Assess where you are now with where you have just established you need to be. Does your team have the skills to fill the gap? Are you capable of taking on the changes required?
- **How can you get there?** What do you need to do first? Work out a way to measure the quality of your service. It could be simple (through tracking your repeat sales) or sophisticated (through the use of analytics), but do something.

Adding Value

Many companies attribute their sales success to their salespeople's value-driven mentality. This type of thinking occurs when companies become less focused on promoting their agenda and become more customer-centric. One company that strives to be customer-led is the grocery chain, Kroger. Their Kroger Plus program rewards loyal customers with offers relevant to their unique shopping preferences. Kroger knows that even their best customers make grocery purchases outside of Kroger.[4] They offer incentives and points for buying items their customers don't usually buy to improve the shopping experience and increase loyalty. Ultimately, they want to make the activity convenient and enjoyable for their customers. Here are two additional examples of value-added service:

> *Salespeople from Caterpillar Tractor promise that their customers will receive ordered parts within 48 hours anywhere in the world. This after-sale service is both appealing and highly successful. The promise is not an idle one. If Caterpillar misses the 48-hour delivery window, the part is free.*

Car manufacturers who use value-added service to enhance the customer experience enjoy 20 percent more after-market revenue than their competitors. Korean automaker Hyundai Motor launched the first-ever online portal for servicing cars to take advantage of this. A sales and marketing director for Hyundai said online shoppers need access to extensive information concerning post-sale servicing, maintenance, and repair. They hope to stand out by making maintenance and service expenses transparent from the start.[5]

The automobile industry estimates that a brand-loyal customer represents a lifetime average revenue of $300,000 to the dealer. If they refer two additional customers, then that one satisfied buyer represents almost $1 million in revenue.[6]

The follow-up activities you perform will determine whether customers reorder and whether they tell their friends, colleagues, and family about the experience. The relationship sales professional is sincerely and unselfishly helpful to clients and prospects alike. Sometimes value-added service costs nothing except thoughtfulness and a few minutes.

Southwest Airlines founder Herb Kelleher wanted to set his airline apart from the others. The company is known for its low fares and attention to customer service. Southwest maintains a high level of customer satisfaction not just because of its convenient flights and low fares, but also because of its value-added service. Exhibit 15.1 tells a story that exemplifies how Southwest Airlines adds value and heart to its service and develops a fiercely loyal customer base.[7]

EXHIBIT 15.1 Southwest Airlines Is On Your Side

Southwest®

A man was headed from a business trip in Los Angeles to his daughter's home in Denver, Colorado, to see his three-year-old grandson for the last time. The boy was being taken off of life support at 9 p.m. that evening so his organs could be used to save other lives. The man's wife called Southwest to arrange the last-minute flight and explained the emergency. Unfortunately, the man was held up by L.A. traffic and long lines at LAX and didn't make it to the gate on time. When he finally made it there 12 minutes after the plane was scheduled to leave, he was shocked to find the pilot waiting for him. He thanked the pilot profusely, and the pilot said, "They can't go anywhere without me, and I wasn't going anywhere without you. Now relax. We'll get you there. And again, I'm so sorry."

Four Keys to Customer Retention

The best way to increase your value as a salesperson is to build a loyal customer base through first-class service. However, keep in mind there is a fine but distinct line between badgering and fostering a customer with regular contact. The difference comes not from *when* you follow up, but *how*. Four keys to customer retention will allow you to stay connected to your customer base. By learning the keys to service after the sale, you will enable your customers to feel as important and valued as they are to you and your organization.

Key #1: Think Like a Customer

People buy from people they like—and this is excellent news for several reasons. First, it allows you to consider your ultimate task to be a matter of finding and connecting with likeminded people. Second, it encourages you to communicate with passion and be genuine with others to establish honest and lasting connections. So, how can you effectively think like a customer? Here are some suggestions:

Get To Know Them. The best way to think like a customer is to get to know your customers better—and not just through an obligatory follow-up call or by following them on Twitter. The best way to get to know them is to ask questions (even after the sale is complete). What made them decide to buy a few months ago may not be their motivating factors today. The only way to know that is to ASK. The important thing is to ask "why" as much as "how." Asking "how" helps you understand what a customer wants to build, while the "why" question leads you to see what they want to accomplish.[8]

Learn More About Their Customers. Your customers' customers are what matters most to them. So, take the time to find out more about their business and how they grow their customer base. One of the first

questions you should ask a new client is, "What is your customer demographic?" and "Why would customers spend money for your service?" Those inquiries can help you identify places where you can trim or add to your existing offering to improve their business (and not just your own).

Communicate Competitive Advantage. Your customers know there are virtually countless companies they could choose that sell some variation of what you sell. So, expect them to question their decision. You know your product or service is superior. Still, you can't assume that even your most loyal customers will continue to think this without occasional reminders. You also have no way of knowing who else has approached your customers since you last spoke with them. So, focus on how you communicate how you are different from other companies. Monitor both traditional and emerging competition. Resolve all customer inquiries quickly, especially questions about pricing and quality.

Send Feedback Requests. One of the best ways to gain insights into your customers is to conduct short surveys asking them what they love (or don't love) about working with you and your company. A lot of companies send out surveys, but the key is to reach back out to customers and tell them how you've implemented their suggestions! There is no better way to communicate with a customer than to show them you were listening. Let the conversation also be an opportunity for more feedback. You want customers to feel like they have an open line of communication

to you at all times—whether that's for praise, complaints, or requests.

Key #2: Go the Extra Mile

Be willing to give your customers more than they demand and far more than they expect. Act from the desire to serve—not the desire to gain. When you make this your policy, you will do whatever you must to be of use and service to your client. Paul J. Meyer, the founder of SMI International, once had a client who made a hobby of collecting rocks containing fossils. When Meyer was on vacation one year, he found a rock with a unique fossil on it. He packed it carefully and mailed it to his client. That kind of extra service, when given from sincere interest, pays rich dividends.

Going the second mile may involve performing a service that is unrelated to your business. Fast-food chain Chick-fil-A has adopted a policy of "second-mile service" for all of its 2,300 nationwide locations. The manager of a Chick-fil-A in Alabama took the policy to heart when he changed a customer's flat tire in the restaurant's parking lot while she ate. Chick-fil-A prides itself on being a company known for going the extra mile. When that same Alabama branch saw a 13 percent sales growth over one year without any menu or aesthetic changes, they couldn't help but believe the increase was due to Chick-fil-A's exceptional service philosophy.[9]

Determining your clients' satisfaction and keeping a constant flow of feedback are the best ways to know if you and your company are consistently going the extra mile. *Benchmarking*, in which organizations compare various aspects of their processes with best practices, is an excellent way to perform "preventative maintenance" on your interactions with customers and prospects.

It pays to go the extra mile. Here are a few ideas for how to provide exceptional follow-up if there is a problem after the sale:[10]

- Offer to personally pick up or deliver goods to be replaced or repaired.
- Give a gift of merchandise to repay for the inconvenience. The gift may be small, but the thought will be appreciated.
- Reimburse for the costs of returning merchandise such as parking fees or gas.
- Provide discounts on office supplies, car rentals, or express shipping.
- Acknowledge the customer's inconvenience with a small token of appreciation, and thank him for allowing you to make it right. Make the wording of the apology sincere and personal.

"I appreciate you going the extra mile, Ted, but now you're a mile away!"

- Follow up to see that the problem was fixed. Don't assume the problem is corrected unless you handled it yourself.

Key #3: Be Sincere in Your Gratitude

For many salespeople, their idea of acknowledging the sale is emailing customers a copy of the receipt or contract. That's no follow-up—that's part of the transaction! Some salespeople think they are doing well when they tweet a thank you to a customer. Saying thanks via social media is helpful, but in most cases, it is simply not enough.

Even when salespeople do reach out and thank customers, research suggests that not all thank you's are equal. Recent statistics indicate that only 38 percent of salespeople send any thank-you note to customers after a meeting, and many who do receive them are getting form letters.[11]

We all want to be thanked for our business and for choosing one company when we could have chosen another. Saying thank you is not only the right thing to do, but it's also a financially advantageous thing to do. Customers who feel their salespeople are exceptional are 10 to 15 times more likely to remain loyal, which means more sales—and more commissions.[12]

Most salespeople can answer the "who, what, when, where, and how" of a business relationship. The missing element is "why." Why do your customers do business with you? Is it because they feel valued, protected, or informed? These "why" factors have a tremendous impact on customer loyalty. Your customers are not expecting to see their names written in the sky. They want a warm, personalized follow-up that conveys your gratitude. If your resources are limited, consider enlisting the help of technology. There are features within most CRM programs that can help generate automatic, personalized email confirmations and thank you messages.

Get Personal. The personal touch goes a long way when it comes to follow-up. Make sure that the greeting itself doesn't offend your customers. With all that technology offers, there is no excuse for sending generic form letters. They need to be personalized, as in "Dear [first name]." Always proof your messages and ensure your information is correct. Don't attempt any other selling or ask for referrals on the initial follow-up. Creating personalized messages to customers doesn't have to take a lot of time or be costly. To have a powerful impact, your thank you letters should follow the Four P's. Thank-you letters should be:

Prompt. Send the message as soon as you have secured their business, preferably within 48 hours.

Personalized. Ensure that you are writing directly to the customer you dealt with (including their first name) and reference their purchase.

Precise. Convey gratitude and explain how any next steps or implementation will proceed.

Positive. Make your customers smile and feel confirmation that they chose the right salesperson and company. Let them know that because of their choice, they are now entering into a long-term relationship with someone who has their best interests at heart.

Customization Vs. Personalization. Personalizing your messages is a must, but be careful not to use customization options in your automated replies as substitutes for the real thing. For example, a university alumnus was asked about his reaction to a fundraising video he'd received from his alma mater. It was innovative, it was different, and it was *customized.* The email he'd received had a subject line with his name in it, and the body of the email had his name in it. The video itself *also* had his name in it![13]

Despite these touches, he said he didn't like it. He felt that all that video told him was that his alma mater paid a lot of money to a video company to stick his name in there in a few places. It was *customized*, but it wasn't *personalized.*

Research suggests that 38 percent of customers judge the quality of customer follow-up according to its level of personalization.[14] Using technology to insert someone's name is not innovative or personal. Taking the time to write a personal note, acknowledge something specific to a customer, hand-address an envelope—those are the actions that say something. It's old fashioned, and that's why it stands out.

Key #4: Treat Every Account Like a Major Account

Thank you letters and follow-up calls are essential, and they should always be a part of your ongoing activities. But keeping customers happy, engaged, and loyal takes more than that. They want to feel special. Their purchase matters the same to them no matter what dollar amount they spent, from your smallest customer to your largest account.

The extent to which salespeople go to thank customers traditionally involves segmenting them (often based on their account size). In other words, only following up with really big clients is a common practice in the sales world. That is a mistake because *every* customer wants to be considered a valuable customer. For example, if you've ever made a small donation to a nonprofit and received no acknowledgment whatsoever, you probably didn't rush to donate again. Some people like to "test out" charities with small donations to see if they want to get involved. Future-focused nonprofits know that a small donor can become a major donor over time. Of course, it takes work on the part of the fundraiser to get them there. Similarly, a small customer can become a large customer with the right care and follow up. Just because a customer placed a small order the first time doesn't mean it will stay that way!

"It's nice to see you again. And thanks so much for the dead mice you sent over."

Never underestimate the power of customer loyalty, regardless of the size of the account.

Consider circulating the names of smaller customers around the office. Ask team members, "Does anyone know this person?" Keep track of the contacts you have with all customers. If you find out something, record the information. Did you find out something that indicates you might need to meet with them again to discuss a new product? Making a personal connection is often the key to more substantial future sales. Large organizations can more easily neglect small sales simply because they have so many. But for smaller companies, every purchase counts.

Letters and emails are not the only ways to express your gratitude. Inexpensive gifts and tokens of appreciation can be great ways to make customers feel appreciated. Consider saying thanks with branded t-shirts, mugs, pens, or totes with your company's logo, or some other token that will both remind your customers of your company and make them feel appreciated. If you have the budget for it, a gift card can go a long way. Even a $10 Starbucks card can make a lasting impression.

Consider your customers to be your portfolio of assets. Find out who they are, what potential they have, and the "why" behind their decision to buy. With the right amount of caring, you will eventually have more big customers than you ever imagined. We all want to feel special and needed, and your smaller customers are no different. The most important thing to remember when it comes to customers of all sizes can be best summed up through the words of Henry James:

> "Three things in human life are important. The first is to be kind. The second is to be kind. And the third is to be kind."

Maximizing Current Customers

Since you invest so much time in finding new customers, attempting to save time by neglecting post-sale follow-up is a costly mistake. A negative buying experience can be a bitter and enduring memory. There is no substitute for salespeople thanking their buyers and asking their customer base what else they can do to help them. All the efforts to retain your customers are certainly not without advantages. It pays to go the extra mile with customers. The payoff of exceptional, consistent customer follow-up can be summed up through the Four R's:[15]

Referrals. Loyal customers encourage others to support your company over another, saving you some of the substantial cost of acquiring new customers. Where yesterday's "word of mouth" could influence a dozen individuals, today's "word-of-mouse" (via email, blogs, and social media) can impact thousands.

Retention. Customers who continue to buy from you provide a solid base for success.

Reputation. Loyal customers speak well of you to others. They increase public support and positive interest from future customers and even the media.

Revenue. Loyal customers give you more of what you and your company need—the resources required to continue growing and prospering.

In addition to providing exceptional service, there are three more ways you can maximize your current customer base:

1. **Sell more.** Call on existing customers and sell them more of what you are already selling to them. Other departments in their company may have a need, so sell them upgrades, enhancements, or additional products. Needs change over time. Sell your current clients something new. Keep them up-to-date on new products. Sell customers on you, strive to become a trusted member of their team, and fresh opportunities will present themselves.[16]

2. **Up-sell.** *Upgrading,* also known as *up-selling,* is the process of persuading the customer to purchase a better-quality product or, perhaps, a newer product. Upgrading is mostly a matter of selling your company and promoting the quality factors of your product and customer image. You ask for the upgrade because the newer or higher-quality product will better serve the

needs of the client. Buyers like to have choices when making a purchase, which is why most companies offer products and services with a range of quality and price.

When you qualify prospects throughout the selling cycle, up-selling becomes easier. You never want to oversell, but giving options is advantageous for both sides. That is especially true since *up-selling* efforts lead to more purchases from 58 to 72 percent of customers.[17] Speak to their genuine needs and focus on selling results—not products.

3. **Cross-Sell.** *Cross-selling* is the process of selling products not directly connected to the primary products purchased. Here is an example of cross-selling in action. During a meeting with your banker to close on a loan, you casually mention how much you dread having to pay your son's college tuition. The banker tells you how you could use a limited trust fund to help pay college expenses and offers to help set one up.

Cross-selling and upgrading have become increasingly important to many companies. Customers have to be convinced that what you have is going to solve a problem or save them money before they're even willing to talk. To be genuinely customer-focused, you have to make as many channels available as your customers are demanding. To do the best job of fostering lifetime loyalty, you need to know what your customers are thinking. When a customer contacts anyone in your company, that employee should be able to access a comprehensive record of every interaction with that customer, no matter how or when it took place. Not only will this enable personalized service, but it will also allow for cross-selling and up-selling opportunities.[18]

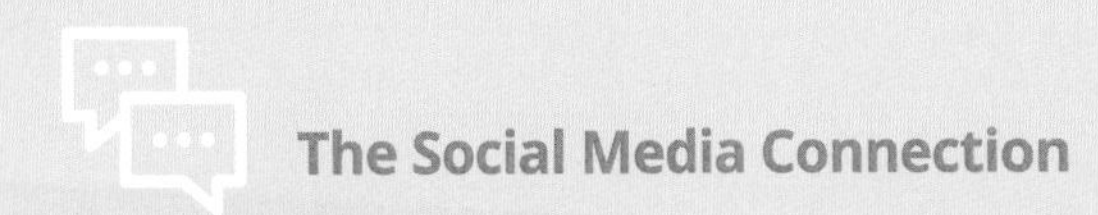

USING SOCIAL MEDIA TO CREATE LIFELONG CUSTOMERS

Can social media help you create loyalty among your client base? Absolutely! Here is a perfect example:

A blogger named Christina McMenemy was in Nashville for a conference and adored the clock in her hotel room at the Gaylord Opryland. During her stay, Christina found herself entranced by one of the features of the alarm clock that played relaxing music, the kind you'd hear in a spa.

Wanting to experience the same serenity at home, the blogger took to Twitter during her stay to ask the hotel where she could purchase one. Their response, essentially, was, "Sorry, it's made just for us, but here's a similar one at The Sharper Image." Unfortunately, the one they recommended lacked the spa music feature. She was disheartened but thanked them for the effort.

When she returned to her room later that day, she found a second clock sitting next to the permanent one. There was also a handwritten note that said, "Christina, thank you for following us on Twitter. We hope you enjoy these spa sounds at home. If you need anything, please let us know."

Opryland recognized an opportunity on social media to make sure a customer had one of the best experiences ever. They didn't just win a customer for life. They also fostered goodwill with conference attendees who subsequently heard the story, as well as anyone who followed Opryland or Christina on Twitter. Christina posted on social media, "You reaffirmed that there are still companies out there focused on great service, and you've made a lifelong fan out of me."[19]

You never know when an opportunity might present itself online to turn a regular or even an on-the-fence customer into a loyal, lifelong partner. So, make sure to read comments and follow up on any questions, whether they're in a tweet, a post, or a picture comment.

Winning Back Lost Customers

In the world of car sales, there's a saying that goes, "Never try to sell someone one car today. Try to sell them five cars over 20 years." If they make the car-buying experience memorable and pleasant—and if they make the customer feel special—the purchase will not be a one-time event.

It is the same no matter what you are selling. If a customer buys once and never buys again, something has gone wrong. Someone or some process within the company has failed that buyer. Repeat customers should be a key component of your financial strategy.

Customers rely on their emotional experiences with salespeople more than any of the traditional factors, according to research by the Peppers & Rogers Group, which showed that:[20]

- Around 60 percent of customers stop dealing with a company because of what they perceive as indifference from salespeople.
- As much as 70 percent of customers leave a company because of poor service from salespeople.
- Nearly 80 percent of defecting customers describe themselves as "satisfied" or "very satisfied" just before they leave. That means that there wasn't anything wrong. However, there also wasn't anything special that motivated loyalty.

Still, you can expect a certain amount of customer attrition for several reasons. Some reasons (such as a change in financial circumstances or no longer needing what you sell) are beyond your control. Other reasons (such as losing interest or merely forgetting) you can overcome with some creativity and personal attention. Those are the customers who will make your efforts worthwhile. Here are four strategies for re-energizing your client base:

1. Concentrate Your Efforts

Winning back customers may require a significant investment of your time and resources. So, plan your efforts to re-engage lapsed accounts before you leap into action. Begin by identifying your best buyers that have left. Consider limiting your search to customers

who stopped purchasing in the last two to three years.

Once you have a list of past customers targeted for recommitment, begin by researching their purchase history. Look for patterns in the way they purchased in the past that can provide critical insights into how to win them back. Consider when they first started doing business with you. What was your company doing at that time that could have induced them to buy? Study the time of year they purchased. Some customers may make seasonal purchases. If this is the case, a simple note with an email subject line that says something like, "We missed you this year!" may be all it takes to re-engage them.

2. Remind Them of Their 'Why'

Every one of your customers was once inspired to say yes to you. So, try to get them thinking about what first drew them to you and your offering. If your company has an important anniversary coming up, throw a party to celebrate it, and invite former customers to get involved in the fun.

Also, consider calling lapsed customers to ask about how they first heard about your company. The idea of calling up a customer to ask them why they *used* to buy may make you uncomfortable. However, if there were no significant reasons for their leaving, it will remind them of why they purchased and may encourage them to come back. On the other hand, if you learn that something went wrong, take the concern seriously, remedy the problem, and ask for another chance to win their confidence.

3. Shake Up Your Email List

There is a term in the world of mass email known as *unemotionally subscribed*. These are people in your email database who have not opened or clicked an email message from you or your company in an extended (several months or more) period. They have not unsubscribed, nor have they marked your message as spam. They either ignore the messages or take the time to delete one every time a message lands in their inbox.

The percentage of your list that is considered unemotionally subscribed can be as high as 30 percent.[21] That means that nearly one out of every three people on your email list are not interacting with your emails. Once you figure out who fits this criterion, you have a few options:

1. Unsubscribe them.
2. Move them to a list where they receive fewer messages.
3. Send a "we miss you" type email.
4. Set up a re-engagement email series in which you actively

pursue former customers through a series of messages with requests for action.

No method is better than the other. If you want to give your unemotionally subscribed followers another chance, consider a "We Miss You" email campaign that provides them with several calls to action. You may send them to a funny video when they select "click here to stay on our list," or send them to a picture of a sad puppy if they choose "click here if you'd like to be removed from our system."

Reaching out to former customers to renew their commitment can be a frustrating process in which a considerable amount of effort and work often yields few results. But with more organizations vying for the attention of an over-messaged and overwhelmed public, the ability to effectively re-energize your existing customer base is becoming an increasingly important component of selling.

4. Calm Angry Customers

It's no fun to lose a customer. Winning back a customer who has turned to a competitor helps your feelings as well as your bank account. The first step in regaining a customer is to discover why you lost their business. If customers leave because they feel they've been poorly treated, it is your responsibility—not the customer's—to mend this relationship. Exhibit 15.2 lists some of the most common excuses given by salespeople for losing accounts.

If you put aside such excuses, then you can uncover the real reasons why a customer left. When you reach out to a lost buyer, do so with sincerity and humility. Do not contradict what the customer tells you, argue, or become angry yourself, no matter how angry or unreasonable the customer may seem to you.

EXHIBIT 15.2 Excuses Salespeople Give for Losing Accounts

That customer is just too picky or unpleasant.

If it isn't price, then it's because the competition uses unfair or unethical tactics.

The customer never cared about anything but price.

It's my company's fault. Delivery is late, and quality has deteriorated.

I don't have time to make all the service calls I'd like to make.

It's not me; it's them! Because I'm doing what I've been doing for years.

"We'd like to hire you for our customer service department. It's practically impossible to look at a penguin and feel angry."

When faced with an angry buyer, you have two choices. First, you can walk away and consider the account lost. Second, you can resolve the conflict and reinforce the relationship.[22] If you listen politely, ask questions, and search for hidden feelings, the act of telling you what is wrong often defuses the negative perceptions of the customer. The former satisfaction that the buyer felt by doing business with you re-surfaces, and the customer may be happy to re-establish your relationship.

Until you discover and acknowledge the real problem, you cannot resolve it. Sometimes the answer is unpleasant. If the problem lies in your actions or attitudes, you must accept responsibility so that you are free to solve the problem and regain the account. If you deny your distinct responsibility, you escape into excuse-making. You then become blind to the options available for restoring the customer's goodwill. On the other hand, when you know what the problem is, you can plan strategies for rebuilding the account.

A Plan for Tracking Follow-Up

With the vital role that customer service and follow up plays in the success of your career, you can't afford to take follow-up planning lightly. You, therefore, need an organized system for tracking follow-up. Use your CRM software to set up files listing the customer's name, date, and type of each contact (meeting, call, text, email, or social media). Whatever system you choose, have a specific, written plan for reaching out to existing clients.

Every customer is essential to your career, but when it comes to major clients, having a plan in place to follow up with them is critical. Here is a simple strategy to retain your most valued customers. This plan also serves as a way to target your most vital prospects:[23]

1. **Start a shortlist of best clients.** Select a manageable number (less than 30) of your best customers and create a separate database with their names.
2. **Create files for each.** Open and work from a record you create for each client.
3. **Identify common partners.** Find centers of influence that you have in common or who know the customer in some way. Be sure to note these names in the appropriate file.
4. **Talk to influencers.** Consult with influencers about this individual or

company and record all findings. You never know what piece of information will prove to be useful down the road.

5. **Pick one player.** Select a primary team member within your organization to deal with the customer. For larger clients, the more experienced that contact is, the better.
6. **Develop a targeted strategy.** Develop a plan for individual customers based on what you know about them, their needs, and their purchase history.
7. **Plan a year ahead.** Map out your moves for the next year with each customer and establish monthly objectives. That move could be as simple as sending an email with some relevant and timely info for their business.
8. **Review and revise.** Record and review results and refine strategy as needed.

The process never ends with the sale. The transaction is not complete until the customer is satisfied and feels appreciated. It is not enough to "pass the buck" and assume the customer will stay engaged through mass emails, social media, or mailings. You carry the responsibility for their satisfaction after the purchase. It takes days, weeks, or even months to earn a customer. Regaining a lost customer is much more expensive and time-consuming than keeping a current customer satisfied.[24]

GAINING A NEW CUSTOMER COSTS FIVE TIMES MORE THAN KEEPING A CURRENT ONE.

Contact Frequency and Medium. Decide how often you will contact each client based on what worked well in the past. Some customers require more work than others. If you come across high-maintenance customers, note that in their file and respond accordingly. Consider the personality and needs of major clients and determine what level of care they need to maintain the relationship. Determine their preferred form of contact and learn which social media platforms your customers prefer. Do not attempt an up-sell or ask for something (like a referral) every time you contact them. Keep your name in front of customers' minds with value-added items such as:

- Information about new products that might interest them.
- An in-house newsletter that includes compelling stories.
- A letter with a self-addressed reply card on which the customer can send in comments or ideas.

Pay close attention to the effectiveness of each type of contact you make. Discard methods that do not work and repeat processes that do. Keep follow-up records as meticulously as data on prospecting. Know what you have done for each customer, what you plan to do next, and when.

"Customer service shouldn't just be a department; it should be the entire company."
Tony Hsieh, Founder of Zappos

SUMMARY

Service after the transaction can be more critical than the sale itself.

Customer follow-up adds value by showing the customer that you care about more than just their money.

A buying decision is a one-time action unless you turn it into a habit with adequate follow-up. Exceptional service creates repeat business.

Service is an ongoing activity. Set goals for regular follow-up and stay top of mind.

Sell current customers more of what you are already selling to them by cross-selling or up-selling.

Service and sincerity are the keys to winning back lost accounts.

No matter what causes the attrition, take responsibility, and make it right for the customer.

Plan, execute, and track visits, calls, and messages to your customers and measure their effectiveness.

Review Questions

1. List the four keys to customer loyalty.
2. What does "value-added" mean when it comes to sales and service? Can you give an example of a time when you experienced extra value as a customer?
3. Think of a situation in which failing to keep up with personnel changes could cause loss of sales for a salesperson.
4. List some types of problems a customer might have that you, as a salesperson, could solve before they become serious by following a regular servicing program.
5. What is the salesperson's responsibility if a piece of machinery or equipment purchased by your customer is defective or missing a part?
6. Discuss the importance of service as an ongoing activity.
7. Explain how you would go about creating a system for follow-up activities.
8. Name particular services that are beneficial to buyers for a retail business.
9. Is prospecting for new customers or servicing existing ones more critical? Justify your answer.
10. Describe specific servicing activities that could be used to win back a lost client.

IN-CLASS EXERCISES

The following in-class exercises help build teams, improve communication, and emphasize the real-world side of selling. They are meant to challenge you, help you learn how to deal with problems with more than one right answer, and use a variety of skills beyond those employed in a typical review question. Read and complete each activity. Then in the next class, discuss and compare answers.

EXERCISE 15.1 Maintaining the Loop

You will work independently on this exercise in class. Imagine that you own a website development, marketing, and hosting company that employs eight people. Five of your staff work in sales and marketing, while three manage the technical backend. There is no separate customer service department. All five of your sales staff do it all: prospect for new customers, sell your services, respond to requests for assistance, and follow up with customer requests and needs. You don't sleep.

As you acquire more customers, you realize that you need to systematize serving their ongoing needs and problems. In other words, you need to develop a customer follow-up and service plan. For the next 15 minutes, jot down as many items as you can think of that you will include in your service plan for this business. Be prepared to explain or justify the items on your list.

EXERCISE 15.2 How Far Should One Go?

For this exercise, you should work independently. Chapter 15 discusses what it means to "go the extra mile" for customers. As you think about the responsibilities of yourself as a salesperson, jot down brief answers to the following questions:

- Should there be limits on what a salesperson is expected to do by way of customer service?
- If so, what are those limits?
- What limits, if any, would you personally adhere to?
- Provide concrete examples of actions that you would refuse to take in the interest of customer service.
- Provide concrete examples of actions that you would consider taking that would be regarded as extraordinary ("going the extra mile") by most people.
- Should salespeople be rewarded or compensated for customer service actions that exceed company requirements?

Case Studies

The following case studies present you with selling scenarios that require you to apply the critical skills discussed in the chapter and give you training through practical learning situations. They are meant to be both engaging and challenging, and like the in-class exercises, they don't have one right answer.

CASE 15.1—To Tweet or Not to Tweet

Nutmeg Appliances operates 35 stores throughout the State of Connecticut and southwestern Massachusetts. They offer complete lines of kitchen appliances, TVs, and home entertainment centers. Competition in this business is fierce. Customers are always shopping for bargains for such products and are often complaining about missed deliveries and malfunctioning equipment. The pace on the sales floor, in operations (delivery and installation), and customer service is intense. In this environment, however, Nutmeg executives take the enlightened and financially prudent view that increasing customer

loyalty must be a top priority. Living off new customers who walk in the door is not a viable option, especially in a stressed economy. Customer retention is vital.

Therefore, Nutmeg routinely holds meetings involving representatives from sales, operations, and customer service to see how they can improve service to their existing customers. This morning's session addresses a controversial matter: how to position the company vis-à-vis social media, specifically Facebook and Twitter. Questions for discussion and decision include the following:

1. How can Nutmeg's Twitter and Facebook accounts be utilized to the best advantage of the company?
2. Should Nutmeg assign one person to monitor these accounts to filter out negative or critical comments? Why should negative comments be filtered out? Why should they be permitted?
3. Should employees from sales, operations, and customer service be alerted whenever someone posts a comment that pertains to their department?
4. Should all employees be encouraged to participate through these accounts, or should Nutmeg restrict participation to designated company employees?

As a representative of sales, you immediately recognize that the decisions taken in response to these questions will affect the company's bottom line and your livelihood. What do you recommend for each of these questions, and why?

CASE 15.2—The Nordstrom Way

Sandra was so frustrated that she was ready to quit on the spot. She loved selling, and she loved selling computers and related equipment. It was her company's lack of commitment to customer service that she hated. She was convinced that the company's refusal to take customer complaints seriously was hurting sales. It was also depriving her of more chances to develop long-term relationships with customers. And that, in turn, deprived her of commissions. She took her complaints directly to her regional vice president, Ernest.

"Okay, Ernie," Sandra declared upon taking a seat in front of Ernest's desk. "I'm here to renew my demand that the company change its policies and devote more resources to customer service."

Clasping his hands behind his head, Ernest replied, "Well, Sandy, you and I have had this conversation before, and the company hasn't changed its mind. Why do you keep pressing?"

"I'm on your case because I know that customer service works," said Sandra. "When I started in sales, I worked for Nordstrom™, a company that has won awards for the highest quality customer service since they were founded in 1901. I made more money because of those policies. More importantly, their stellar customer service helped them expand to 115 stores in 28 states. So, this company is missing out, and I'm missing out."

"Well, how do you expect a computer company to adopt Nordstrom's policies and survive?" asked Ernie. "From what you tell me, we'd go bankrupt in a matter of months."

"I know that Nordstrom's policies are counterintuitive," responded Sandra. "As you may know, Nordstrom instructs all of their sales associates to use their judgment in accepting returns for any reason or no reason. And to always err on the side of the customer. In practice, that means virtually unlimited returns are allowed."

"We can't begin to do that. Our merchandise costs hundreds, sometimes thousands, of dollars per unit," Ernie replied, leaning forward in his chair.

"Well, you should know that at Nordstrom, I regularly accepted $5,000-coats and $1,000-shoes as returns, even when they showed signs of wear and couldn't be resold," Sandra answered. "But over the long term, these same customers bought more than they returned. The company made money, and I made money."

"Sandy, this isn't Nordstrom, and we don't sell shoes." Ernie stood, indicating that this meeting was over. "It appears that you have an important decision to make. Call me to let me know what it is."

Based on your understanding of Chapter 15, who is correct? Should Sandra's computer company adopt Nordstrom's customer service policies? Does the difference in product matter in deciding this issue, as Ernie claims? Would a Nordstrom-like policy of customer service mean more sales for the computer company in the long run? What sort of changes in customer service might the computer company make short of adopting Nordstrom's unlimited return practice? What should Sandra do? Should she quit or not?

Endnotes

Chapter 1

1. Hilton, Conrad. As cited in *Sales success: 62 quotes, a special report*. (2008, Jan 30) Retrieved Apr 20, 2019, from eyesonsales.com/content/downloads/special_report_62_sales_success_quotes.
2. Connor, Tim. (2006, Aug 3). Twelve things every sales super star knows. Retrieved Sep 2, 2019, from ezinearticles.com/?12-Things-Every-Sales-Super-Star-Knows&id=259854.
3. Hodges, Susan. (2003, Feb). Recommissioning your sales. *ELT, 15*(2), 22–28.
4. Anonymous. (2009, Sep). Surveys reveal compensation for call-center sales professionals. *IOMA's Report on Salary Surveys 9*(9), 2.
5. Anonymous. (2010, Jun). Two surveys examine pay for sales and marketing positions. *IOMA's Report on Salary Surveys 10*(6), 9.
6. Bartley, Simon. (2008, Feb). Seeing is believing! Retrieved from TrainingJournal.com.
7. Bersin, Josh. (2014, Feb 4). Spending on corporate training soars: Employee capabilities now a priority. *Forbes*. Retrieved from forbes.com/sites/joshbersin/2014/02/04/the-recovery-arrives-corporate-training-spend-skyrockets/#6b0ae962c5a7.
8. O'Connor, Bob. (2007, Feb). Business sense: Training yourself and your staff to win. *Motor*. Retrieved from motor.com/magazine-summary/business-sense-training-yourself-your-staff-to-win-bob-oconnor-february-2007.
9. Hagel, Dave. (2007, Spring). Why you need to hire the best. *The Canadian Manager 32*(1), 12.
10. Stephens, Charles W. (2000, Feb). Why is training so important? *Industrial Distribution 89*(2), 4.
11. Weber, Lauren. (2015, Feb 6). Why it's so hard to fill sales jobs. *The Wall Street Journal*. Retrieved from wsj.com/articles/why-its-so-hard-to-fill-sales-jobs-1423002730.
12. Mazur, Laura. (2004, Mar 4). UK banks must refocus on the personal touch. Retrieved Dec 16, 2019, from campaignlive.co.uk/article/opinion-uk-banks-refocus-personal-touch/204126.
13. Foster, Jack. (2009, Dec). A novel approach to the market. *Agency Sales 39*(11), 10.
14. See the following sources: Thompson, D.L. (1972, Jan/Feb). Stereotype of the salesperson. *Harvard Business Review 50*(1), 20–29; Cook, R.W. & Hartman, T. (1986, May). Female college student interest in a sales career: A comparison. *Journal of Personal Selling & Sales Management 6*, 29–34; Swenson, M., Swinyard, W., Langrehr, F., & Smith, S. (1993, Winter) The appeal of personal selling as a career: A decade later. *The Journal of Personal Selling & Sales Management 13*(1), 51; Sales strikes out on campus. (1997, Nov). *Sales & Marketing Management*, 13; Selling sales to students. (1998, January). *Sales & Marketing Management*, 15; Harmon, Harry. (1999, Fall). An examination of students' perceptions of a situationally described career in personal selling. *Journal of Professional Services Marketing 19*(1), 119–136; DelVecchio, Susan. An investigation of African-American perceptions of sales careers. (2000, Winter). *The Journal of Personal Selling & Sales Management 29*(1), 43–52.
15. Anonymous. (2003, May). Power of self-image psychology. *The American Salesman 48*(5), 21.
16. Pink, Daniel. (2013). *To sell is human: The surprising truth about moving others*. New York, NY: Riverhead.
17. Halvorson, Heidi Grant. (2013, Feb 19). Yes, you can learn to sell. *Harvard Business Review*. Retrieved Feb 19, 2019, from hbr.org/2013/02/yes-you-can-you-learn-to-sell.
18. Kaplan, S. N., Klebanov, M. M., & Sorensen, M. (2008, Aug). Which CEO characteristics and abilities matter? *Journal of Finance 67*(3), 973–1007. Retrieved from www.law.uchicago.edu/node/53416.
19. Chitwood, Roy. (2015, July 30). Best salesperson in the company should be the CEO. *Puget Sound Business Journal.*
20. Anonymous. (2011, Jan 7). Sales departments are ready to spend money and hire people in 2011 [press release]. *PR Newswire*; Cicelli, David J. (2010, July 31). Smart management: Selling into 2010: A cause for optimism? *Sales and Marketing Management.* Retrieved Mar 20, 2019, from https://salesandmarketing.com/content/smart-management-selling-2010-cause-optimism.
21. Siegel, Sherry. (2014, Jan/Feb). Selling your way to the top. *Success 34*(1), 44.

22. Newton, Derek. (1973). *Sales force performance and turnover,* 3. Cambridge, MA: Marketing Science Institute; Newton, Derek. (1969, Sep/Oct). Get the most out of your sales force. *Harvard Business Review,* 130–143.
23. Donston-Miller, Debra. (2010, Sep 10). How to leverage social networking to get your next job. *The Ladders*. Retrieved Aug 31, 2019, fromtheladders.com/career-advice/how-to-leverage-social-networking-to-get-next-job.
24. McClelland, David. Hiring top performers. (1994, May). *Success 41*(4), 34; Azar, Brian. (1992, Apr). Are you a master salesperson. *Personal Selling Power 12*(3), 27; Qualities to look for when you're hiring. (1995, Aug 13). *Sales and Marketing Management*, 84–87.
25. Feiertag, Howard. (2002, Jul 15). Listening skills, enthusiasm top list of salespeople's best traits. *Hotel and Motel Management 217*(13), 20.
26. Cunningham, T., Woodall, D., Scott, W., & Wheaton, P. (2010, Nov 16). Training new hires for competitive advantage. *Sales and Marketing Management*. Retrieved Jun 20, 2019, from https://salesandmarketing.com/content/training-new-hires-competitive-advantage.
27. Watson Wyatt. (2006, Oct 5). Time management key to successful sales results, Watson Wyatt survey finds [press release]. *PR Newswire*.
28. John, Jim. (2010, Jul 31). Tough times reveal true sales professionals. *Sales and Marketing Management*. Retrieved Apr 20, 2019, from https://salesandmarketing.com/content/tough-times-reveal-true-sales-professionals.

Chapter 2

1. Koch, Lucy. (2019, Apr 17). Did 'clicks' really surpass 'bricks' for share of US retail sales? Not exactly." *eMarketer*. Retrieved Oct 7, 2019, from emarketer.com/content/did-clicks-really-surpass-bricks-for-share-of-us-retail-sales-not-exactly.
2. Smith, Ned. (2012, Jun 15). Will technology advances mark the death of a salesman? *Business News Daily*. Retrieved Sep 2, 2019, from businessnewsdaily.com/2636-technology-impacts-sales-people.html.
3. Congdon, Luis. (2018). Why your website isn't getting you the sales you need. Retrieved Nov 1, 2018, from entrepreneur.com/article/310455.
4. Grönroos, Christian. (2007). *Service management and marketing: A customer relationship management approach, 3rd Ed*. Chichester, UK: John Wiley & Sons.
5. Howell, Debbie. (2006, Mar 27). Selling trust, expertise hits home with customers. *DSN Retailing Today 45*(6).
6. Dasteel, Jeb. (2014, Jan 15). Award-winning companies put customers first. *Forbes*. Retrieved Nov 12, 2019, from forbes.com/sites/oracle/2014/01/15/award-winning-companies-put-customers-first/#24de3202415b
7. Geraghty, Barbara. (2007). *Visionary selling*, 240. New York, NY: Simon and Schuster.
8. McGarvey, R. & Harrison, B. S. (2013, Mar). How tech hip are you? *Selling Power,* 77.
9. Lee, Richard. (2011, Mar 20). Expert touts importance of using social media. *Stamford Advocate*, C1.
10. Brooks, Bill. (2016, Jun). The power of active listening. *The American Salesman 51*(6),12.
11. Abrams, Rhonda. (2009, May 29). Strategies: Make customer retention priority no. 1. *USA Today*. Retrieved Apr 7, 2019.
12. Ng, Hanzo. (2009, Apr 1). After sales service secrets! *Malaysian Business*, 54.
13. Rungtusanatham, M., Ogden, J. A., & Wu, B. (2003). Advancing theory development in total quality management: A 'Deming management method' perspective. *International Journal of Operations & Production Management 23*(7/8), 918.
14. Studer, Quint. (2007, Jul). How to achieve and sustain excellence: there are seven ways to hardwire excellent outcomes. Do you know what they are? *Healthcare Financial Management 61*(6),106-107.
15. Morte, Jude P. (2003, May 29). Special feature: Best employers in the Philippines. *BusinessWorld*.
16. Knotts, Rose. (1992, Jan/Feb). Rambo doesn't work here anymore. *Business Horizons 35*(1), 44–46.
17. Godson, Mark. (2009). *Relationship marketing*, 18. Oxford, UK: Oxford University Press.
18. Deming, W. Edwards. (2000). *Out of the crisis*. Cambridge, MA: MIT.
19. Weinstein, Margery. (2006, Aug). How may I train you? Customer service training programs put the focus on buyer bliss. *Training 43*(8), 28–32.

20. Peters, Tom. (1990, Sep). Meeting the dangers and opportunities of chaos. *Personal Selling Power 10*(6), 49.
21. Anonymous. (2002). TQM: A snapshot of the experts. *Measuring Business Excellence 6*(3), 54–57.
22. Martin, Craig A. (2005). Racial diversity in professional selling: An empirical investigation of the differences in the perceptions and performance of African-American and Caucasian salespeople. *The Journal of Business & Industrial Marketing 20*(6), 285.
23. USA quickfacts. *U.S. Census Bureau*. Accessed Aug 4, 2019, from census.gov/quickfacts/fact/table/US.
24. Bowes, Barbara J. (2007, Dec/2008, Jan). The business case for workplace diversity. *CMA Management 81*(8), 14.
25. Hooker, John. (2008, Dec). Cultural differences in business communication. Tepper School of Business, Carnegie Mellon University. Retrieved Feb 12, 2019, from https://public.tepper.cmu.edu/jnh/businessCommunication.pdf.
26. See more at apple.com/diversity.
27. Gale, Sarah Fister. (2013, May 16). Corporate foreign language training on the rise. *Workforce*. Retrieved from workforce.com/2013/05/16/corporate-foreign-language-training-on-the-rise/
28. Boutelle, Clif. Minority sales personnel have better results in workplaces with supportive diversity climates. *Society for Industrial and Organizational Psychology, Inc.* Retrieved Jun 9, 2019.

Chapter 3

1. Weber, Patricia. Salespeople take note: Let me sell you a bridge or sell ethically! Retrieved Sep 12, 2019, from https://patricia-weber.com/salespeople-take-note-let-me-sell-you-a-bridge-or-sell-ethically.
2. Cragg, A.W. (2006). Business, globalization, and the logic and ethics of corruption. *Business Communication Quarterly 69*(2), 158.
3. Say it with pride: I am a salesman! (2004, Apr 29). *Business Line*. Retrieved from thehindubusinessline.com/todays-paper/tp-brandline/article29142112.ece.
4. McQueeny, Edward. (2006). Making ethics come alive. *Business Communication Quarterly 69*(2), 158.
5. McClaren, Nicholas. (2000). Ethics in personal selling and sales management: A review of the literature focusing on empirical findings and conceptual foundations. *Journal of Business Ethics 27,* 286.
6. Wortruba, Thomas. (1994). A framework for teaching ethical decision-making in marketing. *Marketing Education Review 3*(2), 4.
7. Wilkins, L. & Christians, C.G. (Eds). (2008). *The handbook of mass media ethics*. Abingdon, UK: Routledge.
8. McClaren, Nicholas. (2000). Ethics in personal selling and sales management: A review of the literature focusing on empirical findings and conceptual foundations." *Journal of Business Ethics 27,* 286.
9. Galper, Ari. (2019, Aug 23). Sales ethics: When did it become okay to lie? *Principled Profit.* Retrieved from principledprofit.com/sales-ethics.html.
10. Barnett, T. & Valentine, S. (2003, Fall). Ethics code awareness, perceived ethical values and organizational commitment. *The Journal of Personal Selling 23*(4) , 359.
11. Ingram, T. & Schwepker, C. (1996, Nov). Improving sales performance through ethics: The relationship between salesperson moral judgment and job performance. *Journal of Business Ethics 15*(11), 1151–1160.
12. Rogers, Beth. (2007). *Rethinking sales management.* New York, NY: Wiley.
13. Anonymous. (2018, May 4). International stop-selling day declared by the United Professional Sales Association for May 24th [press release]. *PR Newswire*.
14. Schewpker, C. H., & Good, D. J. (2011). Moral judgment and its impact on business sales. *Journal of Business Ethics 98*, 619.
15. Bragg, Arthur. (1987, May). Ethics in selling, honest. *Sales and Marketing Management 138*(7), 44.
16. Smith, J. Walker. (2008, Jan/Feb). Selling doing good. *Marketing Management*.
17. Schultz, Howard. (2012). *Onward: How Starbucks fought for its life without losing its soul.* New York, NY: Rodale.
18. Ferrell, O.C., Ingram, T., & Schewepker, C. (1997, Spring). The influence of ethical climate and ethical conflict on role stress in the sales force. *Academy of Marketing Science Journal*, 13.

19. Trent, Karen. (1990, Jun). The dangers of groupthink. *Teamwork*.
20. Strout, Erin. (2001, May). Doctoring sales. *Sales and Marketing Management*, 59.
21. Perrone, J. & Vickers, M. H. (2004, Sep). Emotions as strategic game in a hostile workplace: An exemplar case. *Employee Responsibilities and Rights Journal 16*(3), 167.
22. Holsworth, Jeanette. Four ways to curb employee theft. *The Business Report*. Retrieved Dec 10, 2019, from gainevillebizreport.com.
23. Hockenhull, Terence A. (2015, Jun). The selling dilemma. *Business World Online*. Retrieved Nov 30, 2019, from bworldonline.com/content.php?section=Weekender&title=the-selling-dilemma&id=110338
24. Katz, D. (2003). All gifts large and small: Towards an understanding of the ethics of pharmaceutical gift giving. *American Journal of Bioethics 3*(3), 39.
25. Hewlett Packard Enterprise. (2018, Aug). Global business amenities policy. Retrieved from https://h20195.www2.hpe.com/V2/getpdf.aspx/a00000573enw.pdf
26. Hauserman, Nancy R. (1986, Mar/Apr). Whistle-blowing: Individual morality in a society. *Business Horizons 29*(2), 4–9.
27. Wilson, Glenn T. (1984, Jun). Ethics, your company or your conscience. *Working Woman 9*, 67.
28. Dill, Kathryn. (2014, Dec 10).The best places to work in 2015. *Forbes*. Retrieved from forbes.com/sites/kathryndill/2014/12/10/the-best-places-to-work-in-2015/#55a0e3353ca5
29. Zoltners A. A., Sinha, PK, & Lorimer, S. E. (2015, Aug 7). Why sales teams should reexamine territory design. *Harvard Business Review*, Retrieved from https://hbr.org/2015/08/why-sales-teams-should-reexamine-territory-design.
30. Ruiz, Michelle. (2015, Feb 16). What sexual harassment at work really looks like. *Cosmopolitan*, Retrieved from cosmopolitan.com/career/a36462/sexual-harassment-at-work/
31. Lill, David J. (1991, Apr 22–26). Issue of ethics often faces professional salespeople. *Nashville Business Journal*, 5.
32. Stack, Steven M. (1985, Nov). The high risk of dirty tricks. *Sales and Marketing Magazine 135*(7), 58.
33. American Law Institute & National Conference of Commissioners on Uniform State Law. *Uniform Commercial Code*. Retrieved Apr 11, 2018.
34. Todd, Susan. (2010, Jun 6). Drugmakers continue 'off-label marketing' despite large fines. *The Star Ledger*. Retrieved from nj.com/business/2010/06/drugmakers_continue_off-label.html.
35. Evans, David. (2009, Nov 9). Pfizer broke the law by promoting drugs for unapproved uses. *Bloomberg.* Retrieved Nov 1, 2019, from bloomberg.com/politics?pid=20670001&sid=a4yV1nYxCGoA

Chapter 4

1. Jackel, M. & Wollscheid, S. (2007). Time is money and money needs time? A secondary analysis of time-budget data in Germany. *Journal of Leisure Research 39*(1), 77.
2. Morrison, David. (2010, Apr). Setting boundaries on commitments. *Public Management 92*(3), 20.
3. Vanderkam, Laura. (2010, May). *168 hours: You have more time than you think*. New York, NY: Penguin Group.
4. Vanderkam, Laura. (2010, May). *168 hours: You have more time than you think*. New York, NY: Penguin Group.
5. (2010, Jul 18). Time management tips for busy college students. *Daily Herald*. Retrieved Apr 29, 2019, from questia.com/article/1G1-232025529/time-management-tips-for-busy-college-students.
6. Adair J. & Allen M. (2003). *Time management and personal development,* 26. London, England: Thorgood.
7. Berglas, Steven. (2004, Jun). Chronic time abuse. *Harvard Business Review 82*(6), 90.
8. Anonymous. (2004, Mar). Will the piles ever go away? *USA Today 132*(2706), 8.
9. Cox, Tom. (2011, Apr 20). 7 rules of extreme time management. *Oregon Business.*
10. Anonymous. (2004, Apr 5). Get on top of your time management. *Pulse.*
11. Shellenbarger, Sue. (2011, Feb 23). Managing workplace distractions. *The Wall Street Journal*. Retrieved from https://blogs.wsj.com/juggle/2011/02/23/managing-workplace-distractions.

12. Lee, Kevan. (2014, Oct 30). What's the best way to spend 30 minutes of your time on social media marketing? Retrieved Oct 1, 2019, from https://buffer.com/resources/social-media-time-management.
13. Davis, Rick. (2006, Jan). All systems go: A systemized approach to selling can lead to organizational success. *Prosales*. Retrieved May 16, 2019, from prosalesmagazine.com/business/sales/all-systems-go_o.
14. Tyre, Dan. (2019, Apr 17). The 40+ best apps for salespeople who want to win in 2019. *Sales Hacker*. Retrieved Oct 20, 2019, from saleshacker.com/best-apps-salespeople.
15. A brief guide to time management. *Corporate Finance Institute.* Retrieved July 30, 2019, from https://corporatefinanceinstitute.com/resources/careers/soft-skills/time-management-list-tips.
16. Coonradt, Charles. (2013). *Game of work: How to enjoy work as much as play*. Sydney, Australia: Read How You Want Publishers.
17. Kumuyi, William F. (2008, Jul). Setting and scoring your goals: Goals are stated ambitions; and all leaders know they must set them and follow them up till they are accomplished. for, failure to set goals reduces leadership to management by chance and hunches—a sure recipe for corporate disaster. *New African.* Retrieved Apr 29, 2019, from questia.com/magazine/1G1-181728092/setting-and-scoring-your-goals-goals-are-stated-ambitions.
18. Collingwood, Jane. (2018). Organization strategies for ADHD. *Psych Central*. Retrieved Sep 7, 2019, from https://psychcentral.com/lib/organization-strategies-for-adhd.
19. Taylor, Peter. (2009, Jul/Aug). The art of productive laziness. *Industrial Management 51*(4), 18+.
20. Higgins, Kevin. (2014, Jan 9). Six secrets to a successful sales meeting. *Entrepreneur*. Retrieved from entrepreneur.com/article/230689.
21. Atlas, Steve. (2001, Jan/Feb). When the customer isn't right. *Selling Power*.
22. For a more thorough discussion on "How to Run Your Territory Like a Business," see: (1989) Territory management, 6–16 [booklet]. Bureau of Business Practice, Inc.
23. Anonymous. (2004, May). The secrets of time management. *Agency Sales 34*(5), 40–41.

Chapter 5

1. Hoyer, W. D. & MacInnis, D. J. (2010). *Consumer behavior 5th edition,* 3. Mason, OH: Southwestern College Pub.
2. Young, Scott. (2006, Spring). Measuring success: Using consumer research to document the value of package design. *Design Management Review 17*(2), 60–65.
3. Zinkhan, G. M. & Braunsberger, K. The complexity of consumers' cognitive structures and its relevance to consumer behavior. *Journal of Business Research 57*(6), 575.
4. For an expanded description of the model, see: Engel, J. F., Blackwell, R. D., & Miniard, P. W. (1990). *Consumer Behavior.* Hinsdale, IL: Dryden Press.
5. Jefferies, Alex. (2008, Sep 30). Sales 2.0: Social media for knowledge management and sales collaboration. *Aberdeen Group.* Retrieved Dec 5, 2019, from http://gbds.us/clientuploads/downloads/Social_Media_for_Knowledge_Management_and_Sales_Collaboration.pdf
6. O'Cass, Aron. (2004). Fashion clothing consumption: Antecedents and consequences of fashion clothing involvement. *European Journal of Marketing 38*(7), 869.
7. **There are 40 squares in the figure.**
8. Steverman, Ben. (2011, Jan 27). Conspicuous consumption is back: Subdued fashions of the recession years are fading as wealthy Americans again flaunt luxury purchases. *Bloomberg Businessweek*. Retrieved Oct 8, 2019, from bloomberg.com/news/articles/2011-01-27/conspicuous-consumption-is-back
9. Schaub, Kathleen. (2014, Apr). Social buying meets social selling: How trusted networks improve the purchase experience [white paper]. International Data Corporation.
10. Zhang, Y., Winterich, K. P., & Mittal V. (2010, Oct 1). Power distance belief and impulsive buying. *Journal of Marketing Research 47*(5), 945–954.
11. Cummings, Betsy. (2001, May). Selling around the world. *Sales and Marketing Management*.

12. Cayla, J. & Arnould, E. J. (2008, Dec 1). A cultural approach to branding in the global marketplace. *Journal of International Marketing 16*(4), 86–112.
13. Gitomer, Jeffrey. (2004, Jul 23–Aug 5). Where's the sales beef? It's client's buying motive. *Boulder County Business Report 23*(16), 6A.
14. Morgan, James P. (2001, Apr 5). Cross-functional buying: Why teams are hot. *Purchasing.*
15. Ozdemir, V. E. & Hewett, K. (2012, Mar 1). The effect of collectivism on the importance of relationship quality and service quality for behavioral intentions: A cross-national and cross-contextual analysis. *Journal of International Marketing 18*(1), 41–62.
16. Mehrabian, Albert. (1971). *Silent messages.* Belmont, CA: Wadsworth Publishing Company.
17. Varallo, Deb. (2006, Nov). *A Dress for Success Seminar*. Belmont University, Nashville, TN.
18. Chen, Y., Wang, Q., & Xie J. (2011, Apr 1). Online social interactions: A natural experiment on word of mouth versus observational learning. *Journal of Marketing Research 48*(2), 238–254.
19. Nowlis, S. M. & Shiv, B. (2005, May 1). The influence of consumer distractions on the effectiveness of food sampling programs. *Journal of Marketing Research 42*(2),157–168.
20. Dean, D. & Webb, C. (2011, Jan 31). Recovering from information overload. *The McKinsey Quarterly.* Retrieved from mckinsey.com/business-functions/organization/our-insights/recovering-from-information-overload.
21. INSIGHTations: Bits and bytes from around the Blogosphere. Retrieved Jul 19, 2019, from MarketingPower.com.
22. This section on the voice was adapted from: Jacobi, Jeffrey. (2000, Oct). Voice power. *Selling Power*; Peterson R. A., Cannito, M. P., & Brown S. P. (1995, Winter). An exploratory investigation of voice characteristics. *The Journal of Personal Selling & Sales Management 15*(1), 1–15; Melchinger, John H. (2002, Apr). Communication—One key to unlock your sales. *Personal Selling Power 10*(3), 51.
23. Goman, Carol Kinsey, PhD. (2008). *The nonverbal advantage: Secrets and science of body language at work.* San Francisco, CA: Berrett-Kockler Publishers, Inc. This section was inspired by Alessandra, Anthony J. & Wexler, Phillip. (1979). *Non-manipulative selling*, 95–113; Gschwandtner, Gerhard. (1985). *Nonverbal selling power,* 3–80. Englewood Cliffs, NJ: Prentice-Hall; and Molloy, John T. (1981) *Live for success.* New York, NY: Perigord Press.
24. Borg, James. (2008). *Body language: 7 easy lessons to master the silent language*, 37. United Kingdom: Prentice Hall Life.
25. Lambert, David. (2008). *Body language 101: The ulitimate guide to knowing when people are lying, how they are feeling, what they are thinking, and more.* 59–60. New York, NY: Skyhorse Publishing, Inc.
26. www.kevinhogan.net. Retrieved May 11, 2019.
27. Chu, Y., Strong, W. F., Ma, J., & Greene, W. E. (2005, Jan). Silent messages in negotiations: The role of nonverbal communication in cross-cultural business negotiations. *Journal of Organizational Culture, Communications and Conflict 9*(2), 113-129.

Chapter 6

1. Newton, David. (2014, Apr). Sell to the psyche. *Kitchen & Bath Business 51*(4), 41.
2. Jung, Carl G. (1924). *Psychological types.* New York, NY: Harcourt Brace and Co.
3. I am indebted to the following for sharing this valuable information with me: Merrill, D. W. & Reid, R. H. (1981). *Personal styles and effective performance*, Radnor, PA: Chilton Book Company; Mok, Paul. (1982). *Communicating styles technology.* Dallas, TX: Training Associates Press; Wilson, Larry. (2000). *Social styles sales strategies*. Eden Prairie, MN: Wilson Learning Corporation; Alessandra, T., Wexler, P., & Barrera, R. (1987). *Non-manipulative selling.* Englewood Cliffs, NJ: Prentice-Hall.
4. Graham, John R. (1993, Nov/Dec). Four basic categories of prospects. *Personal Selling Power 13*(8), 56.
5. Bledsoe, John L. How to improve your relationships with clients and your staff, too. *The Practical Accountant*. Retrieved Oct 18, 2019.
6. Rega, M. E. & Clayton, L. M. (2003, Nov). Recognizing behavioral buying patterns. *Agency Sales 33*(11), 34.
7. Mok, Dr. Paul. (1975). *Interpretation manual for communicating styles technology*, 5. Richardson, TX: Training Associates Press.

8. Kantin, R. F. & Hardwick, M. W. (1994). *Quality selling through quality proposals*, 28. Anvers, MA: Boyd and Fraser Publishing.
9. Robie, Chet. (2006). Effects of perceived selection ratio on personality test faking. *Social Behavior and Personality 34*(10), 1233–1244.
10. Miller, S. I. & Kavanagh, J. (1975). Emperical evidence. *Journal of Law & Education 4*, 159.
11. Merrill, D. W. & Reid, R. H. (1981). *Personal Styles & Effective Performance*, 88–117. Boca Raton, FL: CRC Press.
12. Alessandra, Anthony J. & Wexler, Phillip. (1979). *Non-Manipulative Selling,* 112. Reston, VA: Reston Publishing, Inc.
13. Nichols, Rod. (2002, Nov/Dec). How to sell to different personality types. *Personal Selling Power 12*(8), 46; and Fleschner, Malcolm. (1998, Jan/Feb). The Microsoft way. *Selling Power*.
14. Thull, Jeff. (2004, Sep). Recognition smarts. *Incentive 178*(9), 120.
15. Seidman, Bruce. (2014, Feb 14). The psychology of the sale, part 1, 2. *SalesDoctors.com*.
16. Duncan, Todd. (1999, Dec). Your sales style. *Incentive*.
17. Alonzo, Vincent. (2001, Jun). Rollcall: Defining your reps' personality types can open a window to motivate. *Sales and Marketing Management*, 34–35; Berman, Helen. (2009, Jun). Selling to different personalities. *Folio: The Magazine for Magazine Management*.
18. Jensen, R. & Spungin, R. (2007, Jul/Aug). Analyze your prospects to a tee. *Selling Power*.
19. Ingrasci, Hugh J. (1991, Jul). How to reach buyers in their psychological "comfort zones." *Industrial Marketing*, 64; Merrill, D. W. & Reid, R. H. (1981). *Personal Styles & Effective Performance*, 88–117.
20. Godin, Seth. (2011, May). The dating game. *Sales and Marketing Management*.
21. Leimbach, Michael. (2010, Jan). Sales versatility: Connecting with customers every time. *Sales & Service Excellence Essentials 10*(1), 10.
22. Newton, David. (2004, Apr). Sell to the psyche. *Kitchen & Bath Business 51*(4), 41.
23. Hoek,Tom, former president of Insurance Systems of Tennessee. (2006, Mar 23). Guest lecture at Belmont University. Nashville, TN.
24. Wilson, Larry. (2006). *Versatile selling: Adapting your style so customers say yes!* (*Wilson Learning Library)* Belgium: Nova Vista Publishing.
25. Schul, P. & Wren, B. (1992, Jul). The emerging role of women in industrial selling: A decade of change. *Journal of Marketing 56*(3), 38.
26. Cole, Henry. (2004). Marketing real estate services: Smart work versus hard work in personal selling. *Services Marketing Quarterly 25*(2), 43.
27. Dugan, John P. (2006, Mar/Apr). Explorations using the social change model: Leadership development among college men and women. *Journal of College Student Development 47*(2), 217–225.
28. Siguaw, J. A. & Honeycutt E., Jr. (1995). An examination of gender differences in selling behaviors and job attitudes. *Industrial Marketing Management 24(1)*, 45–52; Sharoff, Robert. (1994, May). She said, he said. *Selling*.
29. Russ, F. A. & McNeilly, K. A. (1995, Sep). Links among satisfaction, commitment, and performance. *Journal of Business Research 34*(1), 57–61.
30. Cech, E. A. & Blair-Loy, Mary. (2017, Aug). Perceiving glass ceilings? Meritocratic versus structural explanations of gender inequality among women in science and technology. *Social Problems 57(*5), 371–397.
31. Zmudzinski, Paula. (2000, Mar). Gender matters. *Selling Power*.
32. Bachelor, Gary. (1996, Jan/Feb). Selling beyond gender. *Selling Power*.
33. Caykoylu, Sinan. (2010, Jan 7). *Cross-cultural and gender differences in leadership style perspectives: A comparative study between canada and turkey*. Saarbrücken, Germany: LAP Lambert Academic Publishing.
34. Personal interview with Roger H. Reid on Jul 21 2001; Smith, Craig. (2013, Dec 22). How do Myers-Briggs personality types use social media? *DMR.* Retrieved Oct 7, 2019, from expandedramblings.com/index.php/how-do-myers-briggs-personality-types-use-social-media-infographic.
35. The psychology of selling excellence. *Zenith Training and Development.* Retrieved Aug 18, 2019, from https://zenithtraining.ie.
36. Abrams, Fran. (2004, May 21). Learning? It's all in the mind. *The Times Educational Supplement* (4584), F8.

37. Tuckman, B. & Monetti, D. (2011). *Educational psychology*, 168. Belmont, CA: Wadsworth Cengage Learning.
38. Roderique-Davies, Gareth. (2009, Jul). Neuro-linguistic programming: cargo cult psychology? *Journal of Applied Research in Higher Education 1*(2), 58–63.
39. Connolly, Reg. (2019, Apr 18). The NLP eye accessing cues. *The Pegasus NLP Newsletter*. Retrieved from https://nlp-now.co.uk/nlp-eye-accessing-cues.

Chapter 7

1. Anonymous. (2005, Nov 29). Study indicates sales professionals spend little time preparing for calls; preparation for sales calls significantly less than managers and buyers desire [press release]. *Business Wire*.
2. Currie, C.S.M., Cheng, R.C.H., & Smith, H.K. (2008, Aug). Dynamic pricing of airline tickets with competition. *The Journal of the Operational Research Society 59*(8), 1026.
3. Knott, D. G., Boschwitz, J., & Mendes, D. K. (2004, Jul). Know your company's 'DNA.' *Best's Review 105*(3), 46.
4. Wordstream. *Guide to Using Social Media for Marketing* [white paper]. Retrieved Sep 1, 2015, from wordstream.com/social-media-marketing.
5. Williams, Tate. (2004, Apr). The age-old face-off. *Sales and Marketing Management 156*(4), 64.
6. Lager, Marshall. (2007, Jul). The alignment: CRM capabilities and business processes enable technology to shine. *CRM Magazine 11*(7).
7. Markowitz, Eric. (2011, May 3). New tools for sales training. *Inc.* Retrieved Jul 7, 2015, from inc.com/guides/201105/new-tools-for-sales-training.html
8. Retrieved Oct 20, 2015, from www.td.org.
9. Paul Goldner, telephone interview, May 16, 2001; adapted from Rasmussan, Erika. (2000, Sep). Training goes virtual. *Sales and Marketing Management 152*(9), 108.
10. Bedell, Denise. (2005, Nov). Know thy customer's behavior. *Global Finance 19*(10), 54.
11. Stanton, Anne. (2004, Mar/Apr). The "Why" Behind CRM Software. *Infotech Update 13*(2), 5.
12. Bullock, Lillach. (2019, Feb 19). Top 5 lead generation tools that will skyrocket your leads and conversions. *Forbes*. Retrieved from forbes.com/sites/lilachbullock/2019/02/19/5-top-lead-generation-tools-that-will-skyrocket-your-leads-and-conversions/#6d06c97b48f3.
13. Average time spent daily on social media (with 2019 data). *BroadbandSearch.* Retrieved Nov 1, 2019, from broadbandsearch.net/blog/average-daily-time-on-social-media.
14. Giamanco, Barbara. (2011, Mar 10). 6 tips for driving social sales success. *Sales and Marketing Management*. Retrieved Apr 27, 2019, from https://salesandmarketing.com/content/6-tips-driving-social-sales-success.
15. Smith, Craig. (2019). By the numbers: 250 amazing Facebook statistics and facts. *DMR*. Retrieved from https://expandedramblings.com/index.php/by-the-numbers-17-amazing-facebook-stats/
16. Myerhoff, Alice. (2014, Mar 18). 5 steps to maximizing facebook for salespeople. *Salesforce*. Retrieved from salesforce.com/blog/2014/03/salespeople-facebook-gp.html.
17. Bratton, Anna. (2015, Dec 3). Ten tips for using LinkedIn for sales prospecting. *Salesforce.* Retrieved Nov 1, 2019, from salesforce.com/uk/blog/2015/12/ten-tips-for-using-linkedin-for-sales-prospecting.html.
18. Newman, Daniel. Is Twitter really the favorite social network for sales professionals? *Forbes*. Retrieved Jul 7, 2019, from forbes.com/sites/danielnewman/2015/07/07/is-twitter-really-the-favorite-social-network-for-sales-professionals/#339656e2423a .
19. Anonymous. (2010, Nov). Author presents six strategies for motivating employees. *Healthcare Financial Management 64*(11), 26.
20. McGarvey, R. & Harrison, B. S. (2010, Feb). Easy as pie. *Selling Power*.
21. The sections of this chapter dealing with motivation and goal setting were taken largely from: Meyer, Paul J. (1991). *Dynamics of Personal Goal Setting*. (1992). *Dynamics of Personal Leadership*, and (1993). *Dynamics of Personal Motivation*. Waco, TX: Success Motivation.
22. Wilkins, James. (2011, Mar). The 'why' is what drives positivity. *Conference and Incentive Travel*.
23. Werlin, Paul. (2010, Aug). Seven keys to self-motivation. *Bank Investment Consultant 18*(8), 25.

24. Devadason, Rajen. (2011, Jan 1). Thermometer or thermostat? *Malaysian Business*.
25. Cohen, Donna L. (2006, Oct). Plan your way to success and increase sales. *Agency Sales 36*(10), 36.
26. Sabuco, Valentino. (2007, Jul/Aug). What's really important to you?" *The Saturday Evening Post 279*(4), 46.

Chapter 8

1. Farber, Barry. (2000, Feb). Sales success: Get on track. *Entrepreneur*.
2. Petersen, Paul. (2006, Jul). Why sales leads fall through the cracks, and how SFA can make the difference. *Customer Interaction Solutions 25(1).*
3. Patel, Neil. 15 psychological triggers to convert leads into customers. *Kissmetrics*. Retrieved Oct 4, 2015, from https://neilpatel.com/blog/15-psychological-triggers.
4. Beveridge, Dirk. (1991, Jun). Qualifying your prospects. *The American Salesman 36*(6), 6–9.
5. Meyer, Paul J. *Sales Training Material for Distributors of SMI International, Inc.* Waco, TX: Sucess Motivation Institute.
6. Prashad, Sharda. (2005, Oct 20). Tailored sales pitches work best. *Toronto Star*.
7. Gergaghty, Shauna. (2019, Feb 19). 7 Secrets to prospecting using social networks. *TalkDesk*. Retrieved from talkdesk.com/blog/7-secrets-to-prospecting-using-social-networks/
8. Neilsen. (2012, Apr 10). Global trust in advertising and brand messages. *Nielsen's Global Trust in Advertising Survey*. Retrieved from nielsen.com/us/en/insights/report/2012/global-trust-in-advertising-and-brand-messages-2.
9. Cates, Bill. (2000, Oct). Referrals 101. *Selling Power*.
10. Twining, Michael. (2000, Mar). Million to win. *Selling Power*.
11. Bretbarth, Wayne. (2012, Mar 4). LinkedIn infographic: want to know what others are doing? *PowerFormula*. Retrieved Aug 12, 2019, from powerformula.net/2347/linkedin-infographic-want-to-know-what-others-are-doing.
12. Hibma, Maggie. (2013, Sep 24). Got 5 minutes? Use it to find a new prospect on social media. *Hubspot Blogs*. Retrieved Oct 12, 2019, from https://blog.hubspot.com/marketing/social-media-find-prospects-ht.
13. Price, Dan. (2019, Mar 7). The top 20 social media apps and sites in 2019. *MUO*. Retrieved Nov 1, 2019, from makeuseof.com/tag/top-social-media-apps-sites.
14. Vaynerchuk, Gary. (2019). Twitter still has a massive business opportunity for your company. Retrieved Dec 1, 2019, from garyvaynerchuk.com/twitter-still-has-a-massive-business-opportunity-for-your-company.
15. Weiss, Wendy. (2014, Jan). A "warm calling vs. cold calling" rant. *Business Know-How*. Retrieved Jul 24, 2019, from businessknowhow.com/marketing/warm-call.htm.
16. Stewart, Irby F. (2001, Mar). Golden opportunities. *Selling Power*.
17. Fenn, Donna. (2010, Aug 21). 10 ways to get more sales from existing customers. *Inc*. Retrieved from inc.com/guides/2010/08/get-more-sales-from-existing-customers.html
18. Bleier, A., Harmeling, C. M., & Palmatier, R. W. (2019). Creating effective online customer experiences. *Journal of Marketing 83*(2), 98-119.
19. Internet Marketing Strategy Diva. Tips for creating successful sales websites. Retrieved Apr 27, 2019, from internetmarketingstrategydiva.com.
20. Lawal, A. B. (2019). Google Adsense secrets. AB Lawal.
21. Sanford Institute of Philanthropy. (2015, Jan). Basic data analysis and data gathering for fundraisers [seminar].

Chapter 9

1. Fields, Kenneth L. (2012, Mar). There's no substitute for telephone prospecting. *American Agent & Broker 82*(3), 26.
2. Crom, Michael. (2006, Sep 28). How to improve on sales calls. *Gannett News Service*.
3. Kaydo, Chad. (1998, Feb). Lights! camera! sales! *Sales & Marketing Management*.

4. Wilkins, Rich. (1993, Jan/Feb). Visualize your success. *Professional Selling Power 13*(1), 69.
5. Dolphin, Jan R. (2018, Mar). Early birds: Preparation is key to sales success. *Accessory Business & Product News 21*(2), 14.
6. Maddox, Kate. (2006, Dec 11). Lead management takes cooperation. *B to B 91*(17), 3.
7. Keim, Jennifer. (2007, Oct). Eric Kline: Be a confident sales rep. *HME News 13*(10), 82.
8. Adapted from Franco, John J. (1986, Aug). Ring up more telephone sales with well-trained personnel. *Business Marketing 71*(8), 84; and (1994, May/Jun). Telephone closes are up. *Personal Selling Power 14*(4), 20.
9. Greco, Susan. (2007, Apr). The need for speed. *Inc.* Retrieved from inc.com/magazine/20070401/salesmarketing-smart-selling.html?cid=search
10. (2000 Jul/Aug). Getting past the gatekeeper. *Selling Power*; Gelman, Jan. (1994, Jul/Aug). Gatekeeper. *Selling, 2*(1), 54–56; and McCann, Nanci. (1994, May) Protocol. *Selling 1*(9), 79; Foster, Jack (2010, Jul). Maximizing FACE TIME with customers. *Agency Sales. 40*(7), 40.
11. Wallace, Nicole. (2013). How fundraisers can get more out of LinkedIn. *The Chronicle of Philanthropy*. Retrieved Apr 18, 2019, from philanthropy.com/article/How-Fundraisers-Can-Get-More/154971.
12. Boland, Steve. Twitter for nonprofits: It's who (not just how many) you know. *Nonprofit Quarterly*. Retrieved Sep 25, 2019, from https://nonprofitquarterly.org/twitter-for-nonprofits-its-who-not-just-how-many-you-know/.
13. Mansfield, Heather. (2012). *Social media for social good: A how-to guide for nonprofits*. New York, NY: McGraw-Hill.
14. McGinnis, Susan. (2011, Feb). Smart talk: Make an impression. *HME News 17*(2), 19.
15. Jacobi, Jeffrey. (2000, Oct). Voice power. *Selling Power*.
16. Masser B. Z. & Leeds, William M. (1982). *Power-selling by telephone*, 56. West Nyack, NY: Parker Publishing Company.
17. Boe, John. (2010, Nov). Selling is a contact sport: Keys to effective phone calling. *The American Salesman 55*(11), 12.
18. Somaiah, Jasmine. (2019). 8 ways to follow-up in sales without annoying your prospects. Retrieved Nov 30, 2019, from nimble.com/blog/how-to-follow-up-with-prospects/
19. Sawa, Katrina. 10 simple ways to follow up with prospects. *Forbes*. Retrieved Oct 4, 2019.
20. Salesforce. (2014). *The smart guide to successful social selling* [e-book]. Retrieved Nov 1, 2019, from salesforce.com/blog/2014/05/free-e-book-the-smart-guide-to-social-selling-.html.

Chapter 10

1. Dolak, Dave. Sales and personal selling. Retrieved Nov 9, 2019, from davedolak.com.
2. Engleberg, I. N. & Wynn, D. R. (2011). *Think Communication*, 110. Toronto: Allyn & Bacon; Morton, Brian. (2007, May 23). Be prepared to make a good, quick first impression. *Ottawa Citizen*.
3. Laidman, Jenni. (2011, Jun 21). Make it count. *The Tennessean,* D1–2; Kahn, George N. The impression you make. *Smooth Selling 6*(1987), 2.
4. Anonymous. (2007, Apr). Home staging assists sellers. *USA Today,* in collaboration with the Society for the Advancement of Education.
5. Vithyaa, L.R. (2004, Oct 19). Importance of customer service. *Business Times*.
6. Lee, Isabel. (2004, Jul 17). Art of selling one's skills crucial in clinching job. *South China Morning Post*.
7. Leotta, Joan. (2000, Oct) Dressed to sell. *Selling Power*.
8. Alessandra, A. J. & Wexler, P. (1979). *Non-manipulative selling,* 87–93. Reston, VA: Reston Publishing, Inc.
9. Frankel, L. P. (2007). See Jane lead: 99 ways for women to take charge at work. *Business Plus*.
10. Attire guide: Dress codes from casual to white tie. *The Emily Post Institute*. Retrieved Apr 13, 2019, from https://emilypost.com/advice/attire-guide-dress-codes-from-casual-to-white-tie/.
11. Ramsey, Lydia. (2019, April). How to seal the deal in seven seconds. *The Balance*. Retrieved Dec 12, 2019, from thebalancesmb.com/seal-the-deal-in-seven-seconds-2951796
12. Solnik, Claude. (2006, Jul 21). Immaculate receptions: The art of greeting clients to your firm. *Long Island Business News.*
13. Adapted from: (1979). Here's an easy way to remember your customers' names. *Master Salesmanship*. Concordville, PA: Clement

Communications, Inc.; and McCann, Nanci. (1994, Mar). When you forget a prospect's name. *Selling*.

14. Porter, Henry. (1972, Oct 30). Opening for every occasion. *Sales Management 109*(9), 6–8.
15. Mok, Paul P. (1989). CST influencing model. *CST: Communicating Styles Technology*, 3. Dallas, TX: Training Associates Press.
16. Holmes, Chet. (2010). The ultimate sales approach. *Success Magazine*. Retrieved May 3, 2019, from success.com/the-ultimate-sales-approach.

Chapter 11

1. Scheer, Jim. (2006, Jan/Feb). Asking good questions. *Office World News*.
2. Trumfio, Ginger. (1994, Jun). Underlying Motivation. *Sales and Marketing Management*.
3. des Chatelets, Kristen. (2004, Jun). Asking the right questions. *Dealerscope 46*(6), 26.
4. Rudin, Andrew. Just the facts! How asking the right questions will yield the right answers. *SalesVantage.* Retrieved Oct 4, 2019.
5. O'Toole, John. (1994, Jun). The want makes the sale. *Selling*.
6. Schuster, C. P. & Davis, J. E. (1986, May). Asking questions: Some characteristics of successful sales encounters. *Journal of Personal Selling and Sales Management 6*(1), 171.
7. Anonymous. (2006, Jan 17). Probing skills course aims to educate the learner about the role of questions in various situations and the importance of asking the right question at the right time [press release]. *Business Wire*.
8. Ingram, Thomas N. (2012). *Sell, instructor ed.* Mason, OH: South-Western Cengage Learning.
9. Connor, Tim. (1981). *The soft sell*, 67. Crofton, MD: TR Training Associates Intl.
10. Rackham, Neil. (1988) *SPIN® Selling*. New York: McGraw-Hill.
11. Information gathered from *Transworld Systems, Inc*. Retrieved May 2, 2019, from transworldsystems.com.
12. Rackham, Ibid, 89.
13. Youngblood, Todd. (2001, Mar). Let customers sell themselves. *Selling Power*.
14. Using social media to ask the right questions. (2011, Sep 9). *Nielsen*. Retrieved Oct 20, 2019, from nielsen.com/us/en/insights/article/2011/using-social-media-to-ask-the-right-questions.
15. Atlas, Steve. (2000, Sep). When and how to use your favorite close effectively. *Selling Power*.
16. Greshes, Warren. Prospecting skills III [video]. *Brightcove*. Retrieved Jul 30, 2019.
17. Flynn, J., Valikoski T., & Grau, J. (2008). Listening in the business context: Reviewing the state of research. *International Journal of Listening 22*(2), 141–151.
18. DeVito, Joseph. (2008). *Human Communication, 10th Edition*. New York, NY: Longman.
19. Nicholson, N. (2007, Jul). Listening and learning. *Communication World*.
20. Steele, Jonathan. Active listening: Master this skill and master communication. *Nurse Jon's Speechmastery*. Retrieved Aug 4, 2019, from speechmastery.com/active-listening.html.

Chapter 12

1. Brooks, Bill. (2001, Jan). What is the difference between what customers need and what they really want. *The American Salesman*.
2. DiResta, Diane. (1998). *Knockout Presentations*. Worchester, MA: Chandler House Press.
3. Engler, Bill. Marketing magic inspired by P.T. Barnum. *Marketingprofs*. Retrieved May 23, 2019, from marketingprofs.com/6/engler1.asp.
4. Hoover's White Paper Series. How to convert prospects to sales faster with pre call planning. *White Paper Company*. Retrieved May 3, 2019.
5. Schultz, M. & Doerr, J. (2010, May 12). Sales call planning: What to know before every sales call. *Canadian Professional Sales Association.* Retrieved May 3, 2019, from cpsa.com/resources/articles/sales-call-planning-what-to-know-before-every-sales-call.
6. Hannan, Mack. (1976, May). The three C's of selling: A sure cure for the salesman's curse. *Sales and Marketing Management 10*(7), 93.
7. Women's Business Center. Features and Benefits. Retrieved Nov 23, 2019, from sba.gov/offices/headquarters/wbo/resources/7332

8. Taylor, Robert F. (1985). *Back to basic selling,* 75. Englewood Cliffs, NJ: Prentice-Hall.
9. Trumfio, Ginger. (1994, Jun). Underlying motivation. *Sales and Marketing Management.*
10. Arbel, Tali. Proceed with caution: Presentation roadblocks, even the most seasoned salespeople know it: presentations cause anxiety. *Sales and Marketing Management.* Retrieved Aug 4, 2019.
11. Kahn, George N. (1964) You're on stage. *Smooth Selling.*
12. National Sales Development Institute. (1980). *10 steps to greatness in selling,* 10–12. Waterford, CT: The National Sales Development Institute.
13. Marks, Ronald B. Dramatize your presentation or lose the sale. *Advanced Selling.* Retrieved Nov 20, 2019.
14. Mitchell, Olivia. (2009, Dec 14). 9 tips for enriching your presentations with social media. *Mashable.* Retrieved Oct 7, 2019, from https://mashable.com/2009/12/14/presentations-social-media.
15. Holcombe, M. W. &. Stein, J. K. (2008, Jun). How to deliver dynamic presentations: Use visuals for impact. *Business Marketing 71*(6),163–164; Kern, Richard. (2009, Feb). Making visual aids work for you. *Sales and Marketing Management.*
16. Rosenthal, Bill. (2014, Mar 4). How to power up your sales force with tablets. *Sales and Marketing Management.* Retrieved Mar 3, 2019, from https://salesandmarketing.com/content/how-power-your-sales-force-tablets.

Chapter 13

1. Feiertag, Howard. (2012, Oct). Finding out reasons for objections is key to overcoming them. *Hotel and Motel Management 217*(18), 14.
2. Boe, John. (2003, Sep). Overcome objections and close the sale. *Agency Sales 33*(9), 27.
3. Pollock, Ted. (2016, Jun). How good a closer are you? *The American Salesman 48*(6), 18.
4. Ziglar, Zig. (1985). *Zig Ziglar's Secrets of Closing the Sale.* New York: Berkley (Penguin Imprint).
5. Pell, Roger. (1990). The road to success is paved with objections. *Bank Marketing 22*, 16.
6. Huisken, Brad. (2003, Mar). Busting the sales busters, Part II. *JCK 174*(3), 66–67.
7. Huisken, Brad. (2003, Mar). Busting the sales busters, Part II. *JCK 174*(3), 66–67.
8. Lake, Michael. (2008, Mar). Overcoming objections is the key to sales. *Hudson Valley Business Journal.*
9. Gitomer, Jeffrey. (2016, Dec). Make objections obsolete to pave your way to sales. *The Central New York Business Journal.*
10. (2006, Nov). How do you address objections? Here's a few ideas. *Life Association News.*
11. (2004, Mar). Customer objections: Do you have the answers? *Professional Selling 22*(5), 3.
12. Anderson, Wilma G. (2003, May). Nine mistakes to avoid when marketing to seniors. *National Underwriter 107*(20), 22.
13. Roberts-Phelps, Graham. (2002, Nov/Dec). Objections are opportunities to sell. *Personal Selling Power 12*(8), 34.
14. Brooks, Bill. (2013, Feb). Are you responsive enough for your prospects and customers? *The American Salesman 48*(2), 21–23.
15. Kasper, Jim. Objections: Questions in disguise. *SalesVantage.* Retrieved Sep 10, 2019.
16. Brooks, Bill. (2002, Jan). Time, budgets and excuses... how do you overcome them? *The American Salesman 47*(1), 13–15.
17. Weiss, Wendy. (2010, Jan). Eliminate objections: And close more sales this year. *Sales and Service Excellence.*
18. Ramsey, Robert D. (2014, Mar). How to pitch a new idea. *SuperVision 65*(3), 8–9.
19. Graham, John R. (2003, Feb). How to sell more when others are selling less. *The American Salesman 48*(2), 15–20.
20. Natenberg, Todd. Overcoming objections. *Self Growth.* Retrieved Sep 1, 2019, from selfgrowth.com/articles/Natenberg4.html.
21. Smith, Kit. (2019, May 7). 49 Incredible instagram statistics. *Brandwatch.* Retrieved Nov 3, 2019, from brandwatch.com/blog/instagram-stats.
22. N.A. How to control your sales appointment: How salespeople can get and keep the power all throughout their selling interaction. *5min.com.* Retrieved Jul 17, 2019.

23. Farneti, David. (2004, Feb). Opening doors and establishing winning sales relationships. *Agency Sales 34*(2), 28–30.

24. Gross, T. Scott. (2000, Oct). The service factor. *Selling Power*.

25. Weiss, Wendy. (2001, Jan). The price is right? How to handle a customer's objections to price of an item. *American Salesman 46*(1), 6.

26. Chadha, Rhadika. (2004, Jan 22). Sellers of stuff: Salespeople should be trained to meet the demands of the ever-changing marketplace to stay abreast of competition. How do you distinguish your brand from the competition? *Businessline*.

27. Kendy, William F. (2000, Sep). Handling the price objection. *Selling Power*.

Chapter 14

1. Tracy, Brian. (2007). *The Art of Closing the Sale*. Nashville, TN: Thomas Nelson.

2. (2008, Apr 23). Do your salespeople ask for the business every time? *Sales Impact Group*. Retrieved Oct 20, 2019.

3. Anonymous. (2005, Dec 28) Closing the sale can be tough, but guidelines can ease the way. *San Fransisco Chronicle*, C-4.

4. Green, Paul H. (2001, Jul 9). Closing a sale. Retrieved from www.multiplex.com/Greensheet.

5. Gitomer, Jeffrey. (1999). A funny thing happened to me on the way to closing a sale. *Gitomer*. Retrieved from gitomer.com/a-funny-thing-happened-to-me-on-the-way-to-closing-a-sale.

6. Fenton, R. & Waltz, A. (2019). *Go for no!: Yes is the destination, no is how you get there.* Orlando, FL: CourageCrafters.

7. Anonymous. (2010, Jul). The truth about getting prompt buying decisions. *The American Salesman 55*(7), 21.

8. Personal Interview with Jim Duerr, Sep 26, 2012.

9. Selling Power Editors. (2010, Jan 13). Persistence leads to success: Just ask Gerhard Gschwandtner and Joe Sugarman. *Selling Power*. Retrieved from sellingpower.com/2010/01/13/702/persistence-leads-to-successjust-ask-gerhard-gschwandtner-and-joe-sugarman.

10. Cook, Matthew. (2015, Jan 7). Three reasons why persistence matters in sales." *Sales Force Search*. Retrieved from salesforcesearch.com/blog/httpwww-salesforcesearch-combid1557743-reasons-why-persistence-matters-in-sales.

11. Clay, Robert. (2015, Nov 1). Why 8% of sales people get 80% of the sales." *Cool Life CRM*. Retrieved Oct 20, 2019, from coollifecrm.com/news/id/142.

12. Kahle, Dave. (2010, Feb). Closing the Sales. *The American Salesman 55*(2), 3.

13. Boe, John. (2011, Jan). Some will, some won't, so what! *The American Salesman 56*(1), 22.

14. Adapted and modified from (2004, Nov 24). Sometimes I say no. *Selling Power*; Lontos, Pam. (1997, Jun). Rejection conditioning. *Selling Power*; and Reilly, Tom. (1987, July/Aug). Salespeople: Develop the means to handle rejection. *Selling Power 7*(5), 15.

15. Pollock, Ted. (2010, Apr). How good of a closer are you? *The American Salesman 55*(4), 22.

16. Beagelman, Steve. (2008, Feb). The art of closing the sale in 10 easy steps. *Franchising World 40*(2), 52.

17. Anonymous. (2007, Nov 30). Sales technique nonverbal communication: Body language matters. *Travel Trade Gazette*.

18. Sasso, Phil. (2007, Dec). Listening in for more sales. *Professional Distributor 15*(9), 18.

19. Atlas Steve. (2000, Mar). Listening For buying signals. *Selling Power*.

20. Metler, Rhys. (2015, Jan). 3 nonverbal buying signals every top sales person looks for. *Sales Force Search*. Retrieved from salesforcesearch.com/blog/httpwww-salesforcesearch-combid1396223-nonverbal-buying-signals-every-top-sales-person-looks-for/

21. Rosen, Keith. How to avoid a prolonged close. *allBusiness*. Retrieved Jul 23, 2019, from allbusiness.com/how-to-avoid-a-prolonged-close-4001385-1.html.

22. Lappe, Neil. (2012, Nov 15). Trial closings: The key to a 100% closing rate. *Web Strategies*. Retrieved from webstrategiesinc.com/blog/trial-closings-the-key-to-a-100-close-rate.

23. Allon, G. & Hanany, E. (2011, Jul 25). *Cutting in line: Social norms in queues*. Evanston, IL: The Kellogg School of Management.

24. Macfarlane, Iain. (2005, Aug 1). Techniques to improve sales success rate. *Wisconsin State Journal*.
25. Cost of ownership close. *Changing Minds*. Retrieved Jun 24, 2019, from http://changingminds.org/disciplines/sales/closing/cost_ownership_close.htm.
26. Dr. Seuss. (1960). *Green eggs and ham.* New York, NY: Random House.
27. Cohen, Andy. (2006, Mar). Are your reps afraid to close? *Sales and Marketing Management*.
28. Wheeler, Brandy. (2019, Jan 24). Four marketing tricks to achieve top of mind awareness. *Marketing DIY*. Retrieved from https://marketingdiy.wordpress.com/2013/01/24/4-marketing-tricks-to-achieve-top-of-mind-awareness.
29. Florez, Fernando. (2018, Aug 25). How to use social media to close more sales. *B2C*. Retrieved from business2community.com/social-selling/use-social-media-close-sales-0985859.

Chapter 15

1. Brookes, Nicola. (2013, Dec 12). The multibillion-dollar cost of poor customer service. *New Voice Media*. Retrieved from newvoicemedia.com/en-us/news/corporate/the-multibillion-dollar-cost-of-poor-customer-service.
2. RightNow Technology. (2012, Jan 10). 2011 Customer experience impact report. Retrieved from slideshare.net/jperezpgi/2011-rightnow-customer-experience-impact-report
3. Ashton, Leigh. Customer service: Your most important sales tool? *National Association of Sales Professionals*. Retrieved Sep 19, 2019, from nasp.com.
4. Nitzberg, Matt. (2009, Jun 17). Putting the shopper in your shopper marketing strategy. *Shopper Marketing*. Retrieved Apr 14, 2019.
5. Muenich, Uli. (2018, Jul 6). Will shifting to services boost the automotive industry? *Digitalist Magazine*. Retrieved from digitalistmag.com/customer-experience/2018/07/06/shifting-to-services-boost-automotive-industry-06178668.
6. Stevenson, Brett. (2010, Jun 3). Million dollar customers—they're all around you! *Dealer Marketing Magazine*. Retrieved April 14, 2019 from dealermarketing.com.
7. Conradt, Stacy. (2019, Oct 9). 11 of the best customer service stories ever. *Mental Floss*. Retrieved from mentalfloss.com/article/30198/11-best-customer-service-stories-ever.
8. Grubbs, JC. 5 Ways to get to know your customers better. *Business Collective*. Retrieved Oct 4, 2019, from https://businesscollective.com/5-ways-to-get-to-know-your-customers-better/index.html.
9. Hernandez, Andrea V. (2006, Sep 26). Not settling for 'good': Phenix City Chick-fil-A crew embraces 'second-mile service' policy. *Knight Ridder Tribune Business News*.
10. Wilkins, Rich. (2010, Jan 13). Go the extra mile by giving extra service. *Selling Power*. Retrieved Oct 17, 2019, from sellingpower.com/2010/01/13/81/go-the-extra-mile-by-giving-extra-service.
11. 66 Crazy Sales Figures [white paper]. IKO System. Retrieved Sep 26, 2019, from http://go.iko-system.com/rs/ikosystemtrial2/images/eBook_Crazy_sales_figures_IKO.pdf.
12. Dooley, Ken. (2013, Jun 10). The No. 1 reason why customers stay or leave. *Customer Experience Insight*. Retrieved from customerexperienceinsight.com/the-no-1-reason-why-customers-stay-or-leave.
13. Strathy, Maeve. (2015, Jan 2). Customization vs. personalization. *What Gives Philanthropy*. Retrieved from whatgivesphilanthropy.com/2015/01/customization-vs-personalization.
14. Genesys Global Survey, 2009.
15. Beck, T. & Smith, A. (2006, Spring). Four keys to customer loyalty. *The Catalyst* 35(1), 17+.
16. (2000, Oct). Get more from current customers. *Selling Power*, Selling Ideas section, 62.
17. Spielberg, Susan. (2004, Oct 4). You want fries with that? *Nation's Restaurant News 38*(40), 86.
18. Cholewka, Kathleen. (2001, May). CRM: Calling all customers. *Sales and Marketing Management*.
19. Stansberry, Glen. (2010, May 4). 10 examples of shockingly excellent customer service. *Open Forum, American Express*. Retrieved from americanexpress.com/en-us/business/trends-and-insights/articles/10-examples-of-shockingly-excellent-customer-service-1/.
20. Dooley, Ken. (2013, Jun 10). The No. 1 reason why customers stay or leave. *Customer Experience Insight*. Retrieved from customerexperienceinsight.com/the-no-1-reason-why-customers-stay-or-leave.

21. Waldow, DJ. (2013, Sep 19). We miss you! A creative re-engagement email campaign. *Brand Driven Digital*. Retrieved from branddrivendigital.com/email-re-engagement.
22. (1992, Sep). Turn conflict with a customer into a selling opportunity. *Personal Selling Power 12*(8), 73.
23. Lievense, Kathy, CFRE. (2012). Donor centered fundraising [report]. The Summit Group.
24. Brewer, D. Geoffrey. (2008, Feb). How to stay in touch. *Sales and Marketing Management*.